"In *Found in Translation*, prominent scholars offer timely and instructive discussions of two related and endlessly fascinating subjects—the variant texts of the Bible and the perennial challenges of translating it. The charming interview with the honoree, Professor Leonard Greenspoon, offers valuable insights of its own into the profession of biblical scholarship today and the reasons that these subjects remain important and fruitful."

–Jon D. Levenson, Albert A. List Professor of Jewish Studies at Harvard University

"This remarkable volume is no ordinary *Festschrift*. It shines brightly through the immediate, profound, and multidimensional impact Leonard Greenspoon has had on many in both the academy and in the public sphere. The contributions in the book, written by preeminent scholars as they engage with technical, religious, and broader cultural issues, are fresh and make for riveting reading. Surely I will not be alone in being unable to put the book down until reaching the last page!"

–Loren T. Stuckenbruck, Faculty of Protestant Theology at Ludwig Maximilian University of Munich

"The wonderful essays by the leading scholars of biblical translation collected in *Found in Translation* honor Leonard Greenspoon by illustrating the problems and importance of translation. Most of us think of the translation of the Bible as only a diminishment of the original; the chapters of this book illustrate just the opposite—how significant and complex translation is, and how crucial it has been for keeping the Bible alive and vibrant."

–Marc Brettler, Dora Golding Professor of Biblical Literature Emeritus at Brandeis University and Elaine and Morton Lerner Professor of Jewish Studies at Duke University

"Translation is crucial to understanding the Bible itself, and to assessing how the Bible has been understood. Leonard Greenspoon's career has exemplified both cutting edges of this sharp linguistic sword. *Found in Translation* honors his work by explaining and appropriating his insights. At the same time, the volume extends analysis to illuminate the production of ancient texts in Hebrew and Greek, to assess modern attempts to render Scripture, and to fathom how the translation of ancient texts factors into the construction of contemporary culture. Some of the articles are highly detailed and some expository; the volume as a whole is a contribution to learning that honors the act of learning."

–Bruce Chilton, Bernard Iddings Bell
Professor of Religion at Bard College

"An impressive collection of essays by leading scholars, centering on Leonard Greenspoon's interest in ancient (especially Greek) and modern (primarily Jewish) translations of the Bible. A delightful interview with the honoree reflects his personal background, wide-ranging interests, and exuberant personality. Scholars working on the textual history of the Hebrew Bible, translation theory, and modern Jewish views of the Bible will find much of value."

–Frederick E. Greenspahn, Gimelstob Eminent Scholar
of Judaic Studies at Florida Atlantic University

Found in Translation

Found in Translation: Essays on Jewish Biblical Translation in Honor of Leonard J. Greenspoon

Edited by

James W. Barker,

Anthony Le Donne,

and

Joel N. Lohr

Purdue University Press
West Lafayette, Indiana

Printed in the United States of America.
Hardback ISBN: 978-1-55753-781-2
ePDF ISBN: 978-1-61249-496-8
ePub ISBN: 978-1-61249-497-5

Cataloging-in-Publication data is on file at the Library of Congress.
Cover image: Reproduced by kind permission of the Syndics of
Cambridge University Library (Classmark: T-S 12.182).

Leonard J. Greenspoon
Courtesy of Michael Kleveter, Michael K. Photography.

Table of Contents

Part II: Jewish and Christian Scriptures in Modern Translations

Acknowledgments

This book would not be possible without the help of others. First and foremost, we offer thanks to our contributors for working within various deadlines and helping us, through their important contributions, produce a volume worthy of publication and presentation to our honoree. We owe special thanks to Professor Rabbi Jonathan Rosenbaum who, in the final stages of production, provided us with such a suitable Foreword, one that also serves as a helpful introduction to the volume. James Barker gratefully acknowledges a Quick Turnaround Grant from Potter College of Arts & Letters at Western Kentucky University, which facilitated work on this project in Fall 2015, and Joel Lohr thanks University of the Pacific for freeing up time to continue research and writing despite the heavy demands of administration and teaching. James also credits Joel and Anthony Le Donne for conceiving this project and inviting him to contribute to it. Both Joel and Anthony would like to thank James for the extra heavy lifting he undertook to produce this tome. Finally, we are especially grateful to the team at Purdue University Press, especially Peter Froehlich, Katherine Purple, Susan Wegener, Rebecca Corbin, Lindsey Organ, and Bryan Shaffer, for their guidance and assistance in the production of this book.

As expected, we dedicate this book to Leonard Greenspoon. We have learned a great deal from you, Leonard, as scholars, teachers, appreciators of humor, and human beings. Your regular conversations and correspondence with us have enriched our lives. We hope this volume rightly honors you as the kind, humorous, and erudite person you are.

James W. Barker
Anthony Le Donne
Joel N. Lohr

List of Contributors

James W. Barker is Assistant Professor of New Testament at Western Kentucky University.

Adele Berlin is Robert H. Smith Professor of Biblical Studies, Emerita at the University of Maryland.

Kristin De Troyer is Professor of Old Testament/Hebrew Bible at the University of Salzburg

Zev Garber is Emeritus Professor and Chair of Jewish Studies and Philosophy at Los Angeles Valley College.

Edward L. Greenstein is Emeritus Professor and the Meiser Chair in Biblical Studies as well as Head of the Interdisciplinary Graduate Program in Hermeneutics and Cultural Studies at Bar-Ilan University, Israel.

Ronald Hendel is Norma and Sam Dabby Professor of Hebrew Bible and Jewish Studies in the Department of Near Eastern Studies at the University of California, Berkeley.

Anthony Le Donne is Associate Professor of New Testament at United Theological Seminary.

Alan T. Levenson holds the Schusterman/Josey Chair in Judaic History at the University of Oklahoma.

Amy-Jill Levine is University Professor of New Testament and Jewish Studies, Mary Jane Werthan Professor of Jewish Studies, and Professor of New Testament Studies at Vanderbilt Divinity School and College of Arts and Science.

Joel N. Lohr is the President of Hartford Seminary, where he is also Professor of Bible and Interreligious Dialogue.

Michaël N. van der Meer teaches religious education at the Hermann Wesselink College, Amstelveen, and Old Testament at the Protestant Theological University at Amsterdam.

Jonathan Rosenbaum is President Emeritus and Professor Emeritus of Jewish Studies at Gratz College and is a Visiting Scholar at the University of Pennsylvania.

Emanuel Tov is J. L. Magnes Professor of Bible, Emeritus at the Hebrew University in Jerusalem.

Eugene Ulrich is O'Brien Professor Emeritus of Hebrew Scriptures at the University of Notre Dame.

Abbreviations

AB	Anchor Bible (Commentary Series)
ABD	David N. Freedman, ed., *The Anchor Bible Dictionary* (6 vols.; New York: Doubleday, 1992)
AJSL	*The American Journal of Semitic Languages and Literatures*
ANE	Ancient Near East(ern)
AOS	American Oriental Series
ATANT	Abhandlungen zur Theologie des Alten und Neuen Testaments
A[Y]B	Anchor [Yale] Bible (Commentary Series)
BA	*Biblical Archaeologist*
BCE	Before the Common Era
BDB	F. Brown, S. R. Driver, and C. A. Briggs, *A Hebrew and English Lexicon of the Old Testament* (Oxford: Clarendon, 1907)
BETL	Bibliotheca ephemeridum theologicarum lovaniensium
BHK	*Biblia Hebraica*, ed. R. Kittel
BHQ	Biblia Hebraica Quinta
Bib	*Biblica*
BibInt	Biblical Interpretation Series
BIOSCS	Bulletin of the International Organization for Septuagint and Cognate Studies
BJRL	*Bulletin of the John Rylands Library Manchester*
BJS	Brown Judaic Studies
BRev	*Bible Review*
BSNA	Biblical Scholarship in North America
BWANT	Beiträge zur Wissenschaft vom Alten und Neuen Testament
BZAW	Beihefte zur Zeitschrift für die alttestamentliche Wissenschaft
CBET	Contributions to Biblical Exegesis and Theology
CBR	*Currents in Biblical Research*

CBQ	*Catholic Biblical Quarterly*
CE	Common Era
CEB	Common English Bible
CEV	Contemporary English Version
ClQ	*Classical Quarterly*
CurBR	*Currents in Biblical Research (formerly Currents in Research: Biblical Studies)*
CurBS	*Currents in Research: Biblical Studies*
DJD	Discoveries in the Judaean Desert
DSD	*Dead Sea Discoveries*
EBib	Études bibliques
ECL	Early Christianity and Its Literature
ErIsr	*Eretz-Israel*
FAT	Forschungen zum Alten Testament
FOTL	Forms of the Old Testament Literature
FRLANT	Forschungen zur Religion und Literatur des Alten und Neuen Testaments
GCS	Die griechischen christlichen Schriftsteller der ersten Jahrhunderte
GNB	Good News Bible
GNV	Geneva Bible, 1599 Edition
HALOT	L. Koehler, W. Baumgartner, and J. J. Stamm, eds., *The Hebrew and Aramaic Lexicon of the Old Testament*, ed. and trans. under the supervision of M. E. J. Richardson (4 vols.; Leiden: Brill, 1994-1999)
HR	*History of Religions*
HS	*Hebrew Studies*
HSM	Harvard Semitic Monographs
HTR	*Harvard Theological Review*
HUB	*The Hebrew University Bible*
HUCA	*Hebrew Union College Annual*
ICC	International Critical Commentary
IEJ	*Israel Exploration Journal*
IOSCS	*International Organization for Septuagint and Cognate Studies*
JAJSup	*Journal of Ancient Judaism Supplemental Series*
JAOS	*Journal of the American Oriental Society*
JBL	*Journal of Biblical Literature*

JDS	*Judean Desert Studies*
JESOT	*Journal for the Evangelical Study of the Old Testament*
JHebS	*Journal of Hebrew Scriptures*
JPS	Jewish Publication Society
JQR	*Jewish Quarterly Review*
JSCS	*Journal of Septuagint and Cognate Studies*
JSJ	*Journal for the Study of Judaism in the Persian, Hellenistic and Roman Period*
JSJSup	Journal for the Study of Judaism in the Persian, Hellenistic and Roman Period Supplement Series
JSOT	*Journal for the Study of the Old Testament*
JSOTSup	Journal for the Study of the Old Testament Supplement Series
JSS	*Journal of Semitic Studies*
KJV	King James Version
LEC	Library of Early Christianity
LEH	Lust, Johan, Erik Eynikel, and Katrin Hauspie, eds. *Greek-English Lexicon of the Septuagint*. Rev. ed. Stuttgart: Deutsche Bibelgesellschaft, 2003
LHBOTS	Library of Hebrew Bible/Old Testament Studies
LNTS	The Library of New Testament Studies
LSJ	Liddell, Scott, Jones, *Greek-English Lexicon*
LSTS	The Library of Second Temple Studies
MBE	Monumenta Biblica et Ecclesiastica
MS(S)	Manuscript(s)
MT	Masoretic Text
NABR	New American Bible, Revised Edition
NASB	New American Standard Bible
NBf	*New Blackfrairs*
NedTT	*Nederlands Theologisch Tijdschrift*
NETS	Albert Pietersma and Benjamin G. Wright, eds., *A New English Translation of the Septuagint and the Other Greek Translations Traditionally Included under That Title* (New York: Oxford University Press, 2007)
NICOT	New International Commentary on the Old Testament
NIV	New International Version
NJPS	*Tanakh: The Holy Scriptures: The New JPS Translation according to the Traditional Hebrew Text*

NLT	New Living Translation
NovT	*Novum Testamentum*
NovTSup	Novum Testamentum Supplements
NRSV	New Revised Standard Version
NTS	*New Testament Studies*
OBO	Orbis biblicus et orientalis
OG	Old Greek
OTL	Old Testament Library
PG	J. Migne, ed., *Patrologia graeca*
Proof	*Prooftexts: A Journal of Jewish Literary History*
PTA	Papyrologische Texte und Abhandlungen
RB	*Revue biblique*
RCL	Revised Common Lectionary
RSV	Revised Standard Version
SBLSCS	Society of Biblical Literature Septuagint and Cognate Studies
SBLWAW	Society of Biblical Literature Writings from the Ancient World Series
SCS	Septuagint and Cognate Studies
SemeiaSt	Semeia Studies
SJC	Studies in Jewish Civilization
STDJ	Studies on the Texts of the Desert of Judah
SWBA	Social World of Biblical Antiquity
Text	*Textus*
TLNT	Ceslas Spicq, ed.; James D. Ernest, trans., *Theological Lexicon of the New Testament* (3 vols.; Peabody, MA: Hendricksen, 1995)
TSAJ	Texte und Studien zum antiken Judentum
TSK	*Theologische Studien und Kritiken*
TZ	*Theologische Zeitschrift*
VTGSup	Vetus Testamentum Graecum Supplementum
VTSup	Vetus Testamentum Supplements
WUNT	Wissenschaftliche Untersuchungen zum Neuen Testament
YJS	Yale Judaica Series
ZAW	*Zeitschrift für die alttestamentliche Wissenschaft*

Foreword

Jonathan Rosenbaum

Leonard J. Greenspoon personifies the ideals of the academy and of society. As a scholar, teacher, mentor, and community leader, his career and personal deeds are worthy of a *Festschrift* and, even more, of study and emulation by future scholars who seek to reap success.

I first met Leonard in 1972 when we were both graduate students at Harvard studying Hebrew Bible and the ancient Near East. In a cohort that included a number of classmates who would go on to particularly distinguished careers (e.g., Jon D. Levenson, P. Kyle McCarter, James C. Vanderkam, Richard E. Friedman, Baruch Halpern, Robert A. Oden, and Eugene Ulrich, to name a few), Leonard held a prominent place. His encompassing control of Classical languages and his deep knowledge of the Septuagint and the intricacies of Koine Greek earned him the respect of both faculty and classmates.

The faculty consisted of eminent biblical scholars, Assyriologists, linguists, and archaeologists of the ancient Near East. For us, as for most of our fellow students, central among them was the person who would become our *Doktorvater*, Frank Moore Cross. Cross's meticulous scholarship has had a wide-ranging impact on biblical studies and Northwest Semitic epigraphy and paleography. It continues to be frequently cited and to advance research through the work of the roughly one hundred scholars whose dissertations Professor Cross supervised. Leonard's exacting research in the various versions of the Septuagint complemented Cross's own seminal contributions to text criticism. Yet Leonard's qualities—like Cross's—extended beyond academic rigor. He possessed a wit and warmth that would make him a cherished colleague, teacher, and companion.

A *Festschrift* represents a crowning accolade for a scholar, reflecting that person's impact on his/her field and on colleagues and their own research. It builds on the honoree's lifetime of work. It should also incorporate and acknowledge the honoree's particular contribution to scholarship.

This volume exemplifies that ideal. It begins with an unconventional but ingenious introduction. Joel N. Lohr, one of its three editors, draws out Leonard's scholarly achievements, pedagogic philosophy, and personal background with an interview framed by a series of strategic questions. Through this structure, Leonard's prolific scholarly output and his influential contributions to translating both the texts and the fruits of scholarship into language and concepts accessible to the popular reader come into focus.

The volume itself features articles by eminent scholars in two sections that mirror Leonard's sizable contributions: 1) ancient Hebrew Scriptures and Greek translations and 2) Jewish and Christian scriptures in modern translation. The first section opens with a terminological analysis by Emanuel Tov that refines text criticism. Justly regarded by many as the dean of text critical scholars, Tov, like Leonard, was a student of Frank Moore Cross. Michaël van der Meer follows with an examination of the Greek translation of the Book of Joshua by the second-century scholar Symmachus. Leonard's dissertation, later published, was a text critical analysis of the Book of Joshua. Studies of individual biblical passages that have perplexed scholars follow: Kristin De Troyer provides new understandings of King David's war against the Ammonites and of their central city, Rabbah; Eugene Ulrich utilizes Isaiah 40 to compare the Old Greek, the Masoretic Text, and pertinent material from the Dead Sea Scrolls (1QIsa[a]) to uncover the methods of translation used in the Septuagint generally; and James W. Barker vindicates a pivotal position, first proposed by Dominique Barthélemy, regarding the Greek Minor Prophets Scroll from Naḥal Ḥever (8ḤevXIIgr), which Barthélemy designated *Kaige* and the *Quinta*, the "fifth" translation occasionally preserved in the Hexapla, Origen's third-century critical edition comparing the Hebrew Bible and Greek translations. Each of these studies acknowledges inspiration from Leonard's own research.

The detailed text criticism with which Leonard began his scholarly research led him to look more broadly at the function and goals of translations in modernity. The second section of this *Festschrift* mirrors this defining feature of Leonard's work. Ronald Hendel begins with a wide-ranging analysis of various roles of the Exodus in

American culture from the Pilgrims' view of their journey as a new Exodus to its role in African-American slavery and later civil rights to its place in recent popular culture as seen through Hollywood's lenses. Edward L. Greenstein provides a penetrating description of the challenges of translation exemplified by the Hebrew Bible's most linguistically challenging book, Job. Adele Berlin regards the Book of Proverbs as an instructional manual for upper-class adolescent males and contributes a deep analysis of the book's most famous verse, the opening to "A Woman of Valor" (Prov. 31:10). Basing his conclusion on biblical sources, Zev Garber follows with a careful proposal to utilize the term Shoah rather than Holocaust to describe the unique, cataclysmic destruction of European Jewry by the Nazis. Alan T. Levenson employs the German biblical translation of Rabbi Samson Raphael Hirsch (1808–1888) to note the effect that translation can have on education. Building on Leonard's essay, "Translating Jesus and the Jews," Anthony Le Donne confronts the ethnographic (and often anti-Jewish) context of the Greek term *hoi Ioudaioi*, which is especially apparent in the Gospel of John, and proposes a new means of understanding that term.

In an apt conclusion to the volume, Amy-Jill Levine analyzes the breadth of Leonard's approach to translation ranging from Hebrew to Greek, Jew to Christian, and ancient text to popular culture. She then applies these points to perhaps the thorniest issue in post-Shoah New Testament translation, the embedded charge of deicide. She addresses this difficult topic with an unflinching eye and reaches a conclusion about Christian anti-Semitism that is both realistic and rigorous. But she does not end there. She notes that for all Leonard's penetrating analysis of "harmful texts," his approach remains replete with "playfulness and joy."

Professor Levine's final point homes in on the essence of Leonard's multifaceted contributions to both scholarship and society. In the contemporary academy, scholars are typically rewarded for advancing the frontiers of their disciplines through critical, substantive, original research. However, the greatest of scholars do more. They are avid teachers and mentors.

This *Festschrift* differs from the norm in that its editors were not students of the honoree. Leonard influenced them all through his publications and as a mentor. When they needed advice that could advance their own research and careers, he was there. This says a great deal, I think, about Leonard's influence but also his ability to make deep connections, especially with those who might have otherwise been strangers.

Beyond his commitment to colleagues, Leonard's long and distinguished teaching career has shaped an untold number of undergraduate and graduate students. His lasting impact on many may owe a debt to the pedagogic method of Frank Moore Cross. From their first class meeting, Professor Cross treated his graduate students as colleagues. He thus emboldened them to strive to earn the accolade he had so charitably bestowed. Leonard has done much the same thing, not only for his students, but for thousands of others, whom he will never know by name: those who read his popular but learned articles. In writings like his ongoing series, "Bible in the News," published in *Biblical Archaeology Review*, he addresses his readers as partners in scholarly investigation.

Leonard's commitment to the larger society goes further still. A little more than twenty years ago, he called me with a question about Omaha. After twenty years of distinguished teaching and research at Clemson University, he had been offered the Philip M. and Ethel Klutznick Chair in Jewish Civilization at Creighton University in Omaha. Since I had been privileged to spend a decade on the faculty of the University of Nebraska at Omaha, he felt I could provide him with information about the community. Omaha is an academic, cultural, commercial, and social jewel, and Leonard and his beloved Ellie quickly decided to bring their family to Nebraska. Since then, Leonard has contributed mightily to an already vibrant community. A Jewish scholar teaching at a Jesuit university, his empathy, humor, and learning have allowed him to take a central role in both the Christian and Jewish communities. His prolific popular publications can regularly be found in the Omaha *Jewish Press*. Under his guidance, the Klutznick Symposium on Jewish civilization annually brings Judaic scholars to Creighton to present learned but lucid papers under a unifying theme in a forum that is open to all. Together with colleagues, Leonard has then edited those papers and produced numerous scholarly volumes.

Leonard has thus developed an academic exemplar worthy of emulation, that of public scholar. His research has documented the complexity and import of translation from ancient to contemporary times. He has applied its conclusions to achieve a broader goal: translating the products of culturally vital, yet highly complex scholarship into a format accessible to members of the public who lack the specialist's training. The program at Harvard from which Leonard received his Ph.D. required doctoral students to pass noncredit exams in French, German, Latin, and Greek in addition to the Semitic languages that were the primary foci of their training. Conveying the essence of groundbreaking discoveries in so technical a field facilitates society's awareness of the value of original research. The historic power of the humanities to preserve and understand humankind's cultures represents a path to the future of civilization that has never been more crucial. As a translator *par excellence*, a renowned scholar simultaneously dedicated to sharing scholarship's treasures with the public, Leonard J. Greenspoon has earned the admiration of his colleagues and the gratitude of society.

The Life of Leonard

Joel N. Lohr
Hartford Seminary

Like so many young graduates starting out in the academy, I was helped by a number of kind senior scholars. Of course, my professors and doctoral advisors were crucial. In my case I was also helped in particular by one or two people who simply took an interest in me and my work. Leonard Greenspoon is one such person. And, based on conversations I have had with others, I am not alone.[1]

It is not hard to ascertain the basics about Leonard's life and academic career. They can be found in the author bios on his books or in webpages. Leonard was born in Richmond, Virginia and earned a BA and MA in classical studies from the University of Richmond. He earned a PhD from Harvard University in Near Eastern Languages and Civilizations. Leonard was a faculty member at Clemson University for some twenty years before moving to Creighton University in 1996. He still teaches at Creighton, where he holds the Philip M. and Ethel Klutznick Chair in Jewish Civilization and is Professor of Classical & Near Eastern Studies and of Theology. Leonard is the author or editor of some two dozen books and more than two hundred journal articles or book chapters. To say that Leonard's publications are extensive and wide ranging would be an understatement. Some of these, along with the reasons for why he engaged in such a diversity of subjects, will be discussed below. (A list of his publications can be found at the end of this chapter.)

But to find out more about Leonard's *life*, one must dig deeper. There are, in fact, two short articles available, penned by Leonard himself, that tell some of his story. Readers are encouraged to locate these to learn more as background for what follows.[2] But for this piece I wanted to go even deeper. So, in thinking through our hopes for this *Festschrift* in general and for this chapter in particular, I decided that the best way to tackle it was—in honor of Leonard—to defy convention. I would simply ask Leonard some questions—*interview him*—with the hope of learning what makes him tick, what has driven his long and fruitful career, and what caused him to extend kindness to others—indeed strangers like me. What follows, therefore, takes a simple question-and-answer format through eleven prompts. In doing so we get an unusually rich and full glimpse into Leonard's life and work.[3]

(1) In the "Syrian Refugees" article, Leonard, you mention your father's family leaving the Ukraine in the 1920s, having no civic rights or protection there because they were Jews, and then your parents' struggles later, as a young couple unable to rent an apartment in their first-choice location because they were Jewish. In the "Leonard's Story" humanities piece, you mention your journey away from studying Law to ANE Languages and Civilizations. Can you share a little more of your early story, leading up to your life as an academic?

> My sister, two years older than I, and I were the first in our family to go to college. As you mentioned, my father emigrated from Ukraine in the late 1920s, when he was a teenager. My mother, who was born in Richmond, was an extremely smart woman. She completed one year of college, but then her father (my grandfather, the only grandparent I knew) said he wasn't paying for any more—women did not need to go to college. He was what I guess you'd call a hard man, not at all given to emotion or sentiment. But he did use to recite poems, including Poe's "The Raven" and Shakespeare's "Merchant of Venice," starting with the cast of characters.
>
> I actually can't be sure why I thought law was for me, from at least the age of twelve. I had a number of relatives who had studied law, most of whom did not practice it. I'm sure it was thought of as a "Jewish" profession. I'm pretty sure I was not thinking of it as a way to advance in politics. I'm not sure what I would have done with a law degree. Years later, I felt certain that I would have gone into the field of higher education in law, a law professor, at some point had I followed that career path.
>
> As for graduate school, with the goal of becoming a professor, I don't remember any role models in my family or community. I was always very good at traditional education of the sort we

encountered (or endured) in the 50s and early 60s. In college, I started in political science, with the law degree in mind. At my university, in those days there were Saturday classes, and I was actively pledging a social fraternity that had parties every Friday night. My Saturday course was in political science, the professor was (in my memory) boring, and that was that. I had taken Latin, as well as French, in high school, and I found that the professors in the small classics department were very welcoming, and I did well and was happy.

In my senior year, seeing me as a possible "successor" to them as a professor, they pushed me to apply for all sorts of graduate fellowships and I was fortunate to receive them all. I applied to law schools and I applied to grad schools, and I finally decided to pursue graduate education. I accepted an offer to study underwater archaeology at University of Pennsylvania, and we went up there and found an apartment, etc. I was absolutely fascinated by underwater archaeology.

Then I spent the 1967–1968 academic year in Rome on a Fulbright and found out I'd be drafted if I started grad school. So I taught social studies in an all black, Native American public school in a rural area between Richmond and Williamsburg. That was for two years. Then I found out that I had double vision (don't ask!) that was draft deferrable, and I decided to head to Harvard for Classics. For various reasons, I didn't like the Classics grad program and found out about Near Eastern Languages, to which I was able to transfer. I had never heard of Frank Cross, but did know of G. Ernest Wright (through his work on theology).

I never looked back: grad school over law, Near Eastern Languages over Classics. Any of my choices would have been good. I tell that to my students today who have to choose one great medical school over another or one top law school over another. There really aren't any bad choices in these circumstances. We are fortunate to be able to make these choices. They are not inconsequential, but they are clearly not the life-and-death options far too many people worldwide face today.

(2) In the "Leonard's Story" piece, you talk about teaching at Creighton and Clemson, but also elsewhere, such as Santa Barbara, Oxford, New York City, Bucharest, and Jerusalem. Can you talk a little more about what that was like? For instance, how was teaching in these places different from Creighton and Clemson? What did it teach you about yourself, and so on?

I think the greatest contrast is between teaching in the US and in Europe. Starting with Eastern Europe first, I taught several times in the early 2000s in the Jewish Studies program at the University of Bucharest. It was clear that the type of professor students were familiar with was someone (male or female) who came to each class dressed in a dark suit, opened up her or his notes from which she or he read. When the class was due to end, the professor would close the notebook and walk away.

I have always favored a more informal approach: no black suits, no notes to read from. Structured lectures, but totally willing to vary in accordance with student reaction: more time on some topics; less than planned on others; questions, comments, etc., always welcomed. They are not seen as an "interruption" or "intrusion," but as an integral part of the class. Digressions, or what students usually perceive as digressions, are part of what I do—always related in some way to class or maybe just to the larger enterprise of educating, teaching, and learning.

After the first or second class in Bucharest, I remember saying something like, "I saw what looks like a nice bar across the street; I'm going there. Why don't you join me if you can?" It was clear that students had never had that invitation. There was no compulsion, only an invitation: let's get to know each other better. Some students accepted the invitation; others didn't. As I recall, more did as the session continued. Maybe some thought that it was kind of a trick or trap, but I'm really pretty guileless and they caught on.

I taught at Oxford a decade earlier in 1992–1993. By that time, Oxford was already a bit more relaxed than in an earlier period—and that suited me just fine. There seemed to be a general and genuine acceptance of Americans and our typical lack of formality—or maybe it was just my informality. I do remember one older faculty member who lamented to me, "It's become just a bit too American around here."

Wherever I am and whatever I'm teaching, I think that the Leonard Greenspoon in the classroom should be the "real" Leonard Greenspoon. I don't think it makes any sense to put on a different persona as a professor. I think students recognize and, for the most part, accept authenticity. Part of authenticity for me is lack of formality; another part is an insistence on mutual respect and trust. These are characteristics that should serve us all in every context—the classroom is no different.

I'll add one more thing here: I do think that a professor should have near complete autonomy in the classroom—the freedom to explore, to innovate, and to soar—and to fall! I've been fortunate, abroad as in the US: my "superiors" have entrusted me with establishing a hospitable and positive teaching/learning environment, and I don't think I've ever betrayed their trust.

(3) Your area of expertise is not actually that. It's an unusually rich set of *areas* of expertise, in a truly unique way. To my knowledge these include, but are not limited to, the Septuagint, the Hellenistic Period, Bible translation, Dead Sea Scrolls, Jews in popular culture, the Bible in the news and popular culture, humor and the Bible/humor and Judaism, and the Holocaust and the Bible. How and why did you come to be involved in so many areas? What have been the "plusses and minuses" (to borrow Septuagint language) of being involved in so many? And is there any one area that has been especially beneficial, or personally enjoyable (perhaps "a blessing"), and is there another or others being less so (perhaps "a curse")?

It's standard advice in the academic world: until you get tenure and your first promotion, stick to the tried-and-true. Then you can explore or innovate or what have you. I think I probably did that early on—that is, produce mainstream scholarship for mainstream journals and audiences.

But I'm hoping I'm wrong and that I started off, as I've always tried to do, that is, working on topics and in ways that are of interest to me and, I hope, to at least a few others. My early concentration on the Septuagint was natural, I guess, given my interest in classical languages and then in the Near East. And my initial work, philological and textual, was by no means revolutionary (I don't mean that I've ever done anything revolutionary, but, if I did, it certainly wasn't in the early days). But I had different questions in mind than others seem to have had: what was being a scribe all about? How did the translators operate within a (Jewish) communal context? Why did some translate, others revise? In what ways did the LXX serve as the first Jewish translation in a history of Jewish translations? And why wasn't anybody studying Jewish translations, not individual ones, but as a developing phenomenon? And on and on and on.

One question led to another—and you end up with a lot of what I've done. I would not want to make any macro-statements without having done micro-research. Of course, I build on the insights of others, but I want, as much as possible, to be able to move in whatever direction the material takes me in.

I think it was Lévi-Strauss (the French philosopher, not his jeans-making American cousin) who spoke about how after a process of research, the material organizes itself (or, as I can attest, sometimes doesn't). There's a moment, call it mystical or intuitive or whatever, when it all comes together. We have to listen to it, just as we need to interrogate it and interact with it along the way. My students have difficulty in figuring out how someone can interact with, for example, a text, a series of seemingly inert letters. And yet I do my best work interacting with texts in the original or in translation, in word or in images.

So, when the above listing gets to the part about popular culture, is it really all that different? Yes and no. I have always tried to bridge the gap (if there is one) between "academic" and "popular," being fair to the strengths and weaknesses of both realms. This is, in my view, another way in which translation occurs, here from the technical to the more widely understood. Someone once said (I'm not sure who) that if you can't explain what you are doing to a general audience, you should probably ask yourself some serious questions about the level and depth of your engagement in your specialty.

The advantage/benefit of doing things the way I've done them is exactly: I've done things the way I wanted to. If I wanted to work on popular culture, I did. If I wanted to bring my knowledge of the Hebrew Bible into the discussion of how Nazi-supporting German Christians abused the Bible, I could do that—and I did. If I decided it would be perhaps my major contribution to write the first (synthetic) history of Jewish Bible translations, then that's what I did. It's been liberating!

But, at a cost. I'm more knowledgeable than most about the Septuagint—but not really a specialist. I know a lot about Jews and popular culture, but maybe not enough. The breadth of interests and research has almost certainly come at the cost of depth. And the intense relationships that come with specialties and specialists—I think I've missed them. As a result, I've never quite felt like an insider, or at least not one with access to the inner sanctum.

I certainly can't say that I wouldn't change anything, but who can? At the same time, I tell my students (and anybody else who will listen) that it's good, probably necessary, to hear "no" once in a while. At this point in my career, I really don't need to submit proposals of any sort—I've got plenty of people asking me to do plenty of stuff, more actually than I can accomplish. But I'll still submit a paper proposal in an area of interest in which I'm not well known (or even unknown). In such circumstances, I'm bound to hear "no," every once in a while. Rejection is never easy, but I've learned to live with it. And I'm a better person because of it.

(4) Your graduate work in ancient Near Eastern and biblical studies was at a time when these areas were—unless I'm wrong—dominated by Christians, especially Protestants. Can you share a little bit more about that experience? What was it like? What was it like for a Jewish student/scholar (perhaps even "observant Jew") to be in such an environment?

This is a really interesting question. For the most part, I've never felt any substantial or sustained difficulty in working within larger non-Jewish environments. Here are a couple of things that I do remember:

As an undergraduate, I went to the University of Richmond, a school affiliated with the Southern Baptists. Scripture classes were a requirement. We were reading the early portions of the book of Exodus one day and got through the biblical narrative of Moses's early life. At that point, I said to myself (fortunately not out loud): It's just like those Christians; they left out the best part of the story. What was I thinking of? The "biblical" account of why Moses lisped because after he initially put his fingers on a pile of jewels, an angel moved it to the burning coals. Baby Moses could relieve the pain only by putting his finger in his mouth, causing the lisp. No problem, right? Except for the fact that—along with other "biblical" narratives of my youth, including Abraham's being thrown into the fiery pit—it was not biblical at all. They were midrash, which were incorporated into the Bible stories I heard in Sunday School.

I was a pretty active undergraduate, including a two-year stint as editorial writer for the student newspaper. Of course, my views—such as allowing consumption of alcohol by students on campus—were not always popular with the administration. Nonetheless, I heard, on good authority, that the university president spoke of me as "a fine Christian gentleman." I took this—and I'm sure he meant it this way—as a compliment.

Near Eastern Studies at Harvard was very Protestant when I was there in terms of the faculty. I really didn't think too much about it until one day Jon Levenson explained to me that the "scholarly" view our professors were propounding on a particular issue was decidedly Protestant, in this case in terms of the decentralization of worship. Leave it to Jon to be many steps ahead of me in perception—as in so much else.

I also recall that once a Harvard professor (who shall here remain nameless) said: Leonard should read this portion of the Hebrew Bible; it's in his blood.

What I remember most vividly occurred in the fall of 1973, during the Yom Kippur War. One day in class, Frank Cross observed that I looked worried and asked me why. I told him of my anxiety about the conflict. His strong support for the State of Israel was well-known and showed through in his warm and supportive words to me.

(5) Are there other things you'd like share from that time, as a student at Harvard, perhaps reflecting on how much things have changed? I've heard others who studied there during that time say things like, "Oh, well, remember that was a time when PhD students in biblical studies. . . "

Through the first half of the 1970s, when I was a graduate student at Harvard, none of us read papers at conferences, none of us wrote articles for publication in journals. We had no pedagogical discussions. We did not learn how to write a CV or a cover letter, or how to act at an interview. And yet, we all got jobs right away! And I think, as a group, we did pretty well.

But there was more. I don't remember any competitiveness among us that would have focused on someone else in our class as a future competitor for employment. Sure, we all wanted our professors' approval, especially Cross's, but his approval was not a finite substance. I never thought of anyone's success as threatening my own chances for achievement.

Have I got this right? Well, this is the way I remember it. I came to Near Eastern Studies from Classics, as I wrote in response to an earlier question. I felt—and was—unprepared in comparison with most of the other students. But I didn't feel as if I were permanently disadvantaged.

This reminds me of one of my favorite stories. Early on Cross told us we needed to get ahold of the corpus of Donner Röllig, an important collection of ancient inscriptions. But I had no idea of the existence of this book, and I thought he said something like, we need to get ahold of the corpus of Donna Rellig—a prostitute maybe? I mentioned that to Jon Levenson, who chuckled appreciatively and then set me on the right path.

Ah, those were the days!

(6) Your career includes an exceptional publication record. What has that been like, both in terms of things positive and negative? Also, are there specific contributions about which you feel especially proud or you think have been especially important? Are there others that, in looking back, you feel are less important or uninteresting?

> This is an intriguing question. For sure, I've written things that are less important. But I hope I've never written anything that is uninteresting.
>
> The positives and negatives of writing in a number of different fields mirror at least in part parallel features in my scholarship. But the parallel is inexact.
>
> I love writing, and I always have. I think I'm somewhat above average as a writer—well, actually, I think I'm way above average in some genres and in some fields. The actual process of writing has—knock on wood!—never been especially difficult for me. As long as I get the first paragraph right, everything else seems to flow. As might be true with (more) creative writers, I just sort of follow the words, and they usually take me where I want to go—often via paths I wouldn't have thought of.
>
> I don't want this to sound entirely "new-age," however. Whatever I'm going to write about, I immerse myself in—reading everything I can possibly think of that might be relevant. Sometimes I take careful notes as I read, sometimes not. When I start writing, I don't stop for annotating—that will come later. But I also don't jump over some difficult section or where I hesitate about the choice of words. I want to get it right before moving on.
>
> That said, I do tend to over-write, and I would benefit from more demanding editors than I've usually had. There is no question that I almost always use more words than I need to. I hate to cut words that I've written—who does? But more precise editors than I usually have would excise 10%, 20%, or more, and it would probably be all for the better.
>
> Before I write anything (it's the same when I'm making a presentation), I need to know who the audience is. I never cease to be amazed at how many books are written without

any clear audience in mind: too advanced for the beginning, too elementary for the practitioner.

I love writing for popular audiences, and I'm pretty sure that my "Bible in the News" columns are the best read, and possibly most appreciated, writing I'll ever do. And I'm not disappointed by that. I don't think, as some of my colleagues do, that popular writing is somehow or other "second best." If anything someone writes is second best or second rate, that's their fault. I am always surprised at SBL meetings when major, serious scholars, some of whom I've never met, will come up to me and say how much they enjoy the columns. Providing enjoyment, along with some edification, can't be all bad.

And I like writing extended encyclopedia articles, 7,000 words or more. It forces me to be at least a little concise in presentation and to figure out what is really important about the topic and how to get others to understand, appreciate, and perhaps get excited about what excites me in the study of Septuagint or Jewish Bible translations.

It is in the field of Jewish Bible translations that I have done my most sustained and original scholarly work, about which I am unabashedly pretty proud. I think it's safe to say that no one has studied the phenomenon of Jewish Bible translating with the breadth of analysis I have applied to it. Have I made some earth-shattering discoveries in this area? For sure, haven't we all?!? Obviously, there's more than a bit of hyperbole there, but we can shake up our field a bit —and we are all the better because of it.

Now that I've just about completed answering this question, I'm not sure there really are any negatives. To write what I want to, when I want to, for whom I want to—what a blessing!

(7) Your decisions in life (and thus your "career path") have undoubtedly entailed "trade-offs" or perhaps "prices paid." We've already gotten at some of these, but perhaps there are others—for example, I've often wondered if you've regretted not having a steady stream of doctoral students, or perhaps not publishing as many monographs, or perhaps. . .

On the two specific points: Yes and Yes—yes, I wish I could have been more directly involved with doctoral students, and yes I sometimes wonder why I did not produce more monographs.

At the same time, these are not exactly trade-offs. If I haven't directed dissertations (I actually did direct one and have been on several committees), I've had the enormously rewarding experience of working with many graduate students and young scholars through reading their papers, etc., and engaging them in conversations that have often been both personally and professionally positive.

As for the monographs, or lack thereof, sometimes I feel that I just think better in chapters or articles or entries. I especially like editing and here again I've been fortunate, since I've done an amazing amount of editing with an amazing number of scholars. For sure, there are plenty of my colleagues who seem to have managed to do it all. Honestly, my admiration for them is unsullied by jealousy, which I truly consider to be an absolutely useless and harmful trait or characteristic or whatever it is. I once had a colleague who seemed to feel that academic success was a finite item: if I achieved some, he would necessarily achieve less. What a dreary way to live!

(8) Over the years you've organized numerous symposia, conferences, colloquia, etc.—probably more than any other scholar I know, at least in our discipline. What led you to invest so heavily in this? What has that entailed? Do you have regrets? Was it all worth it? What have you learned? Contributed as a result? People met?

Let me say it, right off: I love people. I love interacting with people one-on-one or in groups. I love organizing opportunities for people to come together. I love hosting these events. I even love deciding on menus, hotels, centerpieces, snack foods, etc., etc. It invigorates me, and I have not one regret about the events I've put on—including an annual symposium in Omaha—and hope to continue to put on. While I am far from an objective viewer (who is?), I do know (because lots of people have told me so) that our symposia are among the best organized, most collegial, and enjoyable (at both a personal and professional level) they have ever attended. And, frankly, since I've attended lots of conferences, etc., I don't think that they are entirely wrong.

Since organizational details are not my strongest area, I am again fortunate to have colleagues and staff who excel at these aspects. I think I'm pretty good at making people feel comfortable. In my view, it is in such an environment that we all achieve at our highest level. I'm not entirely averse to controversy or contention, but I certainly don't seek it out. Come to my symposium; it's sort of like coming to my home. You're my guest, and I will consistently treat you exactly like I would want to be treated as a guest.

Most of the symposia, etc., that I've organized lead to publications, which again allows me to practice my "craft" as an editor. This is a process that does, however, have its disappointments, since some people refuse to follow guidelines or even try to make deadlines. Since I myself have been guilty of such academic shortcomings, I can certainly empathize with others who find themselves in similar circumstances. The only thing I can't stand in this regard is people who simply stop communicating, as if that's the way to resolve the issue. It ain't!

(9) In the "Leonard's Story" piece, you mention throwing yourself (your "whole self") into your teaching. Can you share a little bit more about what that means and has meant?

No matter whether it's in (pedagogical) fashion or out of fashion, I tend to get pretty excited about what I'm researching or writing about or simply thinking about. I used to think that I could get my students to be as excited as I am about Bible translations or inscriptions, etc., etc. Over time, I've learned, that's not likely to happen.

But what can happen is that students will transfer my excitement, which is sincere and pretty upfront, to whatever they are passionate about: the sciences, theater, art, whatever. I can't see that there's any advantage, at least for me as a person and as a professor, to be standoffish or aloof when it comes to teaching. If I'm not interested in a subject, why should the students be? If I don't care, why should they care?

That's part of the "whole self," I guess. But there's more. It's very easy for me, as for any other teaching professor, to think that my class is all that really matters for the students and that anything else, academic or personal, that "interferes" with this ought to be avoided or downgraded. It's easy to think that way and act upon such thoughts. Thankfully, I never have.

I guess it's just sort of instinctual for me to at least try to interact with each student as an individual who has lots of obligations other than the assignments in my class. I hope that I am authentic and true to my nature in encouraging students, to the extent that they are comfortable, to come by my office and discuss whatever is on their mind.

Now this approach is of course not without difficulties. Students may be happy to become my "friends" or pretend to be "friends"—and then expect benefits (typically in the form of higher grades). It's a risk that I am, for the most part, willing to take, knowing that I am sometimes (I hope, not often) taken advantage of. I don't mind being something of a role model for some students, but I also have to be aware that there are any number of roles that I am not suited to model. Getting "too much" information can also be a problem. But again, it's something that will happen when you—that is, your whole self—interact with another person, in this case a student—in his/her whole self.

(10) Speaking of one's "whole self," this inevitably will include one's *family*. How has family life been a part of your scholarship and work, if it has?

It is a fairly common observation: the life of a professor can be difficult for her or his family. I'm sure this can be true, but I don't know that the academic world imposes more stresses on its practitioners than those in any other field. Possibly, but I think the stress level may well be about the same across professions, with different levels for different folks.

But there are, within the family of a professor, countervailing benefits that may just outweigh the negatives. For Ellie, my wife, and me, I want to consider a few of them. There were, for example, those five years of graduate school at Harvard, beginning in 1970. "Now we ain't got a barrel of money. . ." was our constant refrain. But, you know, it didn't matter. I can't speak for graduate students in subsequent years, but I know that I wouldn't trade those years for anything—not even for the legal career that had been my alternative career path until I saw the "light" of graduate studies in the humanities.

We moved only twice, not that unusual (I would guess) for someone teaching at a university: first to South Carolina, where I taught for twenty years at a large public university, Clemson. Then, half way across the country to Omaha, NE, where I have been for another twenty years thus far at Creighton, a Jesuit Catholic University. Our two daughters, Gallit and Talya, were both born in South Carolina. Our older daughter's birth preceded by just a bit the completion of my doctoral dissertation. Our younger daughter's birth coincided with our move from the town of Clemson to Greenville, a nearby (roughly forty miles away) city.

Our older daughter had already started her undergraduate study at Boston University when we moved to Omaha. Our younger daughter, then a sophomore in high school, decided to go to New York City—and in New York she will remain the rest of her life. (I don't mean, of course, that she doesn't travel, with some frequency, in fact; only that she will be a resident of the City for most of the rest of her life, I suspect.)

As I've already mentioned, I have been fortunate to be able to work in several different fields and to have outlets, public as well as professional, to write about my experiences—both academic and personal. So it is that, over the years, I have mentioned my family in some of my writings, including the "Bible in the News" columns I wrote for the Biblical Archaeology Society. The examples are many. One comes to mind where I discuss the idea of "Twins in the Bible," a piece that was influenced by the impending birth of our twin grandchildren.[4]

(11) Do you have any other reflections on the past, your life contributions, or your life more generally that you'd like to share? And to close our interview, might you have any advice for others, maybe younger scholars entering the field, that you'd like to share?

Each week, on the second page of the Sunday *New York Times* business section, there is a profile of some big shot or other. Almost always the last question seeks to elicit from the executive some advice she or he can bestow on college graduates. Without fail, I cringe—at the question and the answer (whatever it is).

That said, I will say a couple of things that I hope are not entirely cringe-worthy. First, I am in awe of younger scholars today who enter into an academic world that is constricting even as I speak/write. As I mentioned earlier, all of my Harvard cohort found jobs, without even knowing a thing about teaching or applying for a job. Forget that these days. I now look at applications for entry-level positions that would, not so many decades ago, have been appropriate for tenure and promotion.

But against the odds, these younger scholars persevere. I hope that the essentially competition-free world of Harvard in the first half of the 70s still prevails somewhere, but I doubt it. So, here's my advice, such as it is: You don't move up by downgrading others. There is no meaningful inflation of one's sense of worth that comes at the expense of bursting someone else's bubble (a bit trite, but true). Don't short-change or oversell yourself or your abilities. And don't short-change or undervalue anyone else.

Bibliography of Leonard J. Greenspoon

As already discussed, Leonard's publications are many. What makes his writings especially interesting—indeed unique—has been his unconventional, cross-disciplinary approach. In addition to his scholarly publications listed below, Leonard is well-known for his contributions to the *Bible Review* and *Biblical Archaeology Review*, in particular his regular column titled "The Bible in the News," an accessible one-pager that has appeared in each issue since 2000. A compilation of these articles was published in 2012 (see below).

Authored Books:

Textual Studies in the Book of Joshua. HSM 28. Chico, CA: Scholars Press, 1983.

Max Leopold Margolis: A Scholar's Scholar. BSNA 15 Atlanta: Scholars Press, 1987.

The Bible in the News: How the Popular Press Relates, Conflates and Updates Sacred Writ. Washington, DC: Biblical Archaeology Society, 2012.

Jewish Translations of the Bible. New York: American Bible Society, 2013.

Edited Books:

VIII Congress of the International Organization for Septuagint and Cognate Studies: Paris 1992 (with Olivier Munnich). SCS 41. Atlanta: Scholars Press, 1995.

Representations of Jews Through the Ages (with Bryan LeBeau). Proceedings of the Eighth Annual Symposium of the Philip M. and Ethel Klutznick Chair in Jewish Civilization, September 17–18, 1995. SJC 8. Omaha: Creighton University Press, 1996.

Yiddish Language & Culture: Then & Now. Proceedings of the Ninth Annual Symposium of the Philip M. and Ethel Klutznick Chair in Jewish Civilization, October 27–28, 1996. SJC 9. Omaha: Creighton University Press, 1998.

The Historical Jesus Through Catholic and Jewish Eyes (with Bryan LeBeau and Dennis Hamm). Harrisburg: Trinity Press International, 2000.

Sacred Text, Secular Times: The Hebrew Bible in the Modern World (with Bryan LeBeau). Proceedings of the Tenth Annual Symposium of the Philip M. and Ethel Klutznick Chair in Jewish Civilization, September 14–15, 1997. SJC 10. Omaha: Creighton University Press, 2000.

"*A Land Flowing With Milk and Honey*": *Visions of Israel from Biblical to Modern Times* (with Ronald A. Simkins). Proceedings of the Eleventh Annual Symposium of the Philip M. and Ethel Klutznick Chair in Jewish Civilization, November 1–2, 1998. SJC 11. Omaha: Creighton University Press, 2001.

Millennialism from the Hebrew Bible to the Present (with Ronald A. Simkins). Proceedings of the Twelfth Annual Symposium of the Philip M.

and Ethel Klutznick Chair in Jewish Civilization, October 10–11, 1999. SJC 12. Omaha: Creighton University Press, 2002.

Spiritual Dimensions of Judaism (with Ronald A. Simkins). Proceedings of the Thirteenth Annual Symposium of the Philip M. and Ethel Klutznick Chair in Jewish Civilization, September 17–18, 2000. SJC 13. Omaha: Creighton University Press, 2003.

The Book of Esther in Modern Research (with Sidnie White Crawford). JSOT-Sup 380. London: T&T Clark, 2003.

Women and Judaism (with Ronald A. Simkins and Jean Cahan). Proceedings of the Fourteenth Annual Symposium of the Philip M. and Ethel Klutznick Chair in Jewish Civilization, October 28–29, 2001. SJC 14. Omaha: Creighton University Press, 2003.

Food & Judaism (with Ronald A. Simkins and Gerald Shapiro). Proceedings of the Fifteenth Annual Symposium of the Klutznick Chair in Jewish Civilization-Harris Center for Judaic Studies, October 27–28, 2002. SJC 15. Omaha: Creighton University Press, 2005.

The Jews of Eastern Europe (with Ronald A. Simkins and Brian Horowitz). Proceedings of the Sixteenth Annual Symposium of the Klutznick Chair in Jewish Civilization-Harris Center for Judaic Studies, September 14–15, 2003. SJC 16. Omaha: Creighton University Press, 2005.

American Judaism in Popular Culture (with Ronald A. Simkins). Proceedings of the Seventeenth Annual Symposium of the Klutznick Chair in Jewish Civilization-Harris Center for Judaic Studies, October 24–25, 2004. SJC 17. Omaha: Creighton University Press, 2006.

Love—Real and Ideal—in the Hebrew Bible and the Jewish Tradition (with Ronald A. Simkins and Jean Cahan). Proceedings of the Eighteenth Annual Symposium of the Klutznick Chair in Jewish Civilization-Harris Center for Judaic Studies, September 18–19, 2005. SJC 18. Omaha: Creighton University Press, 2008.

"I Will Sing and Make Music": Jewish Music and Musicians Throughout the Ages. Proceedings of the Nineteenth Annual Symposium of the Klutznick Chair in Jewish Civilization-Harris Center for Judaic Studies, October 29–30, 2006. SJC 19. Omaha: Creighton University Press, 2008.

"The Mountains Shall Drip Wine": Jews and the Environment. Proceedings of the Twentieth Annual Symposium of the Klutznick Chair in Jewish Civilization-Harris Center for Judaic Studies, October 28–29, 2007. SJC 20. Omaha: Creighton University Press, 2009.

Rites of Passage: How Today's Jews Celebrate, Commemorate, and Commiserate. Proceedings of the Twenty-First Annual Symposium of the Klutznick Chair in Jewish Civilization-Harris Center for Judaic Studies, October 26–27, 2008. SJC 21, West Lafayette, IN: Purdue University Press, 2010.

Jews and Humor. Proceedings of the Twenty-Second Annual Symposium of the Klutznick Chair in Jewish Civilization-Harris Center for Judaic Studies,

October 25–26, 2009. SJC 22. West Lafayette, IN: Purdue University Press, 2011.

Jews in the Gym: Judaism, Sports, and Athletics. Proceedings of the Twenty-Third Annual Symposium of the Klutznick Chair in Jewish Civilization-Harris Center for Judaic Studies, October 24–25, 2010. SJC 23. West Lafayette, IN: Purdue University Press, 2012.

Fashioning Jews: Clothing, Culture, and Commerce. Proceedings of the Twenty-Fourth Annual Symposium of the Klutznick Chair in Jewish Civilization-Harris Center for Judaic Studies, October 23–24, 2011. SJC 24. West Lafayette, IN: Purdue University Press, 2013.

Who Is a Jew? Reflections on History, Religion, and Culture. Proceedings of the Twenty-Fifth Annual Symposium of the Klutznick Chair in Jewish Civilization-Harris Center for Judaic Studies, October 28–29, 2012. SJC 25. West Lafayette, IN: Purdue University Press, 2014.

Wealth and Poverty in Jewish Traditions. Proceedings of the Twenty-Sixth Annual Symposium of the Klutznick Chair in Jewish Civilization-Harris Center for Judaic Studies, October 27–28, 2013. SJC 26. West Lafayette, IN: Purdue University Press, 2015.

Mishpachah: The Jewish Family in Tradition and in Transition. Proceedings of the Twenty-Seventh Annual Symposium of the Klutznick Chair in Jewish Civilization-Harris Center for Judaic Studies, October 26–27, 2014. SJC 27. West Lafayette, IN: Purdue University Press, 2016.

"olam ha'zeh v'olam ha-ba": This World and the World to Come in Jewish Belief and Practice. Proceedings of the Twenty-Eighth Annual Symposium of the Klutznick Chair in Jewish Civilization-Harris Center for Judaic Studies-Schwalb Center for Israel and Jewish Studies, October 25–26, 2015. SJC 28. West Lafayette, IN: Purdue University Press, 2017.

Articles and Chapters:

"Max L. Margolis on the Complutensian Text of Joshua." *BIOSCS* 12 (1979): 43–56.

"Ars Scribendi: Max Margolis' Paper 'Preparing Scribe's Copy in the Age of Manuscripts.'" *JQR* 71 (1981): 133–50.

"The Pronouncement Story in Philo and Josephus." *Semeia* 20 (1981): 73–80.

"The Origin of the Idea of Resurrection." Pages 247–321 in *Traditions in Transformation: Turning Points in Biblical Faith*. Edited by Baruch Halpern and Jon D. Levenson. Winona Lake, IN: Eisenbrauns, 1981.

"Ars Scribendi; Pars Reperta." *JQR* 72 (1982): 43–44.

"Theodotion, Aquila, Symmachus, and the Old Greek of Joshua." *Eretz-Israel* 16 (1982): 82–91.

"The Warrior God, or God, the Divine Warrior." Pages 205–31 in *Religion and Politics in the Modern World*. Edited by Peter H. Merkl and Ninian Smart. New York: New York University Press, 1983.

"Max Leopold Margolis: A Scholar's Scholar (A BA Portrait)." *BA* 48 (1985): 103–6.

"'Of These You May Eat': Food and the Bible" (with Donald Turk). Pages 45–51 in *Proceedings of Special Clemson University Symposium, Food and Society, November 5–6, 1986*. Edited by C. Alan Grubb and M. Elizabeth Kunkel. Clemson, SC: Clemson University Press, 1986.

"The Use and Abuse of the Term 'LXX' and Related Terminology in Recent Scholarship." *BIOSCS* 20 (1987): 20–28.

"Herod the Great." Pages 958–63 in *Great Lives from History: Ancient and Medieval Series*. Edited by Frank N. Magill. Pasadena, CA: Salem Press, 1988.

"A Book 'Without Blemish': The Jewish Publication Society's Bible Translation of 1917." *JQR* 79 (1988): 1–21.

"Mission to Alexandria: Truth and Legend about the Creation of the Septuagint, the First Bible Translation." *BRev* 5.4 (1989): 34–41.

"Biblical Translators in Antiquity and in the Modern World: A Comparative Study." *HUCA* 60 (1989): 91–113.

"On the Jewishness of Modern Jewish Biblical Scholarship: The Case of Max L. Margolis." *Judaism* 39 (1990): 82–92.

"Recensions, Revision, Rabbinics: Dominique Barthélemy and Early Developments in the Greek Traditions." *Text* 15 (1990): 153–67.

"The Bible and the Funny Papers." *BRev* 7.5 (1991): 30–33, 41.

"It's All Greek to Me: The Septuagint in Modern English Versions of the Bible." Pages 1–21 in *VII Congress of the International Organization for Septuagint and Cognate Studies (Leuven 1989)*. Edited by Claude Cox. Atlanta: Scholars Press, 1991.

"The Qumran Fragments of Joshua: Which Puzzle are They Part of and Where Do They Fit?" Pages 159–94 in *Septuagint, Scrolls and Cognate Writings: Papers Presented to the International Symposium on the Septuagint and Its Relations to the Dead Sea Scrolls and Other Writings (Manchester, 1990)*. Edited by George J. Brooke and Barnabas Lindars. Atlanta: Scholars Press, 1992.

"Jews and Christians as Bible Translators: A Heritage of Cooperation." [Pamphlet] New York: Layman's National Bible Association, 1992.

"Grading Without Grades." *The Teaching Professor* (May 1992).

"Captain of the Lord's Host" and "Joshua." Pages 127–28 and 416–17 in *Dictionary of Biblical Tradition in English Literature*. Edited by David Lyle Jeffrey. Grand Rapids: Eerdmans, 1992.

"Achan" (1:54), "Aquila's Version" (1:320–1), "Rahab" (5:611–2), "Symmachus, Symmachus's Version" (6:251), "Theodotion, Theodotion's Version" (6:447–

8), and "Versions, Ancient (Greek)" (6:793–4). *The Anchor Bible Dictionary*. Edited by David Noel Freedman. 6 vols. New York: Doubleday, 1992.

(with Bob Du) "Recreation Professional, Religion and Politics." *Parks and Recreation* (July 1993): 66–71.

"New Bible Translations: An Assessment and Prospect (a Response)." Pages 68–75 in *The Bible in the Twenty-First Century*. Edited by Howard Clark Kee. New York: American Bible Society, 1993.

"Judaism in South Carolina." Pages 103–19 in *Religion in South Carolina*. Edited by Charles H. Lippy. Columbia: University of South Carolina Press, 1993.

"From the Septuagint to the New Revised Standard Version: A Brief Account of Jewish Involvement in Bible Translating and Translations." Pages 19–50 in vol. 6 of *The Solomon Goldman Lectures*. Edited by Mayer I. Gruber. Chicago: Spertus College of Judaica Press, 1993.

"The New Testament in the Comics." *BRev* 9.6 (1993): 40–45.

"Non-Masoretic Elements in the Transmission and Translation of the Book of Joshua." Pages 51–58 in *Proceedings of the Eleventh World Congress of Jewish Studies, Division A: The Bible and Its World*. Jerusalem: World Union of Jewish Studies, 1994.

"The IOSCS at 25 Years." Pages 171–81 in *VIII Congress of the International Organization for Septuagint and Cognate Studies: Paris 1992*. Edited by Leonard J. Greenspoon and Olivier Munnich. SCS 41. Atlanta: Scholars Press, 1995.

"It's All Greek to Me: Septuagint Studies Since 1968." *CurBS* 5 (1997): 147–74.

"Tradition in the Modern World: Jewish Perspectives on Illness and Death." Pages 53–71 in *Religious Values of the Terminally Ill: A Handbook for Health Professionals*. Edited by Delfi Mondragón. Scranton, PA: University of Scranton Press, 1997.

"A Preliminary Publication of Max Leopold Margolis's *Andreas Masius*, Together with His Discussion of Hexapla-Tetrapla." Pages 39–69 in *Origen's Hexapla and Fragments*. Edited by Alison Salvesen. TSAJ 58. Tübingen: Mohr Siebeck, 1998.

"The Dead Sea Scrolls and the Greek Bible." Pages 101–27 in vol. 1 of *The Dead Sea Scrolls After Fifty Years: A Comprehensive Assessment*. Edited by Peter W. Flint and James C. VanderKam. STDJ 30. Leiden: Brill, 1998.

"Fairy Tales: Origins and Traditions." Pages 9–13 in *Not for Children Only: Great Books for All Ages*. Edited by Laura M. Zaidman. Columbia: South Carolina State Library, 1998.

"Bringing Home the Gospel: Yiddish Bibles, Bible Societies, and the Jews." Pages 291–304 in *Yiddish Language & Culture: Then and Now*. Proceedings of the Ninth Annual Symposium of the Philip M. and Ethel Klutznick Chair in Jewish Civilization, October 27–28, 1996. Edited by

Leonard J. Greenspoon. SJC 9. Omaha: Creighton University Press, 1998.

"Between Alexandria and Antioch: Jews and Judaism in the Hellenistic Period." Pages 343–82 in *The Oxford History of the Biblical World*. Edited by Michael Coogan. New York: Oxford University Press, 1998.

"Traditional Text, Contemporary Contexts: English-Language Scriptures for Jews and the History of Bible Translating." Pages 565–76 in *The Interpretation of the Bible: The International Symposium in Slovenia*. Edited by Jože Krašovec. JSOTSup 289. Sheffield: Sheffield University Press, 1998.

"Masius" and "Max Leopold Margolis." Pages 123–24 and 134 in vol. 2 of *Dictionary of Biblical Interpretation*. Edited by John H. Hayes. Nashville: Abingdon, 1999.

"Margolis, Max Leopold." In vol. 14 of *American National Biography*. Edited by John A. Garraty and Mark C. Carnes. New York: Oxford University Press, 1999.

"Etched in Stone? Two Tablets, 10 Commandments, a Multitude of Meanings." *Creighton University Magazine* (Winter 1999): 22–29.

"Extra! Extra! Philistines in the Newsroom!" *BRev* 16.4 (2000): 50–53.

"Hellenism" (pp. 237–39), "Hellenistic Literature" (pp. 239–40), and "Joshua, Book of" (pp. 320–22) in *Reader's Guide to Judaism*. Edited by Michael Terry. Chicago: Fitzroy Dearborn, 2000.

"Old Testament Versions, Ancient." Pages 752–55 in *Dictionary of New Testament Background*. Edited by Craig A. Evans and Stanley E. Porter. Downers Grove, IL: InterVarsity Press, 2000.

"Biblical Scholars Need Not Apply: News Media and the Bible." *SBL Forum* (October 2001).

"Jewish Bible Translation." Pages 397–412 in vol. 2 of *The Biblical World*. Edited by John Barton. New York: Routledge, 2002.

"Top Dollar, Bottom Line? Marketing English-Language Bibles Within the Jewish Community." Pages 115–33 in *Biblical Translation in Context*. Edited by Frederick W. Knobloch. Studies and Texts in Jewish History and Culture 10. Bethesda, MD: University of Maryland Press, 2002.

"Joshua: A Man for All Seasons?" *ARCHAEVS: Études d'Histoires des Religions* 6 (2002): 37–51.

"The Birth of a Bible." *Norii* 10 (Summer 2002).

"Another Perspective—Jewish Translations of the Bible." *SBL Forum* (August 2002).

"The Bible and/in Popular Culture." *Norii* 12 (Winter 2002).

"Jewish Bible Translation in/and the Enlightenment." *Studia Hebraica* 2 (2003): 319–28.

"Hebrew into Greek: Interpretation In, By, and Of the Septuagint." Pages 80–113 in vol. 1 of *History of Biblical Interpretation*. Edited by Alan Hauser and Duane F. Watson. Grand Rapids: Eerdmans, 2003.

"From Maidens and Chamberlains to Harems and Hot Tubs: Five Hundred Years of Esther in English." Pages 217–41 in *The Book of Esther in Modern Research*. Edited by Sidnie White Crawford and Leonard J. Greenspoon. JSOTSup 380. London: T&T Clark, 2003.

"The KJV and the Jews." *SBL Forum* (October 2003).

"How the Bible Became the Kynge's Owne English." *BRev* 19.6 (2003): 15–21, 52–54.

"Jewish Translations of the Bible." Pages 2005–20 in *The Jewish Study Bible*. Edited by Adele Berlin and Marc Zvi Brettler. New York: Oxford, 2003.

"Crimes and Punishments: Joshua 7 as Literature." *Studia Hebraica* 3 (2003): 311–24.

"10 Common Misconceptions about Bible Translations." *Creighton University Magazine* (Summer 2004): 12–17.

"The Septuagint and/in Popular Culture." *BIOSCS* 36 (2003): 61–74.

"The Portion: The Politics of Biblical Translation." *The Forward* (January 30, 2004).

"The Portion: Thought Divorced from Action." *The Forward* (July 30, 2004).

"Portrayal of Jews in Comics and in Popular Culture in the Classroom," *SBL Forum* (November 2004).

"Translating Biblical Words of Wisdom into the Modern World." Pages 389–405 in *Seeking Out the Wisdom of the Ancients: Essays Offered to Honor Michael V. Fox on the Occasion of His Sixty-Fifth Birthday*. Edited by Ronald L. Troxel, Kelvin G. Friebel, and Dennis R. Magary. Winona Lake, IN: Eisenbrauns, 2005.

"The Book of Joshua: Text and Versions." *CurBR* 3 (2005): 229–61.

"Texts and Contexts: Perspectives on Jewish Translations of the Hebrew Bible." Pages 64–64 in *Translation and Religion: Holy Untranslatable?* Edited by Lynne Long. Clevedon: Multilingual Matters, 2005.

"The Past, Present, and Future of Jewish Translations of the Bible (with an Emphasis on English-Language Versions)." *Studia Hebraica* 4 (2004): 320–31.

"The Portion: Translations and Transliterations." *The Forward* (October 14, 2005).

"The Portion: Strategies for Remaining True to the Text." *The Forward* (Fall 2005).

"The Book of Joshua and Bible Translation," "The Book of Joshua and Issues of War and Peace," "The Book of Joshua and Jewish Exegesis," and "The Book of Joshua and Popular Culture." Pages 138–44 in *Teaching the Bible: Practical Strategies for Classroom Instruction*. Edited by Mark Roncace and Patrick Gray. Atlanta: Society of Biblical Literature, 2005.

"The Holy Bible: A Buyer's Guide." *BRev* 21.4 (2005): 37–44.

"What America Believes About the Bible." *BRev* 21.5 (2005): 27–29.

"The Septuagint." Pages 595–98 in vol. 3 of *Encyclopaedia Judaica*. Jerusalem: Jerusalem Publishing House, 2006.

"Aristeas, Letter of." Pages 260–61 in vol. 1 of *The New Interpreter's Dictionary of the Bible*. Edited by Katherine Doob Sakenfeld. Nashville: Abingdon, 2006.

"Jews and Judaism in Comic Strips." Pages 255–70 in *American Judaism in Popular Culture*. Proceedings of the Seventeenth Annual Symposium of the Klutznick Chair in Jewish Civilization-Harris Center for Judaic Studies, October 24–25, 2004. Edited by Leonard J. Greenspoon and Ronald A. Simkins. SJC 17. Omaha: Creighton University Press, 2006.

"The *Kaige* Recension: The Life, Death, and Postmortem Existence of a Modern—and Ancient—Phenomenon." Pages 5–16 in *XII Congress of the International Organization for Septuagint and Cognate Studies, Leiden 2004*. Edited by Melvin K. H. Peters. SCS 54. Atlanta: Society of Biblical Literature, 2006.

"The Septuagint." Pages 913–16 in vol. 4 of *The Encyclopedia of Christianity*. Edited by Erwin Fahlbusch et al. Grand Rapids: Eerdmans, 2006.

"Humor in the Bible." *Creighton University Magazine* (Summer 2006): 26–31.

"The Portion: Reconnoitering Translations." *The Forward* (June 23, 2006).

"The Portion: Translating Torah." *The Forward* (July 28, 2006).

"Iesous/Joshua: The Book of Joshua: English Translation, with Introduction." Pages 174–94 in *A New English Translation of the Septuagint*. Edited by Albert Pietersma and Benjamin G. Wright. New York: Oxford University Press, 2007.

"By the Letter?/Word for Word? Scripture in the Jewish Tradition." Pages 141–63 in *The Hebrew Bible: New Insights and Scholarship*. Edited by Frederick E. Greenspahn. Jewish Studies in the Twenty-First Century. New York: New York University Press, 2008.

"'Reclaiming' the Septuagint for Jews and Judaism." Pages 661–70 in *Scripture in Transition: Essays on Septuagint, Hebrew Bible, and Dead Sea Scrolls in Honour of Raija Sollamo*. Edited by Anssi Voitila and Jutta Jokiranta. JSJSup 126. Leiden: Brill, 2008.

"A Short History of Bible Translation." Pages 33–51 in *The Jewish Bible: A JPS Guide*. Edited by Carol Hupping. Philadelphia: Jewish Publication Society of America, 2008.

"Text and the City." Pages 39–52 in *Cities Through the Looking Glass: Essays on the History and Archaeology of Biblical Urbanism*. Edited by Rami Arav. Winona Lake, IN: Eisenbrauns, 2008.

"Old Testament Scriptures." Pages 429–33 in *Encyclopedia of the Historical Jesus*. Edited by Craig A. Evans. New York: Routledge, 2008.

"From Dominion to Stewardship? The Ecology of Biblical Translation." *Journal of Religion & Society* 3 (2008): 159–83.

"The King James Bible and Jewish Bible Translations." Pages 123–38 in *Translation That Openeth the Window: Reflections on the History and Legacy of the King James Bible*. Edited by David G. Burke. New York: American Bible Society, 2009.

"The Taming of the Two: Queen Esther and Queen Vashti in Midrash." *Journal of Religion & Society* 5 (2009): 155–69.

"Versions, Greek" (5:760), "Versions, Jewish" (5:760–65), "The Septuagint" (5:170–77), "LXX" (3:734), "Seventy, The," (5:199), "Symmachus" (5:416), and "Theodotion" (5:555). *The New Interpreter's Dictionary of the Bible*. Edited by Katherine Doob Sakenfeld. 5 vols. Nashville: Abingdon, 2009.

"The Making of a Symposium: Annual Conference on Jews/Judaism Features World Scholars, Unique Topics." *Creighton Magazine* (Summer 2009).

"When Harry Met Max" [article on Harry M. Orlinsky and Max L. Margolis]. Pages 289–304 in *New Essays in American Jewish History: Commemorating the Sixtieth Anniversary of the Founding of The American Jewish Archives*. Edited by Pamela S. Nadell, Jonathan D. Sarna, and Lance J. Sussman. Cincinnati: Jacob Rader Marcus Center of the American Jewish Archives, 2010.

"At the Beginning: The Septuagint as a Jewish Bible Translation." Pages 159–69 in *"Translation Is Required": The Septuagint in Retrospect and Prospect*. Edited by Robert J. V. Hiebert. SCS 56. Atlanta: Society of Biblical Literature, 2010.

"The Septuagint." Pages 1217–20 in *The Eerdmans Dictionary of Early Judaism*. Edited by John J. Collins and Daniel E. Harlow. Grand Rapids: Eerdmans, 2010.

"Money and the Bible." *Creighton Magazine* (Fall/Winter 2010): 14–17.

"Not in An Ivory Tower: Zev Garber and Biblical Studies." *HS* 51 (2010): 369–73.

"The Septuagint." *Oxford Bibliographies Online* (2011).

"Humor in the Bible: Old Testament." *Oxford Biblical Studies Online* (2011).

"Bibelübersetzung." Pages 313–18 in vol. 1 of *Enzyklopädie jüdischer Geschichte und Kultur*. Edited by Dan Diner. Stuttgart: J. B. Metzler, 2011.

"Bible, Translations and Translators," "Cities of Refuge," and "The Ten Commandments." Pages 71–72, 107, and 592 in *The Cambridge Dictionary of Judaism and Jewish Culture*. Edited by Judith Baskin. New York: Cambridge University Press, 2011.

"The Septuagint." Pages 562–65 in *Jewish Annotated New Testament*. Edited by Amy-Jill Levine and Marc Z. Brettler. New York: Oxford University Press, 2011.

"Bickerman, Elias Joseph." Pages 1191–92 in vol. 3 of *Encyclopedia of the Bible and Its Reception*. Edited by Hans-Josef Klauck et al. Berlin: Walter de Gruyter, 2011.

"Humor in the Apocrypha." *Oxford Biblical Studies Online* (2012).

"Translation: The Biblical Legacy to Judaism." Pages 83–97 in *The Wiley-Blackwell History of Jews and Judaism*. Edited by Alan T. Levenson. Malden, MA: Wiley-Blackwell, 2012.

"By the Letter? Word for Word? The Role of Memory in Paul's Citation of Scripture." Pages 9–24 in *Paul and Scripture: Extending the Conversation*. Edited by Christopher D. Stanley. ECL 9. Atlanta: Society of Biblical Literature, 2012.

"Translating 'Jesus' and 'the Jews': Can We Eradicate the Anti-Semitism without also Erasing the Semitism?" Pages 11–27 in *Soundings in the Religion of Jesus: Perspectives and Methods in Jewish and Christian Scholarship*. Edited by Bruce Chilton, Anthony LeDonne, and Jacob Neusner. Minneapolis: Fortress, 2012.

"Humor in the Book of Esther." *Bible Odyssey* (2012).

"The Hebrew Bible." Pages 25–56 in *Bloomsbury Companion to Jewish Studies*. Edited by Dean Bell. New York: Bloomsbury, 2013.

"The Afterlife in the Septuagint." Pages 43–59 in vol. 1 of *Heaven, Hell, and the Afterlife: Eternity in Judaism, Christianity, and Islam*. Edited by J. Harold Ellens. Santa Barbara: Praeger, 2013.

"Humor in the New Testament." *Oxford Biblical Studies Online* (2013).

"Back to Our Environmental Roots: How the Bible Serves to Ground Faith and Action in Roman Catholicism, Protestantism, and Judaism." *Journal of Religion & Society* 9 (2013): 30–45.

"Flusser, David." Pages 263–64 in vol. 9 of *Encyclopedia of the Bible and Its Reception*. Edited by Hans-Josef Klauck et al. Berlin: Walter de Gruyter, 2013.

"The KJV and Anglo-Jewish Translations of the Bible: A Unique and Uniquely Fruitful Connection." Pages 273–95 in *The King James at 400: Assessing Its Genius as Bible Translation and Its Literary Influence*. Edited by David G. Burke, John F. Kutsko, and Philip H. Towner. Atlanta: SBL Press, 2013.

"Interpreting the Sealed Book: Introduction." *JSCS* 47 (2014): 17–20.

"Reflections on a Course: 'Judaism and early Christianity: The Parting of the Ways—When? Where? Why?'" Pages 133–45 in *Teaching the Historical Jesus: Issues and Exegesis*. Edited by Zev Garber. Routledge Studies in Religion 42. New York: Routledge, 2014.

"Textual and Translation Issues in Greek Exodus." Pages 322–48 in *The Book of Exodus: Composition, Reception, and Interpretation*. Edited by Thomas B. Dozeman, Craig A. Evans, and Joel N. Lohr. VTSup 164. Leiden: Brill, 2014.

"Translation Techniques, Ancient Versions." Pages 404–14 in vol. 2 of *The Oxford Encyclopedia of Biblical Interpretation*. Edited by Steven L. McKenzie. 2 vols. New York: Oxford University Press, 2014.

"David and Goliath in Popular Culture." *Bible Odyssey* (2014).

"Joshua." *Bible Odyssey* (2014).

"Goodenough, Edwin." Pages 657–58 in vol. 10 of *Encyclopedia of the Bible and Its Reception*. Edited by Hans-Josef Klauck et al. Berlin: Walter de Gruyter, 2014.

"KJV and Isaiah 9:1." *Bible Odyssey* (2016).

"Jewish Bible Translations." *Oxford Bibliographies in Jewish Studies* (2016).

"Esther, Vashti, Ruth, and Naomi: Kindred Heroines in Megilloth." Pages 20–29 in *Megilloth Studies: The Shape of Contemporary Scholarship*. Edited by Brad Embry. Hebrew Bible Monographs 78. Sheffield: Sheffield Phoenix, 2016.

"Forward." Pages 11–15 in *Near Christianity: How Journeys along Jewish-Christian Borders Saved My Faith in God*, by Anthony Le Donne. Grand Rapids: Zondervan, 2016.

"Between Text and Community: A Characteristic Feature of Jewish Bible Translations." *Open Theology* 2 (2016): 476–93.

In Press and In Preparation:

"Comic Strips." *The Oxford Handbook to the Bible in American Popular Culture*. Edited by Dan W. Clanton and Terry Ray Clark. New York: Oxford University Press, forthcoming.

"The Septuagint." *Jewish Annotated Apocrypha*. Edited by Jonathan Klawans and Lawrence Wills. New York: Oxford University Press, forthcoming.

"Biblical Period: Society, Culture and Demography," and "Biblical Period: Politics and Economics." *Routledge Handbook of Jewish History and Historiography*. Edited by Dean Bell. New York: Routledge, forthcoming.

"Hellenistic Period." *The Oxford Handbook on Ancient Egypt and the Hebrew Bible*. Edited by Susan Tower Hollis. New York: Oxford University Press, forthcoming.

Jewish Translations of the Bible. Atlanta: Society of Biblical Literature/New York: American Bible Society, forthcoming.

The JPS Bible Commentary: Joshua. Philadelphia: Jewish Publication Society of America, forthcoming.

Is Judaism Democratic? Reflections from Theory and Practice Throughout the Ages. Proceedings of the Twenty-Ninth Annual Symposium of the Klutznick Chair in Jewish Civilization-Harris Center for Judaic Studies-Schwalb Center for Israel and Jewish Studies, October 30–31, 2016. West Lafayette, IN: Purdue University Press, forthcoming.

Notes

[1]None of the three editors of this volume studied with Leonard formally, and yet we have similar stories: early in our academic careers Leonard took an interest in our work, in us as individuals, and in our success as budding scholars. In telling our stories to each other, we came to see as a common thread Leonard's kind and selfless giving of time, energy, and wise counsel.

[2]See Leonard J. Greenspoon, "Teaching the Humanities is My Livelihood (Leonard's Story)" in Nebraska Cultural Endowment's *What's Your Livelihood?* column (December 4, 2013). Available at http://nebraskaculturalendowment.org /teaching-the-humanities-is-my-livelihood/. Other elements of Leonard's story can be found in his op-ed article "Deny Syrian Refugees Entry to the US? We've Been Here Before," *History News Network* (December 5, 2015). Available at http:// historynewsnetwork.org/article/161393.

[3]The interview that follows was conducted in January 2016. Leonard's responses are indented to distinguish his words from mine.

[4]See *BAR* 40.6 (2014): 13. In that article, Leonard states: "I do want to let readers know that my new-found interest in twins, in the modern world as well as in the Bible, is not the result of whim or serendipity. Rather, it springs from the announcement by our older daughter, Gallit, and her husband, Elan, that they will soon be the proud parents of twins—meaning that Ellie and I will be the even prouder (if that's possible) grandparents of twins. We don't know what Abraham and Sarah, to say nothing of Jacob and Leah, thought about their bouncing baby grandsons. For sure, I will not be as reticent with my emotions as they apparently were with theirs!"

Part I

ANCIENT HEBREW SCRIPTURES AND GREEK TRANSLATIONS

1

"Proto-Masoretic," "Pre-Masoretic," "Semi-Masoretic," and "Masoretic": A Study in Terminology and Textual Theory

Emanuel Tov
Hebrew University of Jerusalem

The Masoretic Text (MT) is the most common Hebrew version of the Hebrew Bible and the one considered authoritative by Jews for almost two millennia. In modern times, MT is found all over. Even if one thinks that one does not know what MT is or where to find it, one cannot miss it, so to speak, because MT is found in multiple sources. All the printed editions of the Hebrew Bible and most of its modern translations present a form of MT. From the invention of the printing press, all the editions of the Hebrew Bible have been based on a text form of MT, with the exception of publications of the Samaritan Pentateuch or eclectic editions.

In the course of the study of MT several terms have been used. The history of the terms "Proto-Masoretic," "Pre-Masoretic," "Masoretic," "MT-like" and "Semi-Masoretic" is more complicated than one would think at first thought. These complications pertain not only to the terminology used, but also to the textual *Weltanschauungen* in the background. In this conceptual study, I will try to understand when these terms were first used, what they imply, in which sources they are found, and how they are used.

The least problematic is the use of the base term "Masoretic Text" (MT), although also here there are variations. In my *Textual Criticism of the Hebrew Bible* (henceforth *TCHB*), I defined this entity as follows:

> The name *Masoretic Text* refers to a group of manuscripts (the MT group) that are closely related to one another. Many of the elements of these manuscripts, including their final form,

> were determined in the early Middle Ages, but they continue a much earlier tradition. The name *Masoretic Text* was given to this group because of the apparatus of the Masorah attached to it. This apparatus, which was added to the consonantal base, developed from earlier traditions in the 7th to the 11th centuries, the main developments occurring in the beginning of the 10th century with the activity of the Ben Asher family in Tiberias.[1]

Not everyone realizes that the use of the term "proto-Masoretic" is fairly recent, closely related to the discovery of the Dead Sea Scrolls. In 2018 this term commonly designates the precursors of the MT prior to the Middle Ages.

Terminology Used before the Discovery of the Dead Sea Scrolls

I have not found evidence for the use of the term "proto-Masoretic" before 1947, that is, before the discovery of the Dead Sea Scrolls. One could argue that that term could not have been used before the scrolls were found, but that would not be realistic, since some scholars recognized that there was an entity that preceded the medieval MT and that could have been named "proto-MT." I therefore quote some scholars claiming that the medieval texts were preceded by earlier ones, even though the texts themselves were beyond their textual horizon.

The consonantal precursor of MT was often not given a name, and instead the term "textus receptus" was used. Thus Claudius Cappellanus (1667), Erhard Andreas Frommann (1761), Theodor Nöldeke (1868), and Abraham Kuenen (1873) believed that the existence of this "textus receptus" in the first centuries CE can be proven from Scripture quotations in the New Testament and in rabbinic literature.[2]

In an insightful analysis, Justus Olshausen (1853) is aware that there were ancient Hebrew texts similar to the medieval MT in the first century CE.[3]

In concise, abstract terms, Paul de Lagarde proposed in 1863 that all manuscripts of MT derived from one copy (". . . auf ein einziges exemplar zurückgehn"), which served as the "archetype" of the Masoretic Text.[4]

Paul Kahle used the term *Vulgärtext(e)* for the texts preceding MT. Basing his position, on the one hand, on the internal differences between the medieval manuscripts of MT and, on the other hand, on the variants contained in the Cairo Genizah texts and the biblical quotations in the Talmud, Kahle (1915) stressed, against de Lagarde, the difficulty in assuming one original text for MT.[5] The use of a term like proto-MT could have improved the clarity of Kahle's position. Instead, Kahle used other terms that denoted and characterized these early texts. Originally Kahle named the predecessor of MT *Vulgärtext* ("vulgar" text) facilitating the reading;[6] he later used the plural *Vulgärtexte*.[7] He also described the SP and LXX as such texts. Kahle also used the term "textus receptus."[8]

Kahle's views were accepted by Gillis Gerleman[9] (1948) and Alexander Sperber (1929–1966).[10] Neither scholar used the term proto-MT.

Terminology Used after the Discovery of the Dead Sea Scrolls

No specific term

The discovery of the Dead Sea Scrolls brought about many changes in the understanding of specific passages and texts and of the development of the biblical text in general. At the same time, scholars did not immediately comprehend the significance of the new evidence, nor did they integrate that knowledge into the framework of what was known previously.

One of the new categories of knowledge pertains to the discovery of scrolls in the Judean Desert that were close to the medieval MT. The term "proto-Masoretic" was coined in order to describe these sources, influenced by the previously used terms "proto-Theodotion" and "proto-Lucianic" describing textual entities similar to Lucian and Theodotion yet existing before the time of the historical Theodotion or Lucian.[11] However, in the first so many years after the discovery of the scrolls the term "proto-Masoretic" was not yet used.

It was too early for Bleddyn Roberts to have sound knowledge of the scrolls when he published his *Introduction* to textual criticism in 1951.[12] Roberts realized that the medieval MT was preceded by certain ancient scrolls, but he did not give them a name. The very first chapter in his handbook was therefore named, in general, "The Hebrew text before the time of the Massoretes."[13]

In 1956 Moshe Greenberg did not use the term "proto-MT" where, in retrospect, it was expected: "It would thus appear that the forerunner of our received text was extant and current during the last pre-Christian centuries. The Isaiah *b* scroll and Psalter *a* testify to that."[14] Regarding Murabbaʿat, Greenberg adds, "Moreover the biblical fragments—remnants of the Torah and Isaiah—agree in every detail with our text."[15]

Likewise, in 1957 Patrick W. Skehan spoke in general terms about the closeness of the Judean Desert texts to MT without using any specific terms.[16] This applies also to his statements in 1959: "To discuss the MT at this period [i.e., the period of the scrolls] is to affirm that it exists, in a large proportion of the Qumran texts, though not in fully standardized copies. It is also to affirm that the MT in this period is for many books a single recension. . . ."[17]

The terms proto-Masoretic and pre-Masoretic

At one point, scholars started using the term "proto-Masoretic" when describing the Judean Desert scrolls that had a close connection with the medieval texts. If I am not mistaken,[1] this term was first used in 1955 by William F. Albright in an influential study launching his "local texts theory" in which he wrote about the three text "recensions" located in three different localities: Babylonia ("the proto-Masoretic text-tradition"), Egypt ("the Egyptian recension of the LXX"), and Palestine.[18]

Albright's suggestion greatly influenced his student Frank M. Cross, who accepted the local texts theory together with its terminology. Cross developed the theory further, and the new terminology

1. Indeed, the program "Google Books Ngram Viewer" indicates that in the literature written in the English language this term did not appear prior to 1955 (courtesy of Anthony Le Donne).

is first visible in his influential book *The Ancient Library of Qumran* published in 1958, based on his Haskell Lectures for 1956–1957.[19] From that time onwards, Cross systematically used the term "proto-Masoretic,"[20] while in his earlier publication from 1952 this term was not yet used.[21]

The change in terminology is well visible in the various editions of Ernst Würthwein's *The Text of the Old Testament* in German and English. As late as 1988 (fifth German edition) and 1995 (second English edition), this *Introduction* only spoke about MT and never about the proto-MT (see the indexes).[22] Only the third English edition (2014) introduced the notion of proto-MT (see the index).[23]

The change in terminology shows that the acceptance of the term was gradual, more in the writings of American scholars than those of Europeans.[24] The aforementioned studies of Greenberg and Skehan do not yet use the term proto-MT, and likewise the *DJD* volumes hardly use that term. No more than a dozen occurrences of this term together with "proto-rabbinic" can be spotted in all the volumes, especially the later ones.[25]

Pre-Masoretic. Until the time of Dominique Barthélemy, the term "pre-Masoretic" or "vor-Masoretisch" was used infrequently to denote textual witnesses preceding the medieval texts. Basically this term was used as designating the textual status of text preceding the medieval MT. In 1955 Oscar Lofgren spoke about "vormasoretisch" with regard to 1QIsa[a].[26] In 1959 Roberts referred to 1QIsa[b] as "Pre-Masoretic."[27] Likewise, in 1984, when "proto-Masoretic" was the usual term designating early scrolls resembling MT, Giovanni Garbini spoke about "(pré)massorétique."[28] David Clines and Kristin De Troyer used the term in a general sense as referring to the Hebrew text before the stage of the proto-Masoretic text.[29]

With equal frequency, the term "pre-Masoretic" refers to the pronunciation of Hebrew before the Masoretic period. Thus, Kahle often used this term with reference to the linguistic aspects of early scrolls.[30]

What are proto-Masoretic scrolls?

It might seem that there is a consensus regarding the use of the term "proto-Masoretic,"[31] but in actuality there is not, since scholars use this term in different ways. The confusion started in the first years after the discovery of the scrolls with William H. Brownlee and William F. Albright.[32]

When analyzing the use of the term "proto-Masoretic," we make a distinction between the scrolls found in Judean Desert sites outside Qumran (Masada, Murabba'at, Naḥal Ḥever , Naḥal Mishmar, Naḥal Ṣe'elim) and those found in Qumran. We name the former "Judean Desert sites," even though technically Qumran also is in the Judean Desert.

Judean Desert sites

From the very beginning of the publication of the texts from the Judean Desert sites, it was clear to a few scholars that these texts reflect the medieval MT exactly, in contradiction to the Qumran texts.

The Judean Desert texts were found at both the earlier site of Masada (texts written between 50 BCE and 30 CE) and the later sites of Wadi Murabba'at, Wadi Sdeir, Naḥal Ḥever, Naḥal Arugot, and Naḥal Ṣe'elim, dating to the period of the Bar Kochba revolt in 132–135 CE (texts copied between 20 and 115 CE). This identity can be observed best in an examination of the well-preserved texts MasPs[a] (end of the first century BCE), MasLev[b] (30 BCE–30 CE), 5/6ḤevPs (50–68 CE), and MurXII (ca. 115 CE).

Detailed proof of the dichotomy between the texts from the Judean Desert sites and Qumran was provided in later years by Dominique Barthélemy (1992), Ian Young, and Armin Lange.[33] For MurXII the spadework was already performed in the *editio princeps* by Milik, who remarked that this text was copied "a few decennia after the fixation of the received text."[34] Analyzing the corpora as a whole, Young recorded the number of variants from MT (L) included in each text, and then calculated the ratio of variation for the text by dividing the number of preserved words by the variants. The lower that ratio, the greater the divergence from L. In this way, Young demonstrated the difference between the status of the Qumran scrolls as close to MT, yet somewhat distant, and those from the other Judean Desert sites as identical to MT. In his calculation of the number of variants, Young excluded orthographical variants. For example, for MurXII Young records a mere 17 content variants.[35] In his analysis of that scroll the average variant ratio is one variant after every 222 words, while for the Qumran scrolls it is one after 12–22 words.[36] Lange analyzed both orthographic and content variants, and some of the figures provided in his *Handbuch* are included in Table 1.1 in appendix 1 below.

In a similar vein, Cross noted, "The character of textual variation in Qumran texts, where manuscripts belong to different textual families, differs *toto caelo* from the variation exhibited in the biblical texts of Murabbaʿat stemming from the circles of Bar Kochba."[37]

As a result, there is no doubt that the scrolls from the Judean Desert sites need to be distinguished from the Qumran scrolls since they relate differently to the medieval MT manuscripts. The Judean Desert scrolls are clearly proto-Masoretic in the sense that they are the precursors of the medieval manuscripts. In my view, these scrolls do not differ more from Codex L than the medieval texts differ from one another,[38] especially the accurate Tiberian manuscripts differing from the Sephardi, Ashkenazi, and Italian manuscripts.

Qumran

While most scholars now agree that the medieval MT texts are a direct continuation of the Judean Desert texts and ought to be named proto-Masoretic,[39] the opinions expressed on the Qumran texts are less clear. The confusion started with Albright, probably the first scholar to use the term "proto-Masoretic," as he called many scrolls "proto-Masoretic" that we would characterize differently today. Albright described 1QIsa[a] as a text "belonging to the proto-Massoretic type, though it has a much fuller vocalization,"[40] portrayed as "an offshoot of the proto-Massoretic text-tradition in Babylonia."[41] The second Isaiah scroll, 1QIsa[b], is also described as "proto-Massoretic."[42]

Albright may be forgiven for creating some confusion, since he wrote at a time when little was known about the scrolls and when scholars were not yet able to develop a textual outlook. Now that all the data are in front of us, we should be able to make more precise statements. The truth of the matter is that many scholars use the term proto-Masoretic for *all* the scrolls from the Judean

Desert sites that show some kind of affinity to the medieval text, including Qumran. I was guilty of the same confusion myself; until a few years ago, I named scrolls such as 1QIsa^{b} proto-Masoretic. In the second edition of my *TCHB* (2001)[43] I still used that term for that scroll, while in the third edition (2012) I used a different one, "MT-like," to distinguish the Qumran texts from the Judean Desert scrolls that are virtually identical with the medieval tradition. In 1QIsa^{b} I find in a single column (col. XXI) twenty deviations from MT, eleven in orthography and nine in small details.[44] However, it is not conducive for precise scholarship if all the scrolls that have some kind of affinity to MT are given the same name. Realizing the problems involved, Barthélemy, Lange, and Tov developed new terminologies.[45]

Differences in Terminology

The most detailed distinction between the different types of scrolls is by Barthélemy. Barthélemy realized in 1992 that the Judean Desert scrolls are to be subdivided into two Masoretic categories, together with a non-Masoretic group of texts.[46] The recognition of two different Masoretic groups together with a third group was a major innovation, not yet found in Barthélemy's summary of the *Hebrew Old Testament Text Project*, named *Interim Report* (1974–1980).[47] Barthélemy used three different terms for these groups:

1. Pre-Masoretic, e.g. 1QIsa^{b} (cf. Tov's term "MT-like"). These texts display an affinity to MT, but not as close an affinity as the next category. In Barthélemy's system, "pre-" is used in a chronological sense, while "proto-" indicates closeness in content. While the proximity in meaning between "pre-" and "proto-" is confusing, the distinction between these two groups is basic for me as well.

2. Proto-Masoretic, e.g., MurXII. These texts display almost identically with the medieval text.

3. Extra-Masoretic, e.g., 1QIsa^{a}.[48] This category was introduced by Barthélemy in order to illustrate certain aspects of the development of the scrolls. In Barthélemy's terminology all the scrolls that are not designated as either pre- or proto-Masoretic are extra-MT. I do not use this term since it encompasses too many sources, but for

Barthélemy this tripartite division was important in order to support his view of the standardization of the Hebrew text (see below).

The use of these terms served a distinct purpose in Barthélemy's description of the history of the development of the text,[49] worked out only for Isaiah. This terminology cannot be applied to most other Scripture books, since the evidence for the opposition of pre- and proto-Masoretic texts is simply lacking. Barthélemy's terminology was also employed separately by Adrian Schenker and Arie van der Kooij,[50] but I have not seen it used elsewhere.

A. Lange distinguished between two types of texts that previously had been named proto-Masoretic. He named the broader group "semi-Masoretic" and the more limited group of texts that were almost identical with MT, proto-Masoretic.[51] Lange suggested that proto-MT texts differ from MT in as much as 2% of their content. This percentage was probably determined by way of intuition and is confirmed here by an analysis of several scrolls (see appendix 2).

Like Barthélemy, Emanuel Tov distinguished between two circles of early Masoretic texts: an inner circle of *proto-Masoretic* scrolls that are virtually identical with the medieval texts (found in the Judean Desert sites, e.g., MurXII) and a second circle of *MT-like* scrolls that are very similar to it (found at Qumran, e.g., 1QIsa^{b}).[52] While this dichotomy had a central place in my descriptions of the ancient evidence, the terminology itself was used for the first time in my *TCHB*^{3} (2012).

Terminology and Textual Theories

Moving now from terminology to textual theories, we are faced with the problem of explaining the data; among other things, we try to understand the presumed sequence of the text groups. The main issue is whether the typological precursors of the medieval text (that is, the proto-MT) developed from the "MT-like" texts (option 1) or vice versa (option 2). In other words, were variants removed from MT-like texts thus creating a single proto-MT text (option 1), or was there a widening from the proto-MT texts to a looser connection with that text in the MT-like texts (option 2)?

More concretely, was a proto-MT text like 4QGen^b1 created by removing the variants such as those included in a MT-like text such as 4QGen^g (option 1), or did the opposite development take place? That is, were MT-like texts like 4QGen^g created by changing the text of proto-MT 4QGen^b (option 2)? These two Genesis texts are less known, but I cannot exemplify the procedure well for the Isaiah scrolls since no good representative of a proto-MT text of that book has been preserved. Had the Murabbaʿat text of Isaiah (Mur-Isa) been less fragmentary, I could have asked whether that text was the basis for the MT-like text 1QIsa^b (option 2) or whether a reverse development took place (option 1). The options described are typological, since they could have occurred concurrently, and this is actually option 3.

The three options were not presented in this way in previous scholarship since scholars turned mainly to option 1. That option was preferred as the most logical possibility based on the fact that when the Qumran scrolls were written, texts with the looser connection with MT prevailed statistically, while in later times the pure MT texts (proto-MT texts) were predominant. The move from one type of text to another one was supposed to have taken place gradually, although the main change took place after the destruction of the temple at the end of the first century CE, culminating in the "victory" of the proto-MT.

The terminology used, as well as the theoretical descriptions, reveal the intentions behind the views of the scholars. The views of Barthélemy and Lange supported what I named option 1, and the theoretical background of this action was characterized by the assumption of standardization, that is, the move from a multiplicity of texts to a single one, proto-MT. For this purpose Barthélemy used three types of arguments:

1. The later *tefillin* from the Judean Desert are closer to MT than the earlier Qumran *tefillin*.[53]

---

1. The proto-MT scroll 4QGen^b, although classified as a Qumran text, probably derived from one of the Judean Desert sites, and needs to be detached from the Qumran corpus. See James R. Davila, "2. 4QGen^b," in Eugene Ulrich and Frank Moore Cross, eds., *Qumran Cave 4.VII: Genesis to Numbers*, DJD XII (Oxford: Clarendon, 1994 [repr. 1999]), 31.

2. The proto-MT text of the Judean Desert scrolls was created by a process of standardization prior to the second Jewish revolt.[54]

3. The earlier texts were changed towards MT as is shown by ten or eleven corrections in MurXII towards MT.[55]

Barthélemy's arguments are supposed to show the narrowing down from the textual variety in the earlier MT-like texts to the later proto-MT. However, this presumed movement towards standardization cannot be supported by any hard evidence (see notes 55–57 herein).

The main argument in favor of standardization runs as follows. After several centuries of textual plurality, a period of uniformity and stability can be discerned within Judaism at the end of the first century CE. This situation is usually explained as reflecting a conscious effort to stabilize the Scripture text, involving the creation of a standard text for Palestine as a whole. However, textual stability (that is, when all sources reflect the same text) should not be confused with stabilization, that is, an organized attempt to create a stable text, since that stability may have been caused by a number of factors. Stabilization involves a conscious process, since it reflects an attempt to impose a text on a group or certain region. An alternative explanation of the evidence could be an assumed historical coincidence. Thus one could claim—as I do—that after the destruction of the Temple and with the splitting off from Judaism of the Samaritans and Christians, MT was the only text surviving within Judaism, as the central text of the Pharisees, set against textual plurality in earlier times.

Like Barthélemy, Lange assumes a movement toward standardization. To the arguments provided by Barthélemy, Lange added significant statistical data on the diffusion of proto-MT texts after the middle of the first century BCE. It was claimed that the presence of proto-Masoretic scrolls in the late Judean Desert sites from the period of Bar Kochba (135 CE) shows that at that time MT had ousted the other texts in Qumran and elsewhere, already from the second half of the last century BCE onward.[56] However, this assumption is based only on a very small number (six) of presumed proto-MT scrolls at Qumran.[57] These texts are very fragmentary, and with a content of around one hundred fragmentary words, their textual profile cannot be assessed well.[58] In my view, only the first century CE "Qumran" scroll 4QGen[b] (50–100 CE) may be considered truly proto-Masoretic, but the Qumran provenance of this scroll has been greatly doubted.[59] As a result, no certain proto-MT scrolls have been found in Qumran.[60]

Against the assumed reduction of variants, it should further be argued that such a process could only have taken place if early scribes would have constantly compared their scrolls with a central master copy, for which they probably would have had to travel to Jerusalem.

Because of the difficulties inherent with option 1,[61] I lean towards one of two alternative options. The main argument in favor of options 2 and 3 is the refutation of option 1. According to option 2, the proto-MT was often changed slightly. However, neither this view—nor any other one—can be proven with firm evidence. I nevertheless think that this development took place, definitely in the case of the Torah, where most of the textual witnesses further develop a text like the proto-MT. I prefer option 3, according to which two types of development occurred at the same time. In my view, there was no movement from pluriformity to uniformity or from uniformity to pluriformity, but, in the words of Adam van der Woude, "there was a basically uniform tradition *besides* a pluriform tradition in Palestine Judaism in the last centuries BC."[62]

There is no early evidence for the proto-MT, but this is probably a mere historical coincidence. The earliest evidence pertains to MasLev[b] (30 BCE–30 CE), but earlier presence of proto-MT may be inferred from the existence of the MT-like texts.

The nature of 4QJer[a] illustrates the presumed procedure, although it offers no absolute proof. This scroll reflects the exact same spelling as the medieval MT even in the smallest details,[63] but its scribal mistakes and their subsequent correction are much more frequent than in most Qumran scrolls and are uncharacteristic of the Masoretic manuscripts. These data show that the base of this scroll is in the Masoretic tradition, and that this particular scribe carelessly copied the Masoretic tradition.

The date of origin of the Masoretic tradition is unknown, but it must have existed in the background of the MT-like copies at least from approximately 200 BCE onwards (the date of 4QJer[a]). At a later stage, it is found in the hands of the Zealots on Masada and the followers of Bar-Kochba in the Judean Desert sites. At the same time, a slightly free approach towards that tradition is witnessed in less precise copies such as those recorded in appendix 3. These scribes did not go as far as the Qumran Scribal Practice that created such "wild" texts as the large Isaiah scroll and similar texts of the Torah, but remained rather close to MT. *Tefillin* of both scribal traditions, proto-Masoretic and MT-like, are known.

Summary

The Masoretic Text is the most common Hebrew version of the Hebrew Bible and therefore the terms used in connection with the representatives of that text are very meaningful. I hope to have elucidated the meaning and use of the various terms used for the different forms of the Masoretic Text. I also offered an explanation for the presumed development of these texts. (1) MT-like texts are attested for an earlier period, starting with 4QJer^{a} (225–175 BCE). (2) There are no confirmed proto-MT texts from Qumran with the exception of 8QPhyl I. (3) Proto-MT texts from the Judean Desert sites are dated to a relatively late period, between 50 BCE and 30 CE for Masada and between 20 and 115 CE for the Bar-Kochba sites of Wadi Murabba'at, Wadi Sdeir, Naḥal Ḥever, Naḥal Arugot, and Naḥal Ṣe'elim. (4) I presume that, in the period for which we have evidence, the proto-Masoretic and MT-like texts co-existed in different socio-religious environments.

In appendices 2 and 3, I list only relatively well-preserved texts.[64]

Appendix 1: MT-like Scrolls (Selection)

1. 4QpaleoGen-Exod^{l} (100 – 50 BCE).
2. 1QIsa^{b} (50 – 25 BCE).
3. 4QJer^{a} (225 – 175 BCE).
4. 4QJer^{c} (25 – 1 BCE).
5. 4QPs^{c} (50 – 68 CE).
6. 2QRuth^{a} (25 – 1 BCE).

Appendix 2: Well-Preserved Proto-Masoretic Texts

All well-preserved relevant texts from Masada and the other Judean Desert are included in this appendix.

1. MurPhyl (100–125 CE, see J. T. Milik, *DJD* II, 81). The relatively long text of MurPhyl (393 words) contains no variants, neither in content nor in orthography. The passages themselves are in exact agreement with the rabbinic rules. Since the four passages must have been copied from Torah scrolls, it is remarkable that these agreed exactly with MT. The same argument pertains to the two *tefillin* from Ṣe'elim,[65] but they contain very few words (87 and 37 words, mostly complete).

2. 4QGen^b (50-100 CE). While all other proto-MT scrolls are from the Judean Desert sites, this is the only one from Qumran, although it did not derive from controlled excavations.[66] With 358 partially preserved words, this scroll reflects only one variant in spelling and none in content: 1:15 למארת = vv. 14, 16 MT; MT למאורת.

This is a small fragment, but its agreement with MT is striking, even in the form 1:21 התנינם,[67] reflecting a reticence to have two adjacent *plene* syllables. Also, the sense divisions (open sections) agree with MT in 1:5, 8, 13, 19, 23 (complete line). There is one correction of a letter left out by mistake in 1:16. The scroll differs from SP and the LXX.[68]

3. MasLev^b (30 BCE–30 CE). The agreement between MasLev^b and codex L pertains to intricacies of orthography, including the defective [תמי]מם in Lev 9:2, 3 (col. I, lines 11, 13)[69] and the defective *hiphil* form ויקרבו in Lev 9:9 (col. I, line 21).[70] Likewise, among the ancient witnesses only MasLev^b contains the anomalous MT form הוא (Lev 10:17; 11:6) for the third person feminine pronoun, while all other Qumran manuscripts represent this word as היא.

The 96 fragmentary lines of MasLev^b contain no variants (against MT). There is one orthographical difference.

The scroll sides with MT against LXX in nine details (10:9, 15; 11:4, 26, 35, 36, 38, 40, 40), of which six are harmonizations.

There are four corrections of apparent mistakes towards the text that is now MT: 10:17; 11:10, 32, 35. There is one difference in orthography. MasLev^b is closer to MT than to SP in fifteen readings

(9:5, 9; 10:15; 11:7, 25, 26, 27, 28, 29, 31, 32, 35, 36, 37, 38) and four cases of orthography (9:10; 10:9, 9; 11:35), but not in 10:16.

4. The En-Gedi scroll, agreeing with codex L in *all* of its details in Leviticus 1–2 (34 fragmentary lines), and ascribed to the first or second century CE.[71]

Appendix 3: Percentages of Variation between Codex L and Various Ancient Scrolls

The purpose of this appendix is to show that the proto-MT Judean Desert scrolls differ up to 2% from MT,[72] while the MT-like texts differ up to 10%; see Tables 1.1 and 1.2.[73]

Table 1.1: Proto-MT Judean Desert Scrolls Compared with MT

source	word count	content variants	orthographic variants	total variants	% of variation
4QGen[b]	358	0	1	1	0.28
MurExod	119	0	0	0	0
MasLev[b]	456	0	1	1	0.22
En-Gedi scroll	185	0	0	0	0
MasEzek	489	3	8	11	2.24
MurXII	3,605	18	23	41	1.13
MasPs[a]	284	5	4	9	3.16
MurPhyl	393	0	0	0	0

Table 1.2: MT-like Judean Desert scrolls compared with MT[74]

source	word count	content variants	orthographic variants	total variants	% of variation
4QGen[g]	132	4	9	13	10
4Qpaleo Gen-Exod[l]	804	15	30	45	5.6
4QExod[c]	802	37	22	59	7.35

1QIsa^{b} XXI	164	9	11	20	12.2
4QJer^{a}	673	17	16	33	5
4QJer^{c}	631	22	21	43	6.8
4QPs^{c}	320	9	4	13	4
2QRuth^{a}	152	7	2	9	5.9

Notes

This study is dedicated to Leonard Greenspoon, a much appreciated colleague in Septuagint studies and above all a dear friend with a proverbial sense of humor. I always follow his research with great interest and his column in *BAR* with intense pleasure.

[1]Emanuel Tov, *Textual Criticism of the Hebrew Bible*, 3rd ed. (Minneapolis: Fortress, 2012), 24.

[2]Claudius Cappellanus, *Mare rabbinicum infidum seu Quaestio Rabbinico-Thalmudica* (Paris: Gasparo Meturas, 1667), 255–300; Erhard Andreas Frommann, *Quaestio philologica an variae lectiones ad codicem V. T. ex Mischna colligi possiut* (Coburg: ex officina Findeiseniana, 1761); Theodor Nöldeke, *Die alttestamentliche Literatur in einer Reihe von Aufsätzen dargestellt* (Leipzig: Quant & Händel, 1868), 240–42; Abraham Kuenen, *De stamboom van den Masoretischen Tekst des Ouden Testaments* (Amsterdam: C.G. van der Post, 1873).

[3]Justus Olshausen, *Die Psalmen, Kurzgefasstes exegetisches Handbuch zum Alten Testament* (Leipzig: Hirzel, 1853), 18.

[4]Paul de Lagarde, *Anmerkungen zur griechischen Übersetzung der Proverbien* (Leipzig: Brockhaus, 1863), 2–4, here 2; idem, *Mittheilungen*, 4 vols. (Göttingen: Dieterich, 1884), 1:19–26.

[5]Paul Kahle, "Untersuchungen zur Geschichte des Pentateuchtextes," *TSK* 88 (1915): 399–439; repr. in idem, *Opera Minora* (Leiden: Brill, 1956), 3–37.

[6]Kahle, "Untersuchungen," 35; idem, *Die hebräischen Handschriften aus der Höhle* (Stuttgart: Kohlhammer, 1951), 40 and passim.

[7]Kahle, *Die hebräischen Handschriften*, 59; see also Kahle's *The Cairo Geniza* (Oxford: Oxford University Press, 1947; 2nd ed., Oxford: Blackwell, 1959; German ed.: Berlin: Akademie-Verlag, 1962).

[8]Kahle, "Untersuchungen," 26–37.

[9]Gillis Gerleman, *Synoptic Studies in the Old Testament* (Lund: Gleerup, 1948).

[10]Alexander Sperber, *Septuaginta—Probleme: Texte und Untersuchungen zur vormasoretischen Grammatik des hebräischen*, BWANT 3/13 (Stuttgart: Kohlhammer, 1929); idem, *A Historical Grammar of Biblical Hebrew: A Presentation of Problems with Suggestions to Their Solution* (Leiden: Brill, 1966).

[11]I do not know when the term "proto-Samaritan" was coined.

[12]Bleddyn J. Roberts, *The Old Testament Text and Versions: The Hebrew Text in Transmission and the History of the Ancient Versions* (Cardiff: University of Wales Press, 1951).

[13]Roberts, *Old Testament Text and Versions*, 1–29; Roberts gave the Qumran scrolls the unusual name "Jerusalem scrolls" (pp. 2–9).

[14]Moshe Greenberg, "The Stabilization of the Text of the Hebrew Bible Reviewed in the Light of the Biblical Materials from the Judean Desert," *JAOS* 76 (1956): 157–67, here 165.

[15]Greenberg, "Stabilization of the Text," 165.

[16]Patrick W. Skehan, "The Qumran Manuscripts and Textual Criticism," *Volume du Congrès: Strasbourg 1956*, ed. G. W. Anderson, VTSup 4 (1957): 148–60.

[17]Patrick W. Skehan, "Qumran and the Present State of Old Testament Text Studies: The Masoretic Text," *JBL* 78 (1959): 21–25, here 21.

[18]William F. Albright, "New Light on Early Recensions of the Hebrew Bible," *BASOR* 140 (1955): 27–33, here 30.

[19]Frank Moore Cross, *The Ancient Library of Qumran and Modern Biblical Studies* (London: Duckworth, 1958; Garden City, NY: Doubleday, 1961) = *ALQ*[1]; *The Ancient Library of Qumran*, 3rd ed. (Sheffield: Sheffield Academic Press, 1995) = *ALQ*[3].

[20]Cross, *ALQ*[1], 173, 178, 190.

[21]Frank Moore Cross and David Noel Freedman, *Early Hebrew Orthography: A Study of the Epigraphic Evidence*, AOS 36 (New Haven: American Oriental Society, 1952).

[22]Ernst Würthwein, *Der Text des Alten Testaments: Eine Einführung in die Biblia Hebraica*, 5th ed. (Stuttgart: Deutsche Bibelgesellschaft, 1988); idem, *The Text of the Old Testament: An Introduction to the Biblia Hebraica*, trans. E. F. Rhodes, 2nd ed. (Grand Rapids: Eerdmans, 1995).

[23]Ernst Würthwein, *The Text of the Old Testament: An Introduction to the Biblia Hebraica*, revised and expanded by A. A. Fischer, trans. E. F. Rhodes, 3rd ed. (Grand Rapids: Eerdmans, 2014).

[24]In 1956, Moshe H. Goshen-Gottstein used the term "*proto-massoretic* circle" once in his "The History of the Bible-Text and Comparative Semitics: A Methodological Problem," *VT* 7 (1957): 195–201, here 200 [originally included in a lecture delivered in 1956]; repr. idem, *Text and Language in Bible and Qumran* (Jerusalem/Tel Aviv: Orient Publishing House, 1960), 156–62, here 161.

[25]Automatic search based on a scan of the volumes.

[26]Oscar Lofgren, "Zur Charakteristik des 'vormasoretischen' Jesajatextes," in *Donum natalicium H.S. Nyberg oblatum* (Uppsala: Almqvist & Wiksells, 1955), 171–84.

[27]Bleddyn J. Roberts, "The Second Isaiah Scroll from Qumrân (1QIs[b])," *BJRL* 42 (1959): 132–44, here 144: "For this task, and particularly for the implicit support of the likely existence of a pre-Massoretic 'Masoretic' text we must thank 1QIs[b]."

[28]Giovanni Garbini, "1QIsa[b] et le texte d'Esaïe," *Henoch* 6 (1984): 18–21.

[29]David J.A. Clines, *The Esther Scroll: The Story of the Story*, JSOTSup 30 (Sheffield: JSOT Press, 1984), 93–114; Kristin De Troyer, "The Hebrew Text

behind the Greek Text of the Pentateuch," in *XIV Congress of the International Organization for Septuagint and Cognate Studies: Helsinki 2010,* ed. Melvin K.H. Peters, SCS 59 (Atlanta: Society of Biblical Literature, 2013), 15–32, here 21–22.

[30]Paul Kahle, *Die hebräischen Handschriften,* 41, 43; idem, "Pre-Masoretic Hebrew," *The Annual of Leeds University Oriental Society* 2 (Leiden: Brill, 1961), 6–10; idem, "Hebreo premasoretico," *Sefarad* 21 (1961): 240–50.

[31]I do accept the term "proto-Rabbinic," used by several scholars, as very relevant to the proto-MT. However, here it is more relevant to use a term that refers to the medieval MT.

[32]Millar Burrows with the assistance of John C. Trever and William H. Brownlee, *The Dead Sea Scrolls of St. Mark's Monastery, vol. 1: The Isaiah Manuscript and the Habakkuk Commentary* (New Haven: American Schools of Oriental Research, 1950), xiii; Burrows here remarks on the closeness of the large Isaiah scroll to MT: "is substantially that presented considerably later in the MT." See below for discussion of Albright.

[33]Ian Young, "The Stabilization of the Biblical Text in the Light of Qumran and Masada: A Challenge for Conventional Qumran Chronology?" *DSD* 9 (2002): 364–90; Armin Lange, "The Textual Plurality of Jewish Scriptures in the Second Temple Period in Light of the Dead Sea Scrolls," in *Qumran and the Bible: Studying the Jewish and Christian Scriptures in Light of the Dead Sea Scrolls,* ed. Nora Dávid and Armin Lange, CBET 57 (Leuven: Peeters, 2010), 43–96; see below for discussion of Barthélemy.

[34]Jozef T. Milik in Pierre Benoit, O.P., Jozef T. Milik, and Roland de Vaux, *Les grottes de Murabba'ât,* DJD II (Oxford: Clarendon, 1961), 183.

[35]The twenty-three differences in orthography need to be added to this number. The detailed evidence is provided by Dominique Barthélemy, *Studies in the Text of the Old Testament: An Introduction to the Hebrew Old Testament Text Project* (Winona Lake, IN: Eisenbrauns, 2012), 386–87.

[36]I take issue with this system of calculating, since orthographical variants need to be included. All the same, the results would probably be very similar.

[37]Frank Moore Cross, "The History of the Biblical Text in the Light of Discoveries in the Judaean Desert," *HTR* 57 (1964): 281–99, reprinted in idem and Shemaryahu Talmon, eds., *Qumran and the History of the Biblical Text* (Cambridge, MA/London: Harvard University Press, 1975), 177–95, here 184.

[38]In the 31 verses of Isaiah 1 (35 lines in the large Isaiah scroll) the HUB records these differences with Kennicott manuscripts: K 30 (4), K 30 p.m. (4), K 93 (6), K 96 (8), K 96 p.m. (5), K 150 p.m. (10): M.H. Goshen-Gottstein, *The Hebrew University Bible: The Book of Isaiah* (Jerusalem: Magnes, 1995). See further, Jordan S. Penkower, "The Development of the Masoretic Bible," in *The Jewish Study Bible,* ed. Adele Berlin and Marc Z. Brettler, 2nd ed. (Oxford/New York: Oxford University Press, 2014), 2159–65, here 2162.

[39]However, on the basis of his study of MasGen and MasLeva, Eugene Ulrich ("Two Perspectives on Two Pentateuchal Manuscripts from Masada," in *Emanuel: Studies in Hebrew Bible, Septuagint, and Dead Sea Scrolls in Honor of Emanuel Tov,* ed. Shalom M. Paul et al., VTSup 94 [Leiden/Boston: Brill, 2003], 453–64)

challenges the idea of the closeness of these scrolls to MT. Ulrich rightly points to the unusual nature of MasGen, where within the very few preserved words (11), we find two content variants in small details and one spelling variant. This small fragment indeed does not show any closeness to the medieval tradition, but the opposite cannot be claimed either, since the fragment is too small for any type of analysis. Also MasLev[a] is too small for analysis, but at least here the allegiances are clear. The fragment is not close to either the SP or the LXX, while it agrees with MT in all details except for one spelling variant. Both fragments cannot be used for an analysis of the relations between sources, and one should analyze, instead, the longer MasLev[b], MasEzek and MasPs[a] (see below).

[40]Albright, "New Light on Early Recensions," 28–29.

[41]Albright, "New Light on Early Recensions," 30.

[42]Albright, "New Light on Early Recensions," 30.

[43]Emanuel Tov, *Textual Criticism of the Hebrew Bible*, 2nd rev. ed. (Minneapolis: Fortress / Assen: Royal Van Gorcum, 2001).

[44]See *TCHB*2, 31; *TCHB*3, 31–32.

[45]The issue of what exactly is a proto-MT text was also raised by Martin G. Abegg, "1QIsa[a] and 1QIsa[b]: A Rematch," in *The Bible as Book: The Hebrew Bible and the Judaean Desert Discoveries*, ed. Edward D. Herbert and Emanuel Tov (London: British Library and Oak Knoll Press in association with The Scriptorium: Center for Christian Antiquities, 2002), 221–8, here 224; Abegg presented percentages of deviation from MT in the Isaiah scrolls, but he did not employ a new terminology.

[46]Dominique Barthélemy, *Critique textuelle de l'Ancien Testament, 3. Ézéchiel, Daniel et les 12 Prophètes* (OBO 50/3; Göttingen: Vandenhoeck & Ruprecht / Fribourg: Éditions Universitaires, 1992), xcviii–cxvi. The English translation of this work was published posthumously in 2012: Barthélemy, *Studies*, 383–409, here 389.

[47]Dominique Barthélemy et al., *Preliminary and Interim Report on the Hebrew Old Testament Text Project*, vols. 1–5 (1st; 2nd ed.; New York: United Bible Societies, 1974, 1979–1980). In these volumes Barthélemy spoke only about the proto-MT, e.g. p. vii in the identical introduction to all volumes.

[48]Barthélemy, *Studies*, 403. A first formulation is found in idem, *Études d'histoire du texte de l'Ancien Testament*, OBO 21 (Göttingen: Vandenhoeck & Ruprecht / Fribourg: Éditions Universitaires, 1978), 351–55.

[49]The first stage in the development of the MT is the pre-Masoretic text (e.g. 1QIsa[b]), for which no dates are given and the antecedents of which are not described by Barthélemy. Barthélemy only describes "the emergence of the proto-Masoretic text" (header on p. 393) that was created from the pre-MT at the end of the first century CE (e.g. MurIsa), through a process of standardization. See Barthélemy, *Studies*, 404: "The difference between a proto-Masoretic text and a pre-Masoretic text hinges essentially on an event—the textual standardization that took place between the two Jewish revolts. The effects of the standardization are observable."

[50]Adrian Schenker, *Älteste Textgeschichte der Königsbücher: Die hebräische Vorlage der ursprüngliche Septuaginta als älteste Textform der Königsbücher*, OBO 199 (Göttingen: Vandenhoeck & Ruprecht / Friburg: Universitätsverlag, 2004), 9;

idem and Philippe Hugo, "5.2.4 Textual History of Kings," in *Textual History of the Bible, vol. 1B: Pentateuch, Former and Latter Prophets*, ed. Armin Lange and Emanuel Tov (Leiden: Brill, 2017), 315–16. In his analysis of the development of the text of Isaiah, van der Kooij frequently speaks about pre-MT as opposed to proto-MT: "6.1.2.2. After the Qumran Discoveries," in *Textual History of the Bible, vol. 1B*, 461–65.

[51] A. Lange, *Handbuch der Textfunde vom Toten Meer, I: Die Handschriften biblischer Bücher von Qumran und den anderen Fundorten* (Tübingen: Mohr Siebeck, 2009), 16. In this book, Masoretic scrolls are described as either "proto-Masoretic" or "semi-MT." Lange presented a detailed table of these two groups in his study "'They Confirmed the Reading' (y. Taʿan. 4:68a): The Textual Standardization of Jewish Scriptures in the Second Temple Period," in *From Qumran to Aleppo: A Discussion with Emanuel Tov about the Textual History of Jewish Scriptures in Honor of His 65th Birthday*, ed. A. Lange et al., FRLANT 230 (Göttingen: Vandenhoeck & Ruprecht, 2009), 29–80, here 54–55.

[52] Emanuel Tov, "The Text of the Hebrew/Aramaic and Greek Bible Used in the Ancient Synagogues," in idem, *Hebrew Bible, Greek Bible, and Qumran: Collected Essays*, TSAJ 121 (Tübingen: Mohr Siebeck, 2008), 171–88.

[53] Barthélemy refers to the Judean Desert *tefillin* MurPhyl and the one from Naḥal Seʾelim, but they are not necessarily later than the other *tefillin*. The MT-like *tefillin* XḤevSePhyl is equally late. The analysis of the *tefillin* is more complicated than Barthélemy could have known. Three proto-MT *tefillin are* listed above, two of which agree with the instructions of the Rabbis. There is also a group of MT-like *tefillin* and a group copied in the Qumran Scribal Practice, both of which contain several segments beyond the four pericopes accepted by the rabbis.

[54] The Judean Desert texts are indeed fully proto-Masoretic, but this feature is already visible in all the earlier Masada texts that predate the assumed stabilization process.

[55] Several arguments may be adduced against this assumption. (1) In the MurXII scroll, most so-called corrections refer to quantitative differences from MT pertaining to elements omitted by mistake by the first hand, with one possible erasure (Obad 13), subsequently added in the text. On the other hand, the 41 variants in this long scroll (containing 3,605 more or less identifiable words) pertain to qualitative differences in content and orthography. Therefore, in this carefully written scroll, the 10 or 11 corrections probably represent rare mistakes that were corrected according to the scroll's *Vorlage*. It would not be logical to assume that only quantitative differences were corrected, while qualitative variants were left in the text. See in detail my forthcoming study "The Possible Revision of Hebrew texts According to MT." (2) Corrections are found in several scrolls in the Masoretic family as well as in other texts. It is incomprehensible if a few corrections in such an un-Masoretic scroll like 1QIsa[a] be conceived of as approximations towards MT, while the vast majority of its deviations from MT were not corrected.

[56] Lange points to a religious factor as the background of the diffusion of these texts: "The chronological distribution of the manuscripts of biblical books. . . shows, that the proto-Masoretic text was created in the second half of the first century

B.C.E. as part of a concentrated effort to preserve the cultural heritage of Judea. Early proto-Masoretic manuscripts like 4QJer[a] demonstrate that for this purpose existing manuscript traditions were used at least partly" (Lange, "'They Confirmed the Reading,'" 56). The same view has been developed in idem, "The Textual Plurality."

[57]4QXII[e] (75–50 BCE); 4QEzek[a] (50 BCE); 4QDeut[c] (50–25 BCE); 2QRuth[a] (30–1 BCE); 4QDeut[g] (1–50 CE); 4QGen[b] (50–100 CE).

[58]Furthermore, 4QXII[e] is not proto-Masoretic; it reflects a completely different orthography system (רויש, ידעתמה) as well as four corrections and one major variant, in ninety more or less complete words.

[59]This scroll has not been found in controlled excavations. See James R. Davila in E. Ulrich and F. M. Cross, eds., *Qumran Cave 4.VII: Genesis to Numbers,* DJD XII (Oxford: Clarendon, 1994 [repr. 1999]), 31.

[60]The assumption of the rising presence of proto-MT scrolls in Qumran in the second half of the first century BCE is further in jeopardy, since the peak in the presumed presence of proto-Masoretic scrolls is shared with the enlarged production of all scrolls in the second part of the first century BCE. Lange, "They Confirmed the Reading," notes: "It seems that this time was a zenith of scribal culture" (p. 53). This assumption is also confirmed by the statistics in my study, "Some Thoughts about the Diffusion of Biblical Manuscripts in Antiquity," in *Transmission of Traditions and Production of Texts*, ed. S. Metso et al., STDJ 92 (Leiden: Brill, 2010), 151–72; revised version: *Textual Criticism of the Hebrew Bible, Qumran, Septuagint: Collected Writings, Vol. 3,* VTSup 167 (Leiden: Brill, 2015), 60–81.

[61]An extensive refutation of the assumption of standardization is offered in my earlier publications *TCHB*, 174–80 and "The Myth of the Stabilization of the Text of Hebrew Scripture," in *The Text of the Hebrew Bible: From the Rabbis to Masoretes,* ed. E. Martín Contreras and L. Miralles-Maciá, JAJSup 13 (Göttingen: Vandenhoeck & Ruprecht, 2014), 37–45.

[62]Adam S. van der Woude, "Pluriformity and Uniformity: Reflections on the Transmission of the Text of the Old Testament," in *Sacred History and Sacred Texts in Early Judaism: A Symposium in Honour of A. S. van der Woude,* ed. Jan N. Brenner and Florentino García Martínez (Kampen: Kok Pharos, 1992), 151–69, here 163.

[63]Thus, (ו)תהיינה together with (ו)תהיין are the majority spellings of this word in Hebrew Scripture (respectively 30 and 14 times) in contrast to (ו)תהינה occurring twice. The majority spelling (ו)תהיינה occurs three times in Jeremiah, while the minority spelling (ו)תהינה occurs only in 18:21. Remarkably in this detail the scroll agrees with the medieval codices in 18:21 (thus *DJD* XIII, 150).

[64]I exclude (1) most MT-like scrolls in the Torah since they are equally close to the SP; (2) most MT-like Isaiah scrolls since they are equally close to the LXX; (3) MT-like scrolls that are too small for a meaningful analysis.

[65]Publication: Yohanan Aharoni, "Expedition B," *IEJ* 11 (1961): 11–24.

[66]J. Davila, *DJD* XII, 31 mentions Murabba'at or "another cave" as possibilities.

[67]Thus also MT Exod 7:12, Deut 32:33 (differently: תנינים Ps 74:13, 148:7).

[68]SP: The major difference with MT is in v. 14 where SP and LXX have a harmonizing plus להאיר על הארץ. Further small differences between the scroll and SP are in 1:11, 16, 22. Further, the orthography of the scroll is usually more deficient than SP. LXX: Major difference with MT in the large harmonizing plus of the LXX in v. 9. Smaller differences between the scroll and the LXX, especially in harmonizing readings, are in 1:7, 7, 8, 9, 11, 11, 12, 12, 20.

[69]Elsewhere in Scripture the defective form prevails (Exod 29:1; Lev 23:18; Num 28:3, 9, 11, 19, 31; 29:2–36 (10x); Ps 37:18) as against the *plene* form in Lev 14:10; Ezek 43:25, 45:23, 46:4, 6; Prov 1:12, 2:21, 28:10.

[70]The same defective form occurs also in Lev 10:1 and Josh 8:23 as against the *plene* form in Num 7:2, 3, 10, 15:33 and 1 Chr 16:1.

[71]Michael Segal, Emanuel Tov, W. Brent Seales, C. Seth Parker, Pnina Shor, and Yoseph Porath, "An Early Leviticus Scroll from En-Gedi: Preliminary Publication," *Text* 26 (2016): 29–58. Also accessible online: http://www.hum.huji.ac.il/units.php?cat=5020andincat=4972

[72]This figure was first suggested by Lange, "They Confirmed the Reading," 51–52.

[73]The figures of deviation from MT calculated by Abegg (n. 47) are higher for all the Isaiah scrolls, some around 8–9% and others as much as 25%. However, all these scrolls are not considered proto-MT. A very high degree of deviation from MT is found in 1QIsa[a], namely 37%.

[74]On the basis of a complete analysis of 1QIsa[b] XXI, Abegg (n. 47) calculates a deviation from MT of 8% (4.3% variants and 3.7% in orthography), as compared with my calculation of 12.2%.

2

Symmachus's Version of Joshua

Michaël N. van der Meer

The textual history of the book of Joshua is notorious for its complexities.[1] The oldest extant Hebrew witness, 4QJoshua[a], shows major divergences from the later Hebrew tradition,[2] and even the main Masoretic witnesses and the relatively late Syriac Peshitta differ in the section of Levitical cities (Josh 21:36–37). The situation becomes even more complex in the Greek witnesses.[3] The Old Greek differs in numerous quantitative and qualitative details revealing a bewildering variety of variants, particularly in the sections of toponyms (Joshua 13–21). In the first half of the twentieth century, Max Margolis spent most of his academic efforts in a bold attempt to sort out all these variants and reconstruct a critically restored text;[4] he was unaware of the Dead Sea scrolls that would drastically change the scholarly view on the history of both the Hebrew and Greek textual history of the biblical books.

It has been the lasting contribution of the honoree of this volume, friend and colleague Leonard Jay Greenspoon, to have assessed the significance of the Dead Sea Scrolls for the book of Joshua. As soon as the Hebrew scrolls became available to scholarship, Greenspoon published a helpful and balanced study of the fragments of 4QJoshua[a] and 4QJoshua[b].[5] Even more important are his *Textual Studies in the Book of Joshua*,[6] which applied the insights gained from the discovery of the Greek Minor Prophets Scroll from Naḥal Ḥever (8ḤevXIIgr) reflecting the so-called καίγε-Theodotion recension.[7] Dominique Barthélemy published this early (mid- to late-first century BCE) Greek scroll along with a careful examination of its textual character; Barthélemy demonstrated that the revision previously ascribed to the second century CE Jewish scholar Theodotion (from Ephesus? thus Irenaeus, *Haer.* 3.21.1) already pre-dated Christianity. This pre-Christian revision is related not only to the Theodotion sections of Daniel and Job, but also to that of the Greek translation found in Judges

(B text), 2 and 4 Kingdoms (a.k.a. 2 Samuel and 2 Kings), Ruth, 2 Esdras, Lamentations, Canticles, and parts of Jeremiah and Ezekiel. This revision was an attempt to bring the Old Greek translation into conformity with the emergent proto-Masoretic text—that is, the version of the biblical books that would later gain authoritative status and would supersede in Jewish tradition all other text-forms.[8] The Old Greek was based on early Hebrew scrolls that sometimes differed from the proto-Masoretic text-type. This early pre-Christian revision, which is characterized *inter alia* by the fixed rendering of Hebrew וגם (also) with καίγε (even; at least), thus predates the comprehensive attempt by Aquila (early second century CE) to render the whole of the Hebrew Bible in a more literalistic way than the Septuagint. The last of these three Jewish revisions, that made by Symmachus (ca. 200 CE) should then be seen as a deliberate attempt to move away from the literalistic translation style while at the same time adhering to the Hebrew text as found in the proto-Masoretic tradition.

In his landmark studies of Joshua, Greenspoon examined all the readings of Theodotion and their relations with the other Greek versions to delineate the characteristics of the καίγε recension in Joshua. Hence, the first layer of deliberate additions and revisions within the textual history of the Greek Joshua could be ascertained more carefully. At the same time, Greenspoon was able to enlarge the list of characteristic καίγε renderings.

Whereas both the Qumran text and Old Greek version of Joshua have been investigated intensively after Greenspoon's initial studies over the past decades,[9] his work on the later Greek versions of Joshua has hardly been taken up by scholars.[10] This is especially the case of Symmachus's version of Joshua, which heretofore has not been examined in its own right. The reason for this lacuna in biblical scholarship undoubtedly lies in the fragmentary state of the remains of this version, which has only been preserved in marginal readings in Greek and Syriac manuscripts and an occasional scholium in patristic literature. Furthermore, as Greenspoon puts it, "Symmachus is far less useful for the textual critic than is the literalist Aquila. By contrast, the many interpretive elements he introduced make him a valuable source for the study of exegetical traditions."[11]

Such interpretative elements in the ancient versions have nonetheless fascinated me over the years. I have found that redaction and reception are often simply two sides of the same coin; so too formation and reformulation, as well as textual transmission and interpretation.[12] The Greek translation of Symmachus is as fascinating as it is underestimated. Although previous scholarship sought to interpret the readings of Symmachus in light of an alleged Ebionite background, most contemporary scholars examine these readings in light of rabbinic writings as a possible product of Rabbi Meir's pupil Sumkhos ben Joseph.[13] Beyond the aim of rendering the canonized, proto-Masoretic Text of the Hebrew Bible in an intelligible way, Symmachus's version reflects strong interests in the theological themes of anti-anthropomorphism of the Deity, belief in the resurrection, halakhic rulings, and the special status of the land of Israel, as well as the related political aims of compliance with the Roman authorities and endorsement of the rule of Rabbi Juda ha-Nasi.[14] Given Symmachus's proximity in time, place, and religious background, it has also proven meaningful to investigate possible relationships between Symmachus's version and the Targumim.[15] Hence, there are good reasons to examine Symmachus's Greek version as part of the early Jewish reception history of the book of Joshua—especially since the *Wirkungsgeschichte* of Joshua in early Judaism and early Christianity is rather meager compared to the Pentateuch, the Psalter, and the Prophets.[16]

Readings Symmachus Shared with His Predecessors

To reiterate, Symmachus's version has been preserved almost exclusively in readings in the margin of Greek and Syriac hexaplaric manuscripts.[17] All extant material was gathered by Frederick Field in the late nineteenth century.[18] Although new material has come to light for the Pentateuch, the Psalter, and the book of Isaiah,[19] no new readings of Symmachus's version of Joshua have been discovered. In the absence of a new collection and examination of the hexaplaric materials,[20] I therefore rely on the edition of Field.

The number of readings attributed to Symmachus in Joshua amounts to 209, but almost half of them are readings that Symmachus shares with Theodotion and/or Aquila. To trace the peculiar interpretation of Joshua by Symmachus, I first isolate the readings attributed to Symmachus from the readings attributed to the Old Greek and other Greek versions.[21] The hexaplaric notes herein follow the standard reference system for the Septuagint (ο′), Aquila (α′), Symmachus (σ′), and Theodotion (θ′), often by their individual sigla but also collectively as "the Three" (οἱ γ′) or "the others" (οἱ λοιποί or οἱ λ′). Field's Greek retroversions of the Syro-Hexapla (siglum Syh, the Syriac translation of the fifth column of Origen's Hexapla) are marked with a modern asterisk (*).

Readings where Aquila, Symmachus, and Theodotion align against the Old Greek

	Joshua	Variants	LXX	MT
1	1:2	τὸν Ἰορδάνην τοῦτον M 85	τὸν Ιορδάνην ---	את הירדן הזה
2	1:4	τοῦτον M	καὶ τὸν Ἀντιλίβανον (---)	והלבנון הזה
3	1:4	πᾶσαν τὴν γῆν τοῦ Χετταίου M Syh ܟܠܗ ܐܪܥܐ ܕܚܬܝܐ	--- --- --- ---	כל ארץ החתים
4	1:7	σφόδρα M 85	καὶ ἀνδρίζου ---	ואמץ מאד
5	1:7	κατὰ πάντα τὸν νόμον M 85	καθότι --- --- ---	ככל התורה
6	1:8	ἵνα φυλάσσῃς (ποιεῖν) (44,52, 54, 74) Syh ∻ ܕܬܛܪ Lucif (*ut custodias facere*)	ἵνα συνῇς ποιεῖν (Marg)	למען תשמר לעשות
7	1:8	ἐν αὐτῷ ὅτι M 85	πάντα τὰ γεγραμμένα --- --- ---	הכתוב בו כי
8	1:9	χῶρον M	εἰς πάντα (τόπον Marg)	בכל
9	1:11	ἑαυτοῖς M	ἑτοιμάζεσθε ---	הכינו לכם
10	1:11	διαβαίνετε M	διαβαίνετε (var. lect. διαβήσεσθε *O″ C″*)	עברים
11	1:12	λέγων M	---	לאמר

12	1:14	Μωσῆς πέραν τοῦ Ἰορδάνου M	--- --- --- --- ---	משה בעבר הירדן
13	1:15	δοῦλος κυρίου M	--- ---	עבד יהוה
14	1:17	οὕτως M	--- ἀκουσόμεθα	כן נשמע
15	2:2	λέγοντες M	λέγοντες (om A M 15 19)	לאמר
16	2:2	(ἰδοὺ) ἄνδρες εἰσπεπόρευνται ὧδε (τὴν νύκτα) 85	εἰσπεπόρευνται ὧδε ἄνδρες	אנשים באו הנה
17	2:3	πρὸς σὲ οἳ εἰσῆλθον M	τοὺς ἄνδρας τοὺς εἰσπεπορευμένους --- ---	הבאים אליך אשר באו
18	2:4	δύο M	τοὺς --- ἄνδρας	את שני האנשים
19	2:5	ταχέως M	καταδιώξατε	רדפו מהר
20	2:5	⁎ὅτι καταλήψεσθε αὐτούς Syh ܡܛܠ ܕܡܕܪܟܝܢ ܐܢܬܘܢ ܠܗܘܢ ⁘	εἰ καταλήμψεσθε αὐτούς	כי תשיגום
21	2:9	καὶ ὅτι τετήκασι πάντες οἱ κατοικοῦντες τὴν γῆν ἀπὸ προσώπου ὑμῶν M 85	--- --- --- --- --- --- --- --- --- ---	וכי נמגו כל ישבי הארץ מפניכם
22	2:11	αὐτός M	--- θεὸς	הוא אלהים
23	2:12	καὶ δώσετέ μοι σημεῖον ἀληθινόν M (θ′ καὶ δότε 85)	--- --- --- --- ---	ונתתם לי אות אמת
24	2:13	τὰς ψυχὰς ἡμῶν 85	τὴν ψυχήν μου	את נפשתינו
25	2:14	ἐὰν μὴ ἀναγγείλῃς τὸ ῥῆμα τοῦτο, καὶ ἔσται ἂν παραδῷ κύριος ὑμῖν τὴν πόλιν ποιήσομεν μετὰ σου M 85	καὶ αὐτὴ εἶπεν ὡς ἂν παραδῷ κύριος ὑμῖν τὴν πόλιν ποιήσετε εἰς ἐμὲ	אם לא תגידו את דברנו זה והיה בתת יהוה לנו את הארץ ועשינו עמך
26	2:15	ἐν σχοινίῳ, ὅτι ὁ οἶκος αὐτῆς ἐν τῷ τείχει, καὶ ἐν τῷ τείχει αὐτὴ ἐκάθητο M 85	--- --- --- --- --- --- --- --- --- --- --- ---	כי ביתה בקיר החומה ובחומה היא יושבת

27	2:17	ᾧ ὥρκισας ἡμᾶς M 85	--- --- ---	אשר השבעתנו
28	2:19	τὴν θύραν τῆς οἰκίας σου M	τὴν θύραν τῆς οἰκίας σου (τὴν οἰκίαν σου A M 55 71 82 121 Arm)	מדלתי ביתך
29	2:22	ἕως ἐπέστρεψαν M	--- --- --- ---	עד שבו הרדפים
30	3:11	ἔμπροσθεν ὑμῶν M	διαβαίνει --- ---	עבר לפניכם
31	3:12	ἄνδρα M (α' 'Ισραὴλ, ἄνδρα ἕνα τοῦ σκήπτρου 85)	Ισραηλ ἕνα ἀφ' ἑκάστης φυλῆς	ישראל איש אחד איש אחד לשבט
32	3:13	ἄνωθεν M	τὸ καταβαῖνον ---	הירדים מלמעלה
33	3:17	ἑτοίμως M Syh ܐ.ܣ. ܡܛܝܒ̈ܐ = α' σ' ἕτοιμοι?	---	הכן
34	4:3	ἑαυτοῖς M 85	ἀνέλεσθε --- --- ---	שאו לכם מזה
35	4:3	ἀπὸ στάσεως ποδῶν ἱερέων M	--- --- --- --- ---	ממצב רגלי הכהנים
36	4:5	εἰς πρόσωπου κιβωτοῦ 108 Syh ܦܪܨܘܦܐ ܀ ܗ. ܩܒܘܬܐ ܕܡܪܝܐ ܀	ἔμπροσθέν μου πρὸ προσώπου --- κυρίου --- ---	לפני ארון יהוה אלהיכם
37	4:7	τοῦ 'Ισραήλ M	τοῖς υἱοῖς Ισραηλ	לבני ישראל
38	4:10	κατὰ πάντα ὅσα ἐνετείλατο Μωυσῆς τῷ 'Ιησοῦ M	--- --- --- --- --- --- ---	ככל אשר צוה משה את יהושע
39	4:11	καὶ οἱ ἱερεῖς πρότεροι M Procop Syh ܘܟܗܢ̈ܐ	καὶ οἱ λίθοι ἔμπροσθεν αὐτῶν	והכהנים לפני העם
40	4:21	καὶ εἶπεν πρὸς τοὺς υἱοὺς 'Ισραήλ M	--- --- --- --- ---	ויאמר אל בני ישראל
41	5:1	παρὰ τὴν θάλασσαν M	--- ---	ימה
42	5:1	※τῶν Χαναναίων Syh ܕܟܢܥܢ̈ܝܐ	τῆς Φοινίκης	הכנעני
43	5:11	τῇ ἐπαύριον τοῦ πάσχα M	--- ---	ממחרת הפסח
44	5:12	τῇ ἐπαύριον M	--- ---	ממחרת

45	5:13	αὐτοῦ M	καὶ ἡ ῥομφαία ---	וחרבו
46	5:14	καὶ προσεκύνησεν M 85	--- ---	וישתחו
47	5:15	καὶ ἐποίησεν Ἰησοῦς οὕτως M	--- --- --- ---	ויעש יהושע כן
48	6:5	ὑποκάτω αὐτῶν M (α′ *καθ᾽ ἑαυτό Masius)	πεσεῖται αὐτόματα τὰ τείχη τῆς πόλεως	ונפלה חומת העיר תחתיה
49	6:9	ταῖς κερατίναις M	καὶ σαλπίζοντες --- ---	ותקוע בשופרות
50	6:10	οὐ διελεύσεται ἐκ τοῦ στόματος ὑμῶν λόγος M 85	--- --- --- --- --- --- ---	ולא יצא מפיכם דבר
51	6:13	οἱ ἔχοντες M	οἱ φέροντες	נשאים
52	7:3	κοπώσῃς 108 Syh ܠܐ ܬܠܐܬ	μὴ ἀναγάγῃς	אל תיגע
53	8:14	*ἐξῆλθον Syh ܢܦܩܘ	καὶ ἐξῆλθεν	ויצאו
54	9:9	τὴν ἀκοήν 108 (θ′ σ′) Syh܀ܫܡܥܗ .ܬ .ܣ.ܐ	ἀκηκόαμεν γὰρ τὸ ὄνομα αὐτοῦ	כי שמענו שמעו
55	10:1	Ἀδωνιβεζέκ 58 85 (ο′ α′ σ′ θ′)	Ἀδωνιβεζέκ (-σεδεκ F[c] 58 426)	אדני צדק
56	10:2	*πόλεων ※ τῶν βασιλέων . . . Syh ܕܡܕܝܢܬܐ	τῶν μητροπόλεων	ערי הממלכה
57	10:5	τῶν Ἀμορραίων Masius	τῶν Ιεβουσαίων	האמרי
58	10:5	Ἐγλώμ 85 (Αἰγλώμ 58; Ἐγλών, ἢ καὶ Ὀδολλάμ, On)	Ὀδολλάμ	עגלון
59	11:1	Ἰωβάβ 85	Ἰωβάβ (Ἰωάβ 16 30 52)	יובב
60	13:12	τῶν Ῥαφαείμ 54[txt] Syh ܕܪ̈ܦܐܝܡ܀	ἀπὸ τῶν γιγάντων	מיתר הרפאים
61	13:19	τῆς κοιλάδος 85 (τῆς παλλάδος 58[marg])	ἐν τῷ ὄρει Εμακ	בהר העמק
62	16:1	*καὶ ἐξῆλθεν ὁ κλῆρος Syh ܘܢܦܩ ܦܣܐ܀	καὶ ἐγένετο τὰ ὅρια	ויצא הגורל
63	18:17	Ἐδωμείν 85	Αιθαμιν	אדמים

64	19:12	ἡλίου 85 (Σάμ On) Syh ܫܡܫܐ❖	ἀπ' ἀνατολῶν Βαιθσαμυς	מזרח השמש
65	20:7	*καὶ τὴν Καριαθαρβέ Syh ܘܠܩܘܪܝܬ ܐܪܒܥ❖	καὶ τὴν πόλιν Αρβοκ	ואת קרית ארבע
66	21:11	*τοῦ πατρὸς 'Ενάκ Syh ܕܐܒܘܗܝ ܕܥܢܩ❖	μητρόπολιν τῶν Ενακ	אבי הענוק
67	22:33	οἱ υἱοὶ 'Ισραήλ Syh ܒܢܝܐ ܕܐܝܣܪܝܠ❖	καὶ εὐλόγησαν τὸν θεὸν υἱῶν Ισραηλ	ויברכו אלהים בני ישראל

Table 2.1: Readings where Aquila, Symmachus, and Theodotion align against the Old Greek

The Hebrew text of Joshua, particularly that of the first chapters, is rather ponderous in style. This partly results from the literary formation of the book, whereby old conquest narratives were reformulated by Deuteronomistic, Nomistic, and Priestly editors. The style of the Deuteronomistic editor of the book is emphatic and repetitive. In many cases, the Greek translator sought to smooth the text by stylistic shortening; yet in some cases, secondary Hebrew additions to an originally shorter Hebrew *Vorlage*—as reflected by the Septuagint—cannot be ruled out.[22] Regardless of the reasons behind these variants, the younger Greek translators and Origen made numerous adaptations conforming the Septuagint to the standardized Hebrew text. In the sixty-seven cases presented in Table 2.1, Symmachus adopted the corrections and additions that had been made by καίγε-Theodotion and adopted by Aquila. Although Symmachus is often praised for his stylistic elegance, he apparently did not follow the Old Greek in shortening redundant phraseology. Rather, Symmachus retained redundant introductions to direct speech (λέγων in 1:12; 2:2) as well as the emphatic pronouns (1:2, 4, 11; 2:11) and repetitive phrases (2:17; 3:12; 4:3, 21; 6:9, 10).

Readings of all Greek translations vis-à-vis pre-Hexaplaric variant Greek readings

Related to the previous category are readings where ancient witnesses refer to "all" (πάντες) of the Greek translations; see Table 2.2.[23] In these cases, both the Old Greek and the recentiores seem to agree vis-à-vis a variant Greek reading. The different Greek reading is often found in the so-called Lucianic, Antiochene, or Syrian family of Septuagint witnesses.[24]

	Joshua	Reading	LXX	MT
1	4:8	πάντες χω. ὁ θεός M	καθότι ἐνετείλατο κύριος (+ὁ θεός <u>S</u>) τῷ Ἰησοῖ	כאשר צוה יהושע
2	4:24	οἱ λοιποί πάντες· ἐν παντὶ χρόνῳ M 85 Syh ܒܟܠܗ ܙܒܢܐ ÷	ἐν παντὶ ἔργῳ (B 85^mg 120 129* 344^mg 407 Eth)] ἐν παντὶ χρόνῳ (Ra A rell)] (ἐν παντὶ καιρῷ Marg coni.)	כל הימים
3	7:13	πάντες χωρὶς αὐτῶν M	ἐξ ὑμῶν (ἐξ ὑμῶν αὐτῶν Marg > <u>S</u>)	מקרבכם
4	7:25	πα χω τῷ Αχαρ M	καὶ εἶπεν Ἰησοῦς τῷ Αχαρ (τῷ Αχαρ > <u>P</u> <u>C</u>)	ויאמר יהושע

Table 2.2: Pre-Hexaplaric Greek Variants

Apparently the variant Greek readings found in the Antiochene witnesses predate Origen's hexaplaric revision.[25] These readings do not contribute to a better understanding of Symmachus's version of Joshua—except for providing confirmation that Symmachus adopted the corrections of his predecessors here as well.

Readings shared by Symmachus and Aquila

Some thirty-three other alternative readings to the Septuagint text are ascribed to both Aquila and Symmachus; see Table 2.3. In these cases, then, Symmachus adopted the changes introduced by Aquila without further modification.

	Joshua	Reading	LXX	MT
1	1:1	πρὸς Ἰησοῦν υἱὸν Ναυή 108 Syh ܐ.ܗ. ܠܘܬ ܝܫܘܥ ܒܪܗ ܕܢܘܢ	τῷ Ἰησοῖ υἱῷ Ναυη	אל יהושע בן נון

2	1:6	(τοῖς πατράσιν) *αὐτῶν Syh ܐ.ܣ. ܕܐܒܗܘܗܝ̈	τοῖς πατράσιν ὑμῶν	לאבותם
3	2:21	καὶ ἔδησεν τὸ σημεῖον τὸ κόκκινον ἐν τῇ θυρίδι Masius	--- --- --- --- --- --- --- ---	ותקשר את תקות השני בחלון
4	4:7	ἀπεκόπη Syh ܐ. ܐܬܦܣܩܘ (Σ. αποσκοπη [*sic*] 108)	ἐξέλιπεν ὁ Ιορδάνης ποταμὸς	נכרתו מימי הירדן
5	5:10	(καὶ ἐποίησαν) φασέκ 108	καὶ ἐποίησαν οἱ υἱοὶ Ισραηλ τὸ πασχα	ויעשו את הפסח
6	6:27	ἀκοὴ αὐτοῦ 108 Syh ܐ.ܣ. ܫܡܥܐ ܕܝܠܗ܀	καὶ ἦν τὸ ὄνομα αὐτοῦ	ויהי שמעו
7	7:26	κοιλὰς Ἀχώρ M (only σ') On Cat. Niceph. (*s nom.*) (On: Ἀ. Σ. ἐν τῇ κοιλάδι)	Εμεκαχωρ	עמק עכור
8	9:17	*καὶ Καριαθνεαρίν Syh ܐ. ܣ. ܩܘܪܝܬ ܢܥܪ̈ܝܡ ܀ (error for ܝܥܪ̈ܝܡ?)	καὶ πόλις Ιαριν	וקרית יערים
9	10:23	*Ἐγλώμ Syh ܐ. ܣ. ܕܥܓܠܘܡ܀	Οδολλαμ	עגלון
10	10:33	τότε ἀνέβη Ὀραμ βασιλεὺς Γαζὲρ βοηθήσων τῇ Λαχείς (θ' ἀγαζεὶρ βασιλεὺς Λαχείς) 85	τότε ἀνέβη Αιλαμ βασιλεὺς Γαζερ βοηθήσων τῇ Λαχις	אז עלה הרם מלך גזר לעזר את לכיש
11	10:40	καὶ τὸν νότον 85 (44 54) Syh ܐ. ܣ. ܘܠܬܝܡܢܐ܀	καὶ τὴν Ναγεβ	והנגב
12	11:2	κατὰ βορρᾶν Syh ܐ.ܣ. ܠܘܩܒܠ ܓܪܒܝܐ. 44 54 καὶ πρὸς τοὺς ἀπὸ βορρᾶ)	καὶ πρὸς τοὺς βασιλεῖς τοὺς κατὰ Σιδῶνα τὴν μεγάλην	ואל המלכים אשר מצפון
13	11:5	καὶ ὡμολόγησαν Masius	καὶ συνῆλθον	ויועדו
14	11:16	*καὶ πᾶσαν τὴν νότον Syh ܐ.ܣ. ܘܟܠܗ ܬܝܡܢܐ.	καὶ πᾶσαν τὴν Ναγεβ	ואת כל הנגב

15	11:17	*καὶ ἐπάταξεν αὐτοὺς, καὶ ἐθανάτωσεν αὐτοὺς Syh ܐ.ܗ. ܘܡܚܐ ܐܢܘܢ ܘ ܘܐܡܝܬ ܐܢܘܢ ܀	καὶ ἀνεῖλεν αὐτοὺς καὶ ἀπέκτεινεν	ויכם וימיתם
16	12:8	*(καὶ) ἐν τῷ νότῳ (44 54 74) Syh ܐ.ܗ. ܒܬܝܡܢܐ ܀	καὶ ἐν Ναγεβ	ובנגב
17	12:23	ἐθνῶν τῆς Γελγέλ On (Γωεὶν τῆς Γελγέλ. Ἀκ. Σύ. ἐθνῶν τῆς Γελγέλ) Syh ܐ.ܗ. ܕ ܓܠܓܠ ܀	Γωιμ τῆς Γαλιλαίας	מלך גוים לגלגל
18	13:5	*καὶ πάντα τὸν Λίβανον Syh ܐ.ܗ. ܘܟܠܗ ܠܒܢܢ ܀	καὶ (κατὰ G 19 426 Sah VetLat Syh) πάντα τὸν Λίβανον	וכל הלבנון
19	13:9	(καὶ πᾶσαν) τὴν ὁμαλήν On	καὶ πᾶσαν τὴν Μισωρ	וכל המישר
20	13:26	*(ἕως Ῥαμὼθ) Μασφά. Syh ܐ.ܗ. ܕܪܡܝ ܦܩܥܐ ܀	ἕως Ραμωθ κατὰ τὴν Μασσηφα	עד רמת המצפה
21	13:27	(ἐν τῇ κοιλάδι) Βηθαράμ 344 On Syh ܘܒܢܚܠܐ. ܘܒܝܬ ܐܪܡ.	καὶ ἐν Εμεκ Βαιθαραμ	ובעמק בית הרם
22	14:2	(ἐν χειρὶ) Μωυσῆ 108	ἐν χειρὶ Ἰησοῦ	ביד משה
23	15:57	*καὶ αἱ ἐπαύλεις αὐτῶν Syh ܐ.ܗ. ܘܕܝܪ̈ܐ ܀	καὶ αἱ κῶμαι αὐτῶν	וחצריהן
24	17:7	(εἰς) τοὺς κατοικοῦντας On (Ἰασήν [Hieron. *Jaseb*] Ἀκ. Σύμ. τοὺς κατοικοῦντας)	καὶ Ιασσιβ	אל ישבי
25	17:16	*τῆς κοιλάδος Syh ܐ.ܗ. ܕܒܢܚܠܐ ܀	--- --- ἐν τῇ κοιλάδι	ולאשר בעמק
26	19:49	*κληρονομίαν Syh ܐ.ܗ. ܝܪܬܘܬܐ ܀	κλῆρον	נחלה
27	20:5	*καὶ οὐκ ἐκδώσουσι (s. παραδώσουσι) Syh ܐ.ܗ. ܘܠܐ ܢܫܠܡܘܢܝ	--- --- --- (θ′ ? καὶ οὐ συγκλείσουσι)	ולא יסגרו

28	21:9	*ἀπὸ τῆς φυλῆς υἱῶν Ἰούδα, καὶ ἀπὸ τῆς φυλῆς υἱῶν Συμεών Syh ܐ.ܣ. ܡܢ ܫܒܛܐ ܕܒܢ̈ܝܐ ܕܝܗܘܕܐ ܘܡܢ ܫܒܛܐ ܕܒܢ̈ܝܐ ܕܫܡܥܘܢ ܀	ἡ φυλὴ υἱῶν Ιουδα καὶ ἡ φυλὴ υἱῶν Συμεων (÷ καὶ ἀπὸ τῆς φυλῆς υἱῶν Βενιαμιν ↙)	ממטה בני יהודה וממטה בני שמעון
29	21:20	(θ′ ἡ πόλις τῶν ἱερέων αὐτῶν) πόλεις κλήρου αὐτῶν 85 Syh ܕܦܣܐ ܕܠܗܘܢ	πόλις τῶν ὁρίων αὐτῶν	ערי גורלם
30	22:22	*ἰσχυρὸς θεός Masius Syh ܐ. ܫܠܝܛܐ ܀	ὁ θεὸς θεός	אל אלהים
31	22:23	*εἰρηνικήν Syh ܐ.ܣ. ܡܫܝܢܐ ܀	θυσίαν σωτηρίου	זבחי שלמים
32	24:26	ὑπὸ (τὴν) δρῦν 85 (α′) 108 (α′ θ′) Syh (α′ σ′) ܠܬܚܬ ܡܢ ܒܠܘܛܐ	ὑπὸ τὴν τερέμινθον (θ′ ὑποκάτω τῆς δρυός)	תחת האלה
33	24:32	*παρὰ τῶν υἱῶν Ἐμμώρ Syh ܐ.ܣ. ܡܢ ܒܢ̈ܝܐ ܕܚܡܘܪ ܀	παρὰ τῶν Αμορραίων	מאת בני חמור

Table 2.3: Symmachus and Aquila

Readings shared by Symmachus and Theodotion

There are only two cases where Symmachus sides with Theodotion alone; see Table 2.4.

	Joshua	reading	LXX	MT
1	7:24	κοιλάδα Ἀχώρ M 85 (*s nom*) Procop in Cat. Niceph. κοιλάδα ταραχῆς (F[b(*sine nom*)])	Εμεκαχωρ	עמק עכור
2	13:5	Βααλγά (σ′ θ′) Βαεγγά (α′) 85	ἀπὸ Γαλγαλ	מבעל גד

Table 2.4: Symmachus and Theodotion

These cases are not undisputed. The correction of the Septuagint's transliteration of עמק עכור to Εμεκαχωρ, which is ascribed in the margin of codex Coislinianus to Theodotion and Symmachus in Josh 7:25, also occurs in Josh 7:26, where the same correction is ascribed to Aquila and Symmachus in Eusebius of Caesarea's *Onomasticon*. The correction of the transliteration of Εμεκ for עמק is also ascribed to Aquila and Symmachus in 13:27, and the correction of Εμακ into τῆς κοιλάδος is ascribed to the Three in 13:19. The variation in 13:5 between Βααλγά (σ′ θ′) and Βαεγγά (α′) seems to be due to an inner-Greek corruption of the reading ascribed to Aquila.

Interim conclusions

There are good reasons to believe that Symmachus mainly relied on Aquila's revision for Joshua.[26] In all likelihood, kaige-Theodotion was primarily concerned with the quantitative variants between the Old Greek and proto-Masoretic versions of Joshua, so Symmachus supplied the phrases and sentences from his Hebrew text that were missing in the Old Greek. Aquila and Symmachus seem to correct an earlier Greek version of Josh 20:4–6 (see number 27 of the list in Table 2.3), a passage that is absent from the original Greek translation; it thus seems likely that such additions to the Old Greek come from Theodotion, even if they are not explicitly ascribed to him. Likewise, the addition to the shorter Old Greek version of Josh 2:21 (see number 3 of the list in 2.3) should probably be ascribed to Theodotion.

Overall, the readings shared by Aquila and Symmachus mainly deal with qualitative variants—that is, corrections to earlier Greek renderings. In Josh 1:1, for instance, Aquila altered the dative construction τῷ Ἰησοῖ υἱῷ Ναυη into the prepositional, accusative construction πρὸς Ἰησοῦν υἱὸν Ναυή to reflect more accurately the preposition אל in the Hebrew; apparently Symmachus felt no need to restore the more elegant formulation of the Old Greek. In Josh 4:7, Symmachus followed Aquila in his correction of the Septuagint's choice of ἐξέλιπεν ὁ Ιορδάνης ποταμὸς (nicely rendered by Greenspoon in the NETS as "the river Jordan failed") into ἀπεκόπη (was cut off). This translation may reflect the literal meaning of the corresponding Hebrew verb כרת *Niphal* more closely, but it ignores (deliberately) the first Greek translator's rephrasing of the miracle of the waters of the Jordan falling dry. In other cases, Symmachus follows Aquila's corrections too—for example, ἀκοή for ὄνομα in 6:27 (in 9:9 ascribed also to Theodotion) and the correction of the compass's corners south (נגב, transliterated as Ναγεβ by the Old Greek) in 10:40, 11:16, and 12:8, translated as νότος by Aquila and Symmachus. Likewise Symmachus followed Aquila's correction of the Old Greek's paraphrase of Josh 11:2 "the kings from the north" (המלכים אשר מצפון) as "the kings who were by Sidon the great" (τοὺς βασιλεῖς τοὺς κατὰ Σιδῶνα τὴν μεγάλην) into "the kings towards the north" (τοὺς βασιλεῖς κατὰ βορρᾶν).

Symmachus also followed his predecessor(s) in the correction of proper names, such as Ἐγλώμ instead of Οδολλαμ for עגלון in 10:5 (θ′ α′ σ′), 10:23 (α′ σ′), 10:34 (σ′), 10:37 (σ′); τῶν Χαναναίων instead of τῆς Φοινίκης for הכנעני in 5:1 (θ′ α′ σ′); τῶν Ἀμορραίων instead of τῶν Ιεβουσαίων for האמרי in 10:5 (θ′ α′ σ′); and conversely τῶν υἱῶν Ἐμμώρ instead of τῶν Αμορραίων for בני חמור in 24:32 (α′ σ′); τῶν Ῥαφαείμ instead of τῶν γιγάντων for רפאים in 13:12 (θ′ α′ σ′); Ἀδωνιβεζέκ instead of Ἀδωνισεδεκ (MSS F[c] 58 426) for אדני צדק in 10:1 (ο′ θ′ α′ σ′); Ἰωβάβ instead of Ἰωάβ (MSS 16 30 52) for יובב in 11:1 (θ′ α′ σ′); Ἐδωμείν instead of Αιθαμιν for אדמים in 18:17 (θ′ α′ σ′); Καριαθαρβέ instead of πόλιν Αρβοκ for קרית ארבע in 20:7 (θ′ α′ σ′); and Ὀραμ instead of Αιλαμ for הרם in 10:33 (α′ σ′)—to mention only the less problematic examples.

Unique Readings of Symmachus

Besides the approximately one-hundred cases above (where Symmachus seems to have adopted the corrections of his predecessors kaige-Theodotion and particularly Aquila), there are approximately as many cases where ancient witnesses attribute a reading solely to Symmachus. These readings are presented below in four categories: (1) undisputed attributions to Symmachus without rival readings of the other revisors; (2) problematic attributions; (3) Symmachus's revision of corrections made by Theodotion; and (4) similar revisions by readings of Aquila.

Unique and undisputed readings of Symmachus

	Joshua	reading	LXX	MT
1	1:1	*μετὰ δὲ τὴν τελευτὴν Μωυσῆ Syh ܡ. ܒܬܪ ܕܝܢ ܫܘܠܡܗ ܕܡܘܫܐ܀	καὶ ἐγένετο μετὰ τὴν τελευτὴν Μωυσῆ	ויהי אחרי מות משה
2	1:14	φορτίον Masius	καὶ τὰ παιδία ὑμῶν	טפכם
3	3:16	*ἀπὸ Ἀδόμ Syh ܡ. ܡܢ ܐܕܘܡ	μακρὰν σφόδρα σφοδρῶς	הרחק מאד [כ]באדם ([ק]מאדם)
4	3:16	τῆς ἀοικήτου M 85 Syh ܡ. ܕܠܐ ܡܬܥܡܪܢܘܬܐ	κατέβη εἰς τὴν θάλασσαν Αραβα θάλασσαν ἁλός	ים הערבה ים המלח
5	5:13	εἶδε φανέντα (19[txt] 58[txt])	εἶδεν --- --- ἄνθρωπον	וירא והנה איש
6	6:11	*περίοδον μιαν, καὶ ἐπιστρέψει εἰς τὴν παρεμβολήν, καὶ αὐλισθήσεται ἐν τῇ παρεμβολῇ Syh ܡ. ܒܙܒܢܐ ܚܕ ܘܬܗܦܘܟ ܠܡܫܪܝܬܐ. ܘܬܒܘܬ ܒܡܫܪܝܬܐ܀	εὐθέως ἀπῆλθεν εἰς τὴν παρεμβολὴν καὶ ἐκοιμήθη ἐκεῖ	פעם אחת ויבאו המחנה וילינו במחנה
7	7:1	κατεφρόνησεν M 75 85	καὶ ἐπλημμέλησαν	וימעלו
8	8:13	*ἀπὸ δυσμῶν τῇ πόλει Syh ܡ. ܡܢ ܡܥܪܒܐ ܠܡܕܝܢܬܐ܀	--- --- --- (θ′ ? θάλασσαν τῆς πόλεως)	מים לעיר
9	8:18	σὺν τῇ ἀσπίδι *σου ἐπὶ τὴν Γαί Syh ܡ. ܥܡ ܬܪܣܐ ܕܝܠܟ ܥܠ ܓܝ.	ἐν τῇ χειρί σου ἐπὶ τὴν πόλιν	בידך אל העי
10	8:26	ἐν τῇ ζιβύνῃ Syh ܡ. ܒܪܘܡܚܐ.	--- --- --- (θ′ ? ἐν τῷ γαισῷ)	בכידון
11	8:33	*ἀπέναντι τῶν ἱερέων τῶν Λευιτῶν τῶν αἰρόντων τὴν κιβωτὸν τῆς διαθήκης κυρίου Syh ܡ. ܠܘܩܒܠ ܟܗܢܐ ܠܘܝܐ ܗܢܘܢ ܕܫܩܠܝܢ ܩܒܘܬܐ ܕܕܝܬܩܐ ܕܡܪܝܐ܀	καὶ οἱ ἱερεῖς καὶ οἱ Λευῖται ἦραν τὴν κιβωτὸν τῆς διαθήκης κυρίου	נגד הכהנים הלוים נשאי ארון ברית יהוה

12	9:5	ἐπιβλήματα ἔχοντα M 54 85 Syh ܣ. ܕܐܝܬ ܠܗܘܢ ܦܘܪ̈ܩܐ	καταπεπελματωμένα	ומטלאות
13	10:9	ὅλην τὴν νύκτα ἀναβὰς ἐκ Γαλγαλων Masius	ὅλην τὴν νύκτα εἰσεπορεύθη ἐκ Γαλγαλων	כל הלילה עלה מן הגלגל
14	10:37	*τὴν Ἐγλών Syh ܣ. ܠܥܓܠܘܡ܀	Οδολλαμ	לְעֶגְלוֹן
15	10:42	*ἠχμαλώτευσεν Ἰησοῦς μιᾷ ὁρμῇ Syh ܣ. ܫܒܐ ܝܫܘܥ ܒܚܐܦܐ ܚܕ܀ Hier (*uno cepit impetu*)	ἐπάταξεν Ἰησοῦς εἰς ἅπαξ	לכד יהושע פעם אחת
16	11:2	*καὶ εἰς τὴν παραλίαν Δὼρ ἀπὸ δυσμῶν Syh ܣ. ܘܠܣܦܪ ܝܡܐ ܕܕܘܪ ܡܢ ܡܥܪܒܐ	καὶ εἰς Ναφεδδωρ (καὶ εἰς Φενναθ Δωρ καὶ εἰς τοὺς παραλίους Marg.)	ובנפות דור מים
17	11:3	*πρὸς τὸν Χαναναῖον τὸν ἀπὸ ἀνατολῶν, καὶ ἀπὸ δυσμῶν τὸν Ἀμορραῖον Syh ܠܘܬ ܟܢܥܢܝܐ ܕܡܢ ܡܕܢܚܐ. ܘܡܢ ܡܥܪܒܐ ܠܐܡܘܪܝܐ܀	καὶ εἰς τοὺς παραλίους Χαναναίους ἀπὸ ἀνατολῶν καὶ εἰς τοὺς παραλίους Αμορραίους	הכנעני ממזרח ומים והאמרי
18	11:6	*τετρωμένους Syh ܣ. ܟܕ ܡܚܠܠܝܢ	τετροπωμένους (ἐν τῃ τροπῃ Marg. coni.)	חללים
19	12:3	*καὶ ἀπὸ νότου ὑποκάτω Ἀσηδὼθ Φασγά Syh ܣ. ܘܡܢ ܬܝܡܢܐ ܠܬܚܬ ܡܢ ܐܫܕܘܬ ܕܦܣܓܐ܀	ἀπὸ Θαιμαν τὴν ὑπὸ Ασηδωθ Φασγα	ומתימן תחת אשדות הפסגה
20	12:4	*τῶν Ῥαφαείμ (16 18 30 85 128) Syh ܣ. ܪܦܐܝܡ܀	τῶν γιγάντων	הרפאים
21	12:7	*κατὰ διαμερισμοὺς αὐτῶν Syh ܣ. ܐܝܟ ܦܘܠܓܘ̈ܬܐ ܕܝܠܗܘܢ܀	κατὰ κλῆρον αὐτῶν	כמחלקתם

22	12:23	※(Δὼρ) τῆς παραλίας Syh ※ ܕܣܦܪ ܝܡܐ܀	τοῦ Ναφεδδωρ (τοῦ Φενναθ Δωρ Marg. coni.)	לנפת דור
23	13:4	※καὶ εἰς τὸν νότον πᾶσα ἡ γῆ Syh ※ ܘܠܬܝܡܢܐ ܟܠܗ ܐܪܥܐ܀ Hier (*Ad meridiem vero sunt Hevaei, omnis terra* [*Chanaan*])	ἐκ Θαιμαν καὶ πάσῃ γῇ Χαναaν (πάσῃ τῇ γῇ Marg.)	מתימן כל ארץ הכנעני
24	13:6	(. . .) ὑδάτων 108	ἕως τῆς Μασερεφωθ μαιμ (Μασερεφωθ Μαειμ Marg.)	עד משרפת מים
25	13:23	※(Σ. οἱ ἀγροὶ) αὐτῶν (*agros*) Masius	καὶ αἱ ἐπαύλεις αὐτῶν	וחצריהן
26	13:28	※αἱ πόλεις καὶ οἱ ἀγροὶ αὐτῶν Syh ※ ܡܕ̈ܝܢܬܐ ܘܐܓܘ̈ܪܣܐ ܕܝܠܗܘܢ܀	αἱ πόλεις αὐτῶν καὶ αἱ ἐπαύλεις αὐτῶν	הערים וחצריהם
27	14:4	※καὶ τὰ προάστεια αὐτῶν 108^mg (*s nom*) Syh ※ ܘܐܓܘ̈ܪܣܐ ܕܣܘܡ ܡܕ̈ܝܢܬܗܘܢ܀	καὶ τὰ ἀφωρισμένα αὐτῶν	ומגרשיהם
28	15:2	※ἀπ᾽ ἄκρου τῆς θαλάσσης τῆς ἁλυκῆς, ἀπὸ τῆς γλώσσης τῆς βλεπούσης πρὸς νότον Syh ※ ܡܢ ܪܝܫܐ ܕܝܡܐ ܕܡܠܚܐ. ܡܢ ܠܫܢܐ ܗܘ ܕܚܙܐ ܠܘܬ ܬܝܡܢܐ܀	ἕως μέρους τῆς θαλάσσης τῆς ἁλυκῆς ἀπὸ τῆς λοφιᾶς τῆς φερούσης ἐπὶ λίβα	מקצה ים המלח מן הלשן הפנה נגבה
29	15:3	τὸ ἔδαφος 108 On Syh ※ ܠܐܪܥܐ܀	καὶ περιπορεύεται τὴν κατὰ δυσμὰς Καδης (καὶ ἐκπορεύεται τὴν Καδκαδις Marg. coni.)	ונסב הקרקעה
30	15:5	※(ἕως) ἄκρου Syh ※ ܪܝܫܐ܀	ἕως τοῦ Ιορδάνου	עד קצה הירדן

31	15:6	(ἐν τοῖς) περὶ τὴν ἀοίκητον On Hier (*in locis quae juxta inhabitabilem sunt*) Σ. εἰς οἶκον πεδινόν Masius	ἐπὶ Βαιθ αραβα	לבית הערבה
32	15:10	*οἴκου Σάμες Syh ܣ. ܕܒܝܬ ܫܡܫ܀	ἐπὶ Πόλιν ἡλίου	בית שמש
33	15:15	*Σ. Ὁ Ἑβραῖος· Καριαθσεφέρ Syh ܣ. ܥ. ܩܘܪܝܬ ܣܦܪܐ܀	Πόλις γραμμάτων	קרית ספר
34	15:49	*Καριαθσεννά Syh ܣ. ܩܘܪܝܬ ܣܢܐ܀	Πόλις γραμμάτων	וקרית סנה
35	16:3	*καὶ καταβήσεται εἰς δυσμὰς ἐπὶ τὸ ὅριον Syh ܣ. ܘܢܚܘܬ ܠܡܥܪܒܐ ܥܠ ܬܚܘܡܐ܀	καὶ διελεύσεται ἐπὶ τὴν θάλασσαν ἐπὶ τὰ ὅρια	וירד ימה אל גבול
36	17:11	*καὶ αἱ τρεῖς παραλίαι Syh ܣ. ܘܬܠܬܝܗܘܢ ܣܦܪ̈ܝ ܝܡܐ܀	καὶ τὸ τρίτον τῆς Ναφετα	שלשת הנפת
37	17:13	*καὶ ὑπέταξαν τὸν Χαναναῖον ὑπὸ φόρον Syh ܣ. ܘܫܥܒܕܘ ܠܟܢܥܢܝܐ ܬܚܝܬ ܡܕܐܬܐ܀	καὶ ἐποίησαν τοὺς Χαναναίους ὑπηκόους	ויתנו את הכנעני למס
38	17:18	*ἀλλὰ τὸ ὄρος Syh ܣ. ܐܠܐ ܠܛܘܪܐ.	ὁ γὰρ δρυμὸς	כי הר
39	18:2	*οἳ οὐ διεμερίσαντο (διενεμήσαντο) τὴν κληρονομίαν αὐτῶν Syh ܣ. ܗܢܘܢ ܕܠܐ ܦܠܓܘ ܝܪܬܘܬܐ ܕܝܠܗܘܢ܀	οἳ οὐκ ἐκληρονόμησαν	אשר לא חלקו את נחלתם
40	18:15	*τὸ δὲ πρόσωπον τοῦ νότου ἀπ᾽ ἄκρου Καριαθιαρείμ Syh ܣ. ܦܪ̈ܨܘܦܐ ܕܝܢ ܕܬܝܡܢܐ ܡܢ ܪܝܫܐ ܕܩܘܪܝܬ ܝܥܪܝܡ	καὶ μέρος τὸ πρὸς λίβα ἀπὸ μέρους Καριαθ βααλ	ופאת נגבה מקצה קרית יערים

41	18:15	※εἰς θάλασσαν Syh^{M} ܠܝܡܐ	καὶ διελεύσεται ὅρια εἰς Γασιν (Γαειν Marg)	ויצא הגבול ימה
42	18:17	※ἐπὶ τὰ μεθόρια Syh ※. ܥܠ ܬܚܘܡܐ ⁘(ܬܚܘ̈ܡܐ)	ἐπὶ Γαλιλωθ	אל גלילות
43	18:18–19a	εἰς τὴν πεδιάδα ※πρὸς βορρᾶν καὶ καταβήσεται ἐπὶ τὴν πεδιάδα καὶ καταβήσεται τὸ ὅριον ἐπὶ τὸν ὦμον Βαιθαγλὰ εἰς βορρᾶν On Syh ※. ܠܦܩܥܬܐ ܠܘܬ ܓܪܒܝܐ. ܘܢܚܘܬ ܥܠ ܦܩܥܬܐ ܘܢܚܘܬ ܬܚܘܡܐ ܥܠ ܟܬܦܐ ܕܒܝܬ ⁘ܚܓܠܐ ܠܓܪܒܝܐ	κατὰ νώτου Βαιθ αραβα ἀπὸ βορρᾶ καὶ καταβήσεται (+ ἐπὶ Αραβα, καὶ καταβήσεται Marg.) ἐπὶ τὰ ὅρια ἐπὶ νώτου Βαιθ αγλα ἀπὸ βορρᾶ	מול הערבה צפונה וירד הערבתה ועבר הגבול אל כתף בית חגלה צפונה
44	18:21	※καὶ κοιλὰς Κασείς Syh ⁘ ※. ܘܥܘܡܩܐ ܩܣܝܣ	καὶ Αμεκασις (Αμεκ Κασεις Marg)	ועמק קציץ
45	19:13	※εἰς Ῥεμμὼν τὴν ἐπιφανῆ Syh ※. ܠܪܡܘܢ ⁘ܓܠܝܐ	ἐπὶ Ρεμμωνα Αμαθαρ Αοζα (Ανωγα Marg. coni.)	רמון המתאר הנעה
46	19:14	※εἰς φάραγγα On Syh ⁘ ※. ܠܢܚܠܐ	ἐπὶ Γαιφαηλ (Γαι Ιφθαηλ Marg. coni.)	גי יפתח אל
47	19:26	※καὶ κατήντησεν ἐπὶ Κάρμηλον Syh ※. ܘܐܬܐ ܥܠ ⁘ܟܪܡܠܐ	καὶ συνάψει τῷ Καρμήλῳ	ופגע בכרמל
48	19:27	※καὶ ἐν τῇ φάραγγι . . . εἰς βορρᾶν εἰς τὴν κοιλάδα Syh ※. ܘܒܢܚܠܐ ⁘ܠܓܪܒܝܐ ܒܥܘܡܩܐ	καὶ ἐκ Γαι καὶ Φθαιηλ κατὰ βορρᾶν καὶ εἰσελεύσεται ὅρια Σαφθαιβαιθμε καὶ Ιναηλ (καὶ ἐν Γαι Ιφθαηλ . . . ὅρια Σαφθα Βαιθ Εμεκ καὶ Ναειηλ Marg. [coni.])	ובגי יפתח אל צפונה בית העמק ונעיאל
49	19:28	※’Εβδών Syh ⁘ ※. ܥܒܕܘܢ	καὶ Ελβων (Εβρων Marg.)	ועברן (עבדן MT[MSS])

50	19:34	*ἀπὸ δυσμῶν τῷ Ἰούδα Syh ܣ. ܡܢ ܡܥܪܒܐ ܠܝܗܘܕܐ܀	κατὰ θάλασσαν καὶ ὁ Ιορδάνης	מים וביהודה הירדן
51	21:2	καὶ τὰ πρόαστεια αὐτῶν Masius Syh *s nom* ܘܦܪ̈ܘܕܐ ܕܩܘܪܝܗ ܡܕܝܢܬܐ ܀(ܡܕ̈ܝܢܬܐ)	καὶ τὰ περισπόρια	ומגרשיהן
52	21:11	°καὶ τὰ πρόαστεια αὐτῶν Syh ܣ. ܘܦܪ̈ܘܕܐ ܕܩܘܪܝܗ ܀ ܡܕ̈ܝܢܬܐ	καὶ τὰ περισπόρια	ואת מגרשה
53	21:13	*εἰς καταφυγήν Syh ܣ. ܠܒܝܬ ܓܘܣܐ܀	τὴν πόλιν φυγαδευτήριον	את עיר מקלט
54	21:38 (-40)	*πᾶσαι αἱ πόλεις αὗται τοῖς υἱοῖς Μεραρὶ κατὰ τὴν συγγένειαν αὐτῶν, τοῖς λοιποῖς τῆς συγγενείας τῶν Λευιτῶν Syh ܣ. ܟܠܗܘܢ ܡܕܝܢܬܐ (ܡܕ̈ܝܢܬܐ) ܗܠܝܢ ܠܒܢ̈ܝܐ ܕܡܪܪܝ، ܐܝܟ ܐܚܝܢܘܬ ܓܢܣܐ ܕܠܗܘܢ܀ ܠܫܪܟܢܐ ܕܐܚܝܢܘܬ ܓܢܣܐ ܕܠܘ̈ܝܐ	πᾶσαι πόλεις τοῖς υἱοῖς Μεραρι κατὰ δήμους αὐτῶν τῶν καταλελειμμένων	כל הערים לבני מררי למשפחתם הנותרים ממשפחות הלוים
55	22:7–8	*ὅτε μὲν οὖν ἀπέλυσεν αὐτοὺς Ἰησοῦς εἰς τὰς σκηνὰς αὐτῶν, εὐλόγησεν αὐτοὺς, καὶ εἶπε πρὸς αὐτοὺς Syh ܣ. ܟܕ ܡܢ ܗܟܝܠ ܫܪܐ ܐܢܘܢ ܝܫܘܥ ܠܡܫܟ̈ܢܐ ܕܠܗܘܢ. ܒܪܟ ܐܢܘܢ ܘܐܡܪ ܠܘܬܗܘܢ܀	καὶ ἡνίκα ἐξαπέστειλεν αὐτοὺς Ἰησοῦς εἰς τοὺς οἴκους αὐτῶν, καὶ εὐλόγησεν αὐτούς, --- --- ---	וגם כי שלחם יהושע אל אהליהם ויברכם ויאמר אליהם
56	22:8	*διαμερίσατε τὰ σκῦλα τῶν ἐχθρῶν μετὰ τῶν ἀδελφῶν ὑμῶν Syh ܣ. ܦܠܓܘ ܒܙ̈ܬܐ ܕܒܥܠܕ̈ܒܒܐ ܥܡ ܐܚ̈ܝܟܘܢ ܀	διείλαντο τὴν προνομὴν τῶν ἐχθρῶν μετὰ τῶν ἀδελφῶν αὐτῶν	חלקו שלל איביכם עם אחיכם

57	22:10	*εἰς τὰ ὅρια τοῦ Ἰορδάνου Syh ※ ܠܬܚܘܡܐ ܕܝܘܪܕܢܢ ܀	εἰς Γαλγαλα τοῦ Ιορδάνου	אל גלילות הירדן
58	22:11	*ἐπὶ τῶν ὁρίων τοῦ Ἰορδάνου πρὸς τὴν διάβασιν τῶν υἱῶν Ἰσραήλ Syh ※ ܥܠ ܬܚܘܡܐ ܕܝܘܪܕܢܢ ܠܘܬ ܡܥܒܪܬܐ ܕܒܢܝܐ ܕܐܝܣܪܝܠ	ἐπὶ τοῦ Γαλααδ τοῦ Ιορδάνου ἐν τῷ πέραν υἱῶν Ισραηλ (ἐπὶ τοῦ Γαλγαλ . . . Marg. coni.)	אל גלילות הירדן אל עבר בני ישראל
59	22:14	*ἕκαστος δὲ ἄρχων τῶν οἴκων τῶν πατέρων αὐτῶν ἦσαν τῶν χιλιάδων Ἰσραήλ Syh ※ ܟܠ ܚܕ ܕܝܢ ܪܫܢܐ ܕܒܬܐ ܕܐܒܗܬܐ ܕܝܠܗܘܢ ܐܝܬܝܗܘܢ ܗܘܘ ܕܐܠܦܐ ܕܐܝܣܪܝܠ ܀	ἄρχοντες οἴκων πατριῶν εἰσιν χιλίαρχοι Ισραηλ	ואיש ראש בית אבותם המה לאלפי ישראל
60	22:16	*τίς ἡ καταφρόνησις αὕτη ἣν κατεφρονήσατε τοῦ οἴκου Ἰσραήλ Syh *s nom* ܡܢܐ ܗܝ ܡܣܬܪܩܘܬܐ ܗܕܐ ܗܝ ܕܐܣܬܪܩܬܘܢ ܥܠ ܒܝܬܐ ܕܐܝܣܪܝܠ ܀	τίς ἡ πλημμέλεια αὕτη ἣν ἐπλημμελήσατε ἐναντίον τοῦ θεοῦ Ισραηλ	מה המעל הזה אשר מעלתם באלהי ישראל
61	22:25	*κωλύσουσιν Syh ※ ܢܟܠܘܢ.	καὶ ἀπαλλοτριώσουσιν	והשביתו
62	22:25	*ἵνα μὴ λατρεύσωσι Syh ※ ܐܝܟܢܐ ܕܠܐ ܢܦܠܚܘܢ ܀	ἵνα μὴ σέβωνται	לבלתי ירא
63	24:5	*(καὶ ἐπάταξα τὴν Αἴγυπτον) ὃν χρόνον ἐποίησα ἐν αὐτῇ Syh ※ ܘܡܚܝܬܗ ܠܡܨܪܝܢ ܒܗܘ ܙܒܢܐ ܕܥܒܕܬ ܒܗ ܀	ἐν οἷς ἐποίησεν αὐτοῖς (Ra Marg.] ἐν σημειοῖς οἷς ἐποίησεν αὐτοῖς S C)	כאשר עשיתי בקרבו
64	24:19	*καὶ θεὸς ζηλωτής ἐστιν οὗτος (19 58 108) Syh[M]	καὶ ζηλώσας οὗτος	אל קנוא הוא
65	24:33	*ἐν τῷ βουνῷ Syh ※ ܒܪܡܬܐ ܀	ἐν Γαβααθ Φινεες	בגבעת פינחס

Table 2.5: Symmachus's Unique Readings

The most striking observation from the mass of data in Table 2.5 is Symmachus's discernible shift from the first half of Joshua to the second half. Of the readings Symmachus shares with Aquila and/or Theodotion (Tables 2.1 through 2.4), more than three-quarters (86 out of 106) occur in the first half of the book. Conversely, of Symmachus's unique readings (Table 2.5), two-thirds (43 out of 65) occur in the second part of the book. Concommitantly, in the second half of Joshua, there is greater uncertainty regarding the original Greek text of the Septuagint—as seen by the Rahlfs's and Margolis's differing reconstructions. Furthermore, the sources for Symmachus's readings also shift. In the first half of the book, the main witnesses are Greek manuscripts such as M, 85, and 105, along with occasional support from Eusebius's *Onomasticon* or the Syro-Hexapla. For the second part of the book, however, we must rely upon later sources, Eusebius of Caesarea and Jerome. Like Symmachus's, Eusebius's and Jerome's Palestinian provenance reveal a concern to present geographical data as correctly as possible, and such data abound in the second part of the book of Joshua.

Consequently, no fewer than thirty-four out of Symmachus's sixty-five unique readings correct geographical terms and toponyms. In 3:16 (#3 in Table 2.5), the Hebrew sequence הרחק מאד מאדם confused ancient scribes and translators. Already the oldest extant Hebrew manuscript of this passage, 4QJosh^b, reflects traces of scribal correction (frg 2-3, line 3: <מ̇א̊[ד]>מ̇אדם.[27] The Masoretes distinguished between *ketiv* (באדם) and *qere* (מאדם). The Septuagint reading σφόδρα σφοδρῶς seems to reflect a duplication: מאד מאד. Symmachus recognized, in the second of the two similar words, a reference to the place-name Adam (*tell ed-dāmije*; cf. Hos 6:7), the ford at the confluence of the Jabbok and Jordan rivers.[28]

Likewise, Symmachus may have been the only Greek translator who tried to make sense of the problematic expression נפת דור (Josh 11:2; 12:23; 17:11).[29] The Septuagint simply transliterated the phrase either as Ναφεδδωρ (Rahlfs's reconstruction) or Φενναθ Δωρ (Margolis's conjectural emendation) in 11:2 and 12:23 or Ναφετα (Rahlfs and Margolis) in 17:11. Whereas Theodotion and Aquila apparently were content with this solution, Symmachus translated

נפת with *παραλία* (seashore). In Josh 11:2 he rendered the apparently plural Hebrew construction נפות דור as singular construction (*εἰς τὴν παραλίαν Δῶρ*), while in 17:11 he seems to have taken the Hebrew phrase שלשת הנפת as plural, "the three of Napeth" (*αἱ τρεῖς παραλίαι*; cf. 4QJosh[b] הנפות); by contrast, the Old Greek translator understood as "the third part of Napheta" (*καὶ τὸ τρίτον τῆς Ναφετα*).

For the word מים in Josh 11:3, which immediately follows the phrase נפות דור, the Old Greek used the adjective *παράλιος*; Symmachus instead used *ἀπὸ δυσμῶν* (from the west) as he did in 8:13, 16:3 (*εἰς δυσμὰς*; cf. LXX *ἐπὶ τὴν θάλασσαν*), and 19:34 (*ἀπὸ δυσμῶν*; cf. LXX *κατὰ θάλασσαν*). Symmachus did use the literal rendering of ים (sea) with *θάλασσα* in the expression *εἰς θάλασσαν* in 18:12 as substitute for the Old Greek's *εἰς Γασιν*.

Similar translations as substitutions for transliterations can be found in Symmachus's treatment of the Hebrew word for "valley" (גיא) in Josh 19:14, 27. The Old Greek transliterated the word, but Symmachus employed the Greek translation *φάραγξ*. Whereas the Septuagint translator seems to have transliterated the Hebrew word for "plain, broad valley" (עמק) as Εμακ or Αμεκ (Josh 7:16, 24, 13:19, 27; 18:21; cf. 17:16), Symmachus consistently used the Greek word *κοιλάς*, meaning "depression," "low-laying plain."[30] In Josh 24:33 Symmachus rendered the Hebrew word for "hill," (גבעה/*βουνός*), which the Septuagint translator had also left untranslated (Γαβααθ).

Symmachus translated the Hebrew word ערבה (desert, or steppe) with the adjective *ἀοίκητος*, (uninhabited) in Josh 3:16; 4:13; 15:6.[31] The Old Greek versions of Deuteronomy (1:7; 4:49) and Joshua left the word untranslated (Αραβα), although they too used the adjective *ἀοίκητος* occasionally in free renderings.[32] Symmachus also offered a translation for the Hebrew phrase גלילות, "districts" (Josh 18:17; 22:10, 11): *τὰ* (*μεθ-*)*ὅρια* (border areas), while the first Greek translator seems to have varied between Γαλιλωθ (18:17), Γαλγαλα (22:10), and Γαλααδ (22:11).[33]

At the same time, Symmachus transliterated common Hebrew words that the Septuagint had translated. Thus the element שמש—referring to the sun in עין שמש (15:7; cf. LXX *πηγὴ ἡλίου*) and בית שמש (15:10; cf. LXX *πόλις ἡλίου*)—has been transliterated (Σάμες) by Symmachus; yet in Josh 19:12 the reverse seems to be the case (MT: מזרח השמש; LXX: ἀπ' ἀνατολῶν Βαιθ Σαμυς; οἱ λ': ἀπ' ἀνατολῶν ἡλίου). Likewise, the Hebrew and Aramaic word for "village" (קריה), which LXX Joshua duly rendered with πόλις (city) was transliterated by Symmachus as Καριαθ in 9:17 (cf. Aquila), 15:15 and 15:49.

Symmachus further replaced the Old Greek equivalent ἔπαυλις (dwelling) for Hebrew חצר, (settlement); Symmachus used ἀγρός (field) in Josh 13:23, 28; ἀφορισμένον ([land] set apart) in Josh 14:4; and περισπόρια (area surrounding a population centre) in Josh 21:2, 11. Symmachus also replaced Hebrew מגרש (pastureland) with προάστειον (land outside a town) in Josh 14:4; 21:2, 11; cf. LXX Num 35:2, 7. For the Hebrew root חלק (divide), Symmachus preferred the Greek translation διαμερίζω (divide) over LXX κληρονομέω (inherit) in 12:7; 18:2 and instead of LXX διαιρέω (to divide) in 22:8. The Septuagint translated "until the part of" (ἕως μέρους) for Hebrew מקצה (from the end of), but Symmachus corrected "from the extremity of" (ἀπ' ἄκρου) in Josh 15:2 5, 21.

There is somewhat of a concentration of Symmachus's readings in Joshua 22, where eight out of these sixty-five readings (and fourteen out of all 209 of Symmachus's readings in Joshua) are found. Here Symmachus corrects the vocabulary for apostasy. Hebrew מעל, "to violate one's legal obligations," is translated as καταφρονέω, "to treat with contempt" (22:16, 16 cf 7:11 and 22:22); cf. the Septuagint rendering πλημμελέω, "to commit a sinful error." In Josh 22:25, the assertion of the Transjordanian tribes that they had built the stone construction at the other side of the Jordan only to prevent their children from ceasing to fear Yhwh (והשביתו בניכם את בנינו לבלתי ירא את יהוה) is adapted by the Septuagint translator into a statement dealing with the prevention of the tribes of alienating their children from venerating the Lord (LXX καὶ ἀπαλλοτριώσουσιν οἱ υἱοί ὑμῶν τοὺς υἱοὺς ἡμῶν, ἵνα μὴ σέβωνται κύριον). Symmachus, in turn, transformed this into a warning of preventing (κωλύσουσιν) the next generation from "performing their religious duties" (ἵνα μὴ λατρεύσωσι). Since the story of the Transjordanian altar deals with an inner-Jewish conflict about proper cultic worship, one wonders whether Symmachus's version reflects halakhic discussions between rabbinical schools in the second century CE.

Disputed readings of Symmachus

In light of the previous observations concerning Symmachus's translation technique, it seems reasonable to correct the hexaplaric attributions in the manuscript tradition according to Field's proposals; see Table 2.6.

	Joshua	reading	LXX	MT
1	6:14	*μιᾷ ὁδῷ, καὶ ὑπέστρεψεν Syh ܣ. ܚܕܐ ܐܘܪܚܐ ܘܗܦܟܘ܀	ἅπας --- ---	פעם אחת וישבו
2	18:1	Ἄλλος· κατειργάσθη (ὑπετάγη εἰς πρόσωπον) 85	ἐκρατήθη ὑπ' αὐτῶν	נכבשה לפניהם
3	19:29	καὶ ἕως πόλεως τετειχισμένης τῶν Τυρίων 54[txt] *Σ. (fort. Ἀ) . . . ὀχυρώματος Τύρου Syh ܣ. ܘܥܕܡܐ ܠܡܕܝܢܬܐ ܡܚܣܢܬܐ ܕܒ̈ܢܝ ܨܘܪ܀ ܣ. ܚܣܢܐ ܕܒ̈ܢܝ ܨܘܪ܀.	καὶ ἕως πηγῆς Μασφασσατ καὶ τῶν Τυρίων (καὶ ἕως πηγῆς Μαβασαρ τῶν Τυρίων Marg. coni.)	ועד עיר מבצר צר
4	20:9	*Ἄλλος· αἱ τῆς συναγῶγης Syh *s nom* ܗܠܝܢ ܕܟܢܘܫܬܐ܀	αὗται αἱ πόλεις αἱ ἐπίκλητοι	אלה היו ערי המועדה
5	22:10	Ἄλλος· ἐποίησαν βωμόν (16, 30, 52, 85)	ἐκεῖ βωμὸν	שם מזבח
6	22:22	*Ἀ. (potius Σ.) καὶ ἐν καταφρονήσει σήμερον εἰς ΠΙΠΙ, μὴ σῶσαι ἡμᾶς ΠΙΠΙ Syh ܐ. ܘܐܦ ܒܡܒܣܪܢܘܬܐ (ܒܡܒܣܪܢܘܬܐ) ܝܘܡܢܐ ܒܦܝܦܝ. ܠ (ܠܐ) ܢܚܝܘܢ ܠܢ ܦܝܦܝ܀	εἰ ἐν ἀποστασίᾳ ἐπλημμελήσαμεν ἔναντι τοῦ κυρίου μὴ ῥύσαιτο ἡμᾶς	ואם במעל ביהוה אל תושיענו

Table 2.6: Corrections to Hexaplaric Attributions

In Josh 6:14, the Syro-Hexapla attributes the reading *μιᾷ ὁδῷ, καὶ ὑπέστρεψεν to Symmachus (Syh ܣ. ܚܕܐ ܐܘܪܚܐ ܘܗܦܟܘ܀). However, it seems more plausible to ascribe the reading μιᾷ ὁδῷ to Aquila rather than to Symmachus, for in Josh 6:3 equating פעם אחת with μιᾷ ὁδῷ is ascribed to Aquila, whereas in Josh 6:3, 11 Symmachus seems to have used the contextually more appropriate *μιᾷ περιόδῳ* (6:3; cf. *περίοδον μιαν* in 6:11 and *μιᾷ ὁρμῇ* in 10:42). By contrast the reading *καὶ ἐν καταφρονήσει σήμερον εἰς* ΠΙΠΙ, *μὴ σῶσαι ἡμᾶς* ΠΙΠΙ (Syh⁘ ܐ. ܘܐ ܒܡܬܒܣܪܢܘܬܐ (ܒܡܬܒܣܪܢܘܬܐ) ܘܝܘܡܢܐ ܒܦܝܦܝ. ܠ (ܠܐ) ܢܦܪܘܩ ܠܢ ܦܝܦܝ) in Josh 22:22, which the Syro-Hexapla ascribes to Aquila, fits the vocabulary of Symmachus much better. Hence, Field's attribution to Symmachus seems preferable. This would imply that Symmachus adopted the ancient Jewish scribal practice to write the Tetragrammaton in Hebrew, rather than translating the divine name.[34]

In Josh 19:29 the Syro-Hexapla ascribes two distinct readings to Symmachus: ܣ. ܘܥܕܡܐ ܠܡܕܝܢܬܐ ܡܫܘܪܬܐ ܕܨܘܪ̈ܝܐ ⁘ ܣ. ܥܫܝܢܐ ܕܨܘܪ ⁘. Field retroverted these readings into Greek (*καὶ ἕως πόλεως τετειχισμένης τῶν Τυρίων; ὀχυρώματος Τύρου*) and suggested that the second reading be ascribed to Aquila. This division suits the translation techniques of Aquila and Symmachus and seems therefore to be the most plausible explanation.

The three other readings have been transmitted anonymously. In these cases there is good reason to follow Field's proposal to ascribe them to Symmachus. The use of the Greek verb *κατείργω* (press hard, shut in, subdue) in the *Ἄλλος* reading in Josh 18:1 points to Symmachus's use of literary Greek.[35] Based on the equation שׂים/*ποιέω* attested for Symmachus in Deut 7:15, Field ascribed the *Ἄλλος* reading in Josh 22:10 to Symmachus as well. The same applies to the equation מועד/*συναγωγή* attested for Symmachus in Ps 73(74):4 and 74(75):3 which allowed Field to ascribe the *Ἄλλος* reading in Josh 20:9 to Symmachus. The fragmentary nature of the Symmachus readings makes it almost impossible to determine Symmachus's intentions in presenting the six cities of refuge of Joshua 20 as cities belonging to the (jurisdiction of the) synagogue.

Symmachus's corrections to Theodotion

Symmachus's particular profile becomes most apparent where he not only corrects the Old Greek but also departs from the corrections of his predecessors, kaige-Theodotion and Aquila. There are thirty readings where Symmachus's different renderings of either Theodotion or Aquila have been preserved. Again, the distribution between Aquila and Theodotion is very lopsided, since we have only one case where Symmachus corrects a reading of Theodotion, whereas the remaining twenty-nine cases deal with corrections of readings attributed to Symmachus; see Table 2.7.

Joshua	Symmachus	Theodotion	LXX	MT
23:4	ὑπέβαλον ὑμῖν 85	ἔβαλα ὑμῖν 85	ἐπέρριφα ὑμῖν	הפלתי לכם

Table 2.7: Symmachus's Correction of Theodotion

The Hebrew text of Josh 23:4 refers to God's promise to Joshua to cast down (נפל *hiphil*) the remaining non-Israelite people, which alludes to Josh 13:6. In both cases, the Septuagint offers a free rendering of the Hebrew phrase—either with the verb διαδίδωμι (to distribute, Josh 13:6) or ἐπιρρίπτω (to cast over). Probably the imagery of casting lots (as found in Joshua 13–21) influenced these renderings. No hexaplaric reading has been preserved for the passage in Josh 13:6, but in 23:4 MS 85 attributes to Theodotion the reading ἔβαλα ὑμῖν, "I have thrown for you." Apparently, Symmachus subtly adapted this reading by adding the compound ὑπό-βάλλω, which restores the imagery of subjecting the allochthonous people to Israel.[36]

Symmachus's corrections to Aquila

A considerable number of these corrections have already been discussed. In what follows, only a few other changes introduced by Symmachus will be discussed; see Table 2.8.

	Joshua	Symmachus	Aquila	LXX	MT
1	1:10	τοῖς ἐπιστάταις Procop. in Cat. Niceph.	τοῖς ἐκβιβασταῖς *ibidem* Syh ܠܡܟܣܐ	τοῖς γραμματεῦσιν	את שטרי
2	3:11	*δεσπότου Masius	*κυριεύοντος Masius	κυρίου πάσης τῆς γῆς	אדון כל הארץ
3	3:13	ἄσκωμα ἕν M 54 85	σωρὸς εἷς (θ' α') M 54 85	στήσεται --- ---	ויעמדו נד אחד

4	3:16	(ἄσκωμα) ἕν Theodoret	---	ἔστη πῆγμα ἓν ἀφεστηκὸς	קמו נד אחד
5	4:13	*κατὰ τὴν ἀοίκητον Ἱεριχώ Syh .ܣ ܠܡܘܬܒܐ ܠܐ ܡܬܝܬܒܢܝܬܐ ܕܐܝܪܝܚܘ.	*πρὸς ἀραβὼθ Ἱεριχώ Syh .ܐ ܠܘܬ ܥܪܒܘܬ ܐܝܪܝܚܘ.	πρὸς τὴν Ιεριχω πόλιν	אל ערבות יריחו
6	5:6	*ἕως ἀναλώθη πᾶς ὁ λαὸς ἄνδρες πολεμισταὶ οἱ ἐξελθόντες ἐξ Αἰγύπτου Syh .ܣ ܥܕܡܐ ܕܐܬܛܠܠ ܟܠܗ ܥܡܐ ܓܒܪ̈ܐ ܩܪ̈ܒܬܢܐ ܗܢܘܢ ܕܢܦܩܘ ܡܢ ܡܨܪܝܢ܀	*ἕως ἐξέλιπεν πᾶν τὸ ἔθνος ἀνδρῶν πολέμου τῶν ἐξελθόντων ἐξ Αἰγύπτου Syh .ܐ ܥܕܡܐ ܕܫܠܡ ܟܠܗ ܥܡܐ ܕ ܓܒܪ̈ܐ ܕܩܪ̈ܒܐ ܗܢܘܢ ܕܢܦܩܘ ܡܢ ܡܨܪܝܢ ܀	διὸ ἀπερίτμητοι ἦσαν (ἀπηρτίσθησαν ? coni. MNvdMeer) οἱ πλεῖστοι αὐτῶν τῶν μαχίμων τῶν ἐξεληλυθότων ἐκ γῆς Αἰγύπτου	עד תם כל הגוי אנשי המלחמה היצאים ממצרים
7	6:3	μιᾷ περιόδῳ Masius	μιᾷ ὁδῷ Masius	--- --- (θ′ ? ἅπαξ)	פעם אחת
8	6:4	*σάλπιγγας κερατίνας Masius (*buccinas arietinas*)	*σάλπιγγας ἀφέσεως Masius (*tubas remissionis*)	--- --- --- (θ′ ? κερατίνας τοῦ ἰωβὴλ)	שופרות היובלים
9	6:5	*ὅταν δὲ ἑλκύσῃ (μηκύνῃ) τῷ κέρατι τοῦ κριοῦ Syh .ܣ ܐܡܬܝ ܕܝܢ ܕܢܓܘܪ ܒܩܪܢܐ ܕܕܟܪܐ܀	*καὶ ἔσται ἐν σεισμῷ ἐν κερατίνῃ τοῦ ἰωβήλ Syh .ܐ ܘܢܗܘܐ ܒܙܘܥܬܐ ܒܩܪܢܐ ܕܝܘܒܠܐ܀	καὶ ἔσται ὡς ἂν σαλπίσητε τῇ σάλπιγγι	והיה במשך בקרן היובל

10	6:5	*πᾶς ὁ λαὸς ἀλαλαγμὸν μέγαν Syh ܦ. ܟܠܗ ܥܡܐ ܝܒܒܐ ܪܒܐ܀	*ἀλαλάξει . . . Syh ܐ. ܢܝܒܒ܀	ἀνακραγέτω πᾶς ὁ λαὸς ἅμα καὶ ἀνακραγόντων αὐτῶν	יריעו כל העם תרועה גדולה
11	7:21	*ἱμάτιον Σενναὰρ ἓν καλὸν Syh ܦ. ܢܚܬܐ ܕܫܢܥܪ ܚܕ ܫܦܝܪܐ܀	*στολὴν Βαβυλωνίαν μίαν καλήν Theodoret Syh ܐ. ܐܣܛܠܐ ܒܒܠܝܬܐ ܚܕܐ ܫܦܝܪܬܐ	ψιλὴν ποικίλην καλὴν	אדרת שנער אחת טובה
12	8:18	σὺν τῇ ἀσπίδι M 57 85 Procop Theodoret	σὺν τῷ γαισῷ (57)] σὺν τῷ κεσῷ 52 Cat. Niceph.	ἐν τῷ γαίσῳ (ἄλλος θώρακι 57[mg])	בכידון
13	9:5	καὶ πᾶς ὁ ἄρτος τοῦ ἐπισιτισμοῦ αὐτῶν ξηρὸς ἐγενήθη καπυρός 85 Syh ܙܘܕܗܘܢ ܝܒܝܫܐ	καὶ πᾶς ὁ ἄρτος ὁ ἐπισιτισμὸς αὐτῶν ξηρὸς ἐγενήθη καὶ ἐψαθυρωμένος 85 Syh ܙܘܕܗܘܢ ܝܒܝܫܐ	καὶ ὁ ἄρτος αὐτῶν τοῦ ἐπισιτισμοῦ ξηρὸς καὶ εὐρωτιῶν καὶ βεβρωμένος	וכל לחם צידם יבש היה נקדים
14	9:8	τίνες ἐστέ; 108 Syh ܐ.ܦ. ܡܢܘ ܐܢܬܘܢ	τίς ὑμείς; Syh ܐ.ܦ. ܡܢܘ ܐܢܬܘܢ	πόθεν ἐστὲ	מי אתם
15	10:12	ὁ ἥλιος ἐν Γαβαὼν [μὴ] ἡσυχασάτω Masius Syh ܦ. ܫܡܫܐ ܒܓܒܥܘܢ ܠܐ ܬܫܬܘܩ.	ἥλιε, ἐν Γαβαὼν σιώπα Masius Syh ܐ. ܘܐܡܪ ܠܗ̇ ܚܢܢ ܕܐܡܪ ܫܡܫܐ ܒܓܒܥܘܢ ܫܬܘܩ܀	στήτω ὁ ἥλιος κατὰ Γαβαων	שמש בגבעון דום

16	10:13	ἕως ἠμύνατο τὸ ἔθνος τῶν ἐχθρῶν αὐτοῦ Syh ܣ. ܥܕܡܐ ܕ ܢܬܒܥ ܠܥܡܐ ܕܒܥܠܕܒܒܘܗܝ܀	ἕως ἠμύνατο ἔθνος ἐχθρῶν αὐτοῦ Syh ܐ. ܥܕܡܐ ܕ ܢܬܒܥ ܥܡܐ ܕܒܥܠܕܒܒܐ ܕܠܗ.	ἕως ἠμύνατο ὁ θεὸς (τὸ ἔθνος) τοὺς ἐχθροὺς αὐτῶν Marg. coni.)	עד יקם גוי איביו
17	10:19	ὑμεῖς δὲ μὴ ἀποστῆτε, διώξατε κατόπιν 85 344	Καὶ ὑμεῖς μὴ στήκετε, διώξατε ὀπίσω . . . 85 344	ὑμεῖς δὲ μὴ ἑστήκατε καταδιώκοντες ὀπίσω τῶν ἐχθρῶν ὑμῶν	ואתם אל תעמדו רדפו אחרי איביכם
18	10:34	εἰς Ἐγλών Syh ܣ. ܠܥܓܠܘܢ܀	Αἰγλώμ 85	εἰς Οδολλαμ	עגלנה
19	11:2	καὶ εἰς τὴν πεδινήν Masius Syh ܣ. ܘܠܦܫܝܛܘܬܐ܀	Καὶ ἐν τῇ ὁμαλῇ Masius	καὶ εἰς τὴν Ραβα (καὶ εἰς τὴν Αραβα Marg.)	ובערבה
20	11:8	καὶ ἕως Μαστρεφὼθ τῆς ἀπὸ θαλάσσης On Syh ܕܗܝ .ܣ ܀ ܕܡܢ ܝܡܐ܀	καὶ ἕως Μαστρεφὼθ ὕδατος On Syh ܐ. ܘܥܕܡܐ ܠܡܝ̈ܐ ܪܦܘܬ ܕܡܝ̈ܐ ܀	καὶ ἕως Μασερων (Μασερεφωθ Μαιν Marg. coni.)	ועד משרפות מים
21	11:13	ἱδρυμένας ἑκάστην ἐπὶ ὕψους 54 85 Syh ܕܡܬܬ̈ܬܢ	ἑστηκυίας ἐπὶ χώματος 54 85 Syh ܕܩܝ̈ܡܢ ܥܠ ܬ̈ܠܠܐ	τὰς πόλεις τὰς κεχωματισμένας	הערים העמדות על תלם
22	11:17	(τοῦ) λείου On	(τοῦ) μερίζοντος On	ἀπὸ ὄρους Αχελ (ἀπὸ ὄρους Αχελκ Marg. coni.)	מן ההר החלק
23	15:7	(πηγῆς) Σάμες On Syh ܣ. ܕܫܡܫ܀	πηγῆς ἡλίου On	πηγῆς ἡλίου	עין שמש

24	15:9	καὶ ἐξῆλθεν εἰς πόλεις ὄρους (᾿Εφρών) 85	καὶ διεκβάλλει εἰς κώμας ὄρους (᾿Εφρών) 85	καὶ διεκβάλλει εἰς τὸ ὄρος Εφρων	ויצא אל ערי הר עפרון
25	15:21	αἱ πόλεις ἀπ᾿ ἄκρου τῆς φυλῆς 85 Syh ܡܢ ܪܝܫܐ	αἱ πόλεις ἀπὸ τελευταίου τῆς φυλῆς 85	ἐγενήθησαν δὲ αἱ πόλεις αὐτῶν πόλις πρώτη φυλῆς	ויהיו הערים מקצה למטה
26	18:13	˟τὸ ὅριον εἰς Λουζὰ πρὸς τὸν ὦμον Λουζὰ εἰς νότον Syh ܣ. ܬܚܘܡܐ ܠܠܘܙܐ ܠܘܬ ܟܬܦܐ ܕܠܘܙܐ ܠܬܝܡܢܐ܀	˟ἐπὶ τὸ ὅριον Λουζὰ πρὸς ὦμον Λουζὰ πρὸς νότον Syh ܐ. ܥܠ ܬܚܘܡܐ ܕܠܘܙܐ ܠܘܬ ܟܬܦܐ ܕܠܘܙܐ ܠܘܬ ܬܝܡܢܐ܀	τὰ ὅρια Λουζα ἐπὶ νώτου Λουζα ἀπὸ λιβός	הגבול לוזה אל כתף לוזה נגבה
27	20:4	˟καὶ προσδέξονται (s. προσλήψονται) αὐτὸν εἰς τὴν πόλιν πρὸς αὐτοὺς Syh ܣ. ܘܢܩܒܠܘܢܝܗ̇ ܒܡܕܝܢܬܐ ܠܘܬܗܘܢ܀	˟ἐν τῷ ἀνοίγματι τῆς πύλης τῆς πόλεως Syh ܐ. ܒܦܬܚܐ ܕܬܪܥܐ ܕܡܕܝܢܬܐ܀	--- --- --- --- --- --- -- (θ′ ? καὶ ἐπιστρέψουσιν αὐτὸν ἡ συναγωγὴ πρὸς αὐτοὺς	ואספו אתו העירה אליהם
28	21:15	(καὶ τὰ) προάστεια (αὐτῆς) 108	(καὶ) τὰ περισπόρια (αὐτῆς) 108	καὶ τὰ ἀφωρισμένα αὐτῇ	ואת מגרשה
29	22:19	βέβηλος Masius	ἀκάθαρτος Masius	μικρὰ (μιαρά Masius Marg. coni.)	טמאה

Table 2.8: Symmachus's Corrections of Aquila

The precise meaning of the Hebrew word שׁוטר in Josh 1:10 and elsewhere was probably no less problematic for the ancient translators than for modern interpreters, who define the word on the basis of its usage in mainly Deuteronomistic texts and on the basis of Akkadian *šaṭāru* as "civil servant" or "administrator."[37] The Septuagint translator of Joshua (1:10) adopted the translation choice γραμματεύς (scribe, civic) made by the Greek translators of the Pentateuch.[38] Aquila substituted this word for the rather rare Greek title ἐκβιβαστής (someone who executes a sentence; cf. Aq-Deut 16:18; Codex Justiani 9.2.4.2). Symmachus in turn altered the position of this functionary to that of ἐπιστάτης (someone who is assigned to oversee a task, chairman), a title which is applied to rabbi Jesus in the gospel of Luke.[39] As Procopius of Gaza made clear, this Greek title also belonged to the semantic field of jurisdiction and equals the Roman function of *exceptor*.[40]

Particularly interesting is Symmachus's understanding of the miracle at the river Jordan when Israel entered the Promised Land. The Hebrew text of Josh 3:13, 16 narrates that the waters of the river stood as a single wall (נד אחד), a clear allusion to Exod 15:8 where "the streams stood like a dam" (נצבו כמו נד נזלים). The Greek translator of Exodus understood the Hebrew word נד as a "wall" (ἐπάγη ὡσεὶ τεῖχος τὰ ὕδατα). The Septuagint translator of Joshua was less certain and left the word untranslated in 3:13 and employed in 3:16 the rather uncommon Greek noun πῆγμα (anything fastened or joined together, framework).[41] According to manuscripts M, 54, and 85, Theodotion and Aquila supplied the missing translation in Josh 3:13 with the help of the Greek word for "heap" (σωρός), a word that the Septuagint of Joshua used for a heap of stones (Josh 7:26, σωρὸν λίθων, for Hebrew גל אבנים). Thanks to Theodoret of Cyrus (*Questions on Joshua* 2.4), we know that Symmachus corrected this into "wine-skin" (ἄσκωμα), a reading that is also found in the margin of the same manuscripts M, 54, and 85:[42]

> Now, Symmachus rendered the term "heap" as "wine-skin." That is, as the rush of the waters was blocked, they swelled like a wine-skin and piled up, with the Creator's will checking them more firmly than any wall of steel.

Τὸ μέντοι πῆγμα, ἄσκωμα ὁ Σύμμαχος ἡρμήνευσεν· ἐπεχομένη γὰρ τῶν ὑδάτων ἡ ῥύμη, οἷον ἠσκοῦτο καὶ ἐκορυφοῦτο· παντὸς γὰρ ἀδαμαντίνου τείχους πλέον ἐπεῖχεν αὐτὴν ὁ τοῦ δημιουργήσαντος ὅρος.

Interestingly, Targum Jonathan also employs the imagery of a wineskin: רכבה or רוקבה,[43] as does the Peshitta: ܢܩܘܡܘܢ ܠ ܐܝܟ ܙܩܘܡܐ ܚܕܐ ܠܡܠܬܐ ܚܕ. Apparently these translators derived the Hebrew word נד from נאד, "leather bottle," instead of נדד II which can be understood with the aid of Akkadian *nīdu* (mass of water).[44] This Hebrew word נאד (leather bottle) occurs twice in Joshua in the story of the Gibeonites (Josh 9:4 13). Here the Septuagint translator used "bag made of skin" (ἀσκός). In Josh 3:13, 16 Symmachus sides with the roughly contemporaneous Aramaic Bible translators (Targum Jonathan and Peshitta) in interpreting the miracle of the swelling of the water of the river Jordan in terms of a leather wine bag that became inflated or filled. More research is needed in order to determine whether the agreement between Symmachus and the Aramaic versions is a matter of coincidence or reflects a common exegesis in the second century CE.

Joshua 5:4–7 explains the rationale behind the reinstallment of the rite of circumcision: the older generation of Israelites had been circumcised but had failed to circumcise the younger generation. The Hebrew text of Josh 5:6 employs the verb תמם (to be complete, to come to an end), "until the entire people had come to an end" (עד תם כל הגוי). It may be that the Greek translator skillfully rendered this phrase with *διὸ ἀπηρτίσθησαν οἱ πλεῖστοι αὐτῶν, "therefore most of them were finished off."[45] Yet from a very early point in the transmission-history of the Old Greek, the sentence had become the rather problematic statement about the younger generation: "because Israel had dwelt in the desert of Madbaritis for forty-two years, therefore most of them were uncircumcised" (διὸ ἀπερίτμητοι ἦσαν οἱ πλεῖστοι αὐτῶν). Aquila corrected the rather free Greek translation into *ἕως ἐξέλιπεν πᾶν τὸ ἔθνος, "until the whole nation had ceased to exist." The use of ἐκλείπω (to fail, to cease) in the sense of "to die" is not uncommon in the Septuagint and in Classical Greek;[46] apparently, though, this was problematic for Symmachus, who altered the statement into *ἕως ἀναλώθη πᾶς ὁ λαὸς (or ἀνηλώθη Marg.),[47] "until the whole people had been consumed." Symmachus made similar corrections of ἐκλείπω into ἀναλίσκω (to use up, to consume) in Ps 73(72):19 and Ezek 24:10, 11, thereby corresponding to the usage in OG Num 14:33, 35 and 32:13, which also deals with the theme of the extinction of the older generation of Israelites. Whether Symmachus had contemporary concerns in mind when he corrected his predecessors cannot be determined here.

In Josh 6:4 Symmachus altered the designation of the ram's horn trumpets (שופרות היובלים) from Aquila's "trumpets of release (redemption?)" (*σάλπιγγας ἀφέσεως) into the contextually more appropriate "trumpets made of horn" (*σάλπιγγας κερατίνας). The translation "horn of the Iobel" (κέρας τοῦ ἰωβήλ) found in hexaplaric manuscripts of the Septuagint of Josh 6:4—and perhaps originating from Theodotion (?)—is ascribed to Aquila in the following verse (for Hebrew קרן היובל). Here Symmachus seems to have used the more natural phrase "horn of the ram" (κέρας τοῦ κριοῦ).

The miracle of the halting of sun and moon at Joshua's command (Josh 10:12–13) also led to modification in the Greek text. The Hebrew text of Josh 10:12 has Joshua ask the sun to stand still at Gibeon (שמש בגבעון דום). The Septuagint translator used a third-person imperative, "let the sun stand still above Gibeon" (στήτω ὁ ἥλιος κατὰ Γαβαων). Aquila transformed this into an imperative and used his fixed equivalent σιωπάω for Hebrew דמם.[48] Although both the Hebrew and Greek verbs are capable of expressing the notion of "halting," "taking rest," and "remaining silent," Greek σιωπάω primarily expresses the idea of keeping silent, which hardly fits the context of Josh 10:12; there the sun is asked to refrain from proceeding. Hence Symmachus employed the Greek verb ἡσυχάζω (to become restful, to pause), again as a third-person imperative: *ὁ ἥλιος ἐν Γαβαὼν [μὴ] ἡσυχασάτω.

Finally, the description of the Transjordanian territory as "unclean" land (Josh 22:19) deserves attention. As noted above, a considerable number of Symmachus's readings in Joshua is found in Josh 22:9–34, a story that seems to settle disputes over legitimate Yhwh worship outside the land of Israel proper. If the translator Symmachus is identical to rabbi Meir's pupil Sumkhos ben Joseph, known from rabbinic sources,[49] he probably shared his master's view that Israel is a holy land, a cultic center for all the nations (*θρησκεία πάσαις *ταῖς γαίαις*, thus Symmachus in Ezek 20:6).[50] The Hebrew text in Josh 22:19 has the general word for "unclean," טמאה. The original Greek translator may have rendered this as *μιαρά* (thus according to the conjectural reconstruction by Masius and adopted by Margolis), but from a very early point in the transmission history of the Old Greek text this was read as *μι<u>κ</u>ρά*, "(too) small." Aquila restored the notion of "uncleanness" with his Greek adjective *ἀκάθαρτος*, whereas Symmachus employed *βέβηλος*. Since all three Greek adjectives (*μιαρός*, *ἀκάθαρτος*, *βέβηλος*) are almost synonymous,[51] one wonders why Symmachus felt the need to correct Aquila at this point. Perhaps Symmachus wanted to express that the territory that had once belonged to Israel was now "profaned" instead of *a priori* " unclean."

Some Concluding Remarks

This initial survey of readings attributed to Symmachus in the book of Joshua cannot do sufficient justice to the full breadth of his translation. Nevertheless, this overview may be helpful for such an investigation. In the meantime, a few concluding remarks can be made on the basis of the preceding observations.

With respect to Symmachus's knowledge and use of the earlier Greek translations in the Pentateuch, Alison Salvesen demonstrated that Symmachus mainly interacts with Aquila.[52] The same seems to hold true for the book of Joshua. Although there are a few cases (three out of 209) where Symmachus seems to side with, or depart from, Theodotion's version only (see sections 2.4 and 3.3 above), Symmachus seems first of all to adopt and adapt readings by Aquila; yet there also seems to be evidence supporting Greenspoon's statement that "Symmachus used Th. as *a* basis for his further work."[53] However, more than anything else, Symmachus's version of Joshua seems to be a revision of Aquila's. This conclusion may imply that the common distinction between the Old Greek and "the Three" should make way for a distinction between Old Greek renderings of Hebrew supplemented by Theodotion, on the one hand, and the second-century CE revisions by Aquila and Symmachus, on the other.

Symmachus's Palestinian provenance probably explains the preponderance of corrections dealing with topography and geography. Almost three-quarters of Symmachus's unique readings in Joshua concern vocabulary for descriptions of the land of Israel and its toponyms. Given the further concentration of Symmachus's readings in Joshua 22, it may be that Symmachus held a special interest for the interpretation and translation of this part of the book, which deals with the proper cult of God inside and outside the Holy Land.

The extant fragments are often too scanty to allow for an examination of Symmachus's purposes and theology. The use of the Hebrew Tetragrammaton in 22:22 seems to reflect an ancient Jewish scribal practice. In Josh 3:13, 16 Symmachus may reflect ancient Jewish exegesis of the miracle of the waters of the river Jordan swelling like a wineskin.

Further research on Symmachus's version of Joshua might benefit from a comparison of Symmachus's version of the other historical books, an area that remains just as unexplored as the area surveyed here. The relation between Symmachus and the other Greek versions as well as the rabbinic and patristic sources also require further examination. More research along the lines set out by Leonard Greenspoon for Theodotion's version of Joshua is needed to gain more insight in the actual translation and its underlying principles.

Notes

[1]See e.g. Leonard J. Greenspoon, "The Book of Joshua. Part 1: Texts and Versions," *CBR* 3 (2005): 29–61; Michaël N. van der Meer, "3.1. Textual History of Joshua," in *Textual History of the Bible, vol. 1B*, ed. Armin Lange and Emanuel Tov (Leiden: Brill, 2016), 251–56.

[2]See e.g. Michaël N. van der Meer, *Formation and Reformulation: The Redaction of the Book of Joshua in the Light of the Oldest Textual Witnesses*, VTSup 102 (Leiden: Brill, 2004), 479–522.

[3]See e.g. Michaël N. van der Meer, "3.3 Septuagint [Joshua]," in *Textual History of the Bible, vol. 1B*, 269–76.

[4]Max L. Margolis, *The Book of Joshua in Greek According to the Critically Restored Text with an Apparatus Containing the Variants of the Principal Recensions and of the Individual Witnesses*, Publications of the Alexander Kohut Memorial Foundation (Paris: Geuthner, 1931–1938). The originally missing fifth part was retrieved and published by Emanuel Tov in the Annenberg Research

Institute Monograph Series (Philadelphia: Annenberg Research Institute, 1992). For an assessment of Margolis's scholarly contributions, see Leonard J. Greenspoon, *Max L. Margolis: A Scholar's Scholar*, BSNA 15 (Atlanta: Scholars Press, 1987).

[5]Leonard J. Greenspoon, "The Qumran Fragments of Joshua: Which Puzzle Are They Part of and Where Do They Fit?" in *Septuagint, Scrolls and Cognate Writings*, ed. George J. Brooke and Barnabas Lindars, SBLSCS 33 (Atlanta: Scholars Press, 1992), 159–94.

[6]Leonard J. Greenspoon, *Textual Studies in the Book of Joshua*, HSM 28 (Chico, CA: Scholars Press, 1983).

[7]Dominique Barthélemy, *Les devanciers d'Aquila*, VTSup 10 (Leiden: Brill, 1963); Emanuel Tov, ed., *The Greek Minor Prophets Scroll from Naḥal Ḥever (8ḤevXIIgr)*, The Seiyal Collection 1, DJD VIII (Oxford; Clarendon, 1990); Kevin O'Connell, *The Theodotionic Revision of the Book of Exodus*, HSM 3 (Cambridge: Harvard University Press, 1972); Walter Bodine, *The Greek Text of Judges: Recensional Developments*, HSM 23 (Chico, CA: Scholars Press, 1980).

[8]For the term "proto-Masoretic" and the standardization of the Masoretic Text, see the study by Emanuel Tov in this volume.

[9]Also noteworthy is Greenspoon's lucid translation of the Old Greek version for NETS: Leonard J. Greenspoon, "Iesous," in *A New English Translation of the Septuagint*, ed. Albert Pietersma and Benjamin G. Wright (Oxford: Oxford University Press, 2007).

[10]See e.g. Leonard J. Greenspoon, "Theodotion, Aquila, Symmachus and the Old Greek of Joshua," *ErIsr* 16 (1982): 82°–91°.

[11]Leonard J. Greenspoon, "Symmachus, Symmachus's Version," *ABD* 6:251.

[12]Besides my *Formation and Reformulation*, see my studies in Joshua 2, 6 and 18: "Sound the Trumpet! Redaction and Reception of Joshua 6:2–25," in *The Land of Israel in Bible, History and Theology. Studies in Honour of Ed Noort*, ed. Jacques T.A.G.M. van Ruiten and J. Cornelis de Vos, VTSup 124 (Leiden: Brill, 2009), 19–43; "Clustering Cluttered Areas. Textual and Literary Criticism in Josh 18:1–10," in *The Book of Joshua*, ed. Ed Noort, BETL 250 (Leuven: Peeters, 2012), 87–106; "Literary and Textual History of Joshua 2," in *XV Congress of the International Organization for Septuagint and Cognate Studies: Munich, 2013*, ed. Wolfgang Kraus, Michaël N. van der Meer, and Martin Meiser, SBLSCS 64 (Atlanta: SBL Press, 2016), 565–91.

[13]See e.g. Alison Salvesen, *Symmachus in the Pentateuch*, JSS Monographs 15 (Manchester: Manchester University Press, 1991) and my overview article on "Symmachus" in *The Oxford Handbook of the Septuagint*, ed. Timothy Michael Law and Alison Salvesen (Oxford: Oxford University Press, forthcoming) as well as my "Symmachus, the Septuagint and the Sages: An examination of the references to Sumkhos ben Joseph in Mishnah, Tosefta and Talmudim," in *Septuagint, Sages, and Scripture: Studies in Honour of Johann Cook*, ed. Randall X. Gauthier, Gideon R. Kotzé, and Gert J. Steyn, VTSup 172 (Leiden: Brill, 2016), 355–66.

[14]See already the brilliant work of the Jewish scholar Abraham Geiger, "Symmachus, der Übersetzer der Bibel," in *Jüdische Zeitschrift für Wissenschaft und Leben* 1 (1862): 39–64, and further Dominique Barthélemy, "Qui est Symmaque?"

CBQ 36 (1974): 451–65 (repr. in *Études d'histoire du texte de l'Ancien Testament*, ed. Dominique Barthélemy, OBO 21 [Fribourg: Éditions universitaires / Göttingen: Vandenhoeck & Ruprecht, 1978], 307–21); Arie van der Kooij, "Symmachus, 'de vertaler der Joden'," *NedTT* 42 (1988): 1–20; Michaël N. van der Meer, "Entre Léontopolis et Byzance. La version de Symmaque comme étape intermédiaire entre le Vieux Grec d'Isaïe et l'interprétation d'Eusèbe de Césarée," *Semitica et Classica* 3 (2010): 67–83; Michaël N. van der Meer, "Θρησκεία, Terra Incognita, and Terra Devastata: Vocabulary and Theology of Symmachus," in *XIV Congress of the IOSCS: Helsinki, 2010*, ed. Melvin K. H. Peters, SBLSCS 59 (Atlanta: Society of Biblical Literature, 2013) 499–514 and the literature mentioned in the previous footnote.

[15]See e.g. Alison Salvesen, "Symmachus and the Dating of Targumic Traditions," *Journal for the Aramaic Bible* 2 (2000): 233–45.

[16]See e.g. Thomas Elßner, *Josua und seine Kriege in jüdischer und christlicher Rezeptionsgeschichte*, Theologie und Frieden 37 (Stuttgart: Kohlhammer, 2008) and Michaël N. van der Meer, "The Reception History of Joshua in the Septuagint and Contemporary Documents," in *Die Septuaginta: Geschichte—Wirkung—Relevanz*, WUNT (Tübingen: Mohr Siebeck, forthcoming). For the Second Temple Hebrew reworking(s) of Joshua found at Qumran (4Q378, 4Q379, 4Q522, 4Q123, 5Q9) and Masada (Mas 1039-211), see now Ariel Feldman, *The Rewritten Joshua Scrolls*, BZAW 438 (Berlin: de Gruyter, 2014).

[17]The main hexaplaric witnesses for Joshua are codex Coislinianus (M) and the Greek codices in the Vatican library in Rome, Vat.gr. 2058 (Rahlfs number 85) and Vat.gr. 330 (Rahlfs number 108). The Syriac translation of the Hexapla (Syh or Syro-Hexapla) is known from an incomplete manuscript from the British Library (Brit.Mus. Add. 12,133; Syh^{L}) and a lost manuscript used by the Humanist scholar Andreas Masius in his commentary on Joshua: Andreas Masius, *Josuae imperatoris historia illustrate atque explicata* (Antwerp: Plantinus, 1574). Additional leaves from lectionaries have been published by Moshe Goshen-Gottstein, "Neue Syrohexaplafragmente," *Bib* 37 (1956): 162–83 [Josh 7:6–9] and Wim Baars, *New Syro-Hexaplaric Texts* (Leiden: Brill, 1968), 101–3 [Josh 6:16–20]. Additional material is also provided by the Onomasticon of Eusebius of Caesarea (On): Erich Klostermann, *Eusebius: Das Onomastikon der biblischen Ortsnamen*, GCS 11/1 [i.e. Eusebius Werke 3/1] (Leipzig: Hinrichs, 1904) and its Latin translation by Jerome (Hier), the commentary on the Octateuch, book of Kings, and Paralipomena by Procopius of Gaza (Procop in PG 87/1:991–1042) and readings from the Catena Nicephori (Cat. Niceph.). For further references to Greek biblical manuscripts and the Göttingen system of reference, see Detlef Fraenkel, *Verzeichnis der griechischen Handschriften des Alten Testaments*, VTGSup 1.1 (Göttingen: Vandenhoeck & Ruprecht, 2004).

[18]Frederick Field, *Origenis hexaplorum quae supersunt sive veterum interpretum graecorum in totum vetus testamentum fragmenta* (Oxford: Clarendon Press, 1875).

[19]Unfortunately the new Hexaplaric material retrieved from Armenian manuscripts does not yield new Symmachus readings for Joshua; see Claude E. Cox, *Hexaplaric Materials Preserved in the Armenian Version*, SBLSCS 21 (Atlanta:

Scholars Press, 1986) and Claude E. Cox, *Aquila, Symmachus and Theodotion in Armenia*, SBLSCS 42 (Atlanta: Scholars Press, 1996).

[20]See Alison Salvesen, *Origen's Hexapla and Fragments: Papers presented at the Rich Seminar of the Hexapla, Oxford Centre for Hebrew and Jewish Studies, 25th–3rd August 1994*, TSAJ 58 (Tübingen: Mohr Siebeck, 1998); R. Bas ter Haar Romeny and Peter J. Gentry, "Towards a New Collection of Hexaplaric Material for the Book of Genesis," in *X Congress of the International Organization for Septuagint and Cognate Studies, Oslo, 1998*, ed. Bernard A. Taylor, SBLSCS 51 (Atlanta: Society of Biblical Literature, 2001), 285–99; see further: www.hexapla.org.

[21]The task of reconstructing the Old Greek of Joshua corresponding the readings attributed to Symmachus lies beyond the scope of this essay; thus the reconstructions by Rahlfs have been adopted here. In cases where Margolis differs from Rahlfs, I note the former's reconstruction between brackets.

[22]See my *Formation and Reformulation* and the studies mentioned in footnote 12.

[23]The note is often followed by the preposition χωρίς, "without." Since the word following this preposition is usually not attested either in the Old Greek or any of the younger Greek translations, Max L. Margolis, "ΧΩΡΙΣ," in *Oriental Studies Published in Commemoration of the Fortieth Anniversary of Paul Haupt as Director of the Oriental Seminary of the John Hopkins University*, eds. Cyrus Adler and Aaron Ember (Baltimore: The John Hopkins Press / Leipzig: Hinrichs, 1926), 84–92, argued that the preposition originally indicated the absence of the hexaplaric asteriskos.

[24]According to Margolis, *The Book of Joshua in Greek*, this family of witnesses should be subdivided into two sub-families: [1] $\underline{S}_a$: K (codex Lipsiensis), k_1 (54, Paris, Bibl. nat. gr. 5; Colbert 659), k_2 (75, Oxford Univ. coll. 52), $\underline{k}$ (127, Moscou, Syn.bibl. gr. 31), w_1 (118, Paris, Bibl. nat. gr. 6; Colbert 465), w_2 (314, Athens Bibl. nat. 44, Kremos 2) and the Vetus Latina (preserved in Codex Lugdunensis, edited by Ulysse Robert, *Heptateuchi partis posterioris versio Latina antiquissima e codice Lugdunensi; version latine du Deutéronome, de Josué et des Juges antèrieure à saint Jérôme publiée d'après le manuscript de Lyon* [Lyon: Rey, 1900]); and [2] $\underline{S}_b$: t_1 (84, Rome, Vat. gr. 1901), t_2 (134, Florence, Bibl. Med. Laur. Plut. V 1), $\underline{t}_1$ (74, Florence, Bibl. Med. Laur. S. Marco 700), $\underline{t}_2$ (76, Paris, Bibl. nat. gr. 4), f (106, Ferrara, Bibl. comm. 187 I.II & 188 II + 107, Ferrara, Bibl. comm. 188 I), and l (61, Oxford, Bodl. Lib. Laud. gr. 36). See Max L. Margolis, "The K Text of Joshua," *AJSL* 28 (1911): 1–55. Margolis's grouping corresponds very closely to the manuscript grouping for Ruth by Alfred Rahlfs and that for Deuteronomy by John W. Wevers; see Cornelis G. den Hertog, "Studien zur griechischen Übersetzung des Buches Josua" (PhD diss., Justus-Liebig-Universität, Gießen, 1996), 3–23.

[25]See Marcus Sigismund, "Der antiochenische Text im Buch JosuaLXX und seine Bedeutung für die älteste Septuaginta—eine erste Reevaluation," in *XV Congress of the IOSCS*, 13–36.

[26]Cf. Salvesen, *Symmachus in the Pentateuch*, 262.

[27]See Emanuel Tov, "4QJosh[b]," in *Qumran Cave 4.IX Deuteronomy, Joshua, Judges, Kings*, ed. Eugene Ulrich et al., DJD XIV (Oxford: Clarendon Press, 1995), 153–60, here 155–57.

[28]See e.g. J. Simons, *The Geographical and Topographical Texts of the Old Testament*, Studia Francisci Scholten memoriae dicata (Leiden: Brill, 1959), 341 (§825).

[29]See e.g. G. Dahl, "The Three Heights of Joshua 17:11," *JBL* 53 (1934): 381–83; Simons, *Geographical Texts*, 279 ("inexplicable geographically"); Dominique Barthélemy, *Critique textuelle de l'ancien testament* 1. *Josué, Juges, Ruth, Samuel, Rois, Chroniques, Esdras, Néhémie, Esther* (OBO 50/1; Fribourg: Éditions universitaires; Göttingen: Vandenhoeck & Ruprecht, 1983), 47–48; *HALOT* 708b: "the hinterland of Dor."

[30]In Josh 13:9 Symmachus followed Aquila in translating the Hebrew word for "level ground," or "plain," מישׁור, with ἡ ὁμάλη, "the level ground," whereas the Old Greek version has a transliteration (Μισωρ).

[31]Cf. Deut 1:7; 4:49; 32:10; 1 Reg 23:24; Job 39:6; Ps 43[44]:20; 67[68]:5, 8; 68[69]:26. In Josh 18:18 Symmachus rendered the same Hebrew phrase (ערבה cf. LXX Αραβα) with πεδιάς, "flat land" (LSJ 1352a; Rev.Suppl. 244b).

[32]In Deut 13:16(17) and Josh 8:28 the adjective is used in renderings for the Hebrew phrase [שׁממה] תל עולם, "ruin forever"; in Josh 13:3 the adjective seems to match the Hebrew phrase מן השׁיחור, "from (the river) Shichor ([eastern branch of the] Nile)." In Job 15:28; 38:27; Prov 8:26 and Hos 13:5 the adjective occurs as free rendering for various Hebew phrases and in Job 8:14, Wis 11:2; 1 Macc 3:45 no Hebrew counterpart is available.

[33]Margolis conjecturally reconstructs Γαλγαλ in Josh 22:10.

[34]See e.g. Zaky Aly, Ludwig Koenen, *Three Rolls of the Early Septuagint: Genesis and Deuteronomy*, PTA 27 (Bonn: Habelt, 1980), 5–9; Tov, *Greek Minor Prophets Scroll*, 12; Folker Siegert, *Zwischen Hebräischer Bibel und Altem Testament*, Münsteraner Judaistische Forschungen 9 (Münster: Lit, 2001), 202–10; Gunnar Magnus Eidsvåg, "The Paleo-Hebrew Tetragram in 8ḤevXIIgr," *JSCS* 46 (2013), 86–100.

[35]Field, *Origenis hexaplorum*, 375b, refers to Herodotus *Hist*. 1.201, Ὡς δὲ τῷ Κύρῳ καὶ τοῦτο τὸ ἔθνος κατέργαστο, "when Cyrus had conquered this nation also."

[36]See also Greenspoon, *Textual Studies*, 110–11.

[37]Roland de Vaux, *Les institutions de l'ancient Testament* 1 (Paris: Cerf, 1961), 239; *HALOT* 1441a–1442a, 1475b–1476a.

[38]Exod 5:6, 10, 14, 15, 19; Num 11:1, Deut 20:5, 8, 9; Josh 1:10; 3:2; 8:33; 23:2; 24:1. In Exod 18:21, 25; Deut 1:15; 16:18; 29:10(9); 31:28 the Greek translators used the word γραμματοεισαγωγεύς, apparently a Septuagintal neologism.

[39]Luke 5:5; 8:24, 25; 9:33, 49; 17:13.

[40]Field, *Origenis hexaplorum*, I 336a-b: "Procop. in Cat. Niceph. T. II, p. 7: Ταῦτα διὰ τῶν γραμματέων Ἰησοῦς δεδήλωκε τῷ λαῷ· οὓς ὁ μὲν Ἀκ. ἐκβιβαστάς φησιν, ὁ δὲ Σύμ. ἐπιστάτας· ἐοίκασι δὲ κατὰ τοὺς παρὰ Ῥωμαίους ἐκσκέπορας, *Exceptores*, h.e. notarii, qui acta judiciorum describunt, judicis sententiam excipient."

[41]Within the Septuagint the word occurs only here in Josh 3:16 and in 4 Macc 9:21, see further MSL 556a and LSJ 1399b; Rev.Suppl. 250a.

[42]Text and translation: Robert C. Hill, *Theodoret of Cyrus: Questions on the Octateuch*, LEC 2 (Washington, DC: Catholic University of America Press, 2007), 270–71.

[43]See Marcus Jastrow, *Dictionary of the Targumim, Talmud Babli, Yerushalmi and Midrashic Literature* (repr New York: Judaica Press, 1985), 1463b: "[hollow] a goat-skin made into a bag, bottle." cf. Michael Sokoloff, *A Dictionary of Jewish Palestinian Aramaic,* 2nd ed. (Ramat-Gan: Bar Ilan University Press, 1992), 520a: "waterskin."

[44]Cf. *HALOT* 657a, 671a, 672b. For ancient Jewish wineskins from the Judean desert, see Yigal Yadin, *Finds from the Bar Kochba Period in the Cave of Letters,* JDS 1 (Jerusalem: Israel Exploration Society, 1963), 162–64, plates 53–55.

[45]See my dissertation, *Formation and Reformulation*, 360–73.

[46]LSJ 511b–512a with a reference to Plato, *Laws* 856e, Isaeus 11.10; MSL 211a-b; LEH 183b.

[47]Max L. Margolis, "Additions to Field from the Lyons Codex of the Old Latin," *JAOS* 33 (1917), 254–58, here 256.

[48]See Joseph Reider, Nigel Turner, *An Index to Aquila,* VTSup 12 (Leiden: Brill, 1966), 215, 272b–273a.

[49]See footnote 13.

[50]Van der Meer, "Θρησκεία, Terra Incognita, and Terra Devastata."

[51]See e.g. the discussion of βέβηλος in *TLNT* 1:284–86.

[52]Salvesen, *Symmachus in the Pentateuch*, 255–62.

[53]Greenspoon, *Textual Studies*, 255–63.

3

The Final Verses of the Ammonite War Story in 2 Sam 11:1, 12:26–31, and 1 Chron 20:1–3

Kristin De Troyer
Universität Salzburg

In 1982, Hugh G. M. Williamson wrote, "These three chapters, [1 Chronicles] 18–20, are all extracted, with only minor variations, from 2 Sam. 8–21."[1] Williamson then gave three reasons why the Chronicler selected material from this source text: David did not build the Temple himself because he was a man of war; the reign of David was not really a period of rest, and thus not conducive for the establishment of the Temple; David obtained lots of spoils from his wars that he could later dedicate to the work on the Temple.[2] The Chronicler does seem to have rewritten his 2 Samuel source text to create the image of David along the lines indicated by Williamson. In this contribution, I will study the similarities and differences between the ending of the Ammonite war story in its Chronicles and Samuel versions. I suggest a different relationship between the two texts: the ending of the Ammonite war story in 2 Samuel is dependent on 1 Chronicles.

The Ammonite War

The Ammonite War in 2 Samuel

The story of the Ammonite war is told in 2 Sam 10:1–19; 11:1; 12:26–31; the Ammonites are also listed in 2 Sam 8:12 as part of the list of nations subdued by David. In 2 Samuel 10, the old king of the Ammonites died and was succeeded by his son, King Hanun. Encouraged by the Ammonites princes, Hanun decided to shame King David's messengers. In retaliation, King David sent Joab and the warriors to deal with the Ammonites. David's army was confronted with not only the Ammonites but also the coalition partner of the Ammonites, namely the Arameans. The army of the Ammonites gathered "at the entrance of the gate," while the army of the Arameans was stationed in the "open country" (2 Sam 10:8).

The Arameans, however, fled when Joab's army was approaching. The Ammonites, seeing their coalition partners flee, also decided to flee, and they withdrew to the city (2 Sam 10:14).[3] The city is not identified in chapter 10, but it must have been the city where the king lives, as the story begins with the envoys coming to the place where the king resides (2 Sam 10:3). The city is often identified as Rabbah, based on 2 Sam 12:26.[4]

Second Samuel 10:15–19 reports yet another battle against the Arameans. After they fled, they regrouped, added some coalition partners, and prepared to fight. The Arameans were then defeated. Strangely, the battle was not won by Joab, but by King David who had heard about the coalition and gathered his troops to battle it! Whereas Peter Ackroyd considers this an independent section,[5] Anthony Campbell considers it the continuation of the battle against the Ammonites and their coalition partners, the Arameans.[6]

The fight against the Ammonites, however, has not yet finished, as it continues in 11:1 and in 12:25–31. In 2 Sam 11:1a, King David sends Joab to ravage the Ammonites and besiege Rabbah. What Joab does can be found in 12:25ff. and will be analyzed in detail below.

In 2 Sam 11:1b a note indicates that King David remains at Jerusalem. Henry Smith notes, "The siege of a walled town was a tedious matter, so that David can hardly be blamed for remaining at Jerusalem."[7] Ackroyd gives a different explanation: David's remaining in Jerusalem is "a normal procedure, as in 10:1–14, though David on other occasions took the field himself."[8] Similarly, Campbell says that the note "allows the listener or reader to realize that the siege of Rabbah was a relatively minor imperial campaign: it could be entrusted to Joab. The major battle had been with the assembled Aramean forces; that campaign had been led by David."[9]

Ackroyd recognizes three different engagement stories in the battle against the Ammonites: Joab's battle against Ammon and Aram (10:7–14, prefaced by 10:1–6); David's battle against Aram (10:15–19); and Joab (and David) against Ammon (11:1; 12:26–31). The story of Bathsheba and David, Ackroyd remarks, is spliced in:

"Into this group of stories,. . . there has been inserted the story of David and Bathsheba, 11:2–12:25."[10] Similarly, Campbell says, "Between the opening and closing reports of a military campaign (11:1 and 12:26–31) are sandwiched a story about the evil of Israel's greatest king, David, and the birth of his son and successor, Solomon the wise."[11] Knoppers suggests that "this account (10:1–19 + 8:3–8 + 11:1 + 12:25–31) probably derives from contemporary annalistic sources; it was drawn from the royal archives to serve as a framework for the story told in 11:2–12:24."[12]

Moreover, elements of the narrative on the war against the Ammonites are taken up in the David–Bathsheba story. In particular, the David and Bathsheba affair story is tied with the war against the Ammonites story through its main general, Joab. It is the same Joab who sends Uriah, the husband of the wife with whom David falls in love, to the front in the campaign against the Ammonites. The redactor who spliced the story of David and Bathsheba in the Ammonite war story has thus skillfully woven elements from the surrounding verses into the story about David and Bathsheba.[13]

The Ammonite War in 1 Chronicles

The Ammonites had been mentioned in 1 Chron 18:11, and the battle against them begins in 1 Chronicles 19. As in 2 Samuel 10, the battle starts after the Ammonites offended the ambassadors of King David (1 Chron 19:1–5). The Arameans are called in as supporting troops (1 Chron 19:6–9). They encamp לפני מידבה; there is much discussion whether מידבה refers to the city of Medeba or constitutes a misreading of the "city of water" in 2 Sam 12:27 (את-עיר המים), which could have been shortened to "waters of Rabbah" (מירבה).[14] When the battle starts, there are—as in 2 Samuel—two factions: the foreign kings in the field and the Ammonites at the entrance of the city. Joab sees both factions, and he develops his strategy—again as in 2 Samuel. In 1 Chronicles as well, the Arameans flee; the Ammonites entered their town, and Joab returns from the Ammonites and goes to Jerusalem (1 Chron 19:10–15). Then—yet again as in 2 Samuel—a coalition of Arameans is formed, and David deals with them (1 Chron 19:16–19).

In 1 Chronicles 20, David sends out Joab to deal with the Ammonites. As in 2 Sam 11:1, David remains in Jerusalem while Joab goes to Rabbah. This splitting up of the activities—Joab fighting while David stays behind—is in line with the events of 1 Chronicles 19. In 2 Samuel, the note about David remaining behind serves to introduce the events with Bathsheba. In 1 Chronicles, the note is followed by the report on the battle against Rabbah. First Chronicles has no story about David and Bathsheba. As Ackroyd observed, "It is the battle narrative which alone appears in the Chronicler's account in I Chron. 19:1–20:3."[15] There are other narrative sections from 2 Samuel that are not attested in 1 Chronicles, as shown in Table 3.1.

Samuel–Kings	Chronicles
2 Sam 7:1–17	1 Chron 17:1–15
2 Sam 7:18–29	1 Chron 17:16–27
2 Sam 8:1–14	1 Chron 18:1–13
2 Sam 8:15–18	1 Chron 18:14–17
2 Samuel 9 (Mephibosheth)	-
2 Sam 10:1–19	1 Chron 19:1–19
2 Sam 11:1	**1 Chron 20:1a**
2 Sam 11:2–12:25 (Bathsheba, Nathan)	-
2 Sam 12:26–31	**1 Chron 20:1b–3**
2 Sam 13:1–21:14 (Amnon, Absalom)	-
2 Sam 21:15–22	1 Chron 20:4–8
2 Sam 22:1–23:38 (Psalm 18, last words)	-
2 Sam 24:1–17	1 Chron 21:1–17
2 Sam 24:18–25	1 Chron 21:18–27
-	1 Chron 21:28–29:22a
-	(Temple; David's praise of Solomon)
1 Kings 1:1–37, 41–2:11, 13–*fin* (Adonijah, Joab, Shimei)	-
1 Kings 1:38–40; 2:12	1 Chron 29:22b–25
	1 Chron 29:26–30

Table 3.1: Narrative Sequence

The relationship between 2 Samuel and 1 Chronicles has been much debated. Knoppers has summarized the three positions with regard to 1 Chronicles 19 and 2 Samuel 10. First, there are those who hold that "the Chronicler freely rewrites his *Vorlage* resulting in a substantially different, albeit occasionally confused, account from that of 2 Sam 10."[16] Some adherents to this position "think that they can identify the source of the distinctive elements within the Chronicler's text;"[17] others "acknowledge reinterpretation and adaptation in Chronicles, but maintain that MT and LXX Samuel are also developed texts. . . . These scholars believe that the Chronicler's *Vorlage* may have differed somewhat from MT Samuel." Finally, there are those who claim "that both Samuel and Chronicles represent alternate or competing appropriations of an earlier story of Judah's kings."[18] The latter aim at reconstructing that shorter common *Vorlage*.[19] Knoppers underlines at the end of his summary the importance of the work of De Wette, "who influentially argued that Chronicles is dependent on Samuel–Kings."[20] Knoppers himself suggests that "(1) the Chronicler drew upon a divergent text of Samuel with affinities to 4QSam[a] and (2) that multiple textual witnesses existed for these books, especially for Samuel."[21] Differences between 2 Samuel and 1 Chronicles are thus explained by multiple textual stages and witnesses of 2 Samuel; differences are not credited to 1 Chronicles. This holds true for the debate about the relationship between the endings of the Ammonite war story (2 Sam 11:1; 12:26–31; 1 Chron 20:1–3).

To resolve the puzzling relationship between Samuel and Chronicles, numerous witnesses play important roles. There is not just MT 2 Samuel and MT 1 Chronicles, but also the Greek version of 2 Samuel. The Greek version itself divides neatly into an Old Greek portion (2 Sam 1:1–11:1) and a second part reflecting the *Kaige* text (2 Sam 11:2–1 Kgs 2:11).[22] Additional witnesses include the text from 4QSam[a], the Antiochian text of both Samuel and Chronicles, and the text as found in Josephus.

The Ending of the Ammonite War

The last section of the Ammonite war story consists of seven verses in 2 Samuel (11:1 + 12:26–31) and three in 1 Chronicles (20:1–3).

Below are five important points of comparison between MT 2 Samuel and MT 1 Chronicles.

1. David and Joab in MT 2 Sam 11:1a and MT 1 Chron 20:1a

In MT 2 Sam 11:1a, David sends Joab with his officers and all Israel with him to fight. In MT 1 Chron 20:1a, Joab leads out the whole army; Joab is not sent by David, and there is no mention of "all Israel with him."[23] In MT 2 Sam 11:11a, Joab ravaged the children of the Ammonites and besieged Rabbah; in MT 1 Chron 20:1b, Joab ravaged the *country* of the children of the Ammonites, and then he *came* and besieged Rabbah.[24] In MT 2 Sam 11:1a and in MT 1 Chron 20:1, "David remained in Jerusalem."

2. Rabbah in MT 2 Sam 12:26a and MT 1 Chron 20:1b

The Chronicler immediately continues with Joab, the other hero of the story. Joab attacks Rabbah and overthrows it. In MT 2 Samuel, the David and Bathsheba story comprises 11:2–12:25. When the Ammonite war story resumes in MT 2 Sam 12:26, the text is much the same as MT 1 Chron 20:1b. Joab attacks (וילחם) Rabbah; cf. smite (ויך) in 1 Chronicles. Second Samuel also elaborates "Rabbah of the children of the Ammonites" rather than simply naming Rabbah, as in 1 Chronicles. To say that Rabbah is overthrown, MT 2 Sam 12:26 uses וילכד rather than ויהרסה. In MT 2 Sam 12:26, Joab overthrows "the royal city" (את-עיר המלוכה), whereas MT 1 Chron 20:1b names Rabbah explicitly. The change of verbs will be discussed further below.

3. Attacking the "City" Again in MT 2 Sam 12:27–29

The verb לכד occurs four more times in 12:27–29. This short section simply elaborates the first mention of לכד, and the verses are without parallel in 1 Chronicles 20; see Table 3.2.

12:27bβ	גם-לכדתי את-עיר ימים	I [Joab] have taken the city of water
12:28aβ	ולכדה	and take it
12:28bα	פן-אלכד אני את-העיר	or I myself will take the city
12:29b	וילכדה	and he took it

Table 3.2: The Verb לכד in 2 Sam 12:27–29

Joab takes Rabbah in 2 Sam 12:26. He clarifies that he has taken the city of water in v. 27 and then suggests that David take "the city" (not explicitly Rabbah) in 12:28bα. Finally, David takes Rabbah in 12:29b—but only after Joab threatened to take it for himself (12:28b). In both stories, the verb (לכד) is the same, but the subjects differ. This is the most notable difference, since Joab takes the city in 1 Chronicles, but David takes the city in 2 Samuel.

While the verb is systematically the same, the name of the city varies considerably in 2 Samuel; see Table 3.3.

12:26a	רבה	Rabbah
12:26b	את-עיר המלוכה	the royal city
12:27bα	רבה	Rabbah
12:27bβ	את-עיר המים	the city of water
12:28a	העיר	the city
12:28b	העיר	the city
12:29a	רבה	Rabbah

Table 3.3: Naming the City in 2 Sam 12:27–29

In this series of names, the author has subtly changed the city against which Joab is fighting. Originally Joab fought "Rabbah" (12:26a), and David was told to fight "the city" (12:28a); then David actually takes "Rabbah" (12:29a). In the phrases in between, Joab is gently, but surely, dissociated with Rabbah; instead, Joab is involved with "the royal city" (12:26b), "the city of water" (12:27bβ), and "the city" (12:28a, 12:28b). The verb to "take" (לכד) the city at the end of 12:29 is a *Wiederaufnahme* of the end of 12:26, where the MT redactor smartly changed Rabbah into the royal city (את-עיר המלוכה). This necessary change facilitated a second fight, so that David—not Joab—could take Rabbah.

4. The Spoils of War in MT 2 Sam 12:30–31a and MT 1 Chron 20:2–3a

Both in MT 2 Sam 12:30–31a and MT 1 Chron 20:2–3a, David takes the crown of Milcom, brings the spoil out of the city, and brings the people out (to put them to work). In both stories, the crown is placed on David's head—David does not put it on his own head. The crowning is somewhat unexpected; that is, aside from this phrase in 12:30–31a, David is the subject of the verbs.

David's taking of the crown is more confusing in Chronicles than in Samuel. David needs to be in Rabbah to take the crown, bring forth the spoils, and lead out the Ammonite captives. Perhaps the reader "assumes that when the campaign got to the decisive point at which it is necessary for the supreme commander of the forces to be there, then he went."[25] Such an assumption is less likely, given that David expressly remained in Jerusalem according to MT 1 Chron 20:1. However, David's actions make perfect sense in MT 2 Samuel, where David actually fought the battle against Rabbah.

5. "Thus David did. . . and. . . returned to Jerusalem" in MT 2 Sam 12:31b and MT 1 Chron 20:3b

The ending phrase in 1 Chronicles, "Then David and all the people returned to Jerusalem," presumes David's presence in Rabbah. His presence in Rabbah is less unexpected in MT 2 Samuel than in MT 1 Chronicles, where David had not left Jerusalem. Not just David returns to Jerusalem, but "all the people" as well. The expression "all the people" fits better with MT 2 Sam 12:28, where Joab encourages David to take "the rest of the people," and with v. 29, where David is said to gather "all the people."

The penultimate phrase was most likely the original ending of the story of the Ammonite war: "Thus he did with all the cities of the children of the Ammonites" (MT 2 Sam 12:31aβ). The phrase is verbatim to that represented in Chronicles, except that the Chronicler names David explicitly: "Thus David did with all the cities of the children of the Ammonites" (MT 1 Chron 20:3aβ). The explicit naming of David was no longer necessary in MT 2 Samuel 12, as David had been named as subject since 12:29.

Common Explanations

In order to explain the differences between Ammonite war story in MT 2 Samuel and MT 1 Chronicles, it has been suggested that the Chronicler simplified the story of 2 Samuel from two battles against Rabbah to just one battle; this simplification purportedly left traces such as David's returning to Jerusalem in MT 1 Chronicles without ever having left.[26] According to this hypothesis, in the original story the author distinguished between the royal city, which is the fortified city, and the water city, which is a section of the greater Rabbah. The water city was taken by Joab, the larger city by David. Knoppers explains, "if (David) does not assume personal command of the army for the final siege, Rabbah will be regarded thereafter as Joab's own conquest, not that of the king."[27] The different names of the city are explained as follows: "Perhaps 'the Royal Citadel' was the official name used by the narrator and 'the citadel of the water supply' was not a name ('the Citadel of Waters'), but Joab's descriptive way of identifying its strategic importance to David."[28] Knoppers's idea that Joab only took a section of the city and invited King David to come and finish off the city can also be found in Josephus (*Ant.* 7.159–161); Josephus said that Joab laid siege to Rabbah and inflicted damage, but then Joab invited the king to capture the city. In other words, even in antiquity, interpreters were trying to explain how both David and Joab were fighting the same city.

The Other Witnesses

The fragmentary text of 4QSam[a] confirms that the Samuel text with the "second battle" against Rabbah, under the leadership of David, was already part of the text of 2 Samuel.[29] At least, it appears that David was indeed "gathering" his troops, as ו[א]סוף is visible in the scroll. Also, the following verses were already there at the time the scroll was written: in 2 Sam 12:30–31, a letter from the word Milcom, the spoil of the city, and the Ammonites are partially preserved.

The Antiochian text also has the entire history, including the double battle against Rabbah.[30] Antiochian 2 Samuel follows the Old Greek (henceforth OG) closely, albeit with the usual precision in the use of the prepositions; similarly, Antiochian 1 Chronicles follows the OG closely.[31]

A Closer Look at the Details

A more detailed analysis is necessary to define the relationship between the two texts. In what follows, I discuss the differences between 2 Sam 11:1b; 12:26 and 1 Chron 20:1; see Table 3.4.

2 Sam 11:1b; 12:26	1 Chron 20:1
David sent Joab	Joab led out
and his officers with him	the army,
and all Israel;	
they ravaged	ravaged
the Ammonites,	the country of the Ammonites,
	and came
and besieged Rabbah.	and besieged Rabbah.
But David remained at Jerusalem.	But David remained at Rabbah.
Now Joab fought against Rabbah	Joab attacked Rabbah
of the Ammonites	
and took the royal city.	and overthrew it.

Table 3.4: Comparing 2 Sam 11:1b; 12:26 with 1 Chron 20:1

Table 3.5 highlights instances where 2 Samuel and 1 Chronicles use different verbs in parallel phrases.[32]

2 Sam 11:1b; 12:26			1 Chron 20:1		
MT	OG/*Kaige*	Antiochian	MT	OG/*Kaige*	Antiochian
וישחתו	διέφθειραν	διέφθειρον	וישחת	ἔφθειραν	ἔφθειρε
			ויבא	ἦλθεν	ἦλθεν
ויצרו	διεκάθισαν	περιεκάθισαν	ויצר	περιεκάθισεν	περιεκάθισε
ודויד ישב	ἐκάθισεν	κατῴκει	ודויד ישב	ἐκάθητο	ἐκάθητο
וילחם יואב	ἐπολέμησεν	ἐπολέμησεν	ויך	ἐπάταξεν	ἐπάταξεν
וילכד	κατέλαβεν	προκατελάβετο	ויהרסה	κατέσκαψεν	κατεῖλεν

Table 3.5: Comparison of Verbs in 2 Samuel and 1 Chronicles

1. To Fight or To Smite?

In MT 2 Sam 12:26, Joab fights (לחם) against Rabbah. The verb לחם is used in 2:28; 8:10; 10:17; 11:17, 20; 12:26, 27, 29; 21:15. In all these instances, the subject is either Joab (2:28; 11:17, 20; 12:26, 27; 21:15) or David (8:10; 10:17; 12:29). In the majority of cases, the fighting is at Rabbah (11:17, 20; 12:26, 27, 29)—although twice the city is not named explicitly (11:17; 11:20). David only fights at Rabbah in 12:29; otherwise Joab is fighting. It is worth noting that in two of the cases, the fighting against the city is part of the David–Bathsheba story (11:17; 11:20); the fighting at Rabbah is the background for the killing of Uriah, Bathsheba's husband. The MT 2 Samuel redactor, who spliced the David–Bathsheba story in the Ammonite war story, was sure to use the same verb (לחם) as in the immediate context of the story.

In contrast with MT 2 Samuel, the verb לחם is only used three times in MT 1 Chronicles (10:1; 18:10; 19:17). In two of the three cases, David is the one fighting; in the only other case, the Philistines are fighting Israel (10:1). In 1 Chronicles, Joab never fights (לחם), and the verb is never used in relationship with Rabbah. The verb and its usage are thus more typical for MT 2 Samuel than for MT 1 Chronicles. Moreover, MT 2 Samuel seems to emphasize the verb in relation to Joab and Rabbah. In all the cases, the OG/*Kaige* has translated πολεμέω (make war).

In MT 1 Chronicles, the verb נכה (smite) describes the attack on Rabbah. This verb occurs forty-six times in MT 2 Samuel. In only one case does Joab do the smiting; he smites Amasa in 2 Sam 20:10. Everywhere else it is David, David's own conscience, or one of David's companions. Nowhere in 2 Samuel is smiting related to Rabbah. In MT 1 Chronicles, the verb נכה is used twenty-four times. One-third of the time, David does the smiting; other subjects include Elhanan, Benaiah, all Israel, Abishai, and Jonathan, and God is the subject twice (13:10; 21:7)—including God's smiting Israel (21:7). The victims are mostly the Philistines, but others are Moabites, Hadadezer, the Arameans, and even giants and lions. Joab is the subject only once, when he smote Rabbah (20:1). The use of נכה across MT 2 Samuel and MT 1 Chronicles, therefore, shows no exclusive connection between any subject, any war, or any victim. There is, however, a more emphatic use of לחם in MT 2 Samuel: Rabbah is especially fought against, and most of the fighting is attributed to Joab.

2. To Take or To Overthrow?

In MT 2 Sam 12:26, Joab takes (לכד) the royal city. In MT 1 Chron 20:1, Joab tears down (הרס) Rabbah. The verb לכד is only used six times in MT 2 Samuel: David takes Sion (5:7) and Hadadezer (8:4), and the remaining four occurrences have to do with Rabbah (12:26, 27, 28, and 29). In MT 1 Chronicles, the verb only occurs twice, and David is the subject in both cases; David takes Sion (11:5) and Hadadezer (18:4), as in 2 Samuel.

The other verb used is הרס (overthrow), which only appears once in MT 2 Samuel and once in MT 1 Chronicles. The lone usage in 2 Samuel (11:25) occurs toward the end of the report on Uriah. After David hears that Uriah has died, David encourages Joab to continue the attack and tear down the city; the entire phrase reads, "press your attack on the city, and overthrow it, and encourage him" (החזק מלחמתך אל-העיר והרסה וחזקהו). Both the initial command and final exhortation use the verb חזק (strengthen). This verb is used four other times in the surrounding context (twice each in 2 Sam 10:11, 12), where the battle is raging against the Arameans; the parallel text in 1 Chron 19:12, 13 is the same.

Second Samuel 11:25 also contains two words figuring prominently in this study: מלחמתך, which is derived from the verb לחם,

and the verb הרס. A comparison of the verbs used in 2 Sam 11:25, 12:26, and 1 Chron 20:1 may reveal an unexpected link between Samuel and Chronicles; see Table 3.6.

2 Sam 12:26	2 Sam 11:25	1 Chron 20:1
לחם	לחם (derivative noun)	נכה
לכד	הרס	הרס

Table 3.6: The Verbs לחם and הרס

Here again there is a link between the Rabbah story in 2 Samuel and 1 Chronicles, on the one hand, and 2 Samuel's spliced David–Bathsheba story, on the other. As mentioned above, in the middle of the Bathsheba episode, David encourages Joab to press on with the attack on the city and to overthrow it. This command links the beginning and ending of the final phase of the Ammonite war: Joab ravages the Ammonites and besieges Rabbah in 2 Sam 11:1, and then Joab is fighting against Rabbah of the Ammonites in 2 Sam 12:26–31.

More importantly, this link offers a clue about the direction of textual dependence. The use of the verb לחם can surely be credited to the MT Samuel redactor, who *inter alia* spliced the David-Bathsheba affair into the Ammonite war story. Conversely, the use of the verb הרס in 2 Sam 11:25 clearly points to 1 Chron 20:1 or a common text as its source. In other words, the inserted phrase in 2 Sam 11:25 strongly implies that MT 2 Samuel redactor knew the use of the verb in MT 1 Chronicles 20. One could also posit an independent source—an Ammonite war stories source—common to MT 2 Samuel and MT 1 Chronicles. In this case, however, the hypothetical source text would look precisely like the text in 1 Chronicles! See Table 3.7.

2 Sam 12:26	2 Sam:11:25	1 Chron 20:1
לחם MT 2 Samuel Redactor =	לחם MT 2 Samuel Redactor ←	נכה
לכד MT 2 Samuel Redactor ←	הרס ←	הרס

Table 3.7: Direction of Dependence for הרס

3. The extra verb "to come"

In MT 1 Chron 20:1, after Joab has ravaged the country of the Ammonites, he comes (ויבוא) and besieges Rabbah. The addition of the verb may indicate an additional move on the part of Joab: the ravaging of the country of the Ammonites needs to be separated from the besieging of Rabbah. Joab's coming is emphasized a bit more in MT 1 Chronicles than in MT 2 Samuel; see Table 3.8.

1 Chronicles	2 Samuel
Joab came to Jerusalem (19:15)	= 8:5
Joab came and besieged Rabbah (20:1)	-
Joab came to Jerusalem (21:4)	-

Table 3.8: The Verb "To Come"

Joab's coming and going is not emphasized in MT 2 Samuel. The coming of Joab in 1 Chronicles, however, might have inspired the MT 2 Samuel redactor to focus on the coming of David in contrast to the coming of Joab. This contrast is precisely the essence of 2 Sam 12:27–28; in effect, Joab tells David, "I have fought Rabbah, now you have to come!"[33]

Conclusion

The foregoing analysis of the ending verses of the Ammonite war (2 Sam 11:1; 12:26–31) demonstrates that 12:26–29 were added to the story. These additional verses were not only inspired by the Ammonite war story of 1 Chronicles 20 and its parallel in 2 Samuel 10 but also necessitated by 1 Chronicles 20. The MT 2 Samuel redactor created 12:26–29 on the basis of 1 Chronicles 20, and the redactor was sure to use his favorite verb, לחם.

More precisely, the MT 2 Samuel redactor used the muster from the Ammonite war as reported in 2 Samuel 10 (and its parallel text in 1 Chronicles 19): first there was a fight led by Joab (2 Sam 10:6–14; 1 Chron 19:6–15); then there was a fight led by

David (2 Sam 10:15–19; 1 Chron 19:16–19). The redactor created a two-stage battle against the city of Rabbah: Joab led the first stage (2 Sam 12:26–28), and David led the second stage (2 Sam 12:29). Moreover, the MT 2 Samuel redactor used the note that "David did this to all the cities of the Ammonites" (2 Sam 12:31b; 1 Chron 20:3b) to split the battle against Rabbah into two stages.

In order to create this second battle, the MT 2 Samuel redactor expanded the use of לכד, especially in relation to "the city" (12:26–29). The city of Rabbah was split into two sections: the first section, taken by Joab, was labeled "royal city," "water city," or simply "the city," thereby dissociating Joab from Rabbah; David led the battle expressly against Rabbah. The redactor transferred Joab's "taking" (לכד) of Rabbah (2 Sam 12:26; לכדתי, I [Joab] took) to David (2 Sam 12:29; וילכדה, he [David] took it). The redactor also emphasized David's coming—especially to Jerusalem—and not Joab's coming. The hand of the 2 Samuel redactor is especially visible in the change from נכה to לחם.

It is, however, the presence of הרס in 2 Sam 11:25 that reveals the direction of the dependence: the MT of 2 Samuel has elaborated the story of 1 Chronicles 20. In its elaboration, it has also picked up elements from its immediate context and has solved some problems with the story as it was presented.

The final question that needs answering is why David had to be associated with Rabbah. Whereas some scholars have pointed to the minor importance of this battle, I believe Rabbah to have been the ultimate stronghold of the Ammonites and thus the kernel of the Ammonite war story. The sacking of Rabbah is not just the final detail of the war against the Ammonites—it is the culmination of the story: "When Rabbah fell, Ammon was incorporated into the Davidic empire."[34]

Notes

I dedicate this contribution to my wonderful friend and colleague Leonard Greenspoon, who has inspired me to look at textual puzzles!

[1]Hugh G. M. Williamson, *1 and 2 Chronicles*, The New Century Bible Commentary (Grand Rapids: Eerdmans, 1982), 137.

[2]Williamson, *1 and 2 Chronicles*, 138.

[3]Peter R. Ackroyd (*The Second Book of Samuel*, The Cambridge Bible Commentary on the New English Bible [Cambridge: Cambridge University Press, 1977], 97–98) suggests that the two armies in different positions may have been part of a military strategy: one army was in the country ready to fight Joab's army while the latter was going straight for the Ammonites at the city gate; this strategy clearly did not work, as Joab realized the set-up. Anthony F. Campbell (*2 Samuel*, FOTL 8 [Grand Rapids: Eerdmans, 2005], 94) points to the weakness of Ammonites and Aramaeans: "Joab's willingness to fight a battle on two fronts. . . points to the relatively limited strengths of the forces opposing him." It could be argued that the military strategy is the opposite from the strategy used in the battle against Ai as described in the Book of Joshua; see Kristin De Troyer, "The Battle of Ai and the Textual History of the Book of Joshua," *JSCS* 48 (2015): 39-53.

[4]E.g., Ackroyd, *Second Book of Samuel*, 98; Samuel R. Driver, *Notes on the Hebrew Text and Topography of the Books of Samuel, with an Introduction on Hebrew Palaeography and the Ancient Versions and Facsimiles of Inscriptions and Maps*, 2nd ed. (Oxford: Clarendon, 1913), 287; Henry Preserved Smith, *A Critical and Exegetical Commentary on the Books of Samuel*, ICC (Edinburgh: T&T Clark, 1899), 314.

[5]Regarding 2 Sam 10:15–19, Ackroyd (*Second Book of Samuel*, 98) remarks, "These verses appear to relate a quite independent incident. . . ." Similarly, Smith (*Books of Samuel*, 315–16) concludes, "The paragraph breaks the sequence of the narrative however, and is possibly from another source."

[6]Campbell (*2 Samuel*, 92) also points to the two leaders in the battle: on the smaller scale, in the first battle, Joab is the leader; on the larger scale, the second battle, David is the one in charge. Campbell points to David going out to battle and correctly muses: "This ought to give food for thought to those who quibble over David's staying in Jerusalem while Joab besieges the isolated Ammonite capital."

[7]Smith, *Books of Samuel*, 317.

[8]Ackroyd, *Second Book of Samuel*, 100.

[9]Campbell, *2 Samuel*, 96; he also states, "It may therefore be quite appropriate for Joab to lead what may have been minor mopping-up operations" (p. 114).

[10]Ackroyd, *Second Book of Samuel*, 96.

[11]Campbell, *2 Samuel*, 113.

[12]Knoppers, *I Chronicles 10-29*, AB 12A (New York: Doubleday, 2004), 312.

[13]See also Ackroyd, *Second Book of Samuel*, 96. Knoppers (*I Chronicles 10-29*, 728) has also pointed to references to the Ammonite war story in other sections of the succession narrative, e.g. in 20:1–8; i.e., 20:1 is taken from 11:1, and 20:2–3 is taken from 12:30–31. However, Steven L. McKenzie (*King David: A Biography* [Oxford: Oxford University Press, 2000], 157) considers 12:26a secondary. For an analysis of the David–Bathsheba story (and Nathan), see also Kristin De Troyer, "Bathsheba an Nathan: A Closer Look at Their Characterizations in MT, Kaige and the Antiochian Text," in *After Qumran: Old and Modern Editions of the Biblical Texts—The Historical Books*, ed. Hans Ausloos, Bénédicte Lemmelijn, and Julio Trebolle Barrera, BETL 246 (Leuven: Peeters, 2012), 119–42.

[14]For a summary, see Knoppers, *I Chronicles 10-29*, 715; Knoppers translates that they "encamped before the waters of Rabbah," (p. 712), and he later identifies the city with Rabbah, "the royal city of Ammon" (pp. 720–21).

[15]Ackroyd, *Second Book of Samuel*, 96.

[16]Knoppers, *I Chronicles 10-29*, 723.

[17]Knoppers, *I Chronicles 10-29*, 723.

[18]Knoppers, *I Chronicles 10-29*, 723.

[19]Knoppers, *I Chronicles 10-29*, 723.

[20]Knoppers, *I Chronicles 10-29*, 723.

[21]Knoppers, *I Chronicles 10-29*, 726.

[22]This was first identified by Henry St. John Thackeray, *The Septuagint and Jewish Worship: A Study in Origins*, The Schweich Lectures (London: the British Academy, 1923), 17–18; see also Emanuel Tov, *Textual Criticism of the Hebrew Bible*, 3rd ed. (Minneapolis: Fortress, 2012), 143.

[23]This element is emphasized more in MT 2 Samuel than in MT 1 Chronicles.

[24]For a discussion of the extra verb in MT 1 Chron 20:1a, ויבא, see below.

[25]John Jarick, *1 Chronicles*, Readings: A New Biblical Commentary (London: Sheffield Academic Press, 2002), 122.

[26]Panc Beentjes, *1 Kronieken*, Verklaring van de Hebreeuwse Bijbel (Kampen: Kok, 2002), 162.

[27]Knoppers, *I Chronicles 10-29*, 312.

[28]Knoppers, *I Chronicles 10-29*, 310.

[29]See Frank Moore Cross, et al., *4QSama*, in Frank Moore Cross, et al., *Qumran Cave 4. XII: 1-2 Samuel*, DJD XVII (Oxford: Clarendon, 2005), 138–46.

[30]Natalio Fernández Marcos and José Ramón Busto Saiz, with the collaboration of María Victoria Spottorno y Díaz Caro and S. Peter Cowe, *El Texto Antioqueno de la Biblia griega. I. 1–2 Samuel*, Textos y Estudios "Cardinal Cisneros" de la Biblia Políglota Matritense 50 (Madrid: Consejo superior de investigaciones científicas, 1989).

[31]Natalio Fernández Marcos and José Ramón Busto Saiz, with the collaboration of María Victoria Spottorno Díaz Caro and S. Peter Cowe, *El Texto Antioqueno de la Biblia griega. I. 1–2 Crónicas*, Textos y Estudios "Cardinal Cisneros" de la Biblia Políglota Matritense 60 (Madrid: Consejo superior de investigaciones científicas, 1996).

[32]For the OG/Kaige of 2 Samuel and OG of 1 Chronicles, see Alan England Brooke, Norman McLean, and Henry St John Thackeray, *The Old Testament in Greek According to the Text of Codex Vaticanus, Supplemented from Other Uncial Manuscripts, with a Critical Apparatus Containing the Variants of the Chief Ancient Authorities for the Text of the Septuagint, Volume 3*, Cambridge Library Collection (Cambridge: Cambridge University Press, 2009); for the Antiochian, see Fernández Marcos and Busto Saiz, *1-2 Samuel* and *1–2 Crónicas*.

[33]The same MT 2 Samuel redactor also emphasized that David comes with all the people (of Israel): e.g., in 12:29 David returns to Jerusalem and "all Israel (is) with him;" this emphasis is, in my opinion, a typical MT plus.

[34]Knoppers, *I Chronicles 10-29*, 313.

4

The Old Greek Translation of Isaiah 40

Eugene Ulrich
University of Notre Dame

This study offers an analysis of the Greek translator's methods as seen from chapter 40 of the book of Isaiah.[1] The Hebrew book was translated into Greek in the late third or early second century B.C.E. The translation of the poetry and poetic prose of Isaiah into Greek was a formidable task, requiring transformation not only into a different language but into a different family of languages with a different linguistic structure. An added source of problems was that the Hebrew originals had been handed down in oral tradition and written copies for several centuries prior to the translator. The complex relationship between the Masoretic *textus receptus* of Isaiah and the Great Isaiah Scroll (1QIsa[a]), one of the most important of the Dead Sea Scrolls, abundantly illustrates that complexity in the Hebrew. It is also clear that the OG was translated from an alternate Hebrew *Vorlage*, or source text, that differed modestly from both those extant witnesses. This study is designed to examine the translator's attempt at a faithful version of a no-longer-extant Hebrew text that we can largely envision from the Greek text he has bequeathed to us.[2]

Textual variants in the Hebrew Bible can be classified in four mutually independent categories: (1) variant editions of books, that is, newer revised editions showing a number of consciously made and discernibly similar major additions or changes that betray an intentional pattern in the reworking of a text; (2) isolated major insertions of a verse or more, which learned scribes intentionally added, interjecting a significant thought, such as an informational, exegetical, nomistic, pious, or other idea; (3) individual textual variants, which sporadically dot most texts due to scribal lapses or clarifications and which are the customary examples treated in most expositions of text-critical books; and (4) orthography, contrasting alternate legitimate spellings of words but usually entailing no difference in meaning.[3] Only the second and third of these will function in this study. Regarding the first category, variant editions, for the book of Isaiah, although thousands of individual variants occur in the manuscripts, there are no variant editions preserved.[4] Regarding orthography, since the focus is on the LXX, Hebrew orthography will play little part, except in Isa 40:6: ואומרה 1QIsa[a] = καὶ εἶπα (= וָאֹמַר*) OG vs. וְאָמַר MT.

Isolated Insertions

The most extensive variant between the OG and the MT in Isa 40 can be classified in the second category, an intentional isolated insertion: MT's interjection (in italics) into the original proclamation announced to the prophet in 40:7aβ–8a, as shown in Table 4.1.

LXX	(6) φωνὴ λέγοντος Βόησον· καὶ εἶπα Τί βοήσω; Πᾶσα σὰρξ χόρτος, καὶ πᾶσα δόξα ἀνθρώπου ὡς ἄνθος χόρτου· (7) ἐξηράνθη ὁ χόρτος, καὶ τὸ ἄνθος ἐξέπεσε (8) τὸ δὲ ῥῆμα τοῦ θεοῦ ἡμῶν μένει εἰς τὸν αἰῶνα.
1QIsa[a] OG	(6) קול אומר קרא ואומרה מה אקרא כול הבשר חציר וכול חסדיו כציץ השדה *כי רוח . . . . נשבה בוא הכן חציר העם יבש חציל נבל ציץ ודבר אלהינו* (7) יבש חציר נבל ציץ (8) ודבר אלהינו יקום לעולם
MT	(6) קול אמר קרא ואמר מה אקרא כל הבשר חציר וכל חסדו כציץ השדה (7) יבש חציר נבל ציץ *כי רוח יהוה נשבה בו אכן חציר העם* (8) *יבש חציר נבל ציץ* ודבר אלהינו יקום לעולם
English	(6) A voice says, "Proclaim!" And I said, "What shall I proclaim?" "All flesh is grass, their constancy/human glory is like the flower of the field (7) The grass withers, the flower fades, *when the breath of the LORD blows upon it [surely 'the grass' is the people].* (8) *The grass withers, the flower fades, but the word of our God* but the word of our God will stand forever."

Table 4.1 Isa 40:7aβ–8a

That MT-1QIsa$^{a\ 2m}$ is a secondary insertion is dramatically illustrated by 1QIsa^{a*}-1QIsa$^{a\ 2m}$: the original manuscript had the short text, a perfect prophetic salvation oracle, in agreement with the OG, and the insertion (in interlinear italics) was added into 1QIsa^{a} a generation later by a second hand. In addition to the double attestation by 1QIsa^{a} and OG, the *Wiederaufnahme* also weighs in favor of seeing the longer text as an later insertion.

Additional evidence in this regard appears in MT 2:22 and 36:7b, which are two other isolated interjections lacking in the OG but added into, though not quite fitting in the context of, the MT and 1QIsa^{a}. 1QIsa^{a} in fact shows six other isolated insertions lacking in the scroll but added in the MT tradition.[5]

Individual Textual Variants

As we turn from isolated major insertions to individual variants, we must reflect on the condition of the Hebrew manuscript used by the translator. Like 1QIsa^{a}, the *Vorlage*, though generally in good shape, probably had a surface that was marred in some spots, had occasional words and letters cramped at the end of a line, contained ambiguous forms, and included scribal errors already in the early Hebrew text. A survey of a number of the types of variants follows.[6]

Alternate proposals for Ziegler's critical edition

Before considering individual variants, it is important to examine the wording of Ziegler's edition as the point of comparison. Though his critical edition of the Greek text (LXX^{ed}) is of the highest quality, there are three readings in chapter 40 for which I propose alternate readings as the OG (OG*) in line with more recent study of recensional developments.

40:25 *καὶ ὑψωθήσομαι* OG* rel. Syh^{mg}] ואשוה MT 1QIsa^{a} (ואשוא) *καὶ ἰσοθήσομαι* LXX^{ed} Q 86 *α′ σ′ θ′* (ἐξισοθ-) *oI* Vulg. Ziegler chooses ἰσοθήσομαι ("be made equal") for the OG, though it has little and only later attestation, whereas the overwhelming majority of the Greek tradition preserves the erroneous ὑψωθήσομαι ("be raised up").[7] If ἰσοθήσομαι were the original, correct translation from the

Hebrew, it would be difficult to explain ὑψωθήσομαι. That form would be unlikely to creep into the Greek transmission; rather, it must depend on a Hebrew confusion at the time of translating, not during the Greek transmission process. The verb parallel to "to whom will you liken me?" must be שו"ה ("to be like, make like"), but the OG mistakes this for נש"א ("to raise"; note the final א in 1QIsa[a]), a *lectio facilior* that depends on a more common Hebrew word. Thus, it appears that ὑψωθήσομαι was the original translation from the Hebrew and that the early recensionists (σ′ θ′ cf. α′) understood the Hebrew and corrected to ἰσοθήσομαι, followed by some later hexaplaric manuscripts (*oI*) and the Vulgate (*adaequastis*), with the Syro-Hexapla noting the OG reading only in its margin.

40:27 ἀφεῖλεν OG*] יעבור 1QIsa[a] MT; ἀφεῖλεν καὶ ἀπέστη LXX[ed]. As noted below, the OG often translates only one of a pair of poetic parallel forms, but it rarely has a double translation. Rather, ἀφεῖλεν and ἀπέστη are two different translations of יעבור, and this doublet is a combination of the OG (ἀφεῖλεν) plus a recensional revision (ἀπέστη) that was added into the text rather than replacing the older reading.

40:30 νεανίσκοι OG*] ובחורים 1QIsa[a] MT; νεανίσκοι καὶ ἐκλεκτοί LXX[ed]. Similar to the previous reading, the Ziegler text includes a doublet, a recensional parallel in addition to the original Greek. Confirmation of this proposal can be seen in 2 Sam 10:9, where the OG translates ובחורי[ם] with νεανίσκοι while α′ σ′ revise to ἐκλεκτῶν.

Often-confused letters

Most manuscripts, including the OG, contain errors between similar-looking letters.

40:7 נבל 1QIsa[a] MT] ἐξέπεσε OG (= נפל*). The translator or his *Vorlage* erred with ב → פ.

40:9 הרימי... תיראי 1QIsa[a] MT] ὑψώσατε ... φοβεῖσθε OG (=הרימו*). The Greek plurals could be due to paleographic confusion of י → ו or to grammatical revision due to the double subject (the heralds to Zion and Jerusalem).

40:13 תכן 1QIsa[a] MT] ἔγνω OG (= הֵבִן*?). The translator or *Vorlage* may have confused כ → ב; but see 40:12 below.

40:15 כדק 1QIsa[a] MT] ὡς σίελος OG (= כרק*). This reading is due to confusion of ד → ר. The translator may have mistakenly thought he saw רק ("spittle") in the *Vorlage* and translated accordingly; alternatively, he may have seen דק ("fine dust") but not recognized the Hebrew word and translated רק as his best guess (note the free translation of דק in 40:22 below).

40:17 וכאפס 1QIsa[a]] מאפס MT; καὶ εἰς οὐθέν OG (= באפס*?). Though εἰς can translate several prepositions depending on context, it would be an unusual translation of מן or -כ. Moreover, מ/כ/ב are frequently confused.

40:29 ירבה (עוצמה 1QIsa[a]) אונים עצמה MT 1QIsa[a]] καὶ τοῖς μὴ ὀδυνωμένοις λύπην (= עצב*?) OG. This variant phrase is difficult to explain except as a confusion of מ → ב, since the Hebrew words have been correctly translated elsewhere. A less likely alternative is that, since "sorrow to those not grieving" is in stark contrast to "strength to the powerless," it may be an additional example of avoiding repetitious parallelism with "power to the faint."

OG = 1QIsa[a] ≠ MT

The OG sometimes agrees with the Qumran scroll against the MT.

40:20 המסכן תרומה MT 1QIsa[a 2m]] > 1QIsa[a*] OG. The OG agreed with the original text of 1QIsa[a*], lacking the problematic phrase in the MT, which is "a famously difficult expression" whose "meaning remains unclear."[8] The words המסכן תרומה in the MT were supplied by a later hand in 1QIsa[a]. Note the similar agreement of the OG with 1QIsa[a] against the MT in ואומרה 1QIsa[a] = καὶ εἶπα (= וְאֹמַר*) OG ≠ וְאָמַר MT (in 40:6 above), and the agreement of 1QIsa[a*] and OG in lacking the major insertion in 40:7aβ–8a in MT-1QIsa[a 2m].

OG = MT ≠ 1QIsa[a]

Conversely, the OG at other times agrees with the MT against the Qumran scroll.

40:12 מים MT OG] מי ים 1QIsa[a]. The MT-OG reading is less plausible, since the context is dealing with the major constituents of the created universe. Arguably, the original reading was ים, since Second Isaiah knows Canaanite mythic themes: "you cut up

Rahab. . ., dried up Yamm (ים), the waters of the great deep" (51:9–10; see also ים in creation contexts in Exod 20:11 and Prov 8:29). The מי in מי ים of 1QIsa[a] may have been added in light of the parallel עפר in עפר הארץ in the next colon. If the 1QIsa[a] reading had been part of the tradition, then מים may have been a reduction of מי ים.

OG ≠ MT 1QIsa[a]

The OG also disagrees at times with the combined MT-1QIsa[a].

40:5 כי פי יהוה דבר MT 1QIsa[a]] ὅτι κύριος ἐλάλησε OG (> פי). The two expressions are formulaic, כי יהוה דבר and כי פי יהוה דבר. The preserved manuscripts often, but not always, agree in one or the other reading: see 1:2 and 22:25 for agreement in the shorter formula, 1:20 and 58:14 for agreement in the longer formula, but Isa 25:8 for the shorter form in the MT against the longer form in the OG, against the opposite pattern here.

Single translation of parallel readings

Occasionally, where the Hebrew poetic parallelism gives two synonymous terms, the OG renders only one:

40:2 במדבר. . . בערבה MT 1QIsa[a]] ἐν τῇ ἐρήμῳ OG.

40:11 בזרעו יקבץ. . . ובחיקו ישא MT 1QIsa[a]] καὶ τῷ βραχίονι αὐτοῦ συνάξει OG.

40:12 מדד. . . תכן MT 1QIsa[a]] ἐμέτρησε OG (but see 40:13 below).

40:14 וילמדהו בארח משפט. . . ודרך תבונות יודיענו MT 1QIsa[a]] ἢ ὁδὸν συνέσεως τίς ἔδειξεν αὐτῷ OG.

40:15 הן גוים. . . הן איים MT 1QIsa[a]] εἰ πάντα τὰ ἔθνη OG.

40:17 מאפס ותהו MT 1QIsa[a] (וכאפס ותהוו)] καὶ εἰς οὐθέν OG.

Different understanding of the Hebrew Vorlage

The consonantal text presented a number of ambiguous forms, and the OG attempted a faithful rendering of one of its possible meanings:

40:9 ציון. . . ירושלם MT 1QIsa[a] (-לים)] Σιων . . . Ιερουσαλημ OG. The Hebrew intends the vocative: Zion/Jerusalem is the herald. But the Greek understands the two as the recipients of the good news.

40:12 וכל MT 1QIsa[a]] καὶ πᾶσαν OG. The translator did not realize that וכל was the verb כל"ה ("hold, contain") and translated with the *lectio facilior* ("all").

40:13 תכן MT 1QIsa[a]] ἔγνω OG. It is possible that the translator did not understand תכן and had to guess (הבן → ?הבן; see 40:12 above).

40:19 This verse is uncertain, as the *JPS Hebrew-English Tanakh* notes.[9] The wording of the original sentence is by no means clear, but the translator had to, and did, compose a meaningful sentence. This uncertainty is not unique in the book of Isaiah. The translators of Isaiah for the *JPS Hebrew-English Tanakh* record almost one hundred instances of footnotes saying "Meaning of verse uncertain" or "Meaning of Heb. uncertain" plus a similar number of instances of "Emendation yields. . . ." If a highly learned team of specialists with clearly printed texts cannot confidently understand the Hebrew, it is not surprising that the ancient translator did not always find full clarity in his Hebrew scroll which must—like 1QIsa[a] and the MT—have had some problems.

40:22 כדק MT 1QIsa[a] (כדוק)] ὡς καμάραν OG. The Hebrew seems to denote the *material* constituting the sky, a thin curtain, whereas the Greek denotes the *shape*, the vaulted sky. It is unclear whether the translator recognized the Hebrew word designating the material and translated freely, or whether he did not know the word and simply guessed, supplying a parallel to ὡς σκήνην; note the similar problem with דק at 40:15 ὡς σίελος above.

40:23 שפטי ארץ MT 1QIsa[a]] ἄρχειν, τὴν δὲ γὴν OG. The Greek divides differently, *שפט וארץ possibly because of minimal space between words and confusing י → ו.

40:25 ואשוה MT 1QIsa[a] (ואשוא) καὶ ἰσοθήσομαι LXX[ed] Q 86 σ′ θ′ α′ (ἐξισοθ-) *oI* Vulg] καὶ ὑψωθήσομαι OG* Syh[mg]. Though Ziegler chooses ἰσοθήσομαι for the OG (see 40:25 above), the OG mistakes the root שו"ה, rendering the *lectio facilior* נש"א, and the recensionists later correct the mistake.

40:31 יעלו אבר MT 1QIsa[a]] πτεροφυήσουσιν OG. If יעלו were intended as a Qal ("they will mount up with wings"), then this example should be included in this category; but the Greek does give an accurate translation of the Hiphil ("they will grow wings").

40:1–2 אלוהיכם M 1QIsa[a] (אלוהיכמה) σ′ (ὁ θεός ὑμῶν)] ὁ θεός (v. 2) ἱερεῖς LXX (אֶל כֹּהֲנִים*?). A difficult variant to judge is this apparent addition in the Greek at the end of v. 1 or the beginning of v. 2. It is quite possible that אלהיכם in the *Vorlage* was marred at this spot and the best the translator could discern was אֶל כֹּהֲנִים*. An alternative solution to that paleographic suggestion is that the OG translated with ὁ θεός correctly and that during the transmission process—analogous to the Targum—someone supplied a vocative where the subject of דברו is not explicit. The Targum emphasizes the prophets who are to prophesy consolations,[10] and thus an analogous addition of "the priests" as the subject could have happened as well during the Greek transmission process.

Free translations

The OG translation was clearly intended to make sense to its Greek-speaking communities. For a number of Hebrew expressions—such as Hebraisms, corrupt forms, less precise terms, and so forth—it presents a free rendering; for some the different expression conveys the same meaning, while for others it conveys a different meaning:

40:6 חסדו MT 1QIsa[a] (חסדיו)] δόξα ἀνθρώπου OG. This is an explicitation, expressing more clearly what is surely meant by the poet, and presumably considered an important explicitation. Since δόξα κυρίου occurs in the preceding verse referring to God, the distinction between human δόξα and divine δόξα was apparently seen as important.

40:8 יקום MT 1QIsa[a]] μένει OG. The verb μένω gives a somewhat more precise equivalent for the broader verb קום.

40:11 עלות ינהל MT 1QIsa[a]] καὶ ἐν γαστρὶ ἐχούσας παρακαλέσει OG. It is difficult to know the rationale behind the Greek translation. The Hebrew texts refer to sheep nursing their young, whereas the OG denotes pregnant sheep. But the larger picture of the loving care of the shepherd for the sheep is more or less equivalent in each of the formulations.

40:12 וגבעות MT 1QIsa[a]] καὶ τὰς νάπας OG. Again, it is difficult to know why the translator used "forests" as opposed to the Hebrew "hills," in light of the fact that he correctly rendered גבעה

with βουνός in the earlier poetic context of v. 4. Perhaps, since the context is the creator's incomparability, and since וגבעות does not in this prose verse provide much contrast with the preceding הרים, the translator wished to add another major element of creation sometimes included in the routine lists of elements of the universe (cf. νάπαις = גאית Ezek 6:3). Needless to say, α′ σ′ θ′ all correct to καὶ τοῦς βουνούς.

40:13 רוח יהוה ואיש עצתו MT 1QIsa[a]] νοῦν κυρίου καὶ τίς σύμβουλος αὐτοῦ ἐγένετο OG. The translator, while giving a free and stylistically different formulation, provides a version that is good Greek and perfectly conveys the intended meaning of the Hebrew.

40:15 וכשחק MT 1QIsa[a]] ὡς ῥοπή OG. The Greek translation is curious and seemingly against the sense of the verse. The Hebrew meaning is that the "fine dust" on the scale is insignificant, having no effect, whereas the Greek "inclining or turning" of the scale indicates that the balance of the scale has been affected. Nonetheless, no Greek variants are recorded for ῥοπή.

40:16 וחיתו MT 1QIsa[a]] τὰ τετράποδα OG. The Greek expression gives a somewhat more precise equivalent for the more generic חיה.

40:24 זרעו . . . נטעו MT 1QIsa[a]] σπείρωσιν φυτεύσωσιν (. . . זרעו נטעו* OG). The Greek shows a transposition of the two verbs, perhaps mechanically or perhaps thinking that "sowing" ought to come before "planting." But again, it is probable that the OG is a faithful mirror of its *Vorlage* which already contained the transposition.[11]

40:26 לא נעדר MT 1QIsa[a]] οὐδέν σε ἔλαθεν OG. The insertion of "you" is anomalous in this third-person description of the awesome control of the creator. A possibility is, as in the Psalms, a switch of persons to direct address.

40:28–31 ויעף MT 1QIsa[a]] πεινάσει OG. In each of the next four verses the Hebrew יע"ף = "to be weary" is translated with πεινάω = "to be hungry." This may be due, not to the translator's failure to understand the words, but to resistence to the triple repetitious parallelism of יע"ף with יג"ע (also = "to be weary"); see also *Single translation of parallel readings* above.

40:30 כשול יכשלו 1QIsa[a]] ἀνίσχυες ἔσονται OG. Again, the Greek ("be powerless") differs from this Hebraism in wording and syntax, but it conveys the general meaning of the Hebrew.

Theological translations

The idea of intentional variants with theological significance is certainly a possibility and offers attraction to scholars. For example, the translation τὸ ὕδωρ in 40:12 might be alleged to be a theological variant from ים or מי ים, on the suspicion that it may have been changed to echo מים in the creation context of Gen 1:2, 6, etc. But even if that hypothetical motive were operative, the fact that מים occurs already in the MT vitiates the claim that it was the work of the translator.

The only Greek reading in Isa 40 that could appear to be a theologically motivated variant is the following:

40:5b וראו כל בשר יחדו MT 1QIsa[a]] καὶ ὄψεται πᾶσα σὰρξ τὸ σωτήριον τοῦ θεοῦ. This reading can be seen as a theological variant. Joseph Blenkinsopp[12] and Shalom Paul[13] describe the extant evidence (the presence of σωτήριον in LXX vs. its absence in the MT) as a theological addition in the LXX, not addressing the issue whether the Greek reading was introduced by the translator or inherited by him. Brevard Childs[14] does not mention the Greek variant at all, nor does Klaus Baltzer.[15] But an immediate question is whether the reading is due to the OG translator or, rather, whether it was already in the Hebrew *Vorlage* which the translator rendered exactly.[16] Not only is the latter quite possible, it is arguably more likely since וראו כל אפסי ארץ את ישועת אלהינו occurs at 52:10b in the Hebrew of both MT and 1QIsa[a] as well as in the OG.[17]

The implicit object of וראו in MT-1QIsa[a] in 40:5b is parallel to the כבוד/δόξα in v. 5a and could well be envisioned as "the salvation of God" as a result of God's manifestation. It is the coming of the כבוד/δόξα that will save the people,[18] and note that a prophetic salvation oracle immediately follows in 40:6–8.

Ziegler, Troxel, and others discuss the prominent theological theme of δόξα in the OG of Isaiah.[19] But Childs, Paul, and Baltzer note that כבוד is already a prominent theme in the Hebrew book. Childs remarks that "in chapter 40 a sign of the inbreaking of a new age of salvation is that the glory of God will now be revealed to all flesh."[20] Paul comments, "the prophet emphasizes that at the time of redemption God's presence will appear to all the nations. . . ."[21] Similarly, Klaus Baltzer states that "the whole of humanity witnesses to his saving activity in history."[22] All three recognize the combined theme of כבוד with ישועת אלהינו as well attested in the Hebrew book, and it is thus not surprising that it shows up in the Greek tradition.

Therefore, though it is true that there is a theological variant in the OG text that is not attested in any extant Hebrew text, little weight can that observation bear. If the variant were not in the Hebrew *Vorlage* used by the OG but introduced by the translator, it still could not be properly and adequately claimed as a notable theological variant in the OG; it can only be claimed that it echoes a major theme already in the Hebrew book and already occurring virtually verbatim by the combined Hebrew-Greek at 52:10b. If, as is more likely, the OG simply faithfully translates its *Vorlage*, chapter 40—though only one of the sixty-six chapters—presents no sign of intentional theological innovation in the Septuagint.

Conclusion

This examination of the OG translation in comparison with the Hebrew of the MT and 1QIsa[a], though focusing on only a single chapter of Isaiah, albeit a theologically rich chapter, hopefully helps illuminate the question of the method and intentions of the Greek translator. Where, on the spectrum from "faithful translation" to "actualizing exegesis," does the translator register?[23] Although this study focuses on only Isa 40, the examples discussed coalesce with the character of the translation visible in the remainder of the book. It is a faithful, if at times somewhat free, translation of what the translator saw, or thought he saw, in his Hebrew source. For example, though the OG lacks a long reading that occurs in the MT at 40:7aβ–8a, the fact that 1QIsa[a*] also lacks the reading shows that the OG is simply following its Hebrew *Vorlage*.

The OG agrees now with the MT, now with 1QIsa[a], now with neither. That indicates—as we should suspect in light of the many variants in the other twenty Qumran Isaiah scrolls—that the Hebrew used by the translator, though mostly similar to those preserved manuscripts, differed somewhat from them.

Discerning the character of the translation requires awareness of several factors. The manuscript used by the translator must be envisioned, not as a clearly printed text, but as a scroll similar to the Great Isaiah Scroll. It must have had occasional flawed spots, ambiguous forms (due to the unvocalized consonantal text), errors already in the Hebrew tradition, and so forth. Moreover, it is the result of a transfer not only into a different language but into a different family of languages, the structure of which is quite different.

The translation shows many types of differences from the Hebrew texts, due to various factors. Like most texts, it displays some confusion between similarly written letters, such as נבל → נפל (40:7). There were ambiguous forms: was יעלו (40:31) to be understood as Qal or Hiphil? The elevated poetic style entailed the problem that the translator (and modern scholars) did not know or recognize every Hebrew word, such as וכשחק (40:15), כדק (40:15, 22), and תכן (40:12, 13).

The translator also exercised a certain degree of freedom, since he had to produce a text that made sense to his Greek-speaking communities. He remained mostly faithful to the Hebrew—such as translating *νοῦν κυρίου* for רוח יהוה (40:13)—though sometimes using different wording while still conveying the general sense of the Hebrew—such as *ἐν γαστρὶ ἐχούσας* for עלות (40:11). Other expressions remain obscure; for example, 40:19 is an uncertain verse, but, though an intelligible translation had to be produced, it contains nothing theologically distinctive. Something of an exception is *καὶ τὰς νάπας* for וגבעות (40:12). The translator clearly knew the word וגבעות but perhaps wanted to add a different element often occurring in routine lists of nature's elements (cf. Ezek 6:3), though again entailing no theological significance.

Stylistically, he occasionally rendered only a single term where the Hebrew parallelism had two. He also clarified certain words through explicitation, such as *δόξα ἀνθρώπου* for חסדו (40:6), since the previous verse also contained *δόξα*, which referred to the Lord.

None of the examples cited immediately above can be categorized as a theological variant introduced by the OG translator. The only possible candidate in Isa 40 for being classified as a theological variant is *τὸ σωτήριον τοῦ θεοῦ* in place of יחדו (40:5). But as explained above, first, it is plausible that the OG translation is based on its Hebrew *Vorlage* (cf. the virtually identical 52:10b), and second, the theme of salvation as linked with the divine כבוד is strong throughout the Hebrew book of Isaiah and thus its appearance in the Greek—even if it were by the hand of the translator—is not meaningful. Chapter 40 of Isaiah presents no sign of intentional theological innovation by the Septuagint translator.

Notes

It is a pleasure to honor long-time friend Leonard Greenspoon for his lifetime of study, teaching, and writing about the Hebrew Bible and especially the Septuagint for both scholarly circles as well as wide public audiences.

[1]The Greek text is cited from Joseph Zeigler, *Isaias*, Septuaginta: Vetus Testamentum Graecum auctoritate Academiae Litterarum Gottingensis editum vol. 14, 3rd ed. (Göttingen: Vandenhoeck & Ruprecht, 1983).

[2]The most recent learned and comprehensive treatment of the translator of Isaiah is Ronald L. Troxel, *LXX-Isaiah as Translation and Interpretation: The Strategies of the Translator of the Septuagint of Isaiah*, JSJSup 124 (Leiden: Brill, 2008).

[3]These categories are discussed more fully in Eugene Ulrich, *The Dead Sea Scrolls and the Developmental Composition of the Bible*, VTSup 169 (Leiden: Brill, 2015), 40–45, and are illustrated throughout the volume.

[4]See DJD XXXII, Part 2:91–92, 208; Ulrich, *Developmental Composition*, 29, 139. The closeness between 1QIsa^{b} and the Masoretic witnesses warrants seeing them as a text family, but their differences from 1QIsa^{a} and the OG are not systematic and patterned and thus do not show intentional variant editions.

[5]DJD XXXII, 2:90–91.

[6]In general, minor commonplace variants such as the presence or absence of frequent differences (e.g., -ו, כי, כל) or inconsequential contrasts of singular vs. plural forms or stylistic prepositions will not be considered here.

[7]In fact, Rahlfs' *Septuaginta* prints ὑψωθήσομαι since all the major uncials have this reading; he does not even list ἰσοθήσομαι as a variant.

[8]Joseph Blenkinsopp, *Isaiah 40–55: A New Translation with Introduction and Commentary*, AB 19 (New York: Doubleday, 2002), 189; Shalom M. Paul, *Isaiah 40–66: Translation and Commentary* (Grand Rapids: Eerdmans, 2012), 147.

[9]*JPS Hebrew-English Tanakh* (Philadelphia: Jewish Publication Society of America, 1999), 936.

[10]Note that Blenkinsopp (*Isaiah 40–55*, 180) comments: "The prologue begins, then, with a summons to prophets in general, or to a specific prophetic group, to proclaim a message of comfort and hope to Yahveh's people. . . ."

[11]See Troxel's statement in note 17 below.

[12]Blenkinsopp, *Isaiah 40–55*, 178.

[13]Paul, *Isaiah 40–66*, 132.

[14]Brevard S. Childs, *Isaiah*, OTL (Louisville: Westminster John Knox, 2001), 298–300.

[15]Klaus Baltzer, *Deutero-Isaiah*, Hermeneia, trans. Margart Kohl, ed. Peter Machinist (Minneapolis: Fortress, 2001), 49, 56.

[16]An example of a theological variant in the Hebrew, not the Greek, that is illuminated by a newly discovered manuscript occurs in 1 Sam 1:23. Regarding Elkanah's comment about Hannah's vow, the OG describes it as simply what has come forth from her mouth, whereas the MT changes to God's word. For στήσαι κύριος τὸ ἐξελθὸν ἐκ τοῦ στόματος σου in the OG, the MT has יקם יהוה את דברו. The discovery of 4QSam[a] with יקם יהו]ה היוצא מפיך] provided the Hebrew basis and confirmed the fidelity of the OG translation.

[17]Regarding readings in the OG not attested in extant Hebrew manuscripts, Troxel (*LXX-Isaiah as Translation*, 75) says they are "so commonplace in our extant Hebrew manuscripts that denying they stood in the translator's *Vorlage* amounts to special pleading, unless one can mount persuasive arguments about why the translator rendered against the grain of his *Vorlage*."

[18]Troxel discusses the "association of δόξα with Israel's salvation" and the "close association of the revelation of divine δόξα and the arrival of τὸ σωτήριον τοῦ θεοῦ" in *LXX-Isaiah as Translation*, 130–31.

[19]Joseph Ziegler, *Untersuchungen zur Septuaginta des Buches Isaias* (Münster: Aschendorffschen Verlagsbuchhandlung, 1934), 108; Troxel, *LXX-Isaiah as Translation*, 130–32.

[20]Childs, 55, 298–300, esp. 299.

[21]Paul, *Isaiah 40–66*, 132.

[22]Baltzer, 56.

[23]For discussion of this issue, see Ulrich, *Developmental Composition*, 229–33.

5

The Equivalence of *Kaige* and *Quinta* in the Dodekapropheton

James W. Barker
Western Kentucky University

In 1952 Bedouin discovered the Greek Minor Prophets Scroll from Naḥal Ḥever (8ḤevXIIgr), a manuscript dating near the end of the first century BCE.[1] Soon thereafter Dominique Barthélemy designated the text as *kaige*, given its tendency (e.g., in Zech 9:2) to translate וגם (also) as καίγε (even; at least).[2] *Kaige* clearly intended to revise the Old Greek (hereafter OG) into closer conformity with a proto-Masoretic *Vorlage*.[3] Barthélemy also postulated the equivalence of *kaige* and *Quinta*, the "fifth" translation—besides the LXX, Aquila, Symmachus, and Theodotion—occasionally preserved in the Hexapla.[4] This position gained initial acceptance,[5] but subsequent scholars have questioned it.[6] This essay vindicates Barthélemy's conclusion.

The essay divides into four parts. First, I give examples of lesser and greater extents of *kaige's* revision of the OG. Second, I discuss Justin Martyr's use of *kaige* for the Minor Prophets. Sometimes Justin quoted *kaige* verbatim, but at other times he conflated it with the OG. Third, I reexamine the relationship between *kaige* and *Quinta*. Based on the extant evidence from Justin, Origen, and Jerome, one can reasonably conclude that *kaige* and *Quinta* were the same in the Dodekapropheton. The prevailing counterargument contends that *kaige* influenced *Quinta* no more than *kaige* also influenced Justin, the Coptic versions, Codex W, and Aquila.[7] The concluding section shows this argument to be specious by weighing internal and external evidence.

Kaige's Revision of the Old Greek

This section presents three examples of *kaige's* revision of the OG.[8] Sometimes *kaige* bears relatively little resemblance to the OG, but at other times *kaige* follows the OG closely. As shown in Table 5.1, *kaige* Hab 2:18 remains very close to the OG, which reads, "What is the use of a carving, for he carved it? He shaped it, an image, a false fantasy. For the shaper trusts in his shape when making dumb idols."

OG Hab 2:18	8ḤevXIIgr Hab 2:18
τί ὠφελεῖ γλυπτόν, ὅτι ἔγλυψεν αὐτό; ἔπλασεν αὐτὸ χώνευμα, φαντασίαν ψευδῆ, ὅτι πέποιθεν ὁ πλάσας ἐπὶ τὸ πλάσμα αὐτοῦ τοῦ ποιῆσαι εἴδωλα κωφά.	τί ὠφέλησεν γλυπτόν, ὅτι [ἔγλυψε]ν αὐτό; ὁ πλάσας αὐτὸ χώνευμα [καὶ φα]ντασίαν ψευδῆ, ὅτι πέποιθεν ὁ πλάσας ἐπὶ τὸ πλάσμα αὐτοῦ ἐπ' αὐτὸ [π]οιῆσαι εἴδωλα κωφά.

Table 5.1: Hab 2:18

Kaige changes the tense of ὠφελέω (benefit) from the present or imperfect to the aorist to match the perfect aspect of the Hebrew. *Kaige* changes the finite verb ἔπλασεν (he shaped) to the participle ὁ πλάσας (the shaper); these represent different vocalizations of יצרו, but *kaige* reads incoherently, "the shaper it an image." Before the infinitive ποιῆσαι (to make), *kaige* changes the definite article (τοῦ) to ἐπ' αὐτό (in it) based on עליו (unto it or unto himself). The OG and *kaige* have in common φαντασίαν, which would reflect מראה (appearance) rather than the MT's מורה (teacher), and *kaige* adds καί. The Coptic versions and Codex W are nearly identical to the OG in this instance, and they show no influence from *kaige*.[9]

Vis-à-vis the OG, Hab 2:7 shows slightly more variation than the preceding example; see Table 5.2. *Kaige* Hab 2:7 reads, "Will not the ones who bite you suddenly arise, and will not the ones who shake you sober up, and you will be booty to them?"

OG Hab 2:7	8ḤevXIIgr Hab 2:7
ὅτι ἐξαίφνης ἀναστήσονται δάκνοντες αὐτόν, καὶ ἐκνήψουσιν οἱ ἐπίβουλοί σου, καὶ ἔσῃ εἰς διαρπαγὴν αὐτοῖς.	οὐχὶ ἐξαί[φνη]ς ἀναστήσονται δάκνοντές σε, καὶ ἐγνή[ψους]ιν οἱ σαλεύοντες σε, καὶ ἔσῃ εἰς διαρπαγὰς αὐτ[οῖς;].

Table 5.2: Hab 2:7

In the OG the verse is a statement, which *kaige* turns into a question as in the Hebrew. That is, *kaige* changes ὅτι (for) to οὐχί (not), which more closely matches הלוא (is it not?). *Kaige* also changes αὐτόν (him) to σε (you), which matches the Hebrew suffix. *Kaige* changes οἱ ἐπίβουλοί σου (your schemers) to οἱ σαλεύοντες σε (the ones who shake you), which matches מזעזעיך. *Kaige* changes the singular διαρπαγήν (booty) to plural, as in the Hebrew. Both the OG and *kaige* understand למו as plural (see GKC §103.2.a). Once again, the Coptic versions and Codex W are nearly identical to the OG, despite *kaige's* more substantial revisions.[10]

Compared to the OG, nearly every word of *kaige* Hab 3:14 is changed; see Table 5.3. In this instance, *kaige* looks like an independent translation: "You cut in two with his staffs a head of his unfortified areas; they will be shaken to scatter us—their exultation just like a poor man eating in secret."

OG Hab 3:14	8ḤevXIIgr Hab 3:14
διέκοψας ἐν ἐκστάσει κεφαλὰς δυναστῶν, σεισθήσονται ἐν αὐτῇ· διανοίξουσι χαλινοὺς αὐτῶν ὡς ἔσθων πτωχὸς λάθρᾳ.	διέτρη[σα]ς ἐν ῥάβδοις αὐτοῦ κεφαλὴν ἀτει[χίσ]των αὐτοῦ σεισθ[ή]σονται τοῦ σκο[ρπίσ]αι ἡμᾶς τὸ γαυρίαμα αὐτῶν καθ[ὼς ἐσ]θίων πτωχὸν κρυφῇ.

Table 5.3: Hab 3:14

The opening word of *kaige*, διέτρησας, means to pierce, which accords with the Hebrew נקב, as compared with the synonymous διακόπτω (cut through) in the OG. *Kaige* not only corrects the odd word ἔκστασις (ecstasy) to ῥάβδος for מטה (staff) but also adds the possessive αὐτοῦ, which is present in the Hebrew. *Kaige* makes *head* singular, and the meaning is a *chief* of the unfortified areas (ἀτείχιστοι), which reflects the Hebrew פרזות (open country); the MT's פרזו is dubious, and the BDB renderings *warriors* or *leaders* are simply based on the OG's δύνασται (masters, from δύναμαι). *Kaige's* "to scatter us—their exultation" (σκορπίσαι ἡμᾶς τὸ γαυρίαμα αὐτῶν) matches להפיצני עליצתם; the OG's "they will open their bridles" (διανοίξουσι χαλινοὺς αὐτῶν) is peculiar. *Kaige* here prefers καθώς (just like) to ὡς (like), and it spells *eating* ἐσθίων rather than ἔσθων. *Kaige* prefers κρυφῇ to λάθρᾳ, both of which mean *secretly,* and it inflects the poor man in the accusative (πτωχός/πτωχόν).[11] In Hab 3:14 Codex W matches the OG verbatim, and the Coptic here shows no influence from *kaige*. Aquila's purported rendering (τοῦ διασκορπίσαι [με]· γαυριάματα αὐτῶν τοῦ φαγεῖν πένητας ἀποκρύφως) nowhere matches *kaige*.[12]

These three verses exemplify greater and lesser extents of *kaige's* revision of the OG. In the OG, these verses contain fifty-three words (including articles), and *kaige* made twelve changes, none of which influenced Aquila, Codex W, or the Coptic versions. To be sure, *kaige* influenced these texts elsewhere, yet here these witnesses do not match *kaige's* thoroughgoing revision of the OG. More particularly, Codex W and the Coptic versions clearly remain in the OG's textual tradition, whereas *kaige* is readily identifiable as a distinct—albeit dependent—tradition.[13]

Justin Martyr's Use of Kaige

This section explains Justin Martyr's use of *kaige*. Scholars had long known that Justin Martyr's Old Testament quotations do not always match the OG.[14] One of Justin's longest quotations in *Dialogue with Trypho* is of Mic 4:1–7, which mentions beating swords into ploughshares. Upon discovery of 8ḤevXIIgr, Barthélemy identified *kaige* as the source of Justin's quotation.[15] Given its significance, I will explain it in detail; see Table 5.4.

OG Mic 4:1–7	Justin Martyr *Dial.* 109.2–3
1 καὶ ἔσται ἐπ᾽ ἐσχάτων τῶν ἡμερῶν ἐμφανὲς τὸ ὄρος τοῦ κυρίου, ἕτοιμον ἐπὶ τὰς κορυφὰς τῶν ὀρέων, καὶ μετεωρισθήσεται ὑπεράνω τῶν βουνῶν· καὶ σπεύσουσι πρὸς αὐτὸ λαοί, 2 καὶ πορεύσονται ἔθνη πολλὰ καὶ ἐροῦσι Δεῦτε ἀναβῶμεν εἰς τὸ ὄρος κυρίου καὶ εἰς τὸν οἶκον τοῦ θεοῦ Ιακωβ, καὶ δείξουσιν ἡμῖν τὴν ὁδὸν αὐτοῦ, καὶ πορευσόμεθα ἐν ταῖς τρίβοις αὐτοῦ· ὅτι	1 καὶ ἔσται ἐπ᾽ ἐσχάτου τῶν ἡμερῶν ἐμφανὲς τὸ ὄρος κυρίου, ἕτοιμον ἐπ᾽ ἄκρου τῶν ὀρέων, καὶ ἐπηρμένον αὐτὸ ὑπὲρ τοὺς βουνούς· καὶ ποταμὸν θήσονται ἐπ᾽ αὐτῷ λαοί, 2 καὶ πορεύσονται ἔθνη πολλά, καὶ ἐροῦσι· Δεῦτε, ἀναβῶμεν εἰς τὸ ὄρος κυρίου καὶ εἰς τὸν οἶκον τοῦ θεοῦ Ιακωβ, καὶ φωτιοῦσιν ἡμᾶς τὴν ὁδὸν αὐτοῦ, καὶ πορευσόμεθα ἐν ταῖς τρίβοις αὐτοῦ· ὅτι ἐκ Σιων ἐξελεύσεται

ἐκ Σιων ἐξελεύσεται νόμος καὶ λόγος κυρίου ἐξ Ιερουσαλημ. 3 καὶ κρινεῖ ἀνὰ μέσον λαῶν πολλῶν καὶ ἐλέγξει ἔθνη ἰσχυρὰ ἕως εἰς μακράν, καὶ κατακόψουσι τὰς ῥομφαίας αὐτῶν εἰς ἄροτρα καὶ τὰ δόρατα [cf. W: τὰς ζιβύνας] αὐτῶν εἰς δρέπανα, καὶ οὐκέτι μὴ ἀντάρῃ [cf. W: ἀνθ᾽ ἄρῃ] ἔθνος ἐπ᾽ ἔθνος ῥομφαίαν, καὶ οὐκέτι μὴ μάθωσι πολεμεῖν. 4 καὶ ἀναπαύσεται ἕκαστος ὑποκάτω ἀμπέλου αὐτοῦ καὶ ἕκαστος ὑποκάτω συκῆς αὐτοῦ, καὶ οὐκ ἔσται ὁ ἐκφοβῶν, διότι τὸ στόμα κυρίου παντοκράτορος ἐλάλησε ταῦτα. 5 ὅτι πάντες οἱ λαοὶ πορεύσονται ἕκαστος τὴν ὁδὸν αὐτοῦ, ἡμεῖς δὲ πορευσόμεθα ἐν ὀνόματι κυρίου θεοῦ ἡμῶν εἰς τὸν αἰῶνα καὶ ἐπέκεινα. 6 ἐν τῇ ἡμέρᾳ ἐκείνῃ, λέγει κύριος, συνάξω τὴν συντετριμμένην καὶ τὴν ἐξωσμένην εἰσδέξομαι καὶ οὓς ἀπωσάμην· 7 καὶ θήσομαι τὴν συντετριμμένην εἰς ὑπόλειμμα καὶ τὴν ἀπωσμένην εἰς ἔθνος ἰσχυρόν, καὶ βασιλεύσει κύριος ἐπ᾽ αὐτοὺς ἐν ὄρει Σιων ἀπὸ τοῦ νῦν καὶ ἕως εἰς τὸν αἰῶνα.	νόμος καὶ λόγος κυρίου ἐξ Ιερουσαλημ. 3 καὶ κρινεῖ ἀνὰ μέσον λαῶν πολλῶν καὶ ἐλέγξει ἔθνη ἰσχυρὰ ἕως μακράν· καὶ συγκόψουσι τὰς μαχαίρας αὐτῶν εἰς ἄροτρα καὶ τὰς ζιβύνας αὐτῶν εἰς δρέπανα, καὶ οὐ μὴ ἄρῃ [cf. 8ḤevXIIgr: ἀνθάρῃ] ἔθνος ἐπ᾽ ἔθνος μαχαίραν, καὶ οὐ μὴ μάθωσιν ἔτι πολεμεῖν. 4 καὶ καθίσεται ἀνὴρ ὑποκάτω ἀμπέλου αὐτοῦ καὶ ὑποκάτω συκῆς αὐτοῦ, καὶ οὐκ ἔσται [cf. 8ḤevXIIgr: ἔστιν] ὁ ἐκφοβῶν, ὅτι στόμα [cf. 8ḤevXIIgr: τὸ στόμα] κυρίου τῶν δυνάμεων ἐλάλησεν. 5 ὅτι πάντες οἱ λαοὶ πορεύσονται ἐν ὀνόματι θεῶν [cf. 8ḤevXIIgr: [θε]οῦ] αὐτῶν, ἡμεῖς δὲ πορευσόμεθα ἐν ὀνόματι κυρίου θεοῦ ἡμῶν εἰς τὸν αἰῶνα. καὶ ἔσται 6 ἐν τῇ ἡμέρᾳ ἐκείνῃ [λέγει יהוה fits here in 8ḤevXIIgr] συνάξω τὴν ἐκτεθλιμμένην καὶ τὴν ἐξωσμένην ἀθροίσω καὶ ἣν ἐκάκωσα, 7 καὶ θήσω τὴν ἐκτεθλιμμένην εἰς ὑπόλειμμα καὶ τὴν ἐκπεπιεσμένην εἰς ἔθνος ἰσχυρόν· καὶ βασιλεύσει κύριος ἐπ᾽ αὐτῶν ἐν τῷ ὄρει Σιων ἀπὸ τοῦ νῦν καὶ ἕως τοῦ αἰῶνος.

Table 5.4: Mic 4:1–7

There are several inconsequential differences between the OG and Codex W,[16] and there are a few inconsequential differences between 8ḤevXIIgr and Justin.[17] The more substantial differences between 8ḤevXIIgr and Justin are as follows. In Mic 4:3 Justin's shortened ἄρῃ (raise up) is idiosyncratic; ἀντάρῃ/ἀνθάρῃ (raise up against) would be the original reading. Similarly, the OG and 8ḤevXIIgr align against Justin's anarthrous στόμα (mouth) in v. 4, and there Justin's infinitive ἔσται (to be) is likely influenced by the OG, since 8ḤevXIIgr uses the finite ἔστιν. In v. 5 Justin's plural gods is as likely as 8ḤevXIIgr's singular—"in the name of their god(s);" Justin and *kaige* use the plural "their" (αὐτῶν), whereas the Hebrew uses the singular possessive "his god(s)" (אלהיו). Justin likely omitted "says the Lord" in v. 6; λέγει יהוה is included in Tov's reconstruction of 8ḤevXIIgr.

There are numerous differences between the OG and *kaige*. *Kaige* Mic 4:1 has singular ἐσχάτου (end) rather than plural ἐσχάτων, omits the definite article before the Lord, and has ἄκρου (farthest point) rather than κορυφάς (highest points). *Kaige's* "having lifted it above the hills" (ἐπηρμένον αὐτὸ ὑπὲρ τοὺς βουνούς) is synonymous with the OG's "it will be raised high above the hills" (μετεωρισθήσεται ὑπεράνω τῶν βουνῶν), but *kaige's* "and peoples will put a river at it" (καὶ ποταμὸν θήσονται ἐπ' αὐτῷ λαοί) does not make as much sense as the OG's "and peoples will speed to it" (καὶ σπεύσουσι πρὸς αὐτὸ λαοί); the Hebrew uses the verb נהר (flow). In v. 2 *kaige's* "and they will enlighten us" (καὶ φωτιοῦσιν ἡμᾶς) and the OG's "and they will show us" (καὶ δείξουσιν ἡμῖν) both differ from the Hebrew "and he will teach us" (ויורנו). In v. 3—as in the parallel saying in OG Isa 2:4—*kaige* not only uses the complex element συν- (with) rather than κατα- (against) with the verb κόπτω (cut) but also prefers μάχαιρα (short sword) and ζιβύνη (spear) to the OG's ῥομφαία (long sword) and δόρυ (spear) for חרב (sword) and חנית (spear) respectively;[18] to say, "not at all again," *kaige* divides οὐ μὴ . . . ἔτι rather than combining οὐκέτι μή.

Furthermore, in v. 4 *kaige* omits the definite article before στόμα (mouth) and ταῦτα (these things), and *kaige* changes ἀναπαύσεται (rest) to καθίσεται (sit), ἕκαστος (each one) to ἀνήρ (man), διότι (therefore) to ὅτι (for), and παντοκράτωρ (almighty) to τῶν δυνάμεων (of the hosts/armies); ἀνήρ, ὅτι, and τῶν δυνάμεων are characteristic *kaige* revisions. In v. 5 *kaige* omits ἕκαστος and changes τὴν ὁδὸν αὐτοῦ (his road/way) to ἐν ὀνόματι θεοῦ/θεῶν αὐτῶν (in the name of their god/gods), which matches the Hebrew בשם אלהיו; *kaige* also omits καὶ ἐπέκεινα (and beyond) after "forever," and it adds ἔσται (it shall be) to begin the ensuing sentence. In v. 6 the OG's συντετριμμένην (ground up), εἰσδέξομαι (receive in), and ἀπωσάμην (push away) are respectively changed in *kaige* to ἐκτεθλιμμένην (squeezed out), ἀθροίσω (gather together), and ἐκάκωσα (afflict); *kaige* also uses a singular rather than a plural relative pronoun. In v. 7 *kaige* changes the active (θήσω) to the middle voice (θήσομαι) for "I will put," συντετριμμένην (ground up) to ἐκτεθλιμμένην (squeezed out) as in v. 6, and ἀπωσμένην (pushed away) to ἐκπεπιεσμένην (squeezed out); *kaige* also prefers the genitive to the accusative with ἐπί—both being grammatically correct. Finally, *kaige* adds a definite article before "Mount Zion" and omits the preposition εἰς with "forever."

By my count, the OG contains 196 words, and *kaige* makes forty-four changes, only one of which influences Codex W. Additionally, W adds land (γῆν) to clarify faraway (μακράν); this clarification also appears in the Achmimic. As in *kaige,* the Bohairic reflects singular ἐσχάτου in v. 1, and the Achmimic is closer to *kaige's* ἐκάκωσα (afflict) than the OG's ἀπωσάμην (push away). The Coptic versions here show no further influence from *kaige.* Without specifying a source, the Syrohexapla notes ἐν ὀνόματι θεοῦ—as opposed to τὴν ὁδὸν αὐτοῦ—in the margin at v. 5,[19] so the presumption is that Aquila, Symmachus, and Theodotion all shared this reading with Justin and *kaige.* There are no other known agreements between Aquila and *kaige* in Mic 4:1–7. Accordingly, there is no basis for assuming that our extant MSS of Justin's works have been contaminated by Aquila's text.[20]

It is a vast understatement to describe *kaige* as merely "influencing" Justin.[21] As Barthélemy pointed out, Justin's quotation of Mic 4:1–7 is "substantially identical" to the text of 8ḤevXIIgr.[22] Justin's quotation totals 192 words, and there is only one instance of contamination from the OG, namely ἔσται rather than ἔστιν. It would be superfluous to posit Justin's knowledge of Aquila here, since Justin shares none of Aquila's other attested variants.[23] The single most important variant in Codex W is the change from τὰ δόρατα to τὰς ζιβύνας in Mic 4:3, which agrees with Justin and 8ḤevXIIgr; there is a slight chance that OG Isaiah influenced W here, but in any event W shows no more than one word of influence from *kaige.* The significance of Justin's Micah quotation cannot be overstated, for it recovered *kaige* as the long lost source of Justin's non-LXX quotations of the Minor Prophets in the *Dialogue with Trypho.*

Another non-LXX text appears in *Dial.* 107.4. There Justin quotes Jonah 4:10–11, the conclusion to the book wherein God chastises Jonah for worrying more about a gourd that he did not plant than about the thousands of human and animal inhabitants of Nineveh. These verses do not appear in Column 4 of 8ḤevXIIgr, but in all likelihood Justin purely preserves *kaige;* see Table 5.5.

OG Jonah 4:10–11	Justin Martyr *Dial.* 107.4
σὺ ἐφείσω ὑπὲρ τῆς κολοκύνθης, ὑπὲρ ἧς οὐκ ἐκακοπάθησας ἐπ' αὐτὴν καὶ οὐκ ἐξέθρεψας αὐτήν, ἣ ὑπὸ νύκτα ἐγενήθη καὶ ὑπὸ νύκτα ἀπώλετο. ἐγὼ δὲ οὐ φείσομαι ὑπὲρ Νινευη τῆς πόλεως τῆς μεγάλης, ἐν ᾗ κατοικοῦσι πλείους ἢ δώδεκα μυριάδες ἀνθρώπων, οἵτινες οὐκ ἔγνωσαν δεξιὰν αὐτῶν ἢ ἀριστερὰν αὐτῶν, καὶ κτήνη πολλά;	σὺ ἐφείσω περὶ τοῦ σικυῶνος, οὗ οὐκ ἐκοπίασας ἐν αὐτῷ, οὔτε ἐξέθρεψας αὐτόν, ὃς ὑπὸ νύκτα αὐτοῦ ἦλθε καὶ ὑπὸ νύκτα αὐτοῦ ἀπώλετο· κἀγὼ οὐ φείσομαι ὑπὲρ Νινευΐ τῆς πόλεως τῆς μεγάλης, ἐν ᾗ κατοικοῦσι πλείους ἢ δώδεκα μυριάδες ἀνδρῶν, οἳ οὐκ ἔγνωσαν ἀνὰ μέσον δεξιᾶς αὐτῶν ἢ ἀνὰ μέσον ἀριστερᾶς αὐτῶν, καὶ κτήνη πολλά;

Table 5.5: Jonah 4:10–11

Justin's text uses the preposition περί rather than ὑπέρ, both of which mean *concerning*, and Justin omits the second instance of ὑπέρ. Justin's text also uses ἐν (in) rather than ἐπί (at) for ב, σικυώνη (cucumber) rather than κολόκυνθα (colocynth, a gourd) for קיקיון (castor-oil plant), κοπιάω (toil) rather than κακοπαθέω (suffer ill) for עמל (toil), and οὔτε (neither) rather than καὶ οὐκ (and not) for ולא (and not). Justin's text adds αὐτοῦ (its) modifying *night* in both instances, and he uses ἔρχομαι (come) rather than γίνομαι (become) for היה (be, become) as well as κἀγώ (and I) rather than ἐγὼ δέ (but I). Justin inflects Nineveh with a *iota*, and he uses the article οἵ rather than the pronoun οἵτινες for אשר. Most significantly, Justin uses ἀνήρ (man) rather than ἄνθρωπος (person) for איש (man), a characteristic *kaige* revision;[24] finally he adds ἀνὰ μέσον (in the middle of) to reflect בין (in between) with the right and left hands. Compared with the OG, Justin's quotation deletes two words, adds six words, and alters seventeen other words; this amounts to twenty-five changes to a string of fifty-two words. Codex W contains none of these alterations,[25] and the Achmimic has only one, namely οὔδε like Justin's οὔτε; there is no comparative data for Aquila. As was the case with Justin's Micah quotation, *kaige* appears to be Justin's sole source for this text.

The aforementioned Jonah and Micah quotes establish that Justin sometimes quoted *kaige* very precisely. Surprisingly Justin nowhere quotes the OG of the Dodekapropheton verbatim.[26] However, Justin occasionally presents mixed quotations, partly OG and partly *kaige*. Mixed quotations are identifiable based on conflations of the OG and variant readings. As the earliest known revision of the OG, *kaige* offered corrective variants, but *kaige* did not make any conflations. For example, *kaige* uses μάχαιρα (short sword) and ζιβύνη (spear) rather than ῥομφαία (long sword) and δόρυ (spear) in Mic 4:3. In other words, the OG's terms were replaced altogether, not juxtaposed with *kaige's* variants; such would-be conflations occur nowhere in 8ḤevXIIgr. In *Dial.* 22.2–5, Justin gives a mixed quotation from the book of Amos; see Table 5.6.

OG Amos 5:18–6:7
5:18 Οὐαὶ οἱ ἐπιθυμοῦντες τὴν ἡμέραν κυρίου· ἵνα τί αὕτη ὑμῖν ἡ ἡμέρα τοῦ κυρίου; καὶ αὐτή ἐστι σκότος καὶ οὐ φῶς, 19 ὃν τρόπον ἐὰν [cf. W and Justin: ὅταν] φύγῃ [cf. Justin: ἐκφύγῃ] ἄνθρωπος ἐκ προσώπου τοῦ λέοντος καὶ ἐμπέσῃ [cf. Justin: συναντήσῃ] αὐτῷ ἡ ἄρκος, καὶ εἰσπηδήσῃ εἰς τὸν οἶκον αὐτοῦ καὶ ἀπερείσηται τὰς χεῖρας αὐτοῦ ἐπὶ τὸν τοῖχον καὶ δάκῃ αὐτὸν ὁ ὄφις. 20 οὐχὶ σκότος ἡ ἡμέρα τοῦ κυρίου καὶ οὐ φῶς; καὶ γνόφος οὐκ ἔχων φέγγος αὐτῇ. 21 μεμίσηκα, ἀπῶσμαι ἑορτὰς ὑμῶν καὶ οὐ μὴ ὀσφρανθῶ ἐν ταῖς πανηγύρεσιν ὑμῶν· 22 διότι ἐὰν ἐνέγκητέ μοι ὁλοκαυτώματα καὶ θυσίας ὑμῶν, οὐ προσδέξομαι αὐτά, καὶ σωτηρίου ἐπιφανείας ὑμῶν οὐκ ἐπιβλέψομαι. 23 μετάστησον [cf. Justin: ἀπόστησον] ἀπ' ἐμοῦ ἦχον [cf. Justin: πλῆθος] ᾠδῶν σου, καὶ ψαλμὸν ὀργάνων σου οὐκ ἀκούσομαι· 24 καὶ κυλισθήσεται ὡς ὕδωρ κρίμα καὶ δικαιοσύνη ὡς χειμάρρους ἄβατος. 25 μὴ σφάγια καὶ θυσίας προσηνέγκατέ μοι τεσσαράκοντα ἔτη [cf. Justin: ἐν τῇ ἐρήμῳ; cf. Acts 7:42: ἔτη τεσσεράκοντα ἐν τῇ ἐρήμῳ], οἶκος Ισραηλ; [Justin and the Bohairic add here λέγει κύριος] 26 καὶ ἀνελάβετε τὴν σκηνὴν τοῦ Μολοχ καὶ τὸ ἄστρον τοῦ θεοῦ ὑμῶν Ραιφαν, τοὺς τύπους αὐτῶν [Acts 7:43, Justin, and the Bohairic omit αὐτῶν], οὓς ἐποιήσατε ἑαυτοῖς. 27 καὶ μετοικιῶ ὑμᾶς ἐπέκεινα Δαμασκοῦ, λέγει κύριος, ὁ θεὸς ὁ παντοκράτωρ ὄνομα αὐτῷ.
6:1 Οὐαὶ τοῖς ἐξουθενοῦσι [cf. Justin: οἱ κατασπαταλῶντες] Σιων καὶ τοῖς πεποιθόσιν ἐπὶ τὸ ὄρος Σαμαρείας· [Justin adds here οἱ ὠνομασμένοι ἐπὶ τοῖς ἀρχηγοῖς] ἀπετρύγησαν ἀρχὰς ἐθνῶν, καὶ εἰσῆλθον ἑαυτοῖς. οἶκος τοῦ Ισραηλ, 2 διάβητε πάντες [W and Justin add here εἰς Χαλάνην] καὶ ἴδετε καὶ διέλθατε ἐκεῖθεν εἰς Εμαθ Ραββα [cf. Justin: τὴν μεγάλην] καὶ κατάβητε ἐκεῖθεν εἰς Γεθ ἀλλοφύλων, τὰς κρατίστας ἐκ πασῶν τῶν βασιλειῶν τούτων, εἰ πλείονα τὰ ὅρια αὐτῶν ἐστι τῶν ὑμετέρων [cf. Justin: ὑμῶν and word order] ὁρίων. 3 οἱ εὐχόμενοι [cf. Justin: ἐρχόμενοι] εἰς ἡμέραν κακήν [cf. Justin: πονηράν], οἱ ἐγγίζοντες καὶ ἐφαπτόμενοι σαββάτων ψευδῶν, 4 οἱ καθεύδοντες [cf. Justin: κοιμώμενοι] ἐπὶ κλινῶν ἐλεφαντίνων καὶ κατασπαταλῶντες ἐπὶ ταῖς στρωμναῖς αὐτῶν καὶ ἔσθοντες ἐρίφους [cf. Justin: ἄρνας] ἐκ ποιμνίων καὶ μοσχάρια ἐκ μέσου βουκολίων

γαλαθηνά, 5 οἱ ἐπικροτοῦντες πρὸς τὴν φωνὴν τῶν ὀργάνων ὡς ἑστῶτα ἐλογίσαντο καὶ οὐχ ὡς φεύγοντα· 6 οἱ πίνοντες τὸν διυλισμένον [cf. Justin: ἐν φιάλαις] οἶνον [Coptic versions add here ἐν φιάλαις] καὶ τὰ πρῶτα μύρα χριόμενοι καὶ οὐκ ἔπασχον οὐδὲν ἐπὶ τῇ συντριβῇ Ιωσηφ. 7 διὰ τοῦτο νῦν αἰχμάλωτοι ἔσονται ἀπ' ἀρχῆς δυναστῶν, [Justin adds here τῶν ἀποικιζομένων, καὶ μεταστραφήσεται οἴκημα κακούργων] καὶ ἐξαρθήσεται χρεμετισμὸς ἵππων ἐξ Εφραιμ.

Table 5.6: Amos 5:18–6:7

Codex W shows a tendency to omit the definite article and add καί,[27] whereas Justin tends to add the definite article and omit καί.[28] Each witness has one or two minor differences in spelling,[29] and there are several inconsequential variants in Codex W.[30] Undoubtedly reflecting *kaige,* Justin's quotation in *Dial.* 22.2–5 shows numerous differences vis-à-vis the OG. In Amos 5:19 Justin has ὅταν (whenever) rather than ἐὰν (if); Codices W and Alexandrinus also have this variant. Justin also has the synonymous ἐκφύγῃ (escape) rather than φύγῃ as well as συναντήσῃ (meet with) rather than ἐμπέσῃ (fall upon) in v. 19. In v. 23 Justin has ἀπόστησον (be away) rather than μετάστησον (take away) as well as πλῆθος (abundance) rather than ἦχον (sound); for the latter, the Hebrew word המון can mean both *sound* and *abundance*. In v. 25 the Hebrew says, "in the desert forty years," and the quotation in Acts 7:42 says, "forty years in the desert;" Justin simply has ἐν τῇ ἐρήμῳ (in the desert), whereas the OG, W, and the Bohairic simply have τεσσαράκοντα ἔτη (forty years). At the end of v. 25, Justin and the Bohairic add λέγει κύριος, which also appears in Alexandrinus but is not in the Hebrew. In v. 26 Justin, Acts 7:43, and the Bohairic omit αὐτῶν (their), which should be ὑμῶν (your) according to the Hebrew. In v. 27 Justin has παντοκράτωρ (almighty) as in the OG; surely *kaige* would have made the characteristic change to τῶν δυνάμεων (of the armies).

In Amos 6:1 Justin has οἱ κατασπαταλῶντες (those living excessively or self-indulgently) rather than τοῖς ἐξουθενοῦσι (those considered useless). After Σαμαρείας in 6:1 Justin adds "those named among the leaders" (οἱ ὠνομασμένοι ἐπὶ τοῖς ἀρχηγοῖς), which must have been *kaige's* alternative to "they harvested the authorities" (ἀπετρύγησαν ἀρχὰς); the OG considers Hebrew נקב in the active voice (pluck), but *kaige*—as in the MT—considers it passive (distinguished or designated).[31] In v. 2 W and Justin add εἰς Χαλάνην (into *Chalanēh*) after πάντες (all); the MT has a proper name כלנה (vocalized כַּלְנֵה, *Kalnēh*), but πάντες in the OG probably reflects כלה (vocalized כֻּלָּה, meaning 'all of it'),[32] so this would be a conflation. In v. 2 Justin has πορεύθητε (be brought) rather than διέλθατε (pass through), and he has the translation τὴν μεγάλην (great) rather than the transliteration Ραββα for רב; also in v. 2 Justin has the synonymous ὑμῶν (your) for ὑμετέρων as well as a different word order than the OG.[33] In v. 3 Justin has ἔρχομενοι (coming) rather than εὐχόμενοι (praying) as well as πονηράν (evil) rather than κακήν (bad). In v. 4 Justin has κοιμώμενοι (falling asleep) rather than καθεύδοντες (sleeping) as well as ἄρνας (lambs), which matches כרים, as opposed to ἐρίφους (young goats). In v. 6, as compared with the OG's "those drinking filtered wine" (οἱ πίνοντες τὸν διυλισμένον οἶνον), Justin has, "those drinking wine in bowls" (ἐν φιάλαις), which matches the Hebrew; Coptic versions conflate "those drinking filtered wine in bowls;" see Table 5.7.

MT Amos 6:7	לכן עתה יגלו בראש גלים וסר מרזח סרוחים
OG Amos 6:7	διὰ τοῦτο νῦν αἰχμάλωτοι ἔσονται ἀπ' ἀρχῆς δυναστῶν, καὶ ἐξαρθήσεται χρεμετισμὸς ἵππων ἐξ Εφραιμ.
Dial. 22.5b	διὰ τοῦτο νῦν αἰχμάλωτοι ἔσονται ἀπὸ ἀρχῆς δυναστῶν τῶν ἀποικιζομένων, καὶ μεταστραφήσεται οἴκημα κακούργων, καὶ ἐξαρθήσεται χρεμετισμὸς ἵππων ἐξ Εφραίμ.
MT Amos 6:7	Therefore now they will be exiled at the head of exiles, and the cry of the licentious will go out.
OG Amos 6:7	Therefore now they will be captives at the first of the powerful, and neighing of horses will be removed from Ephraim.
Dial. 22.5	Therefore now they will be captives at the first of the powerful of exiles, and a house of wickedness will turn, and neighing of horses will be removed from Ephraim.

Table 5.7: Amos 6:7

Although ἀπ' ἀρχῆς is always temporal in the New Testament, "from the beginning," the sense of the Hebrew is "at the head [i.e., front] of the line of exiles" (בראש גלים) in v. 7.[34] The OG and Justin use δυναστῶν (captives), but Justin adds ἀποικιζομένων (exiles), which must have stood in *kaige*. The OG and Justin also say "and neighing of horses will be removed from Ephraim," which does not easily derive from the Hebrew. The OG somehow read סוסים (horses)—or perhaps a more graphically similar, albeit morphologically unattested, form סוסות (mares)—for סרוח, which refers to lazy people sprawling on a couch;[35] the same Hebrew word appears in v. 4, where the OG rendered these people κατασπαταλῶντες (living excessively or self-indulgently). The Hebrew word מרזח only occurs here and in Jer 16:5, where it is a cry of mourning; once horses entered the Greek verse, however, their *cry* was translated specifically as *neighing* (χρεμετισμός). Here Justin would conflate *kaige*, which most likely read instead, "a house of wickedness (οἴκημα κακούργων);[36] *house* is inexplicable, but *wickedness* would be synonymous with the *self-indulgent* rendering of סרוח in the OG of v. 4. *Kaige* also would have had μεταστραφήσεται (turn around; change) rather than ἐξαρθήσεται (go out), either of which work for סור (BDB: turn or depart [*qal*]). The Hebrew does not mention Ephraim, but Justin and the OG do.[37]

Including definite articles, the OG contains 292 words, thirty-three of which are changed somehow in Justin's quotation (fifteen alternate words, seventeen added words, and one subtracted word). Justin shares three word changes with W and five word changes with the Coptic; the only *kaige* readings in W are ὅταν in Amos 5:19 and εἰς Χαλάνην in 6:2. The Bohairic aligns with Justin in adding λέγει κύριος in Amos 5:25 and (along with Acts 7:43) omitting αὐτῶν in 5:26; in a conflation, Coptic versions include "in bowls" in 6:6. Justin shares none of Aquila's attested revisions,[38] thereby nullifying Barthélemy's suspicion that Aquila's version contaminated the fourteenth-century MS of Justin's works.[39] Such seeming contamination results instead from Justin's conflating *kaige* with the OG. Justin's conflation of these two known sources eliminates the need for a hypothetical *testimonium* as one of Justin's sources.[40]

In summary, sporadic variants show that *kaige* definitely influenced Codex W and the Coptic versions. The Coptic and W nonetheless remain faithful to the OG line by line. On the contrary, Justin's Jonah and Micah quotations are taken practically word for word from *kaige* with minimal contamination from the OG. Justin's Amos quotation is a more difficult case, for without comparative data from 8ḤevXIIgr, one cannot reasonably assume that *kaige* left the OG unchanged in all the places where Justin's quotation agrees with the OG.[41] One can, however, reasonably conclude that Justin quotes *kaige* variants wherever his Amos quotation diverges from the OG. *Kaige* and the OG sufficiently account for Justin's sources for the Dodekapropheton in the *Dialogue with Trypho,* so there is no need to posit hypothetical *testimonia* as additional sources.

The Relationship between Kaige and Quinta

This section argues for the equivalence of *kaige* and the *Quinta* in the Dodekapropheton. The case studies are Origen's quotation of *Quinta* Zech 9:9 and Jerome's quotations of *Quinta* Hab 2:15, 3:13, and Mic 5:6, as well as Hos 8:6. I offer a few correctives to Barthélemy's work, but overall I show that his main conclusion withstands George Howard's counterarguments regarding the relationship between *kaige* and the *Quinta.*

As shown in the preceding section, Justin's Jonah and Micah quotations come solely from *kaige.* On that basis, some scholars have mistakenly assumed that Justin exactly reproduced *kaige* when quoting Zech 9:9 in *Dial.* 53.3.[42] However, this is a mixed quotation, as was the case with Justin's Amos quotation in *Dial.* 22; see Table 5.8.

OG Zech 9:9	Justin Martyr *Dial.* 53.3
χαῖρε σφόδρα, θύγατερ Σιων· κήρυσσε, θύγατερ Ιερουσαλημ· ἰδοὺ ὁ βασιλεύς σου ἔρχεταί σοι, δίκαιος καὶ σῴζων αὐτός, πραῢς καὶ ἐπιβεβηκὼς ἐπὶ ὑποζύγιον καὶ πῶλον νέον.	χαῖρε σφόδρα, θύγατερ Σιων, ἀλάλαξον, κήρυσσε, θύγατερ Ιερουσαλημ· ἰδοὺ ὁ βασιλεύς σου ἥξει σοι δίκαιος καὶ σῴζων αὐτὸς καὶ πραῢς καὶ πτωχός ἐπιβεβηκὼς ἐπὶ ὑποζύγιον καὶ πῶλον ὄνου.

Table 5.8: Zech 9:9

As I have demonstrated elsewhere,[43] Justin changed ἔρχεται (comes) to ἥξει (will have come); the "prophetic future perfect" is a redactional *Tendenz* that Justin shows elsewhere.[44] Justin then conflated *kaige's* ἀλάλαξον (shout) with the OG's κήρυσσε (proclaim) as well as *kaige's* πτωχός (poor) with the OG's πραΰς (humble); to reiterate, as the earliest known revision of the OG, *kaige* would have contained no such conflations. Last, Justin's phrase πῶλον ὄνου (a colt of an ass) was influenced by John 12:15, not by any extant Greek version of Zechariah.[45]

For Zech 9:9b, Origen lists full Hexaplaric data including the *Quinta;* see Table 5.9.[46]

OG Zech 9:9b	πραΰς καὶ ἐπιβεβηκὼς ἐπὶ ὑποζύγιον καὶ πῶλον νέον
Aquila	πραΰς καὶ ἐπιβεβηκὼς ἐπὶ ὄνου καὶ πώλου υἱοῦ ὀνάδων
Symmachus	πτωχὸς καὶ ἐπιβεβηκὼς ἐπὶ ὄνον καὶ πῶλον υἱὸν ὀνάδος
Theodotion	ἐπακούων καὶ ἐπιβεβηκὼς ἐπὶ ὄνον καὶ πῶλον υἱὸν ὄνου
Quinta	πτωχὸς καὶ ἐπιβεβηκὼς ἐπὶ ὑποζύγιον καὶ πῶλον υἱὸν ὄνων

Table 5.9: Zech 9:9b

Howard accepted that Justin used *kaige,* but since Justin's quotation does not exactly match Origen's *Quinta,* Howard rejected Barthélemy's equating *kaige* and the *Quinta.*[47] However, neither Barthélemy nor Howard recognized that Justin conflated the OG with *kaige.* By removing Justin's redactions, I reconstruct *kaige* Zech 9:9 as follows: χαῖρε σφόδρα, θύγατερ Σιων· ἀλάλαξον, θύγατερ Ιερουσαλημ· ἰδοὺ ὁ βασιλεύς σου ἔρχεται σοι, δίκαιος καὶ σῴζων αὐτός, πτωχὸς καὶ ἐπιβεβηκὼς ἐπὶ ὑποζύγιον καὶ πῶλον υἱὸν ὄνων.

Justin shows that—as in the *Quinta—kaige* preferred πραΰς (humble) to πτωχός (poor) for עני, which can mean either *humble* or *poor;* the translation πτωχός for עני also appears in 8ḤevXIIgr Hab 3:14. Symmachus also had πτωχός in Zech 9:9, but he did not work until a few decades after the death of Justin. It is also important that Aquila kept πραΰς, for there is no reason to suppose that later scribes conformed Justin's text to Aquila's recension.[48] Another key agreement between *kaige* and *Quinta* is leaving the OG's ὑποζύγιον unchanged; Aquila, Symmachus, and Theodotion unanimously preferred ὄνος. In Zech 9:9 Codex W is identical to the OG, and Coptic versions show no Hexaplaric influence.[49]

Regarding Zech 9:9, then, Justin alone gives evidence that *kaige* preferred ἀλάλαξον to the OG's κήρυσσε. Justin also shows that *kaige* changed πραΰς to πτωχός but left ὑποζύγιον unchanged. Origen's *Quinta* likewise read πτωχός and ὑποζύγιον. Justin's πῶλον ὄνου—as opposed to the OG's πῶλον νέον or the *Quinta's* πῶλον υἱὸν ὄνων—comes from the quotation of Zech 9:9 in the Gospel of John. Accordingly, as compared with Origen's *Quinta,* Justin's main disagreement did not derive from *kaige*. Moreover, the shared agreements between Justin's *kaige* and Origen's *Quinta* line up against the OG, Aquila, Symmachus, and Theodotion. One can thus reasonably infer the equivalence of *kaige* and *Quinta* in Zech 9:9.

Zechariah 9:9 is Origen's lone extant quotation of the *Quinta,* but Jerome cites the *Quinta* twenty-six times in the Minor Prophets.[50] Only three references can be checked against 8ḤevXIIgr, yet in all three cases *kaige* is identical to Jerome's *Quinta*. For Hab 2:15, Jerome cites Aquila, Symmachus, Theodotion, the *Quinta,* and two others. The OG proclaims woe on someone who gives a neighbor ἀνατροπῇ θολερᾷ to drink; LSJ here understands ἀνατροπῇ as *poured out*, but it can also mean something *upsetting*, and θολερᾷ means *muddy* or *cloudy*. According to Jerome, the *Quinta* changed θολερά to θυμός (wrath), but the *Quinta* retained ἀνατροπή, albeit in the genitive rather than the dative. In 8ḤevXIIgr a fragment of Column 18 preserves ανατ in Hab 2:15, so *kaige* and *Quinta* here line up against every other attested revision of the OG.

The Hebrew word סלה appears in Hab 3:3, 9, 13. The OG translated διάψαλμα, but Jerome relates the translations ἀεί (always) by Aquila, εἰς τὸν αἰῶνα (until the aeon) by Symmachus, and εἰς τέλος (until the end) by Theodotion as well as the transliteration σελα by the *Quinta*. Although Habakkuk 3 is very fragmentary in 8ḤevXIIgr, this transliteration—albeit spelled σελε—stands in *kaige* Hab 3:13; by contrast, Codex W and the Coptic maintain the OG's διάψαλμα. In this instance, *kaige* and *Quinta* align the OG to the Hebrew in exactly the same way *and* in contrast to Aquila, Symmachus, and Theodotion.[51]

The prophet Micah imagines a remnant of Israelites ruling the Assyrians: "And they will shepherd the land of Asshur with a sword and the land of Nimrod with a פתחיה" (MT Mic 5:5a; OG v. 6). The Assyrian cities Nimrod and Asshur clearly stand in parallelism, and so would חרב (sword) and פתחיה. Nonetheless OG Mic 5:6a reads: "And they will shepherd Assour with a sword and the land of Nebrod with her ditch." The Greek phrase ἐν τῇ τάφρῳ αὐτῆς (with her ditch) would reflect Hebrew בפתחה, the segolate פתח (opening, doorway) with the preposition *bet* and 3fs suffix *he*. Symmachus's ἐντὸς πυλῶν αὐτῶν and Theodotion's ἐν πύλαις αὐτῶν show the same understanding of the Hebrew noun. Aquila's *in lanceis eius* (with her spears) and the *Quinta's* ἐν παραξίφεσιν αὐτῶν (with their daggers) understand the Hebrew word in 5:5aβ as פתיחה or פתוחה for *drawn sword* or *dagger,* which restores the parallelism with *sword* (חרב) in 5:5aα. Most importantly, εν παρα in Column 9 of 8ḤevXIIgr shows that *kaige* here aligns with Jerome's *Quinta* reading.

Especially in Hosea 4–9, Barberini MS 86 designates a number of marginal variants with the siglum ε′. The question is whether these come from the *Quinta*. Hosea 8:6 is most important because Jerome gives a different *Quinta* reading than the ε′ note in MS 86. Here Hosea decries Israel's idolatry, specifically "the calf of Samaria" (cf. 1 Kings 12); see Table 5.10.

MT Hos 8:6	והוא חרש עשהו ולא אלהים הוא כי-שבבים יהיה עגל שמרון
OG Hos 8:6	καὶ αὐτὸ τέκτων ἐποίησε, καὶ οὐ θεός ἐστι· διότι πλανῶν ἦν ὁ μόσχος σου, Σαμάρεια
MS 86 ε′ Hos 8:6	τὸ ὑπὸ τέκτονος γενόμενον οὐκ ἂν ᾖ θεός· παραπλησίως τῷ τῆς ἀράχνης ἱστῷ.
MT Hos 8:6	And it, a carpenter made it, and it is not a god, for the calf of Samaria will become splinters.
OG Hos 8:6	And a carpenter made it, and it is not a god; therefore your calf, Samaria, was misleading.
MS 86 ε′ Hos 8:6	What came into being by a carpenter should not be a god, resembling a spider's web . . .

Table 5.10: Hos 8:6

The Hebrew word שבבים is *hapax legomenon*. The rendering *splinters* (see BDB and HALOT) is supported by Targum Jonathan's phrase, "for the calf of Samaria will become sawed boards" (ארי לנסרי לוחין יהי עגלא דשומרון).[52] Jerome observes that the OG's πλανῶν represents שׁובבום, based on שׁוב (cf. *qere* שׁובבום for *ketiv* שׁובבים in Jer 50:6a), which denotes *turn* or *turn back* but can connote *turning away* or *apostasy*. Jerome gives full Hexaplaric data for this word. Aquila said *errantibus* (wandering) or *conversis* (turn around or turn back), whereas the *Quinta* said ῥεμβεύων (roaming). Symmachus put ἀκαταστατῶν (unstable), and Theodotion kept the OG's πλανῶν (wandering, misleading). The *Quinta's* ῥεμβεύων does not match παραπλησίως, the ε′ note in MS 86; for comparison, MS 86 attributes to Symmachus ἀκατάστατος, which does correspond to Jerome's evidence.

Jerome's translation of Hos 8:6b in the Vulgate reads, "since the bull of Samaria will turn into a spider web" *(quoniam in aranearum telas erit vitulus Samariae)*. According to Jerome's commentary, Hosea was saying that a thin web disappears into thin air, just as Samaria's greatness will diminish. Moreover *aranearum fila* (spider web) is Jerome's understanding of Hebrew שבבים, which he transliterates *sababim*. Barthélemy speculated that Jerome was influenced by Syriac ܫܒܒ, which can mean "to descend by means of a rope."[53] A clearer explanation has gone unrecognized until now: Jerome actually misreads שׂבבים as שׂבכים, which signifies interwoven things such as a net (Job 18:8) or lattice-work (1 Kgs 7:17); cf. Aramaic שׂבכא for a lyre, which is strung or threaded. Jerome thus mistakes a graphically similar *kaph* for *bet; sin* and *shin* are indistinguishable in unpointed MSS.

I accept Barthélemy's hypothesis that MS 86 ε′ is dependent on Jerome's Vulgate and his commentary on the Minor Prophets.[54] At the same time, it is difficult to determine the origin of that Greek text because it is not a direct translation of the Vulgate. There are two unparalleled features, namely omitting "and" as well as the shift to the subjunctive; "should not be a god" (οὐκ ἂν ᾖ θεός) differs from the Vulgate's *et non est Deus,* which matches the OG and the MT.[55] The main problem in v. 6b is παραπλησίως, which seems to be related to, or a revision of, πλανῶν. That is, παραπλήσιος is a Greek word with a dual meaning: one pertains to movement (coming alongside), and the other is used for comparison (resembling). The OG's πλανῶν connotes movement, but Jerome apparently introduced the notion of comparison in this verse. In the OG the calf image instrumentally caused Israel to sin, whereas the MT says that Samaria's calf will be materially chopped to pieces. In other words, the Hebrew does not say that the calf will become *like* splinters, but that it literally will be turned into splinters. Jerome's "spider web" mistranslation necessitates a figurative interpretation, and the discussion in Jerome's commentary—not the Vulgate itself—presumes Hosea to have compared Samaria's bull to a spider web. Therefore the comparative aspect of παραπλήσιος makes the most sense in view of Jerome's interpretation.

Jerome did not find the "spider web" reading anywhere in the Hexapla or even in the Old Latin, which closely follows the Old Greek—particularly the participle *seductor* (one who misleads) for πλανῶν.[56] There is no evidence for a Hebrew *Vorlage* reading "spider web," a misunderstanding arising from Jerome's own exegesis in the late-fourth century. Had he known of a Greek version like the MS 86 ε′ reading, Jerome could have quoted it as "others say," as he does for the *Sexta* and the *Septima*. I consider it too much of a stretch to see the Greek MS 86 ε′ as independent of, or prior to, Jerome. In any event, Jerome's *Quinta* reading of ῥεμβεύων does not match παραπλησίως in MS 86 ε′, and I confidently concur with Barthélemy's dissociation of MS 86 ε′ from the Hexapla's *Quinta;* although they share the same siglum, they are not the same text. Since Jerome's *Quinta* does not match *kaige* here but does match it elsewhere, the marginal notes in MS 86 do not challenge the equivalence of *kaige* and *Quinta* in the Dodekapropheton.

In summary, there are admittedly few examples, but in every verifiable instance *kaige* and *Quinta* turn out to be equivalent with no contrary evidence. In previous research, the greatest difficulty came from dissimilar quotations of Zech 9:9 in Justin Martyr's *kaige* and Origen's *Quinta*. Upon closer inspection, however, Justin was conflating the OG with *kaige*. By subtracting the OG conflations, *kaige* is shown to agree with the *Quinta* there. Moreover, Jerome's quotations of *Quinta* Hab 2:15, 3:13, and Mic 5:6 match *kaige*, as evidenced by 8ḤevXIIgr. Jerome's witness to *Quinta* Hos 8:6 further establishes that the ε′ notations in MS 86 do not refer to the *Quinta*, and so Barthélemy rightly excluded MS 86 ε′ readings from consideration. I have offered occasional refinements to Barthélemy's discussions, but overall I hope to have vindicated his carefully weighed conclusion based on internal evidence that *kaige* and *Quinta* are equivalent in the Dodekapropheton.

Conclusion: Weighing Internal and External Evidence

Howard paid insufficient attention to external evidence, and so he inaccurately asserted that *kaige* and *Quinta* were no more closely related than *kaige* was to Justin, the Coptic versions, Codex W, or Aquila.[57] The OG is by definition the earliest known Greek translation. As the earliest known revision of the OG, *kaige* dates no later than the first century BCE, since the physical artifact of 8ḤevXIIgr dates near the turn of the era. The scroll's discovery in the Cave of Horror shows that this artifact remained in use in Palestine until the Bar Kokhba Revolt (132–135 CE). Soon thereafter, Justin Martyr used *kaige* for his *Dialogue with Trypho*, which dates between 155 and 167.[58] To reiterate, *kaige* did not simply influence Justin—*kaige* was the discernible, independent source that Justin used alongside the OG for the Minor Prophets.[59]

Aquila's revision dates to ca. 125 CE, so it was a potential source for Justin; it appears not to have been an actual source, however, since Justin's work nowhere reveals traces of Aquila's revision. As Barthélemy demonstrated, Aquila was himself dependent on *kaige*.[60] As a revision of *kaige*, Aquila's would not have been identical—as were Justin's verbatim quotations. Nevertheless, Aquila would show much closer affinity to *kaige* than does Codex W or the Coptic versions, all of which only reveal *kaige* variants sporadically.

The recensions by Symmachus and Theodotion traditionally date to ca. 200 CE.[61] Third-century biblical translations reflect scholarly interests that culminated in Origen's Hexapla. Codex W dates to the mid- to late-third century, and W incorporates variants from Aquila, Symmachus, and the *Quinta*. Henry Sanders inferred that W's parent text included marginal Hexaplaric glosses similar to those of MS 86, except that the sources might not have been identified.[62] The same type of Hexaplaric influence appears in Coptic translations, which did not emerge until the mid- to late-third century.[63] In particular, Coptic versions of the Minor Prophets incorporate variants from Aquila, Symmachus, Theodotion, and the *Quinta*.[64]

Since Codex W and the Coptic versions date to the third century, they can and do occasionally attest Hexaplaric readings that did not exist in Justin's era. Yet it is essential to recognize that W and the Coptic firmly stand in the OG tradition. For example, in Mic 4:1–7 W and the Coptic each show >99% agreement with the OG, whereas Justin's *kaige* shows <78% agreement with the OG. Howard relativizes these textual traditions as though *kaige* exerted similar influence across the board. Quantifiably, out of all the examples included herein, *kaige* changed approximately one out of every five words of the OG, yet very few of those variants (<6%) went on to contaminate Codex W or the Coptic versions; Aquila would assume more of those variants because it stands in the new tradition forged by *kaige*.

In conclusion, Howard justifiably questioned the equivalence of *kaige* and *Quinta* given such limited data.[65] But if, in the Minor Prophets, *kaige* is not the *Quinta*, then what is it? Jerome cites the *Sexta* (ϛ′) and *Septima* (ζ′) for Hab 1:5 and 2:11. He gives an additional *Sexta* reference for Hab 3:13, which reads "through Jesus, your Christ." None of the *Sexta* or *Septima* quotes can be checked against 8ḤevXIIgr, but the *Quinta* definitely differed from these two, and the *Sexta* was clearly a Christian revision. As a pre-Christian revision of the OG, *kaige* thus cannot be the same as the *Sexta*. And if the positive evidence connecting *kaige* and *Quinta* is insufficient or indeterminate for some scholars, then neither could *kaige* be identified with the *Septima*, for which there is no overlap at all. I do not draw conclusions for *kaige* or *Quinta* beyond the Dodekapropheton, but in terms of parsimony I validate Barthélemy's argument for their equivalence in the Minor Prophets as the surest hypothesis moving forward. Otherwise *kaige* must be posited as an *eighth* Greek version of the Minor Prophets, one that Justin Martyr knew but Origen did not—even though Origen was "more textually aware than almost anyone else one could name in the history of ecclesiastical scholarship."[66]

Notes

This essay furthers my argument in "The Reconstruction of *Kaige/Quinta* Zechariah 9,9," *ZAW* 126 (2014): 584–88. That was my first peer-reviewed publication, and Leonard Greenspoon graciously provided such helpful feedback on it; I am honored to dedicate this essay to him. I thank Emanuel Tov, Kristin De Troyer, and Michaël N. van der Meer, as well as David Leonhardt for offering very helpful comments and corrections for this essay.

[1]Emanuel Tov, with the collaboration of R. A. Kraft and a contribution by P. J. Parsons, *The Greek Minor Prophets Scroll from Naḥal Ḥever (8ḤevXIIgr)*, The Seiyâl Collection 1, DJD VIII (Oxford: Clarendon, 1990), 26.

[2]Dominique Barthélemy, "Redécouverte d'un chaînon manquant de l'histoire de la Septante," *RB* 60 (1953): 18–29; idem, *Les Devanciers d'Aquila: première publication intégrale du texte des fragments du Dodécaprophéton*, VTSup 10 (Leiden: Brill, 1963). My references to "*kaige*" are intended only for the revision of the Dodekapropheton.

[3]Robert A. Kraft (review of Dominique Barthélemy, *Les Devanciers d'Aquila*, *Gnomon* 37 [1965]: 474–83, here 477) initially questioned whether the *kaige* scroll would show systematic dependence on the OG. This question has been answered affirmatively; see Tov, *Greek Minor Prophets Scroll*, 102–6, 145–53. On the term "proto-Masoretic," see Tov's essay in this volume.

[4]Hexaplaric data for the Minor Prophets appear in Joseph Ziegler, *Duodecim prophetae*, 2d ed., Septuaginta 13 (Göttingen: Vandenhoeck & Ruprecht, 1967); see also Frederick Field, *Origen Hexapla*, 2d ed., 2 vols. (Oxford: Clarendon, 1875), 2:937–1034.

[5]Kraft, review of Barthélemy, 477.

[6]George Howard ("The Quinta of the Minor Prophets: A First Century Septuagint Text?" *Bib* 55 [1974], 15–22) rejects Barthélemy's equating *kaige* and the *Quinta*. Natalio Fernández Marcos (*The Septuagint in Context: Introduction to the Greek Version of the Bible*, trans. Wilfred G. E. Watson, [Atlanta: Society of Biblical Literature, 2000], 157–58) and Joshua L. Harper (*Responding to a Puzzled Scribe: The Barberini Version of Habakkuk 3 Analysed in the Light of the Other Greek Versions*, LHBOTS 608/The Hebrew Bible and Its Versions 8 [London: Bloomsbury T&T Clark, 2015], 15) seem to concur with Howard's dissent.

[7]Howard, "Quinta of the Minor Prophets," 22. For Codex W, see Henry A. Sanders and Carl Schmidt, *The Minor Prophets in the Freer Collection and the Berlin Fragment of Genesis*, University of Michigan Studies, Humanistic Series 21 (New York: Macmillan, 1927). Coptic variants are collected in Willem Grossouw, *The Coptic Versions of the Minor Prophets: A Contribution to the Study of the Septuagint*, MBE 3 (Rome: Pontifical Biblical Institute, 1938).

[8]The OG text is from Ziegler, *Duodecim prophetae* (see n. 4 above).

[9]In Hab 2:18 Codex W is identical to the OG except for plural verbs ἔγλυψαν and ἔπλασαν; the Achmimic and Bohairic versions also have the plural ἔπλασαν, and there is no comparative data for Aquila.

[10]In Hab 2:7, instead of ἐκνήψουσιν, Codex W has a solecism ἐκνήψονται, which is simply influenced by the ending of ἀναστήσονται on the line directly above; there is no comparative data for Aquila or the Coptic.

[11]Literally someone is secretly eating the poor man, as Harper (*Responding to a Puzzled Scribe*, 253) points out. However, I assume that 8ḤevXIIgr intends καθὼς ἐσθίον πτωχὸν κρυφῇ. It is not unusual to inflect similes in the accusative, and at least once 8ḤevXIIgr writes *omicron* for *ōmega*, namely Hab 1:8 (see Tov, *Greek Minor Prophets Scroll*, 144); moreover, there is no direct object marker (את) before עני.

[12]Field, *Origen Hexapla*, 2:1010, there citing Bernard de Montfaucon's reference to Codex Coislinianus.

[13]Barthélemy (*Études d'Histoire du Texte de l'Ancien Testament*, OBO 21 [Göttingen: Vandenhoeck & Ruprecht, 1978], 392–93) made a similar point in reply to Howard.

[14]The Greek text of Justin's works is from Edgar J. Goodspeed, *Die ältesten Apologeten: Texte mit kurzen Einleitungen* (Göttingen: Vandenhoeck & Ruprecht, 1914).

[15]Barthélemy, "Redécouverte d'un chaînon manquant;" idem, *Devanciers d'Aquila*, 205–7.

[16]In Mic 4:1 Codex W has αὐτόν rather than αὐτό. In v. 2 W adds ἐπ' αὐτό after πορεύσονται, has dittography of τὴν before ὁδόν, and says the law and word of God (θεοῦ) rather than Lord (κυρίου). In v. 3 W has ὡς (as) rather than ἕως (until); adds land (γῆν) to clarify faraway (μακράν); and has ἐπί (at) rather than εἰς (into) before plows (ἄροτρα). In v. 7 W uses ἀπερριμμένην (thrown away) rather than ἀπωσμένην (driven away), and W describes the nation as capable (δυνατόν) rather than strong (ἰσχυρόν).

[17]8ḤevXIIgr uses an initial *sigma* for ζιβύνας and [ἐ]φ' rather than ἐπ' before ἔθνος in v. 3; the scroll elsewhere shows this tendency to aspirate. 8ḤevXIIgr also uses plural [καθίσ]ονται rather than singular in v. 4.

[18]Cf. OG Isa 2:4b: καὶ συγκόψουσιν τὰς μαχαίρας αὐτῶν εἰς ἄροτρα καὶ τὰς ζιβύνας αὐτῶν εἰς δρέπανα, καὶ οὐ λήμψεται ἔτι ἔθνος ἐπ' ἔθνος μάχαιραν, καὶ οὐ μὴ μάθωσιν ἔτι πολεμεῖν. Leonard Greenspoon (*Textual Studies in the Book of Joshua*, HSM 28 [Chico, CA: Scholars Press, 1983]) identified many *kaige* characteristics including a discussion of μαχαίρα and ζιβύνη.

[19]Antonio Maria Ceriani, ed., *Codex Syro-Hexaplaris Ambrosianus* (London: Williams & Norgate, 1874), 102v.

[20]*Pace* P. Katz, "Justin's Old Testament quotations and the Greek Dodekapropheton Scroll," in *Studia Patristica*, vol. 1, pt. 1, ed. Kurt Aland and F. L. Cross (Berlin: Akademie Verlag, 1957), 343–53, here 348.

[21]Howard, "Quinta of the Minor Prophets," 22.

[22]Barthélemy, *Devanciers d'Aquila*, 205.

[23]The Syrohexapla notes that Aquila, Symmachus, and Theodotion differed from the MT by saying God (θεοῦ) rather than Lord (κυρίου) in v. 1; this influenced W. Also, Aquila and Symmachus preferred μεταξύ to ἀνὰ μέσον in v. 3, and Aquila and Theodotion had ὑπό instead of ὑποκάτω in v. 4.

[24]See Barthélemy, *Devanciers d'Aquila*, 48–54, here 51; *kaige* more characteristically changes ἕκαστος (each) to ἀνήρ (man), but Barthélemy also observes ἀνήρ for ἄνθρωπος (person) in 2 Chr 6:29.

[25]Codex W has one instance of haplography, omitting καὶ ὑπὸ νύκτα, and W reverses the right and left hands.

[26]Justin's use of Mic 5:2 in *1 Apol.* 34.1 and *Dial.* 78.1 quote Matt 2:6 verbatim—not the OG or *kaige*.

[27]Codex W omits the definite article in 5:18 before κυρίου (Lord), in 5:19 before ὄφις (snake), and—according to Sanders's reconstruction—in 5:22 before ὁλοκαυτώματα (whole burnt offerings); Justin omits the definite article in 6:1 before Ισραηλ, and the article is not present in the Hebrew. W adds καί in 5:18 between κυρίου and ἵνα, in 5:22 between διότι and ἐάν, and in 5:26 after Ραιφαν.

[28]Justin adds the definite article in 5:20 before ἑορτάς (feasts; the article is present in Hebrew), in 5:22 before θυσίας (sacrifices; absent in Hebrew), in 5:24 before δικαιοσύνη (righteousness; absent in Hebrew), in 6:2 before ἀλλοφύλων (foreign tribes; the Hebrew is anarthrous Philistines), and in 6:4 before ἐσθίοντες (the ones who are eating); Justin omits καί in 6:1 between ἐθνῶν (nations) and εἰσῆλθον (entered; *waw* is present in Hebrew) and in 6:4 before ἐσθίοντες (present in Hebrew).

[29]Codex W spells ἄβατος with two *bētas* in 5:24, and Justin omits the *iōta* in Ραιφαν (5:26) but adds a *iōta* to ἔσθοντες (6:4).

[30]Codex W has the future ἀπώσομαι rather than the perfect ἀπῶσμαι in 5:21, and W omits αὐτά after προσδέξομαι in 5:22; according to Sanders's reconstruction, W also changed σωτηρίου to σωτηρίους in 5:22. W has αὐτοί rather than ἑαυτοῖς in 6:1, and after κατάβητε in 6:2 W has dittography of διέλθετε, which is on the line directly above.

[31]Cf. the phrase נקבו בשמות (designated by the names) in Num 1:17; 1 Chr 12:32; 16:41; 2 Chr 28:15; 31:19; Ezra 8:20.

[32]BHQ nonetheless considers πάντες elusive (Anthony Gelston, ed., *The Twelve Minor Prophets*, Biblia Hebraica Quinta 13 [Stuttgart: Deutsche Bibelgesellschaft, 2010], 48).

[33]Justin has εἰ πλειόνά ἐστι τὰ ὅρια αὐτῶν τῶν ὁρίων ὑμῶν rather than εἰ πλέονα τὰ ὅρια αὐτῶν ἐστι τῶν ὑμετέρων ὁρίων.

[34]Cf. "at the end of the street" (בראש דרך/חוץ) in Ezek 16:31; 21:24 (Eng. v. 9); 42:12; Nah 3:10.

[35]Cf. סרח as the part of a curtain that hangs or folds over in Exod 26:12; perhaps also contributing to *horses* in OG Amos 6:7 is the reference to horses in v. 12.

[36]*Kaige* likely also translated סרוחים as κακοῦργοι in vv. 4 and 7; *kaige* likely reserved κατασπαταλῶντες for שאננים (people who are secure, at ease, or arrogant) in v. 1.

[37]For comparison, Ephraim and a horse (מאפרים וסוס) are juxtaposed in Zech 9:10.

[38]Vis-à-vis the OG, Aquila transliterates ναβλων rather than translating ὀργάνων in Amos 5:23 according to MS 86; according to Jerome, Aquila prefers the synonymous συσκιάσμους rather than σκηνὴν for *shade* in v. 26 and (including 2pl. suffix) transliterates מלכּכם as Μολχομ rather than Μολοχ and כיון (Saturn) for Ραίφαν in v.

26; finally Aquila translates πολλήν rather than transliterating Ραββα in 6:2 according to the Syrohexapla, and Aquila gives the more accurate οἱ ἀποκεχωρισμένοι (separating) instead of οἱ ἐρχόμενοι (coming) for המנדים (putting away) in v. 3 according to MS 86.

[39] Barthélemy, *Devanciers d'Aquila*, 208–9.

[40] *Pace* Pierre Prigent, *Justin et l'Ancien Testament: l'argumentation scripturaire du traité de Justin contre toutes les hérésies comme source principale du Dialogue avec Tryphon et de la première Apologie*, EBib (Paris: J. Gabalda, 1964), 260–61; Oskar Skarsaune, *The Proof from Prophecy: A Study in Justin Martyr's Proof-Text Tradition*, NovTSup 56 (Leiden: Brill, 1987), 124. Prigent and Skarsaune averred that Justin used *kaige*, but they maintained Justin's reliance on a testimony-book. Appeals to a *testimonium* here are based on the quotation of Amos 5:25–26 in Acts 7:42–43: μὴ σφάγια καὶ θυσίας προσηνέγκατέ μοι ἔτη τεσσεράκοντα ἐν τῇ ἐρήμῳ, οἶκος Ἰσραήλ; καὶ ἀνελάβετε τὴν σκηνὴν τοῦ Μόλοχ καὶ τὸ ἄστρον τοῦ θεοῦ [ὑμῶν here is omitted in B and D but present in $\mathfrak{P}^{74}$, ℵ, and A *et al.*] Ῥαιφάν, τοὺς τύπους οὓς ἐποιήσατε προσκυνεῖν αὐτοῖς, καὶ μετοικιῶ ὑμᾶς ἐπέκεινα Βαβυλῶνος.

[41] E.g., Jerome does not cite any Hexaplaric data for Hab 3:14, where *kaige* changed nearly every word of the OG; Codex Montefiore attests thoroughgoing revision of Hab 3:14 by Aquila and Symmachus as well.

[42] E.g., Prigent, *Justin et l'Ancien Testament*, 284; Skarsaune, *Proof from Prophecy*, 76.

[43] Barker, "Reconstruction of *Kaige/Quinta* Zechariah 9,9," 588.

[44] In *Dial.* 49.3 Justin described John the Baptist as a prophet who cried out that one stronger than he "will have come" (ἥξει). Justin's *Vorlage(n)* would have said that someone either "comes" (ἔρχεται; Mark 1:7b; Luke 3:16c) or "is coming" (ἐρχόμενος; Matt 3:11a; John 1:27).

[45] Justin also quotes Zech 9:9 in *1 Apol.* 35.11; there his sources were the OG and the quotations of Zechariah in the Gospels of Matthew (21:5) and John (12:15): χαῖρε σφόδρα θύγατερ Σιων· κήρυσσε θύγατερ Ιερουσαλημ· ἰδοὺ ὁ βασιλεύς σου ἔρχεταί σοι· πρᾶος ἐπιβεβηκὼς ἐπὶ πῶλον ὄνον υἱὸν ὑποζυγίου; the missing καί between πρᾶος/πραῢς and ἐπιβεβηκώς is also attested in Codex Bezae at Matt 21:5. In *1 Apology* Justin misattributed the verse to Zephaniah, for OG Zeph. 3:14a and OG Zech. 9:9aα begin verbatim, "Rejoice greatly, daughter Zion; proclaim, daughter Jerusalem." As I have pointed out elsewhere (James W. Barker, *John's Use of Matthew*, Emerging Scholars [Minneapolis: Fortress, 2015], 79), it is possible that Justin read from the Book of the Twelve and arrived at Zephaniah 3 prior to Zechariah 9. After copying as far as "daughter Jerusalem," Justin could have relied on Matt 21:5 and John 12:15 for the remainder of his quotation without further recourse to any OT text. Justin's *1 Apology* nowhere reflects knowledge of *kaige*.

[46] Origen lists the Hexaplaric evidence in his commentary on the Gospel of Matthew (16.16.180–193); see Erich Klostermann and Ernst Benz, *Origenes Werke X: Matthäuserklärung I*, GCS 40 (Leipzig: J. C. Hinrichs, 1935).

[47] Howard, "Quinta of the Minor Prophets," 21–22.

[48] *Pace* Katz, "Justin's Old Testament Quotations."

[49]E.g., "a yoke animal and a young colt" (ⲟⲩϥⲁⲓⲛⲁϩⲃϥ̄ ⲁⲟⲩ ⲟⲩⲥⲓϭ ⲛⲃ̄ⲣⲣⲉ) in the Achmimic matches the OG exactly; the Achmimic is taken from Carl Wessely, "Duodecim porphetarum minorum versionis Achmimicae: Codex Rainerianus," *Studien zur Palaeographie und Papyruskunde* 16 (1915): 257.

[50]Jerome's Hexaplaric data come from M. Adriaen, ed., *Hieronymus: Comentarii in prophetas minores,* 2 vols., CCSL 76–76A (Turnhout: Brepols, 1964–1969). According to Field, Jerome lists *Quinta* variants in Hos 8:6; 13:14; Joel 3:14; Amos 1:1, 5; 4:13; 7:14; 9:7; Obad 18; Mic 4:13; 5:1, 5; 6:2, 8; 7:18; Nah 1:8, 14; Hab 2:1, 11, 16; 3:1, 3, 5, 13; Zeph 1:3; 2:5. An additional example is Hab 2:4, regarding which Jerome says, "And where the Septuagint has put, 'But the righteous will live by *my* [μου] faith,' everyone alike has translated, 'will live by *his* [αὐτοῦ] faith.' Only Symmachus says, interpreting distinctively, 'the righteous will live by *his own* [ἑαυτοῦ] faith.'" Similarly, the Syrohexapla (Ceriani 107r) notes that "these" (ܗܠܝܢ)—i.e., Aquila, Symmachus, and Theodotion—say that the righteous one "lives from his faith" (ܡܢ ܗܝܡܢܘܬܐ ܕܝܠܗ ܚܐܐ). Column 17 of 8ḤevXIIgr preserves καιος εν πιστει αυτου ζησετ, which agrees verbatim with Eusebius's attribution to Aquila in *Dem. evang.* 6.14 (*PG* 22:439, 441). Migne's Hexapla (*PG* 16:2985, 2987) mistakenly extends Symmachus's reading to Theodotion, *Quinta, Sexta, and Septima.*

[51]Barthélemy (*Devanciers d'Aquila*, 176) and Howard ("Quinta of the Minor Prophets," 20) reconstructed the rest of Hab 3:13 differently, and Howard concluded that "there is no certainty whatever that Quinta and R are the same in this passage"; yet Howard neglected the key agreement of σελα/σελε, which does not require reconstruction.

[52]The Peshitta reflects the OG's πλανῶν in the sense of *error* (ܛܘܥܝܘܬܐ); Grossouw lists no variants for the Coptic.

[53]Dominique Barthélemy, "Quinta ou Version selon les Hébreux," *TZ* 16 (1960): 342–53, here 344; A. A. Macintosh (*A Critical and Exegetical Commentary on Hose*, ICC [Edinburgh: T&T Clark, 1997], 310) considers this suggestion "too uncertain to commend itself."

[54]Barthélemy, "Quinta ou Version selon les Hébreux," 344. Howard ("Quinta of the Minor Prophets," 17–18) further suggested that Jerome could have mistakenly copied the *Quinta* and that MS 86 could have copied a contaminated *Quinta*. However, there is no basis for doubting that Jerome took ῥεμβεύων from the *Quinta,* and contamination (e.g., *kaige's* influence on Codex W and Coptic versions) typically consists of a word here or there, not an unparalleled string of thirteen words.

[55]The shift to the subjunctive in MS 86 ε′ further distances this text from *kaige,* for the subjunctive is relatively infrequent in OG, and only once does 8ḤevXIIgr change an indicative to a subjunctive: OG's ἥξουσι becomes [ἔλ]θωσιν for יבאו in Zech 8:20 (Tov, *Greek Minor Prophets Scroll*, 124).

[56]Old Latin Hos 8:6 reads verbatim in the fifth-century Constance text and the ninth- or tenth-century Sangallensia text: *et ipsum faber fecit et non est ds· propter quod seductor erat vitulus tuus samaria* (P. Alban Dold, *Konstanzer Altlateinische Propheten- und Evangelien-Bruchstücke mit Glossen nebst zugehörigen Prophetentexten aus Zürich und St. Gallen,* Texte und Arbeiten [Leipzig: Otto Harrassowitz, 1923]).

[57] Howard, "Quinta of the Minor Prophets," 22.

[58] Craig D. Allert, *Revelation, Truth, Canon and Interpretation: Studies in Justin Martyr's* Dialogue with Trypho, Supplements to Vigiliae Christianae 64 (Leiden: Brill, 2002), 27–34.

[59] I agree with Tessa Rajak's ("Theological Polemic and Textual Revision in Justin Martyr's *Dialogue with Trypho the Jew*," in *Greek Scriptures and the Rabbis*, ed. Timothy Michael Law and Alison Salvesen, CBET 66 (Leuven: Peeters, 2012), 127–40, here 140) caution regarding Justin's polemics, yet I would qualify that he still plays an important part in textual reconstruction.

[60] Barthélemy, *Devanciers d'Aquila*, 246–52.

[61] Peter J. Gentry ("Pre-Hexaplaric Translations, Hexapla, post-Hexaplaric translations," in *Textual History of the Bible, vol. 1A*, ed. Armin Lange [Leiden: Brill, 2016], 211–34, here § 1.3.1.2.4) has recently re-dated Theodotion to 25 BCE–25 CE, working contemporaneously within the *kaige* tradition. The relation between *kaige/Quinta* and Theodotion in the Dodekapropheton needs further study; presently, though, two points are clear: Theodotion readings in the Minor Prophets are distinguishable from *kaige/Quinta*, and Theodotion did not influence Justin's quotations.

[62] Sanders, *Minor Prophets in the Freer Collection*, 33.

[63] Christian Askeland, "The Coptic Versions of the New Testament," in *The Text of the New Testament in Contemporary Research: Essays on the* Status Quaestionis, ed. Bart D. Ehrman and Michael W. Holmes, 2nd ed. (Boston: Brill, 2013), 201–29, here 209; see also Frank Feder, "Coptic Translations," in *Textual History of the Bible, vol. 1A*, 331–44, here § 1.4.2.4.

[64] This phenomenon recurs in Armenian translations: Claude E. Cox, *Hexaplaric Materials Preserved in the Armenian Versions*, SBLSCS 21 (Atlanta: Scholars Press, 1986); idem, *Aquila, Symmachus and Theodotion in Armenia*, SBLSCS 42 (Atlanta: Scholars Press, 1996).

[65] Howard, "Quinta of the Minor Prophets," 16.

[66] R. G. Jenkins, "Hexaplaric Marginalia and the Hexapla–Tetrapla Question," in *Origen's Hexapla and Fragments*, ed. Alison Salvesen, TSAJ 58 (Tübingen: Mohr Siebeck, 1998), 73–102, here 74.

Part II

JEWISH AND CHRISTIAN SCRIPTURES IN MODERN TRANSLATIONS

6

The Exodus in America

Ronald Hendel
University of California, Berkeley

As Leonard Greenspoon is wont to say, popular culture "relates, conflates, and updates Sacred Writ" in ways that are, by turns, wise, witty, or awful.[1] In this spirit, I wish to explore some variations on the theme of the Exodus in American culture, beginning with the Pilgrims and ending with Hollywood. Many of these Exodus variations reverberate in modern American culture—in literature, media, and scholarship showing how past cultural memories of the Exodus are related, updated, and conflated as we perennially renegotiate our American identity. The Exodus was a major theme in the birth of the nation, and Americans still draw on these Exodus memories in articulating our hopes and anxieties about the contemporary American dream.

I will address three extended episodes in the American reimagining of the Exodus: the concept of migration to America as a new Exodus, beginning with the Pilgrims' settlement to the Revolutionary War; the Exodus in African-American culture from slavery to the civil rights movement; and the Hollywood Exodus in the classic film *The Ten Commandments*, seen as a Cold War drama. This is a small selection, but it shows the long life of the Exodus story in American culture. The biblical narrative has a multiplicity of themes and nuances, and provides a broad palette for the articulation of varied and often contradictory meanings. Its multiple themes can be mobilized for causes both conservative and revolutionary by a dizzying array of speakers: Puritans and atheists, slaves and aristocrats, artists and merchants, preachers and politicians. It is the combination of traditional authority and thematic multivalence that makes the Exodus such a rich source for American self-fashioning from the Pilgrims to the present day.

The New Exodus: From Pilgrims to Revolution

The Mayflower Pilgrims and their Puritan compatriots saw in their migration to the New World a new Exodus, an escape from the corruption of Europe, and the birth of a new Israel across the sea. Since they were accustomed to reading the Old Testament typologically, they read their own journey as a new chapter of sacred history, a New Exodus. As the Puritan divine Richard Mather wrote, "so many things that literally concerned the Jewes were types and figures, signifying the like things concerning the people of God in these latter dayes."[2] The Pilgrims and other Puritan émigrés were, in their view, the community of saints, whom God would soon redeem in these latter days. In a 1629 pamphlet advocating Puritan migration to New England, John Winthrop invoked the Exodus as an analogy and foreshadowing of the new errand in the wilderness: "So He carried the Israelites into the wilderness and made them forgette the fleshpotts of Egipt."[3]

The Old World, in this Exodus typology, was not only a spiritually corrupt Egypt, ruled by papists and other sinful Christians, but was also on the verge of apocalyptic judgment. As Winthrop wrote to his wife in 1629, while still in England, "I am verily perswaded that God will bringe some heavye Affliction upon this lande, and that speedylye."[4] This combination of apocalypse and new Exodus was adumbrated in the book of Isaiah, and was a familiar theological notion. The Puritan separatists fashioned their sectarian identity by inserting themselves into this eschatological scenario as the righteous remnant on the verge of the end-time. As Avihu Zakai observes:

> In accordance with the Exodus type of religious migration, theirs was a migration based upon a flight from the impending divine judgments which would soon come upon England and the old corrupt European world; theirs was the flight of God's chosen remnant whom the Lord chose to save from the general conflagration.[5]

In his introduction to a sermon preached at Plymouth, New England, in 1621, Robert Cushman laid out the eschatological backdrop of the Pilgrims' "errand into the wilderness":

> And if it should please God to punish his people in the Christian countries of *Europe* (for their coldnesse, carnality, wanton abuse of the Gospel, contention, &c.) either by Turkish slavery, or by Popish tyrannie, which God forbid, yet if the time be come, or shall come (as who knoweth) when Satan shall be let loose, to cast out his flouds against them, *here* is a way opened for such as have wings to flie into this Wildernesse.[6]

The Pilgrim settlement was an eschatological Israel in the New World, for the Egypt of the Old World was to be blasted away for its sins. In Cushman's words, "I cannot thinke but that there is some judgement not farre off."[7]

But for the Pilgrims, the New Israel in Plymouth was not yet a paradise. It was a wilderness, filled with tests and travails, just as the Israelites had their travails in the wilderness. In the light of this difficult transition, William Bradford, a governor of Plymouth, composed a prayer of thanksgiving that conflated the wilderness travails with the Exodus deliverance:

> Ought not the children of these fathers rightly say: "Our faithers were Englishmen which came over this great ocean, and were ready to perish in this wilderness; but they cried unto the Lord, and he heard their voice, and looked on their adversitie, &c." Let them therefore praise the Lord.[8]

In this biblical pastiche, the first Pilgrims are at once the patriarchs and the Exodus generation, echoing the biblical verses, "my father was a perishing/wandering Aramean" (Deut 26:5–7), and "the Israelites were groaning. . . and God heard their cry" (Exod 2:23–25). The Pilgrim fathers—as they are still called—are the typological instantiations of the biblical ancestors, founding a new sacred polity in the wilderness of Canaan. As a consequence of this Puritan discourse, the Exodus typology became basic to the American self-image. As Melville later wrote, "Out of some past Egypt, we have come to this new Canaan."[9]

The Pilgrims and Puritans of New England used the biblical concept of the new Exodus as a connective paradigm, linking their experiences with the Bible's sacred history and eschatology.

However, the Puritans' sectarian intolerance (viz. expelling and occasionally executing nonconformists) limited their influence in the new colonies as immigrants with other motivations and backgrounds arrived. As one critic wrote, the New England Puritans were "Colluvies of wild Opinionists, swarmed into a remote wilderness to find elbow-roome for phanatick Doctrines and practices."[10] The Puritan divine Roger Williams, who was placed under arrest for his unorthodox views and escaped to Rhode Island, denounced the Exodus typology as spiritually arrogant. With biting sarcasm, he responds to a critic, "Doth he count the very Land of *England* literally *Babel*, and so consequently *Egypt* and *Sodom* (Rev 11:8) and the Land of new England *Judea, Canaan*?"[11] But the concept of the American Exodus was not easily dislodged.

A century later, the republican values of the Enlightenment were ascendant. The leaders of the American Revolution were mostly liberal Christians—a mix of deists, Episcopalians, and Presbyterians—and an atheist or two. But they knew their Bible well. They reinterpreted the Exodus in a way that suited their situation: as a call to resist tyranny and establish a free people.[12] As it was for the Pilgrims, England was Egypt, the house of bondage. But the kind of bondage was different: the slavery imposed by this Pharaoh, George III, consisted of unjust laws and taxes, imposed without colonial representation. This was not a prelude to apocalypse and divine deliverance, but a prelude to political revolution, a secular kind of apocalypse. In this new situation, the traditional Exodus themes were transposed into a political key.

So John Adams described the Boston Tea Party in 1773 as resistance to Egyptian slavery. To let the tea be unloaded, he writes, would mean "subjecting ourselves and our Posterity forever to Egyptian Taskmasters—to Burthens, Indignities, to Ignominy, Reproach and Contempt, to Desolation and Oppression, to Poverty and Servitude."[13] The offense of taxation without representation becomes a new kind of Egyptian slavery. The colonies, as the new Israel, must resist its Egyptian taskmasters, lest it accept the ignominy of poverty and servitude. These are powerful words, which reimagine the American Exodus in a novel way.

In his electrifying and influential pamphlet, *Common Sense* (1776), Thomas Paine castigated King George as "the hardened, sullen tempered Pharaoh of England," whom the colonists must disdain and reject.[14] By drawing on the Exodus and other biblical texts, Paine recast the Revolution as a biblically authorized battle against the tyranny of the English Pharaoh. This is a strategy laced with irony, since Paine was a notorious atheist. But he marshalled the Bible adroitly to advance his criticism of monarchy and his advocacy of a republic. He writes: "Monarchy is ranked in scripture as one of the sins of the Jews," whereas prior to the sinful ascent of kings "their form of government (except in extraordinary cases where the Almighty interposed) was a kind of republic, administered by a judge and the elders of the tribes. Kings they had none."[15] The biblical republic, based on the just laws of the covenant, is presented as a model and justification for an American republic. The rejection of Pharaoh entails a Hebrew/American republic, based on the will of God and the consent of the people (viz. a covenant). The United States would be "a kind of republic," just as Israel was in the era from Moses to Samuel.

On July 4, 1776, the Continental Congress appointed a committee to create a Great Seal for the newly declared republic. Its members were Benjamin Franklin, Thomas Jefferson, and John Adams. Franklin proposed a design that represented the new republic as a New Exodus:

> Moses standing on the Shore, and extending his Hand over the Sea, thereby causing the same to overwhelm Pharaoh who is sitting in an open Chariot, a Crown on his Head and a Sword in his hand. Rays from a Pillar of Fire in the Clouds reaching to Moses, to express that he acts by Command of the Deity. Motto, *Rebellion to Tyrants is Obedience to God*.[16]

The motto crystallizes the meaning of the Revolutionary Exodus, as obedience to God becomes a political duty, "rebellion to tyrants." Pharaoh is the face of tyranny. Jefferson liked the motto so much that he adopted it in his personal seal. For the Great Seal, Jefferson offered a different Exodus motif. As Adams reported, "Mr Jefferson proposed The Children of Israel in the Wilderness, led by a Cloud by day, and a Pillar of Fire by night."[17] Franklin's and Jefferson's Exodus designs were rejected by Congress, as was

Adams' design, which used Roman allegorical motifs. Many years later, an amalgam of Franklin's and Jefferson's design was published in *Harper's Monthly,* as shown in Figure 6.1.[18]

Figure 6.1: 1856 Great Seal of the United States

This design was perhaps too complicated or possibly too biblical. In 1783 Congress adopted a Great Seal design featuring a bald eagle, a simpler form of heraldry.[19]

The Exodus imagery of Franklin's and Jefferson's designs shows the power of the Exodus themes in their own understanding and promotion of the meaning of the American revolution. America was still the Israel of the New Exodus; yet, rather than a communion of Puritan saints, it was now a secular republic founded by political rebellion from tyranny. In the Revolutionary Exodus, God's law commands the natural rights of liberty and justice. The Exodus typology now transposes America's teleological role in sacred history into a justification of America's political constitution. This secularization of Exodus themes is linked to a new kind of civil religion, where God—who requires rebellion from tyranny and the creation of a republic—is non-denominational but still recognizably biblical. This is a God of republican virtues who is the divine agent of the American Exodus.

Let My People Go: The African-American Exodus

The great tragedy of the American republic was its lawful acceptance of slavery, whose denial of liberty and natural rights directly contradicted the ideals of the Revolution. This internal contradiction generated the radically different meanings of the Exodus narrative in African-American culture.[20] As Albert Raboteau writes:

> White Christians had represented their journey across the Atlantic to America as the exodus of a New Israel from the bondage of Egypt into the Promised Land of milk and honey. For black Christians, the imagery was reversed: the Middle Passage had brought them to Egypt land, where they suffered bondage under a new Pharaoh. White Christians saw themselves as the New Israel; slaves identified themselves as the Old. This is. . . one of the abiding and tragic ironies of our history: the nation's claim to be the New Israel was contradicted by the Old Israel still enslaved in her midst.[21]

African-American slaves naturally construed the typological meanings of the Exodus differently than white Americans. For slaves, America was Egypt, the house of bondage. The freedom from bondage in the Exodus typology meant either the release of death and ascent to heaven, or—increasingly with the rise of the abolition movement—political emancipation.

Maria Stewart, a free black abolitionist, used these Exodus themes in a speech in Boston in 1831:

> America, America, foul and indelible is thy stain!. . . . You may kill, tyrannize, and oppress as much as you choose, until our cry shall come up before the throne of God; for I am firmly persuaded that he will not suffer you to quell the proud, fearless and undaunted spirits of the Africans forever; for in his own time, he is able to plead our cause against you, and to pour out upon you the ten plagues of Egypt.[22]

The cry of the slaves rising up to God and the ten plagues powerfully evoke the Exodus in this indictment of America as sinful Egypt. By using the biblical language of Exodus, abolitionists were able to appeal to white Americans' religious values, and further, to their commitment to America as the new Israel in the Exodus paradigm. The idea that America was the new Egypt was a shocking claim, but, as the abolitionists pointed out, its logic was sound. The Exodus, as a discursive network of authoritative themes, provides an ethical orientation that entails the liberation of the slaves. To deny the slaves their freedom is to deny the efficacy and religious authority of biblical religion. This is the paradox, and the tragedy, of the American Exodus in antebellum white and African-American culture.

The liberationist meanings of the Exodus were obvious to the slaves. As a slave named Polly explained to her mistress, "We poor creatures have need to believe in God, for if God Almighty will not be good to us some day, why were we born? When I heard of his delivering his people from bondage, I know it means the poor Africans."[23]

Not surprisingly, the Exodus (along with the book of Revelation) was the central biblical canon in slave society. A white chaplain in the Union Army working among freed slaves complained about the slaves' fascination with the Exodus:

> There is no part of the Bible with which they are so familiar as the story of the deliverance of Israel. Moses is their ideal of all that is high, and noble, and perfect, in man. I think they have been accustomed to regard Christ not so much in the light of a spiritual Deliverer, as that of a second Moses who would eventually lead them out of their prison-house of bondage.[24]

The chaplain's disapproval stems from the different valences of the Exodus for whites and African-Americans. For whites, the American Exodus had already happened, and the future deliverance was primarily spiritual. For black slaves, deliverance entailed material and spiritual meanings—heaven, the Kingdom of God, and political emancipation were different dimensions of deliverance from "their prison-house of bondage." As Raboteau writes:

> Slaves prayed for the future day of deliverance to come, and they kept hope alive by incorporating as part of their mythic past the Old Testament exodus of Israel out of slavery. . . . The Christian slaves applied the Exodus story, whose end they knew, to their own experience of slavery, which had not ended.[25]

This painful longing for freedom, as articulated through Exodus themes, is most potent in the slave spirituals. Frederick Douglass recalled the impact of what he called the "sorrow songs": "Every tone was a testimony against slavery, and a prayer to God for deliverance from chains. . . . The songs of the slave represent the sorrows of his heart; and he is relieved by them, only as an aching heart is relieved by its tears."[26]

The spirituals were oral multiforms, with floating motifs continually recombined, as in the song, "Let God's Saints Come In." The first stanza is the chorus, and the refrain, "And let God's saints come in," repeats after each line in the verses:[27]

Come down angel and trouble the water,
Come down angel and trouble the water.
Come down angel and trouble the water,
And let God's saints come in.
Canaan land is the land for me,
Canaan land is the land for me,
There was a wicked man,
He kept them children in Egypt land.
God did say to Moses one day,
Say, Moses go to Egypt land.
And tell him to let my people go,
And Pharaoh would not let 'em go.

God did go to Moses' house,
And God did tell him who he was.
God and Moses walked and talked,
And God did show him who he was.

Notice that the content of the spiritual—featuring angels, saints, and biblical persons and events—would be unobjectionable to the ears of Christian slaveholders. It is an expression of pure biblical piety. However, since it was sung by slaves, it has what James Scott calls a "hidden transcript."[28] The multiple meanings of the African-American Exodus—including the subversive ones—were masked by using plain biblical language. These expressions were, on the surface, simply biblical hymns. The multivalence of the Exodus themes serves as a discursive camouflage, a way to avoid the suspicion of subversion. As W. E. B. DuBois observed, "Deception is the natural defence of the weak against the strong, and the South used it for many years against its conquerors."[29] By using the Exodus paradigm that was embraced by the dominant white culture, the slaves were able to mingle Christian piety with a deep-rooted desire for emancipation.

For slaves who were literally escaping from bondage (by the Underground Railroad or other means) this multivalence could serve as an effective code. As Frederick Douglass relates, when he and his fellow slaves planned their escape to the North, "A keen observer might have detected in our repeated singing of "O Canaan, sweet Canaan, I am bound for the land of Canaan," something more than a hope of reaching heaven. We meant to reach the *north*—and the north was our Canaan."[30]

Similarly, Harriet Tubman used the spiritual "Go Down Moses" to announce her presence to slaves hiding at the appointed spot for their northward flight to freedom. As her biographer and friend, Sarah Bradford, describes this scene:[31]

To make certain that it is their leader who is coming, she breaks out into the plaintive strains of the song, forbidden to her people in the South, but which she and her followers delight to sing together:

Oh go down, Moses,
Way down into Egypt's land,

Tell old Pharaoh,
Let my people go.
Oh Pharaoh said he would go cross,
Let my people go.
And don't get lost in de wilderness.
Let my people go.
. . . .
You may hinder me here, but you can't up dere,
Let my people go.
He sits in de Hebben and answers prayer,
Let my people go!

Bradford states that this song was "forbidden to her people in the South." Its barely veiled expression of the subversive, liberatory meanings of African-American Exodus had been perceived by the slaveholders.

"Go Down Moses" or "Let My People Go," in various versions, became well-known during the Civil War. The song was sung by escaped slaves ("contrabands") at Fort Monroe, Virginia and published by their Union chaplain in 1861.[32] At a celebration on the eve of emancipation (December 31, 1862), escaped slaves at a contraband camp in Washington DC sang this spiritual several times. According to former slave William Wells Brown, shortly after midnight, "A sister broke out in the following strain, which was heartily joined in by the vast assembly: Go down, Abraham | Away down in Dixie's land | Tell Jeff Davis | To let my people go."[33] This new version, which joyfully unpacked and updated the song's hidden transcript, circulated widely among the newly freed slaves.[34]

Booker T. Washington recalled his last days of slavery with a similar account of the exposure of hidden transcripts in the spirituals:

> As the great day [of emancipation] grew nearer, there was more singing in the slave quarters than usual. It was bolder, had more ring, and lasted later into the night. Most of the verses of the plantation songs had some reference to freedom. True, they had sung those same verses before, but they had been careful to explain that the "freedom" in these songs referred to the next world, and had no connection with life in this world. Now

> they gradually threw off the mask; and were not afraid to let it be known that the "freedom" in their songs meant freedom of the body in this world.[35]

Like the collapse of light-waves into particles, the Exodus typology collapsed into an explicit expression of political liberation at the time of emancipation, much as it did for the founders in the era of Revolution. The partial secularization of the Exodus into a paradigm of political transformation unites these two instantiations of the New Exodus in America. But they soon drew apart, again tragically, by the post-War imposition of Jim Crow laws, enforced segregation, and other innovations in institutional racism.

The themes of the African-American Exodus persisted in the liturgy and sermons of the black church. From this reservoir of affective and authoritative themes, Martin Luther King, Jr. developed his biblical eloquence in the cause of civil rights. As Gary Selby comments on King's use of Exodus themes:

> With a word or phrase—the "long night of captivity," the "wilderness," the "Promised Land"—King evoked the larger body of social knowledge that had been such a prominent part of African American cultural history. He thus treated his audience as insiders, with himself, to the cultural code, inviting them to supply the larger body of content and the appropriate emotional reaction, which, as the audience reaction. . . [to] his speeches demonstrates, they did gladly.[36]

At times King made use of the Exodus expansively. In a 1956 speech in Montgomery celebrating the Supreme Court decision banning bus segregation, he described this step as progress in the Exodus journey:

> We have been in Egypt long enough, and now we've gotten orders from headquarters. The Red Sea has opened for us, we have crossed the banks, we are moving now, and as we look back we see the Egyptian system of segregation drowned upon the seashore. We know that the Midianites are still ahead. We see the beckoning call of the evil forces of the Amorites.

> We see the Hittites all around us but, but we are going on because we've got to get to Canaan.[37]

More often, as Selby observes, King expressed his Exodus themes with a word or phrase, drawing on his audience's tacit knowledge of the biblical resonance. By inviting his audience to supplement his cues with their personal affirmations, rooted in the Exodus language of the black church, King effectively recruited African-Americans to the movement. Equally important, his carefully modulated Exodus language brought liberal whites—particularly liberal white clergy—into this inner group. He was inviting them to enter into a shared covenant of Exodus values to which they were already committed, even though it entailed a restructuring of the conventional themes of the American Exodus in white culture.

When he used Exodus language in his eloquent and resonant style, it seeded a receptive soil, as in his first speech during the Montgomery bus boycott:

> We who have been oppressed so long, are tired of going through the long night of captivity. And now we are reaching out for the daybreak of freedom and justice and equality. May I say to you, my friends, as I come to a close, that we must keep God in the forefront. . . . But I want to tell you this evening that it is not enough for us to talk about love. Love is one of the pivotal points of the Christian faith. There is another side called justice.[38]

Moses's justice and Christ's love come together in this exhortation, framed by Exodus themes. It is irresistible to any who are committed to the inner meanings of Exodus in its American incarnations. King's Exodus language was a key feature in appeal to all Americans, black and white.

In his last speech, on the eve of his assassination, King invoked Moses looking into the Promised Land from Mount Nebo (Deuteronomy 34). This was Moses's last act. By this point, King was viewed by many as a modern Moses. In his emotional testament, King said:

> I don't know what will happen now we've got some difficult days ahead. But it really doesn't matter with me now, because I've been to the mountaintop. And I don't mind. Like anybody, I would like to live a long life—longevity has its place. But I'm not concerned about that now. I just want to do God's will. And He's allowed me to go up to the mountain. And I've looked over, and I've seen the Promised Land. I may not get there with you. But I want you to know tonight that we, as a people, will get to the Promised Land.[39]

This speech is a synthesis of the African-American Exodus. It is a semi-secular prophecy from a modern-day Moses that America will fulfill its destiny as a new Promised Land. This promise combines the ideals of the Revolutionary Exodus—liberty, justice, and the defeat of tyranny—with the emancipatory ideals of the African-American Exodus. Notice the verbal combination of "we, as a people," echoing the Constitution's preamble, with the urgent journey and imminent arrival, "will get to the Promised Land."

This is a New Exodus that reconfigures the American dream. In its biblically-infused discourse, it brings to bear God's promises to the biblical ancestors and the eschatological promise of the Kingdom of God. This combination, sealed by King's martyrdom and his national holiday, is now a permanent part of American civil religion and cultural memory. Through his work and legacy, the different faces of the New Exodus in America have been brought together, incompletely but irreversibly.

Hollywood's Exodus and the Cold War

In the same year as King's 1956 Exodus speech, Cecil B. De Mille released his biblical epic, *The Ten Commandments*.[40] The movie opens with the director speaking to the audience, drawing a Cold War frame around the widescreen spectacle:

> The theme of this picture is whether men are to be ruled by God's law, or whether they are to be ruled by the whims of a dictator like Rameses. Are men the property of the state,

> or are they free souls under God? This same battle continues throughout the world today.

In De Mille's popular entertainment—spiced with sex, melodrama, and special effects—the theme is the battle between godless Communism and American freedom under God.[41] The Exodus is reconfigured as a Cold War drama.[42]

This explicit theme is doled out discreetly in the movie. De Mille was too accomplished a storyteller to do otherwise. He was an ardent anti-Communist during the 1950s, alongside his colleague Ronald Reagan and others. In an address to the Protestant Film Commission in 1949, he described his strategy: "Let the story itself carry the message. Do not put propaganda speeches into the dialogue. Convey the message through what the characters do."[43] The only explicit propaganda speech in *The Ten Commandments* is his own introduction, sparing the characters this burden. But there are many bits of dialogue and action that articulate this theme in the movie.

For instance, when Moses first tells Pharaoh to let his people go, the dialogue expresses the clash of ideologies between totalitarianism and democracy:

> Rameses: "The slaves are mine—their lives are mine—all that they have is mine. I do not know your God—neither will I let Israel go."
>
> Moses: "Who are you to make their lives bitter in hard bondage? Men shall be ruled by Law—not by the will of other men."

This dramatic exchange expresses clearly the Cold War theme. Moses stands for American political values in the fight against totalitarianism. This exchange recalls the wording of Ayn Rand's 1947 anti-communist pamphlet, *Screen Guide for Americans*: "The whole world is torn by a great political issue—Freedom or Slavery, which means Americanism or Totalitarianism."[44] This bit of dialogue makes the Cold War subtext clear: slavery equals Communism and freedom equals Americanism.

De Mille was a founder of The Motion Picture Alliance for the Preservation of American Values, the group that commissioned

Rand's "Screen Guide." De Mille was dedicated to fighting Communist influence in Hollywood and to promoting American values as he saw them. At a meeting of the executive committee of the MPA in 1953, he exhorted: "We have two missions—to fight subversion in our own industry and to make the pictures we produce effective carriers of the American ideals we are pledged to preserve."[45] *The Ten Commandments* was the most successful carrier of De Mille's American ideals.

But it was more than mere propaganda. The film is a Hollywood Exodus that unites conservative politics, semi-orthodox Protestant theology, and popular spectacle. *Time* magazine decried the movie as "almost a sort of Sexodus,"[46] but their criticism missed the point. When the beautiful Princess Nefretiri says to her rugged, bare-chested boyfriend, "Oh, Moses, Moses, you stubborn, splendid, adorable fool," we know how to respond. It is a soap opera and a love triangle overlaid on a biblical epic. It is irresistible eye-candy and filmmaking, which we know how to take both seriously and comically, like Shakespeare's groundlings.

The anti-Communist animus is focused on Rameses, played magnificently by Yul Brynner, whose Asiatic features (he was born in Russia) perfectly combine an Oriental Pharaoh with a USSR Premier. Rameses' father, Sethi, is a genial and principled man, who informs his son that he will appoint his successor on the basis of merit, not inheritance. By this standard, Moses is the rightful successor, not Rameses. This is an American success story, where success is earned by merit and hard work, not bloodline. It is not quite a democracy, but a meritocracy. Sethi is a liberal Pharaoh, not a tyrant.

Moses earns his success by two achievements, military victory and urban construction. Like a good Cold Warrior, Moses not only defeats Ethiopia, but he earns the conquered people's respect and gratitude. Moses is a biblical Eisenhower, a victorious liberator who creates new allies. The beautiful Ethiopian princess is clearly in love with Moses, but he does not seem to notice. Interestingly, Moses's victory over the black African nation gives rise to the possibility of miscegenation—all things seem to be possible in the land of liberty. But this possibility is not realized, for Moses is in love with Princess Nefretiri, Pharaoh's daughter. This is as close as De Mille's Exodus gets to the themes of the African-American Exodus, which would confuse and complicate his Cold War message.

Moses's successful construction of the city honoring Sethi is a decisive victory over Rameses, who was previously unable to build it. The Communist industrial system, based on slave labor and government control, is a failure. Moses succeeds by raiding the government storehouses, feeding the laborers, and providing them a day of rest (the Sabbath). By giving an honest wage for a day's work, he releases the workers' untapped capacity for labor and builds a great city. The climactic scene where he erects the great obelisk for Sethi, overruling the cautions of his master builder, marks Moses as a master architect—like the self-made genius architect in Ayn Rand's novel, *The Fountainhead* (1943), a paean to American free-market values. Moses, the great industrialist and beloved conqueror, is the epitome of the successful self-made man, whose courage, hard work, and intelligence enable him to rise to the top. Moses is a fusion of Eisenhower and Howard Roark (Ayn Rand's fictional hero), and Moses will soon become a biblical savior. He is the natural leader in the inevitable victory over Pharaonic tyranny.

While at his height, the Pharaoh Rameses offers a striking critique of Egyptian religion: "What gods? You prophets and priests made the gods that you may prey upon the fears of men." This Marxist critique activates the Cold War frame and exposes Pharaoh as a Communist atheist. However, after he witnesses the miraculous destruction of his army, Rameses ruefully admits, "His God *is* God." These are Rameses' last words. His system has failed, and he has a final moment of religious clarity. In this Cold War drama, Rameses' moment of truth grants the inevitable victory of biblical/American way. The same year as *The Ten Commandments*, the U.S. adopted "In God We Trust" as the national motto. Rameses' brief moment of true religion affirms the triumph of America's trust in God over the godless scourge of Communism. As De Mille stated, the film was "a means of welding together all faiths against the common enemy of all faiths, atheistic Communism."[47]

At the movie's end, Moses's last words, spoken from Mount Nebo on the threshold of the Promised Land, underscore this victory. His command is a slight revision of the biblical verse (Lev 25:10) inscribed on the Liberty Bell. He says, "Go: proclaim liberty throughout all the lands, unto all the inhabitants thereof." In these closing words, the Cold War frame reappears: the liberty achieved by the slaves is an American liberty, echoing the themes of the Revolutionary Exodus. This is emphasized in the 1956 souvenir program for the movie, which has an illustration of Charlton Heston as Moses standing before the Liberty Bell with its inscription legible.[48] However, Moses's words make a small change to the biblical verse. Whereas Leviticus and the Liberty Bell read "land" in the singular, Moses now says "lands."[49] The revision is subtle, but has a clear message. Liberty belongs not to one land, but to all lands. It is incumbent on Moses's New Israel to spread liberty to all the peoples of the world, particularly to those under tyranny. The triumph of American liberty *and* the imperative to expand its global reach are expressed by Moses's last words. It is a resonant final chord in a Cold War drama.

Compared to the real dramas of the Pilgrim Exodus, the Revolutionary Exodus, and the African-American Exodus, the fictional Cold War drama of the Hollywood Exodus may seem contrived. As Cold War propaganda, it has not worn well. But as epic melodrama and visual spectacle, it remains a classic. It is, in a sense, a simulacrum of the Exodus, in which Moses's and Pharaoh's rippling muscles and Nefretiri's Oriental sensuality feature as much as biblical miracles and Cold War subtexts.[50]

De Mille's claim in the movie's introduction that everything in the movie has been scrupulously drawn from historical sources is laughably false. And yet the film remains a basic substrate for American biblical religions, particular of the fundamentalist kind. The evangelist Billy Graham praised De Mille as "a prophet in celluloid who has had the privilege of bringing some of the Word of God to more people throughout the world than any other man."[51] The American Exodus, as a Cold War drama, remains a religious touchstone.

The effects of the movie's ideology still resonate in modern American politics. There has been a decades-long controversy over the constitutionality of the public display of monuments of the Ten Commandments. These monuments originated in the publicity campaign for the movie, when De Mille teamed with the Fraternal Order of Eagles to place some two hundred granite monuments of the Ten Commandments across the country, usually in public places. In 2005 the Supreme Court narrowly affirmed the legality of one of them, at the Texas State Capitol, by a 5-4 vote.[52] Similar cases are under adjudication. The American Exodus, in its Cold War version, is still raising questions about the relationship of the Bible to American civil religion and constitutional law. The Revolutionary Exodus's separation of church and state is blurred by the legacy of the Cold War Exodus.

Conclusions

Each of these extended episodes in the life of the Exodus in America was complicated by the others, and each resounds in American life. The Pilgrim Exodus—with its emphasis on the immigrants as God's chosen people initiating a new era in sacred history—is embraced by the Christian right. The Revolutionary Exodus—with its focus on liberty, natural rights, and secular governance—revised and secularized the Pilgrim vision. The African-American Exodus powerfully criticized the dominant American Exodus narrative, thereby effecting significant change. The election of Barack Obama was a signpost in this evolutionary spiral of American Exoduses. In his words, President Obama belongs to the "Joshua generation," charged with fulfilling the work of Martin Luther King and the civil rights movement, who were the "Moses generation."[53] The language and themes of the Exodus narrative continue to resonate in our culture.

There are other complications, however. For Native Americans, the America Exodus narrative is stained by genocide. As Robert Allen Warrior, a member of the Osage nation, observes, "those parts of the story that describe Yahweh's command to mercilessly annihilate the indigenous population" have been used to justify the annihilation of America's indigenous people.[54] He rightly cites Walter Benjamin's adage, "There is no document of civilization which is not at the same time a document of barbarism."[55] The American Exodus traditionally addressed the Native Americans as Canaanites, a heathen people to be destroyed, their remnants assimilated. African-Americans, women, and other marginalized groups can and have been included in an evolving American Exodus narrative, but for Native Americans the narrative is irredeemable. Warrior asks,

"With what voice will we, the Canaanites of the world, say 'Let my people go and leave my people alone?'"[56] And yet here, by his pointed mimicry of the Exodus, the narrative provides a medium for a powerful critique.

Another group, to which I turn last, has a distinctive claim on the Exodus in America—the Jews. For many Jewish immigrants in the nineteenth and twentieth centuries, America was the Promised Land in a biblical and existential sense. The Old World was a land of persecution, pogroms, and, at times, genocide. For these wander-

Figure 6.2: Emile Pissis, *Moses Presenting the Ten Commandments to the Children of Israel at Yosemite*, stained glass, 1905.

ing Jews, America was the land of liberty and opportunity, where anti-Semitism was generally mild and sometimes nonexistent. This was particularly true in the American West, where new communities were more egalitarian than the older Eastern cities, dominated by hierarchical Protestant elites.

The early Jewish community in San Francisco is a notable example. Jacob Voorsanger, a prominent local rabbi and the first Professor of Semitic Languages and Literatures at the University of California in Berkeley (chair established in 1894), described California to his colleagues in the Reform movement in lush Exodus language: "This dear California is a gorgeous edition *de luxe* of Palestine of old of which the Midrash says with effusive tenderness that every spot in it has its hills and dales. Our holy land, our promised land is this golden spot."[57]

This view of California as the Promised Land is strikingly illustrated by a stained glass window commissioned in 1905 by Congregation Sherith Israel for its new building in San Francisco; see Figure 6.2. In the center, Moses is giving the Ten Commandments to the tribes of Israel, each holding its flag. But the locale is not Mount Sinai. Rising behind Moses are the recognizable silhouettes of Half Dome and El Capitan. Moses and the children of Israel are in the Yosemite Valley, with its famous peaks as the New Sinai. The Exodus journey has brought the Jews to the Promised Land in northern California. In this Jewish version of the American Exodus, the ages-long burden of Pharaonic oppression has finally been lifted, and Moses gives the Law anew in the splendor of the High Sierra. This updating of the Exodus celebrates the new birth of freedom that Jews experienced in the American West. It is a compelling image of the alchemy of cultural memory, as it reconfigures the Exodus narrative to illuminate the present.

Notes

[1] Leonard J. Greenspoon, *The Bible in the News: How the Popular Press Relates, Conflates and Updates Sacred Writ* (Washington, DC: Biblical Archaeology Society, 2012).

[2] Richard Mather, *An Apologie of the Churches in New-England for Church-Covenant* (London: Allen, 1643), 2; quoted in Sacvan Bercovitch, *The American Jeremiad*, 2nd ed. (Madison: University of Wisconsin Press, 2012), 46.

[3]John Winthrop, "Reasons to be Considered, and Objections with Answers" (1629), quoted in Avihu Zakai, *Exile and Kingdom: History and Apocalypse in the Puritan Migration to America* (Cambridge: Cambridge University Press, 1985), 65.

[4]John Winthrop, "John Winthrop to his Wife" (1529), quoted in Zakai, *Exile*, 132–33.

[5]Zakai, *Exile*, 123.

[6]Robert Cushman, *A Sermon Preached at Plimmoth in New-England* (London: Bellamie, 1622), 2; quoted in Zakai, *Exile*, 124.

[7]Cushman, *Sermon*, quoted in Zakai, *Exile*, 124.

[8]William Bradford, *History of Plymouth Colony* (1680), in *Chronicles of the Pilgrim Fathers of the Colony of Plymouth, From 1602 to 1625*, ed. Alexander Young (Boston: Little and Brown, 1841), 107.

[9]Herman Melville, *Pierre; or The Ambiguities* (New York: Harper, 1852), 42.

[10]Nathaniel Ward, *The Simple Cobler of Aggawam in America* (1647); ed. R. M. Zall (Lincoln: University of Nebraska Press, 1969), 6; quoted in Bercovitch, *Jeremiad*, 40.

[11]Roger Williams, *Mr. Cotton's Letter Lately Printed, Examined, and Answered* (London, 1644), 26; quoted in Bercovitch, *Jeremiad*, 41.

[12]Eran Shalev, *American Zion: The Old Testament as a Political Text from the Revolution to the Civil War* (New Haven: Yale University Press, 2013), 15–49.

[13]John Adams, diary, December 17, 1772; quoted in John Coffey, *Exodus and Liberation: Deliverance Politics from John Calvin to Martin Luther King Jr.* (New York: Oxford University Press, 2014), 67.

[14]Thomas Paine, *Common Sense* (Philadelphia, 1776), 25; quoted in Coffey, *Exodus*, 68.

[15]Paine, *Common Sense*, 11.

[16]Benjamin Franklin, "Proposal for the Great Seal of the United States," ca. August 14, 1776, in *The Papers of Benjamin Franklin: Digital Edition* (Yale University). Online: http://franklinpapers.org/franklin/framedVolumes.jsp?vol=22&page = 562b.

[17]John Adams, letter to Abigail Adams, August 14, 1776, in *Adams Family Papers: An Electronic Archive* (Massachusetts Historical Society). Online: http://www.masshist.org/digitaladams/archive/doc?id=L17760814ja.

[18]Benson John Lossing, "The Great Seal of the United States," *Harper's New Monthly Magazine* 13 (June 1856), 180. Online image: commons.wikimedia.org/wiki/File:FirstCommitteeGreatSealReverseLossingDrawing.jpg.

[19]In 1784 Franklin (letter to Sarah Bache, January 26, 1784, in *Papers*) wryly commented in a letter to his daughter, "I wish the Bald Eagle had not been chosen as the Representative of our Country. He is a Bird of bad moral Character." Online: http://franklinpapers.org/franklin/framedVolumes.jsp?vol=41&page= 281.

[20]See Albert J. Raboteau, "African-Americans, Exodus, and the American Israel," in *African-American Christianity: Essays in History*, ed. P. E. Johnson (Berkeley: University of California Press, 1994), 1–17; Allen Dwight Callahan, *The Talking Book: African Americans and the Bible* (New Haven: Yale University Press, 2006), 83–137.

[21]Raboteau, "Exodus," 9.

[22]Maria W. Stewart, "Religion and the Pure Principles of Morality" (1831), in *Maria W. Stewart, America's First Black Woman Political Writer: Essays and Speeches*, ed. Marilyn Richardson (Bloomington: Indiana University Press, 1987), 39–40; quoted in Raboteau, "Exodus," 12.

[23]Raboteau, "Exodus," 13.

[24]Raboteau, "Exodus," 13.

[25]Albert J. Raboteau, *Slave Religion: The "Invisible Institution" in the Antebellum South*, 2nd ed. (New York: Oxford University Press, 2004), 311.

[26]Frederick Douglass, *Narrative of the Life of Frederick Douglass, an American Slave*, 3rd ed. (Wortley: Barker, 1846), 14–15.

[27]William Francis Allen, Charles Pickard Ware, and Lucy McKim Garrison, eds., *Slave Songs of the United States* (New York: Simpson, 1867), 76.

[28]James C. Scott, *Domination and the Arts of Resistance: Hidden Transcripts* (New Haven: Yale University Press, 1990), 18–19: "hidden transcripts" enact a "subordinate group politics. . . of disguise and anonymity that takes place in public view but is designed to have a double meaning or to shield the identity of the actors."

[29]W. E. B. DuBois, "Of the Faith of the Fathers," in *The Souls of Black Folk: Essays and Sketches* (Chicago: McClurg, 1903), 204.

[30]Frederick Douglass, *My Bondage and My Freedom* (New York: Miller, Orton & Mulligan, 1855), 278; quoted in Raboteau, *Slave Religion*, 247.

[31]Sarah H. Bradford, *Harriet Tubman: The Moses of Her People* (New York: Lockwood, 1886), 37–38.

[32]Dena J. Epstein, *Sinful Tunes and Spirituals: Black Folk Music to the Civil War*, 2nd ed. (Urbana: University of Illinois Press, 2003), 243–50.

[33]William Wells Brown, *The Negro in the American Rebellion: His Heroism and his Fidelity* (Boston: Lee & Shepard, 1867), 111, 118; quoted in Eileen Southern, *The Music of Black Americans: A History*, 3rd ed. (New York: Norton, 1997), 215.

[34]Raboteau, *Slave Religion*, 249.

[35]Booker T. Washington, *Up From Slavery: An Autobiography* (Garden City, NY: Doubleday, 1901), 19–20; quoted in Raboteau, *Slave Religion*, 249.

[36]Gary S. Selby, *Martin Luther King and the Rhetoric of Freedom: The Exodus Narrative in America's Struggle for Civil Rights* (Waco: Baylor University Press, 2008), 122.

[37]Address to the Montgomery Improvement Association, November 14, 1956, in *The Papers of Martin Luther King, Jr. Vol. 3: Birth of a New Age, December 1955–December 1956*, ed. C. Carson et al. (Berkeley: University of California Press, 1997), 433; quoted in Selby, *King*, 80.

[38]Address to the MIA, December 5, 1955, in *Papers*, 3:73; quoted in Selby, *King*, 76.

[39]King, "I've Been to the Mountaintop," Memphis, April 3, 1968, in *Martin Luther King Online Encyclopedia* (Stanford University): http://kingencyclopedia.stanford.edu/encyclopedia/documentsentry/ive_been_to_the_mountaintop/; see Selby, *King*, 165–66.

[40]*The Ten Commandments* (Hollywood, CA: Paramount Pictures, 1956), script by A. MacKenzie, J. L. Lasky, Jr., J. Gariss, and F. M. Frank.

[41]The phrase "under God" was added to the Pledge of Allegiance in 1954; Eisenhower described this law as a means to "strengthen those spiritual weapons which forever will be our country's most powerful resource, in peace or war"; see T. Jeremy Gunn, *Spiritual Weapons: The Cold War and the Forging of an American National Religion* (Westport, CT: Praeger, 2009), 2.

[42]See Tony Shaw, *Hollywood's Cold War* (Edinburgh: Edinburgh University Press, 2007), 103–34; Alan Nadel, *Containment Culture: American Narratives, Postmodernism, and the Atomic Age* (Durham, NC: Duke University Press, 1995), 90–116; Melanie J. Wright, *Moses in America: The Cultural Uses of Biblical Narrative* (New York: Oxford University Press, 2003), 89–127; and Sumiko Higashi, "Antimodernism as Historical Representation in a Consumer Culture: Cecil B. DeMille's *The Ten Commandments*, 1923, 1956, 1993," in *The Persistence of History: Cinema, Television, and the Modern Event*, ed. Vivian Sobchack (London: Routledge, 1996), 91–112.

[43]Shaw, *Hollywood*, 118–19.

[44]Ayn Rand, "Screen Guide for Americans" (Beverly Hills, CA: The Motion Picture Alliance for the Preservation of American Ideals, 1947), 2; quoted in Shaw, *Hollywood*, 103.

[45]Shaw, *Hollywood*, 115.

[46]*Time* vol. 68 no. 20 (November 12, 1956), 123; see also "perhaps the most vulgar movie ever made" (p. 122).

[47]Shaw, *Hollywood*, 116.

[48]Higashi, "Antimodernism," 102.

[49]The plural "lands" is in the script.

[50]See Ilana Pardes, "Moses Goes Down to Hollywood: Miracles and Special Effects," *Semeia* 74 (1996): 15–31.

[51]Shaw, *Hollywood*, 114.

[52]*Van Orden v. Perry* (2005); Judge Breyer's deciding opinion called this "a borderline case," but affirmed the secular purpose of the monument since "the State intended the display's moral message—an illustrative message reflecting the historical 'ideals' of Texans—to predominate." (*Van Orden v. Perry*, 702; quoted in Ann Althouse, "Let's Take a Look at that 10 Commandments Monument." Online: http://althouse.blogspot.com/2007/04/lets-take-look-at-that-10-commandments.html.

[53]See David Remnick, "The Joshua Generation: Race and the Campaign of Barack Obama," *The New Yorker*, November 17, 2008. Online: http://www.newyorker.com/magazine/2008/11/17/the-joshua-generation.

[54]Robert Allen Warrior, "Canaanites, Cowboys, and Indians: Deliverance, Conquest, and Liberation Theology Today," *Christianity and Crisis* 49 (1989): 262.

[55]Walter Benjamin, "Theses on the Philosophy of History," in *Illuminations: Essays and Reflections*, ed. Hannah Arendt (New York: Schocken, 1968), 256.

[56]Warrior, "Canaanites," 264.

[57]Jacob Voorsanger, letter, July 10, 1896; quoted in Fred Rosenbaum, *Cosmopolitans: A Social and Cultural History of the Jews of the San Francisco Bay Area* (Berkeley: University of California Press, 2009), 105.

7

Challenges in Translating the Book of Job

Edward L. Greenstein
Bar-Ilan University

I have been occupied for several years in producing a new translation of the Book of Job. I have been engaged in translation theory,[1] and—to a limited extent—I have engaged in Hebrew Bible translation,[2] so it behooves me to reflect on what I have been trying to do as well as the challenges I have been trying to meet in this endeavor. Translation from source-text to target-text is always a challenge. It is impossible to achieve in an ideal fashion, but is nevertheless performed by many people all the time.

One of the earliest translations of the book of Job was into Aramaic in the first century BCE (11QtgJob), but that translation—as much as any other—makes one keenly aware of what is lost in translation.[3] That Aramaic version of Job not only misses or guesses at many of the senses of the Hebrew, but the Aramaic also sometimes flattens the parallelism of its poetry into prose sentences. Consider the following example (col. 31:2–4 = MT Job 38:25–26): "Who has appointed a time for the rain and a way for the light clouds | To bring (them) down upon the land of the unpopulated wilderness."[4] The Hebrew verb פלג (*piel*), "to split (into rivulets)," is replaced by the banal "to put" (שוי; here rendered "appointed"). The Hebrew word תעלה, "channel," is apparently misread as two words עת לה, "time for it."[5] The poetic term שטף, "flood, downpour,"[6] is rendered by the commonplace מטר, "rain." The rare word חזיז, "thunder-bolt, lightning-flash,"[7] is translated "clouds" (עננין). And the familiar Hebrew term for "thunder," קול (in the plural: קלות) is mistakenly derived from the adjective קל, "lightweight." Of course, the repeated sounds in the Hebrew of the first line, mainly *l*, are not duplicated in the Aramaic translation. In the first verse, at least the parallelism between the two lines of the couplet is preserved. Not so, however, in the second verse. There the doubling of the parallel phrases in the Hebrew—"land of no person" (ארץ לא איש), "desert with no human in it" (מדבר לא אדם בו)—is reduced to a single expression, thereby demolishing the poetic parallelism.

It is indeed difficult, if not impossible, to render poetry from one language into poetry in another. As the American poet Robert Frost has famously said, poetry is precisely what is lost in translation. The process of translation is well reflected in the Latin etymology of the term: "to carry across." Knowing that one can only transfer some elements of a source to the target, a translator needs to decide, either in general or on a case by case regimen, what aspects of a source can and will be conveyed and which ones will inevitably be relinquished. How much of the semantic sense, how much of the form, how many of the affective aspects of a text will be conveyed? Poetry arouses sentiments, perceptions, conceptions, images, associations, and allusions through unique expressions in language. Such a constellation can hardly be conveyed by any other than the original configuration of language—much less the conversion of one set of linguistic forms into another. As shown above, the Aramaic translator of Job sometimes abandoned even the most fundamental rubric of ancient verse, namely its structuration as couplets (or triplets) in parallelism.

Translation Theory vis-à-vis the Book of Job

Even the most sophisticated of translators—and, since the Renaissance, good translators have honed their skills to a remarkable degree—must make a basic decision before setting out to translate. They must choose, as the German Romantic theorist Friedrich Schleiermacher put it, whether to bring the audience to the text or bring the text to the audience.[8] In the author- or text-oriented approach, the translator must somehow confront the audience with the strangeness of the language, anthropology, and world-view of the source.[9] In the contemporizing or audience-oriented approach, the translator must transform the source into an idiom and conceptual framework that will resonate with the readership.[10] In bringing the audience to the source, there is a likelihood of losing comprehension. In bringing the text to the audience, there is a likelihood of losing the sense and/or its impact. The text-oriented approach tends toward a literal method (sometimes word-for-word), and such translators may regard the idiomatic approach as sleight of hand. Conversely, the audience-oriented approach tends toward a conversion of foreign expression to local idiom and, in the most extreme instances, to the replacement of one poem by another that is meant to produce similar sentiments and effects in the reader; these translators may regard the literalists as missing the whole point of translation, namely to perform a carryover. Ancient, premodern, and early modern Bible translations favor a more text-oriented approach, while most relatively recent translations favor a moderate version of the audience-oriented approach.

Returning to the metaphor (itself a term indicating translation) of translation as a conveyance from text to target, these two translational tendencies fall along a spectrum. At one end is hyper-literalism, such that the translation is almost mechanically word-for-word with little regard for intelligibility; the other end is hyper-idiomatic, such that the source text is barely recognizable in the translation. Nearly all translations, especially those of the Bible, fall somewhere in the middle range of the spectrum—some favoring the literal, others favoring the idiomatic.

The Book of Job presents the translator, who is highly challenged in the best of circumstances, with a number of special challenges. None is unique, but in their convergence they present a challenge of an unusual order. First, the Book of Job is "a drama of words," in which the rhetoric is more than a means—it is in some important respects the medium itself; and the medium is the message.[11] How can the effects of a particular arrangement of words—with their particular sounds, rhythms, and nuances—be reproduced? Second, the Book of Job is full of tropes, whereby particular forms and features are interwoven in unique fashions.[12] One can hardly reproduce the full complement of tropes in translation. Third, the language of Job is dense and peculiar in a variety of ways. It is highly poetic and often archaic, making frequent use of foreign vocabulary and forms.[13] It is inventive in usage and in producing new words; it is sui generis and often polysemous.[14] It is often figurative, and sometimes vacillates between the literal and figurative sides of a metaphor.[15] It is richly intertextual and allusive, both within the work itself and within the Hebrew literary tradition to which it belongs.[16]

Fourth, it is evident that the Book of Job has suffered some damage in its textual transmission.[17] There are errors in copying, on the level of the letter and the word, as well as apparent accidents of misplacement, on the level of certain verses, passages, and even chapter-length texts. Although these are concentrated in the center of the book, there are displacements of a limited number and on a more modest scale elsewhere in the book.[18] Ariel and Chana Bloch compare their translation of the Song of Songs to the cleaning of the breathtaking painting by Michelangelo on the ceiling of the Sistine Chapel.[19] They understand their mission not only to translate the received Hebrew text but to restore the text in the course of translating it. I also see my project of translating Job as restorative. However, the textual state of the Book of Job is, at least in places, not like that of the Sistine Chapel ceiling—an intact work the colors and details of which are obscured by centuries of fading and accumulated dirt. With regard to Job, it is as though the plaster had fallen down in places and had been re-set in an erroneous secondary arrangement. Restoring the text of Job to a more original state is no more difficult than divining the meaning of difficult words and phrases; yet the effort is still a challenge, not least because there is no other ancient text of Job to compare to it. (The various ancient translations and manuscripts of parts of Job are centuries later and often at a loss in grasping the sense of the text.[20])

Fifth, as just suggested, the sometimes dubious text of Job together with the difficulties of its peculiar language and linguistic usages pose a substantial philological challenge. It is clear to any competent Hebraist and Semitist that much of what has passed for translation of Job has little or no basis; translations follow a convention that has not undergone sufficient critical scrutiny. It is sometimes sheer guesswork, with little or no effort spent on seeking a more convincing understanding of a word or a point. A responsible translation of Job must, to my mind, make patient and scrupulous use of the linguistic and textual resources that are available at this time; must take stock of the full gamut of expressions, motifs, figures, and arguments within the Book of Job; and must take stock of the full inventory of language and literary expression that one finds in the ancient Near East in general and within the Hebrew scriptures in particular.[21] Most if not all of the philological interpretations and reconstructions can be supported by sources and parallels within the known linguistic and textual inventories of the Bible and of ancient and classical Near Eastern literature. As I will show below, the number of intertextual connections that have been missed, even within the Book of Job, is remarkable.

Finally, there is a sixth challenge that confronts the translator—like all other interpreters—of Job. The author, the poet, does not just treat a sore subject—the theological conundrum of innocent suffering in a world believed to be governed by a just deity—in an unconventional manner, namely by questioning the deity's justice. The poet also flouts conventional forms of conception and expression in his images and linguistic idiom. His thinking and writing are "out of the box," and few readers, commentators, and translators have followed the unanticipated directions the poet has taken. Instead, some have made the source of Job conform, thereby distorting its plain sense in order to produce a more palatable or familiar one.[22]

Case Studies in Translating the Book of Job

Translations of Job 3:10 (כי לא סגר דלתי בטני ויסתר עמל מעיני) blatantly distort the plain sense of the text. Job curses the night he was conceived because that night, here personified, did not shut the "doors" of his (yes, his) womb and prevent him from seeing the light, that is, the experiences of life, which Job now regards as full of pain and anguish.[23] In this monologue, Job parodies Jeremiah's characterization of his birth as "accursed" (Jer 20:14–18). Whereas Jeremiah had mentioned the persons involved in his birth (his mother, his father, and the messenger who informed his father of his birth), Job excludes everyone. That is, Job refers to his mother only as "breasts" for suckling and his father only as "knees" for receiving him (Job 3:12), and Job personifies the messenger as the "night" he was conceived (3:3).[24] Job expresses the loneliness he feels by focusing on himself alone.[25] Accordingly, he pictures himself in the womb, in which he experiences only himself in a closed space, and speaks only of his own womb—"my womb."

Most translators fail to comprehend Job's point of view and its corresponding rhetoric and so transform the womb into his mother's. Compare the examples presented in Table 7.1.[26]

JPS *Tanakh*	Because it did not block my mother's womb, And hide trouble from my eyes.
NRSV	Because it did not shut the doors of my mother's womb, And hide trouble from my eyes.
Robert Alter	For it did not shut the belly's doors To hide wretchedness from my eyes. [Alter comments on *belly*, "An ellipsis for 'my mother's belly.'"]

Table 7.1: Translations of Job 3:10

Good and Scheindlin render "the belly," also avoiding the Hebrew's "my belly/womb."[27] This example, which goes back to the King James Version and beyond,[28] demonstrates the failure of translators to comprehend the peculiar conceptions that characterize much of Job's poem. Translators reveal their proclivity to present the text in more familiar terms, thereby blunting its edge. My perspective is instead influenced by the project of Martin Buber and Franz Rosenzweig, their Anglophone disciple Everett Fox, and the well-known essay of Walter Benjamin. In this view, one of the purposes of translation is to make strange the work at hand by sharpening its difference from what is familiar to the audience, thereby stimulating its imagination and broadening the horizons of linguistic expressibility.[29]

The reader may suspect that this example is an accident of misunderstanding, but it is not. The character Job's reference to the womb in which he gestated as his own is key to interpreting a similar reference of his in a later discourse. In chapter 19, Job laments that his family and servants have distanced themselves from him because they interpret his affliction as a stigma of divine displeasure. In that vein, Job complains that his breath repulses his wife and that his smell (reading וצחנתי, "my stench")[30] repulses "the sons of my womb" (רוחי זרה לאשתי וחנתי לבני בטני; v. 17). Predictably, translators assume (as have many commentators and lexicographers),[31] that these must be Job's children, the fruit of his loins. After all, the phrase בן בטן in Hebrew (Isa 49:15) and בר בטן in Aramaic (Prov 31:2; Proverbs of Aḥīqar 139) indicate a "son."[32] Compare the translations presented in Table 7.2:[33]

New JPS	My odor is repulsive to my wife; | I am loathsome to my children.
NRSV	My breath is repulsive to my wife; | I am loathsome to my own family.
Robert Alter	My breath became strange to my wife; | I repelled my very own children.

Table 7.2: Translations of Job 19:17

These, and other, translations not only misinterpret the phrase but they also turn to paraphrase, so that the reader learns nothing of the striking expression "my womb," which reappears in the Hebrew. "Sons (or children) of my womb" is reduced to "my children," etc.

This rendering should have given pause because it creates a factual contradiction between Job's speech and the book's opening narrative, according to which Job had ten children who were all killed (1:19). E. M. Good asks, "Has (Job) forgotten that they are dead?" He continues, "Does the convention of the lament require reference to them regardless of the facts? I know of no way to decide between those alternatives, and I can think of no third."[34] There is a third possibility, however, if readers, interpreters, and translators can grasp the somewhat idiosyncratic use of language in Job. The speaker establishes a peculiar way of seeing, such that the womb from which he was born is *his*. Accordingly, for Job the "children of *my* womb" are his siblings, who gestated in that same place. Those siblings are referenced more conventionally in Job 19:13, "My brothers (relatives) He has kept distant from me"—and more idiosyncratically in verse 17: "My breath is foul to my wife; | And my odor to the sons of my womb (i.e., my siblings)."[35] The poet gives his characters a good deal of linguistic flexibility, enabling them thereby to produce and manipulate unorthodox expressions.

In Job 4:3–5, Eliphaz is the first of Job's companions to respond. Eliphaz seeks to calm his friend by reminding him that others have suffered trauma and that Job was the one who tried to comfort them. A typical translation is that of the JPS *Tanakh*, as shown in Table 7.3.

(3) See, you have encouraged many; You have strengthened failing hands.	הנה יסרת רבים וידים רפות תחזק
(4) Your words have kept him who stumbled from falling; You have braced knees that gave way.	כושל יקימון מליך וברכים כרעות תאמץ
(5) But now that it overtakes you, it is too much; It reaches you, and you are unnerved.	כי עתה תבוא אליך ותלא תגע עדיך ותבהל

Table 7.3: Job 4:3–5

The first four lines describe Job's acts of assistance toward those enfeebled by tragedy. The second, third, and fourth lines each describe Job's beneficence in starkly physical terms—strengthening hands, holding up the stumbling, stiffening buckling knees. The first line, "You have encouraged many," although philologically sound, is poetically limp, lacking in a physical reference.

The poet behind Job thrives on odd usage and polysemy, and he makes regular use of phrases found in earlier Hebrew poetry—for example, the prophets Isaiah, Jeremiah, Hosea, and Amos. Attention to these references can produce a more vivid understanding of the language.[36] Eliphaz's advice to Job draws directly on a verse in Isaiah (35:3), which the JPS *Tanakh* renders: "Strengthen the hands that are slack; | Make firm the tottering knees" (חזקו ידים רפות וברכים כשלות אמצו). These phrases resound in the second and fourth lines of the passage in Job 4. The verb featured in the first line in the desired sense of "fortifying" (*piel* יסר) is found in Hos 7:15a, which the JPS *Tanakh* renders, "I braced, I strengthened their arms" (ואני יסרתי חזקתי זרועתם).[37] Thus, we have the following sense for the first line: "You have fortified many."

Moreover, the word for "many," רַבִּים, can with a small change in its vocalization be read רָבִים, "those who shudder." Although this verb is best known from its Akkadian cognate *rābu*, it has been long recognized that the poet behind Job enriches his language by drawing from Babylonian.[38] This particular verb has long been identified in Job 33:19, "He is reproved by pains on his bed, | And the trembling in his bones is constant" (JPS *Tanakh;* והוכח במכאוב על-משכבו [וריב] ורוֹב עצמיו אתן). The same verb may be found in Job 4:14 as well (פחד קראני ורעדה ורב עצמותי הפחיד). The JPS *Tanakh* reflects its understanding of the verbal noun רב, "trembling," in its somewhat loose translation of the verse: "Fear and trembling came upon me, | Causing all my bones to quake with fright." The JPS seems to render רב doubly as both "all (my bones)" and "quake."

At this point, it helps to realize that the poet is adapting another "biblical" expression, in this case from Jeremiah (23:9).[39] There the prophet describes his trembling as, "All my bones shuddered" (רחפו כל-עצמותי). Here the verb "shudder" is predicated of the "bones" as the grammatical subject of the sentence. The poet of Job remade Jeremiah's *qal* verb into the *hiphil* causative (הרחיף), thereby coining a new word.[40] The phrase was meant to read: ורב עצמותי הרחיף, "As shivers set my bones to shaking" (my translation). Unfortunately, a later copyist was unfamiliar with the neologism and—finding the common term "fear" (פחד) nearby—misread the verb הרחיף; that is, an early copyist attempted a correction by writing "he frightened" (הפחיד) instead. The copyist mistook the *resh* for a *dalet* and metathesized the letters.[41] Such a scribal error is easy to explain. In fact, one finds an almost identical variation between two different versions of the Wisdom of Ben Sira.[42] One reads a word as מפחדת, "she fears," the other as מחפרת, "she causes shame." Recognizing the poet of Job's use of "trembling" (רוב) and his Jeremiah-inspired coinage of הרחיף עצמות in Job 4:14 yields an elegant and sensible verse: "Fear overcame me, and trembling; | As shivers set my bones to shaking."

The presence of רוב, "trembling," elsewhere in chapter 4 enhances its likelihood in verse 3, in the form רָבִים. Thus the most fundamental sense of the line is, "It is you who have fortified the trembling." One may then ask why the learned and ingenious poet would choose words that are so unfamiliar. What does he gain? The answer is, a double meaning.[43] In addition to the primary meaning there is a secondary one, namely, "You have chastened many." According to Eliphaz, Job has steadied the trembling and thereby taught them a lesson in life.

The meaning of many expressions and phrases in Job depends on a close acquaintance with the Hebrew literary tradition. Job 3:23, for example, is easily interpreted once one realizes that it borrows from Isa 40:27. The verse in Job reads, "(Why should light be given) to a man. . .?" Compare the two leading translations presented in Table 7.4.[44]

Hebrew	לגבר אשר-דרכו נסתרה ויסך אלוה בעדו
New JPS	(Why does He give light) To the man who has lost his way, Whom God has hedged about?
NRSV	Why is light given to one who cannot see the way, Whom God has fenced in?

Table 7.4: Translations of Job 3:23

According to these versions, the "way" of the "man" is "hidden" from the man himself. The second line is then understood as an explanation for the man's path being obscure—the deity has obstructed it. This interpretation differs from the similar, probable source from Isaiah.

Isaiah 40:27 reads: "Why do you say, O Jacob, and state, O Israel, 'My way is hid from the Lord. . .?'" (JPS *Tanakh*). The phrase clearly means that the Israelites ask why the deity does not look upon their ways. Accordingly, the verse in Job 3, which seems to borrow its language from Isaiah, should be understood: "(Why give light) to a man whose path is hidden (from God), | whom God has screened off (from his sight)?" This interpretation is corroborated by a later reference to the same idea by Job and by an elaboration of that idea by Eliphaz in a reply. In Job 21:22, Job describes the deity as remote, "he passes judgment from on high" (והוא רמים ישפוט). In Job 22:13–14, Eliphaz is annoyed at Job's imputation of ignorance to God. Eliphaz paraphrases Job at length and alludes not only to Job's brief comment in the preceding discourse but apparently also to Job's point in 3:23:

You say, "What can God know?
Can He govern (ישפוט) through the dense cloud?
The clouds screen Him (עבים סתר לו) so he cannot see
As He moves about the circuit of heaven" (my translation).

The responsible translator of Job must seek out the interconnections within the book and those between the book and its predecessors.

The greatest obstacle before the translator of Job, however, is the necessity to overcome the many presuppositions that have accompanied the book since antiquity. Perhaps the most stubborn of these presumptions is the notion that, because the deity not only condones Job's brutal God-talk but approves it (42:7–8), Job must have withdrawn the harsh indictment of the deity he had made. Indeed, Job 42:6 has almost universally been understood to relate Job's acquiescence in the presence of divine power. Compare the translations presented in Table 7.5.[45]

Hebrew	על-כן אמאס ונחמתי על-עפר ואפר
New JPS	Therefore, I recant and relent, | being but dust and ashes.
NRSV	Therefore I despise myself, | and repent in dust and ashes.
Robert Alter	Therefore do I recant, | And I repent in dust and ashes.

Table 7.5: Translations of Job 42:6

Much has been written about this troubling verse.[46] The explicit verb מאס has been derived from a different root (מסס, מוס), and previous scholarship has made false claims about its usage (i.e., that it must be transitive). The phrase "dust and ashes" (which appears two other times in the Bible, one of them in Job) is taken differently from the way it functions there. And the syntax of the last phrase has been presumed to be valid, but it is not.

I address the problem with four interpretative principles in hand: first, the overall sense of the verse should not be presupposed; second, the verse should be interpreted as part of its immediate context; third, the words and phrases should be taken in their usual meanings, unless there is a compelling reason to interpret them otherwise; and fourth, all things being equal, the language should be examined in relation to known grammar and usages.[47]

Accordingly, the prevailing interpretation of Job 42:6 must be rejected, for it not only assumes that Job must be capitulating to the brow-beating deity but also fails to account for the tone of the preceding passage, which is parodic. The "repentance" interpretation renders some of the phrases contrary to their attested usage and seemingly ignores alternative meanings that make fewer presuppositions. In what follows, I shall summarize the considerations supporting my own interpretation.[48]

I render Job 42:6 (without emendation or repointing) as follows: "I am therefore fed up, | And take pity on 'dust and ashes.'" This rendering can serve as a default interpretation, principle by principle. First, seeing that the deity has not only failed to respond to Job's burning desire to receive an explanation of his suffering (see, e.g., Job 13:23–24) but has verbally abused him as well, one may wonder why Job should be assumed to recant his critique of divine justice. Elie Wiesel, for one, expressed strong dismay at Job's apparent submission.[49] Contrary to the conventional, pious reading of Job, one should allow for contrary reading.

Second, the preceding verses are suffused with irony. Job begins his reply to the divine discourse by asserting, "I know that you can do everything, | That nothing you propose is impossible for you" (JPS *Tanakh* Job 42:2). As many have noted (yet few have applied exegetically), Job sums up his understanding of the whirlwind speech by acknowledging God's omnipotence. But then Job alludes to God's comment about the builders of the Tower of Babel, "nothing that they propose to do will be out of their reach" (JPS *Tanakh* Gen 11:6b). In Hebrew, Job's language echoes the deity's even more closely. Job's noun מזמה, "scheme," evokes God's verb יזמו "they schemed" (from the related roots זמם and יזם), and the phrase "cannot be blocked" (לא-יבצר מן) appears in both verses. Job's acknowledgement of divine power is, therefore, negative.[50] Moreover, Job intersperses his own words with very close paraphrases of the deity's addresses to him. Job's formulations, "Who is this who conceals counsel without knowledge" (42:3a) and "Hear now, and I will speak; | I will ask you questions, and you will inform me" (v. 4) are in fact mimicry of the

Lord's words in 38:2–3 and 40:7. Mimicry, according to Simon Dentith, is the very quintessence of parody.[51] Such critical and parodic discourse forms the background of Job's remark in 42:6.

Third, אמאס is all too often taken as an ellipsis of a transitive phrase, "I retract/abandon/detest something." However, when it appears without an explicit object, the verb is intransitive.[52] Indeed, the verb is used intransitively—in the sense of "I am fed up"—in Job 7:16, 34:33, and possibly 36:5. This usage is well recognized, as in this translation of מאסתי in 7:16 by the JPS *Tanakh*: "I am sick of it." It is likely that this intransitive usage of מאס devolved from a fuller expression such as מאס חיים / נפש, "to despise one's life" (see, e.g., Job 9:21); yet, there is no gainsaying the fact that the default meaning of אמאס in Biblical Hebrew in general and in Job in particular is simply, "I am fed up!"

Similarly, the phrase "dust and ashes" (עפר ואפר) occurs, as is well known, in only two other places in the Bible; in Gen 18:27, Abraham humbly describes his lowly status as "dust and ashes," and Job (30:19) elsewhere describes the state to which he has deteriorated as "dust and ashes." The expression is classically figurative and not literal. And yet, most Biblical translators render "dust and ashes" literally, as the ground on which Job stands as he recants his critical theology. Unfortunately, such a rendering is for all intents and purposes impossible.

Hence the fourth principle guiding my treatment of Job 42:6. The verse does not relate that Job is standing, sitting, lying, or otherwise even being in "dust and ashes." As I have argued elsewhere,[53] in Biblical Hebrew some such verb is necessary to describe someone's posture when they are *in* dust or ashes. Yet there is no verb in connection with this phrase. Consequently, "dust and ashes" in Job 42:6 does not refer to Job's literal location, but rather figuratively to the abject state of humankind—described by both Abraham and earlier by Job as "dust and ashes."

All that remains is to decide the meaning of the polysemous phrase ונחמתי על, which most others understand as "I repent," but which no longer makes sense in context. Would Job conclude, "I am fed up, and I repent over miserable humanity"? This does not work. There is, however, another established meaning for the phrase נחם על (in the *niphal*), namely "to have compassion, to take pity."[54]

For example, in Ps 90:13 (שובה יהוה עד-מתי והנחם על-עבדיך), the JPS *Tanakh* properly translates, "Turn, O Lord! How long? | Show mercy to Your servants." In fact, Job 42:6 was interpreted in precisely this manner by the liturgist who wrote the following line in a *piyyut*, or poetical prayer for the evening service of Yom Kippur: "May You take pity on dust and ashes" (תנחם על עפר ואפר), that is, on us humans. In this final declaration to the God who has, in Job's mind, afflicted him for no good reason, Job is saying, "I am disgusted! I feel only pity for miserable humanity."

A final example of the challenges in translating the book comes in Job's initial discourse, an outcry into the void (3:3); see Table 7.6.

Hebrew	יאבד יום אולד בו והלילה אמר הרה גבר
New JPS	Perish the day on which I was born, | And the night it was announced, "A male has been conceived!"
NRSV	Let the day perish in which I was born, | And the night that said, "A man-child is conceived."
Robert Alter	Annul the day that I was born, | And the night that said, "A man is conceived."

Table 7.6: Translations of Job 3:3

Before addressing issues of semantics in the verse, I would first point out that none of these translations adequately conveys the elegance of each line of the couplet, particularly the rhyming *yō*, *ʾô*, *bô* in the first line and of the repetitive sonants *l* and *r* in the second. The echo of sound makes a profound impact on the hearer, for the transition from day to night is accompanied by a shift in acoustics.

It is surprising that the translations above included the pronouns "that" and "in which," even though they are frequently omitted in Biblical Hebrew verse—especially in the archaizing poetry of Job.[55] Dispensing with relative pronouns altogether in Job 3:3 would help achieve a balanced rhythm. Further regarding rhythm, the translations above treat the verse as a triplet, with three relatively balanced lines, even though it is unmistakably a couplet. The verse divides in two, for Job refers to his accursed birth in two stages—birth by day and a prior conception at night.

I definitely appreciate the translator's problem here: another line seems required to convey the two short Hebrew words spoken by the personified night of his conception. However, here is a different solution, one that preserves the duality of the verse's structure. The first line can be lengthened to balance the second. My translation reads, "Let the day disappear, the day I was born, | And the night that announced: A man's been conceived." Admittedly, for the sake of rhythm, balance, and assonance, I have repeated the word "day," and I too have made explicit the underlying pronoun "that." Yet I have done so both for intelligibility and for the preservation of an anapestic rhythm. In the Hebrew, the metrical emphasis in Job 3:3b is trochaic, but it is consistent: *we-ha-LA-ye-la ʾA-mar HO-ra GA-ver*. My repetition of anapests is meant to convey a similar rhythmic thrust.

The impact of Job's opening couplet is also important to translate. That is why the well-known translator Stephen Mitchell rendered the first line of this couplet: "God damn the day I was born."[56] Unfortunately, in mirroring the assonance, Mitchell has (not unlike Robert Alter and other translators[57]) misrepresented a crucial semantic aspect. In this part of the soliloquy, Job does not address the deity—although in the next verse Job does bid Eloah not to bring about the night of his accursed conception (3:4b); Job's only other reference to God in this discourse is in the third-person, as in v. 4. Job's calculated avoidance of the deity is evident throughout this speech. Job asks, for example, why the light of day and life in general are given to those who suffer (vv. 20–23), but he does not direct his rhetorical question to the deity in the second-person. Job, in his opening outburst, seems deliberately to employ the third-person jussive, "let it disappear" (יאבד), without invoking the deity. Job instead uses a verb that conventionally indicates a curse (cf., e.g., Judg 5:31).[58] Even if God alone could impose a curse on the day of Job's birth, Job is not in a mood to appeal to the deity. Job's rhetoric embodies his attitude, and that is part of what a translator should aim to convey.

I would add in conclusion just one more aspect of the semantics of Job 3:3. Job here refers to himself, at the time of his conception, not as "male child"[59] or "man-child" but as גבר, a "man." Translators as well as commentators have difficulty coping with this seemingly odd usage.[60] However, one can suggest at least three reasons for this peculiar choice of words. First, by using this term, Job identifies himself with the "man" (גבר) whose "path" in life is ignored by the deity, as Job complains later on in the discourse (v. 23).[61] Second, throughout the speech Job has eliminated the occasion of his birth. Thus, in the same way he does not refer to his parents or any other circumstances of his birth, he does not refer to himself as a child.[62] And third, the term גבר, "man," is a technical term in ancient Near Eastern as well as biblical parlance for the type of the pious sufferer. The best known parallel is in Lam 3:1, where a Job-like lamenter introduces himself (or herself—it is a type, not a person) as הגבר—"the man" (who saw affliction).[63] By identifying himself as a "man," Job therefore arouses a typological association and provides rhetorical cues reflecting his attitude toward his birth and toward life in general.

One can hardly expect such a wealth of meanings to be conveyed by any choice of words in the target language. Translation, it has been said, is an art of failure.[64] Nevertheless, it behooves the translator not only to come to grips with the strangeness or oddity of a source's formulation but also to convey it to the reader, who will in turn be challenged to come to grips with a startling expression and manner of thought. In the case of Job, the reader of the original is hardly less challenged than the translator. In my own experience, the effort of translating Job has made me a very much better reader of the book.

Notes

I am pleased to dedicate this essay to a long-time friend and colleague, Leonard Greenspoon, who has enlivened our field with his wit as well as enriching it with his scholarship.

[1]See esp. Edward L. Greenstein, "Theories of Modern Bible Translation," *Proof* 3 (1983): 9–39; slightly expanded in idem, *Essays on Biblical Method and Translation*, BJS 92 (Atlanta: Scholars Press, 1989), 85–118.

[2]Edward L. Greenstein, "The Scroll of Esther: A New Translation," *Fiction* 9/3 (1990): 52–81. I have also benefited from years of working as a consultant and

friendly critic with the great modern Bible translator, Everett Fox, and I have translated some ancient Near Eastern texts into English and Hebrew, esp. the Ugaritic epic "Kirta," in *Ugaritic Narrative Poetry*, ed. Simon B. Parker, SBLWAW (Atlanta: Scholars Press, 1997), 9–49. For a critical discussion of my diverse translation styles, see Simon B. Parker, "Pushing the Limits: Issues in Jewish Bible Translation," in *Hesed ve-Emet: Studies in Honor of Ernest S. Frerichs*, ed. Jodi Magness and Seymour Gitin, BJS 320 (Atlanta: Scholars Press, 1998), 73–79.

[3]For a fine analysis of the translation approach of 11QtgJob with extensive bibliography, see Sung Jin Park, "The Text and Translations of Job: A Comparative Study on 11QtgJob with Other Versions in Light of Translation Techniques," *JESOT* 2 (2013): 165–90.

[4]Translated by Michael Sokoloff, *The Targum to Job from Qumran Cave XI* (Ramat-Gan: Bar-Ilan University Press, 1974), 89; for the text, see p. 88.

[5]I am indebted to Dr. Noam Mizrahi for this insight.

[6]See, e.g., *BDB*, 1009a.

[7]See, e.g., *BDB*, 304a.

[8]Friedrich Schleiermacher, "On the Different Methods of Translation," trans. André Lefevere, in *German Romantic Criticism*, ed. A. Leslie Willson (New York: Continuum, 1982), 1–30.

[9]See, e.g., George Steiner, *After Babel: Aspects of Language and Translation* (New York: Oxford University Press, 1975).

[10]See, e.g., Willis Barnstone, *The Poetics of Translation: History, Theory, Practice* (New Haven: Yale University Press, 1993).

[11]Cf. Edward L. Greenstein, "The Job of Translating Job," in idem, *Essays*, 119–23.

[12]See Edward L. Greenstein, "Features of Language in the Poetry of Job," in *Das Buch Hiob und seine Interpretationen*, ed. Thomas Krüger et al., ATANT (Zurich: Theologischer Verlag, 2007), 81–96.

[13]See Edward L. Greenstein, "The Language of Job and Its Poetic Function," *JBL* 122 (2003): 651–66; idem, "The Poetic Use of Akkadian in the Book of Job," in *The Avi Hurvitz Festschrift*, ed. S. Fassberg and A. Maman, Mehqarim be-Lashon 11-12 (Jerusalem: Hebrew University of Jerusalem, 2008), 51–68 (in Hebrew with English abstract).

[14]See Edward L. Greenstein, "The Invention of Language in the Poetry of Job," in *Interested Readers: Essays on the Hebrew Bible in Honor of David J. A. Clines*, ed. James K. Aitken, Jeremy M. S. Clines, and Christl M. Maier (Atlanta: Society of Biblical Literature; 2013), 331–46.

[15]See Greenstein, "Features of Language," 95–96; idem, "Some Metaphors in the Poetry of Job," in *Built by Wisdom, Established by Understanding: Essays on Biblical and Near Eastern Literature in Honor of Adele Berlin*, ed. Maxine L. Grossman (Bethesda, MD: CDL Press, 2013), 179–95.

[16]See Katharine Dell and Will Kynes, eds., *Reading Job Intertextually*, LHBOTS 574 (New York: Bloomsbury T&T Clark, 2013); JiSeong James Kwon, *Scribal Culture and Intertextuality*, FAT 85 (Tübingen: Mohr Siebeck, 2016).

[17]See, e.g., Marvin H. Pope, *Job*, AB 15 (Garden City, NY: Doubleday, 1965), xxxix–xlii.

[18]See, e.g., Ken Brown, *The Vision in Job 4 and Its Role in the Book*, FAT 2/75 (Tübingen: Mohr Siebeck, 2015).

[19]Ariel and Chana Bloch, *The Song of Songs: A New Translation with an Introduction and Commentary* (New York: Random House, 1995), 41.

[20]See, e.g., Robert Althann, "Job 3 in the Masoretic Text and the Septuagint," *Orientalia* 78 (2009): 348–57; John Gray, *The Book of Job*, ed. David J. A. Clines (Sheffield: Sheffield Phoenix, 2010), 76–91. It has been maintained that "the translator [of the Hebrew Bible] is not called upon to re-write the original. A translation destined for the people can only follow the traditional text": Max L. Margolis, *The Story of Bible Translations* (Philadelphia: Jewish Publication Society of America, 1948), 126. However, I see no academic value in translating a text that I determine to be neither original nor sound. The position taken by Margolis is valid only when one is interested not in the text when it was composed but only in the text as it has been transmitted in a particular tradition. Even the JPS *Tanakh* translators often assume, without any note, a differently vocalized or spelled word from that in the Masoretic Text. I point some of these out in my annotations to Job in *The Jewish Study Bible*, ed. Adele Berlin and Marc Z. Brettler, 2nd ed. (Oxford: Oxford University Press, 2014), 1489–1556.

[21]Cf., e.g., Samuel R. Driver, "Preface to the Second Edition," *Notes on the Hebrew Text and the Topography of the Books of Samuel*, 2nd ed. (Oxford: Clarendon, 1913), xi–xii.

[22]See Edward L. Greenstein, "'Difficulty' in the Poetry of Job," in *A Critical Engagement: Essays on the Hebrew Bible in Honour of J. Cheryl Exum*, ed. David J. A. Clines and Ellen van Wolde (Sheffield: Sheffield Phoenix; 2011), 186–95.

[23]See Greenstein, "Features of Language," 84–86. For the image of the womb as a house or room with bolted doors, see my ""The Book of Job and Mesopotamian Literature: How Many Degrees of Separation?" in *Subtle Citation, Allusion, and Translation in the Hebrew Bible*, ed. Ziony Zevit (London: Equinox, 2017), 149; cf. Karen Langton, "Job's Attempt to Regain Control: Traces of a Babylonian Birth Incantation in Job 3," *JSOT* 36 (2012): 53–63.

[24]See Edward L. Greenstein, "Jeremiah as an Inspiration to the Poet of Job," in *Inspired Speech: Prophecy in the Ancient Near East: Essays in Honour of Herbert B. Huffmon*, JSOTSup 378 (New York: T&T Clark, 2004), 102–3.

[25]See my "Loneliness of Job," in *The Book of Job in Scripture, Thought, and Art*, ed. Lea Mazor (Jerusalem: Mt. Scopus Publications, 1995), 43–53 (in Hebrew).

[26]Robert Alter, *The Wisdom Books: Job, Proverbs, and Ecclesiastes* (New York: Norton, 2010), 20.

[27]Edwin M. Good, *In Turns of Tempest: A Reading of Job with a Translation* (Stanford: Stanford University Press, 1990), 55; Raymond P. Scheindlin, *The Book of Job* (New York: Norton, 1998), 59. Buber's German translation, which is meant to echo the Hebrew closely, does have "meines Mutterleibes," but because the German term for "womb" that he chose incorporates the word for "mother,"

the result is ambiguous; see Martin Buber, *Die Schriftwerke* (Stuttgart: Deutsche Bibelgesellschaft, 1992), 4:281.

[28]Saadia Gaon (early tenth century) resorts to paraphrase: "For had the portals of the womb been shut against me. . ."; see Lenn E. Goodman, *The Book of Theodicy: Translation and Commentary on the Book of Job by Saadiah Ben Joseph Al-Fayyūmī*, YJS 25 (New Haven: Yale University Press, 1988), 181.

[29]See, e.g., Martin Buber and Franz Rosenzweig, *Scripture and Translation*, trans. Lawrence Rosenwald with an introduction by Everett Fox (Bloomington: Indiana University Press, 1994); Everett Fox, *The Five Books of Moses*, Schocken Bible 1 (New York: Schocken, 1995); idem, *The Early Prophets*, Schocken Bible 2 (New York: Schocken, 2014); Walter Benjamin, "The Task of the Translator," *Illuminations*, ed. Hannah Arendt, trans. Harry Zohn (New York: Schocken, 1969), 69–82; and see my "Theories of Modern Bible Translation" (cited above). Cf. George Steiner, "An Exact Art," *No Passion Spent: Essays 1978–1995* (New York: Yale University Press, 1996), 202.

[30]See Joel 2:20; see also, e.g., *BHK* and consider the parallelism.

[31]E.g., *BDB*, 106a.

[32]For this lineation of Aḥīqar, see Bezalel Porten and Ada Yardeni, *Textbook of Aramaic Documents from Ancient Egypt, vol. 3: Literature, Accounts, Lists* (Jerusalem: Magnes, 1993), 24–53.

[33]Alter, *Wisdom Books*, 82. Note that Alter also mistakes the verb זור "to be loathsome" (*BDB*, 266b) for its more common homonym "to be strange."

[34]Good, *In Turns of Tempest*, 256.

[35]Buber (*Die Schriftwerke*, 303) translates "sons of my womb" in accordance with the phrase in Job 3:10.

[36]See Greenstein, "Language of Job," 656; idem, "Features of Language," 93–94.

[37]It is likely that the reading of the verb in Hosea was corrupted from יסד; however, the author of the passage in Job found the form יסר and used it, apparently for its oddity and the resultant double entendre.

[38]See esp. Greenstein, "Poetic Use of Akkadian."

[39]I am indebted to my teacher, Prof. H. L. Ginsberg, for this ingenious insight. See my published note in "Poetic Use of Akkadian," 53 n. 13.

[40]See on this phenomenon Greenstein, "Invention of Language."

[41]Readers should recall that when Job was first written, there was no distinction between medial and final *peh*.

[42]See Moshe Zvi Segal, ספר בן סירא השלם, 2nd ed. (Jerusalem: Mossad Bialik, 1972), 287.

[43]See Greenstein, "Language of Job," 656.

[44]In this instance, Alter's translation (*Wisdom Books*, 21) is ambiguous.

[45]Alter, *Wisdom Books*, 177.

[46]For a recent discussion, see, e.g., Thomas Krüger, "Did Job Repent?" in *Das Buch Hiob und seine Interpretationen*, ed. idem et al., 217–29. For a more somewhat more elaborate discussion, see Ellen J. van Wolde, "Job 42, 1-6: The Reversal

of Job," in *The Book of Job*, ed. W. A. M. Beuken, BETL 114 (Leuven: Peeters, 1994), 223–50.

[47]For my analyses, see "In Job's Face/Facing Job," in *The Labour of Reading: Desire, Alienation, and Biblical Interpretation*, ed. Fiona C. Black, Roland Boer, and Erin Runions, SemeiaSt 36 (Atlanta: Society of Biblical Literature, 1999), 301–17; "The Problem of Evil in the Book of Job," in *Mishneh Todah: Studies in Deuteronomy and Its Cultural Environment in Honor of Jeffrey H. Tigay*, ed. Nili Sacher Fox, David A. Glatt-Gilad, and Michael J. Williams (Winona Lake, IN: Eisenbrauns, 2009), 333–62, esp. 356–61.

[48]Cf. esp. John B. Curtis, "On Job's Response to Yahweh," *JBL* 98 (1979): 407–511.

[49]Elie Wiesel, *Messengers of God: Biblical Portraits and Legends*, trans. Marion Wiesel (New York: Simon & Schuster, 1975), esp. 231–34; cf. Mark Larrimore, *The Book of Job: A Biography* (Princeton: Princeton University Press, 2013), 222–25.

[50]The New Testament's apparent reading of this verse is entirely without irony: "With men this is impossible, but with God all things are possible" (Matt 19:26).

[51]Simon Dentith, *Parody* (London: Routledge, 2000), esp. 3.

[52]In addition to Curtis, "On Job's Response" (see n. 48 above) and my own treatments (see n. 47 above), see Michael V. Fox, "Job the Pious," *ZAW* 117 (2005): 351–66, here 365.

[53]Greenstein, "Problem of Evil," 360.

[54]See *BDB*, 636b–7a.

[55]See, e.g., David Noel Freedman, "Prose Particles in the Poetry of the Primary History," in *Biblical and Related Studies Presented to Samuel Iwry*, ed. Ann Kort and Scott Morschauser (Winona Lake, IN: Eisenbrauns, 1985), 49–62.

[56]Stephen Mitchell, *The Book of Job* (San Francisco: North Point, 1987), 13.

[57]E.g., Scheindlin, 59: "Blot out the day when I was born."

[58]See Greenstein, "Features of Language," 86–87.

[59]See, e.g., E. Dhorme, *A Commentary on the Book of Job*, trans. Harold Knight (London: Thomas Nelson, 1967), 24–25; Gray, *The Book of Job*, 139. Pope (*Job*, 25) renders "boy"; cf. 28. However, the term גבר denotes an adult male; see, e.g., John E. Hartley, *The Book of Job*, NICOT (Grand Rapids: Eerdmans, 1988), 92. Although it may seem that the Septuagint read זכר, "a male," instead of the MT's גבר, their rendering is probably an effort to convey a "rational" sense; see S. R. Driver and G. B. Gray, *The Book of Job*, ICC, 2 vols. (New York: Scribner's, 1921), 2:16–17.

[60]Compare an analogous distortion in translations of Franz Kafka's "The Metamorphosis": while Kafka refers to the protagonist Gregor's immediate family as "the mother," "the father," and "the sister," translators seem to thwart Kafka's purpose by rendering them in a less awkward fashion as "his mother," etc. See Donna Freed, "Translator's Afterword," in Franz Kafka, *The Metamorphosis and Other Stories: A New Translation* (New York: Barnes and Noble, 1996), 216.

[61]Greenstein, "Features of Language," 86.

[62]Greenstein, "Features of Language," 86; cf. Greenstein, "Jeremiah as an Inspiration," 102–3.

[63]See my Hebrew article, "A Woman's Voice in Lamentations 3," *Shnaton: An Annual for Biblical and Ancient Near Eastern Studies* 24 (2016): 167–76, here 174–76 with references. For this usage, see also Ps 88:5; 94:12.

[64]E.g., John Ciardi, "Translation: The Art of Failure," *Saturday Review*, 7 October 1967, 17–19.

8

On Translating Proverbs 31:10

Adele Berlin
University of Maryland

Leonard Greenspoon has given us much insight into Bible translations, so I dedicate to him some thoughts on English translations of the opening verse of the *Eshet Ḥayil* (אשת חיל) poem, that is, the honorable woman of Prov 31:10–31. My understanding of this verse is especially influenced by two excellent, recent commentaries on Proverbs by Michael V. Fox and by Avigdor (Victor) Hurowitz,[1] with whose views I by and large agree (except when I do not). I will be in dialogue with these commentaries, with other scholarship, and with a number of English translations presented below.[2] Translators, whether they opt for a literal or a dynamic translation, must first understand the Hebrew text and then find the right English word or phrase to convey their understanding. There is room for differing opinions in both parts of the operation, and often the choice is between several good options from which the translator may select only one. Like most biblical scholars, I will be concerned first and foremost with the meaning of the Hebrew, but I will also attend to English vocabulary and usage as well as comment on how some of the translations might sound to contemporary readers.

I view the book of Proverbs as concrete, practical advice addressed to upper-class young men on how to succeed in life. It is "establishment" literature; that is, it wants young men (adolescents) to assimilate societal norms. Being addressed to adolescents, the book constantly stresses heeding parental advice (e.g., 4:1–2). Proverbs also focuses on activities and behaviors typical of teenagers. The book warns, for example, against joining gangs that engage in petty theft (1:10–19). Since young men think so much about sex, a certain amount of the book's advice concerns the type of woman to avoid—a married seductress, the אשה זרה. By contrast, the *Eshet Ḥayil* poem in Prov 31:10–31 portrays the type of woman to seek.

This poem gives advice regarding the type of woman to marry, the kind of woman best suited to the kind of man Proverbs molds. The "son," that is, the young male addressee, will become noble, and the virtuous woman will ensure the young man's success in society—she is a crown for her husband (Prov 12:4). To put it somewhat tautologically, the אשת חיל is the fitting mate for the איש גבור חיל (Ruth 2:1). It is reasonable to think that the young man is being directed to choose a wife from his own socioeconomic class, for such a woman would know how to manage her husband's household and promote his interests; she would likely add to his wealth as well. This scenario may well reflect the actual activities of upper-class women of the Persian period.[3] It is at least possible that this passage also served an instructional purpose for socially well-placed young women.

The woman pictured is a type, as Fox has noted.[4] She is a model wife, a composite of the attributes that were valued in an upper-class wife. She is an ideal, but not unattainable. I am not persuaded that she is a personification of Wisdom, despite the verbal similarities that have been observed between the woman in chapter 31 and the descriptions of Wisdom elsewhere in Proverbs.[5] Yair Zakovitch suggested that this composite is a conservative response to the woman of Song of Songs, whom he reads as more liberated and more proactive in her relationship with her lover; Zakovitch also compares her with Ruth, as does Samuel Goh.[6] Both scholars' comparisons are based on similarities in expressions and motifs. But such similarities do not prove that one text was written with the other in mind, as Zakovitch argues. It may be that they all use the same conventions in portraying women—conventions that include physical and bodily descriptions, actions and skills, as well as social and moral qualities. An author may manipulate these conventions to draw the portrait that fits his purpose.

Proverbs 31:10 in Translation

Sixteen English translations of Prov 31:10 are presented in Table 8.1.

Robert Alter	"A worthy woman who can find? Her price is far beyond rubies."
American Standard Version (ASV)	"A worthy woman who can find? For her price is far above rubies."
Common English Bible (CEB)	"A competent wife, how does one find her? Her value is far above pearls."
Contemporary English Version (CEV)	"A truly good wife is the most precious treasure | a man can find!"
Michael Fox	"A woman of strength, who can find? Her price is greater than rubies."
Good News Bible (GNB)	"How hard it is to find a capable wife! She is worth far more than jewels!"
Geneva Bible (GNV)	"Who shall find a virtuous woman? for her price is far above the pearls."
Jewish Publication Society, 1917 (JPS)	"A woman of valour who can find? for her price is far above rubies."
King James Version (KJV)	"Who can find a virtuous woman? for her price is far above rubies."
New American Bible, revised edition (NAB)	"Who can find a woman of worth? | Far beyond jewels is her value."
New American Standard Bible (NASB)	"An excellent wife, who can find? For her worth is far above jewels."
New International Version (NIV)	"A wife of noble character who can find? She is worth far more than rubies."
New Jewish Publication Society (NJPS)	"What a rare find is a capable wife! Her worth is far beyond that of rubies."
New Living Translation (NLT)	"Who can find a virtuous and capable wife? She is more precious than rubies."

New Revised Standard Version (NRSV)	"A capable wife who can find? She is far more precious than jewels."
Revised Standard Version (RSV)	"A good wife who can find? She is far more precious than jewels."

Table 8.1: Translations of Prov 31:10

חיל

The dictionaries and commentaries have amply discussed the semantic range of the Hebrew term חיל. Its basic meaning is "strength, power," and it may refer to wealth, social position, and prominence as well as physical or military prowess, or even spiritual and intellectual fortitude. No single English word can capture the range of meanings of חיל, and that accounts for the wide variations in the way it is rendered. All the translations above are correct to one degree or another, but some seem more apt than others.

The passage is commonly known as *a woman of valour* (see JPS, 1917), but most translations do not use this expression. Such a rendering probably does not resonate with today's readers; to the extent that it might, it conveys the notion of military bravery. According to the *Oxford English Dictionary*, the first meaning of *valour* or *valor*, now obsolete, is "Worth or importance due to personal qualities or to rank." It was used in the fourteenth century of women and of men. Fox translates the basic meaning, "strength," which is also the broadest, including many of the attributes spelled out in the rest of the poem. But I am not sure how most modern readers understand this. Without a modification such as "strength of character," many readers might think only of physical strength. To be sure, that is not entirely absent in the description (v. 17), but it is not a primary attribute. *Worthy* or *woman of worth* carries the sense of "value" and also denotes "honorable, meritorious, of good character." It is close to the now obsolete "valour" and echoes "her price" in the second part of the verse. Several translations use *excellent* (NASB) or *truly good* (CEV) or *good* (RSV), which may get to the heart of the issue; yet these renderings are overly bland for חיל. Character and morality are conveyed by *virtuous* (GNV and KJV) and *of noble character* (NIV), but this is only one aspect of the woman portrayed (she gives to the poor, she is wise). The other aspect is her activities and her skill in carrying them out (managing the household), captured by *capable* (GNB, NJPS, NRSV) and *competent* (CEB); Zakovitch calls her "industrious." I am not sure that today's readers would be impressed by these adjectives; they may sound rather like a minimum standard in a wife. NLT's *virtuous and capable* includes both character and activities but must use two words to do it.

אשה

There is a quibble about rendering אשה as *woman* or *wife*. In this case, it makes little difference since marriage is the context. Hebrew אשה often means "wife" or "married woman," but not always. The word may denote a woman of any marital status or even non-humans or inanimate objects that are grammatically feminine. For example, in Ezek 1:9, the wings of the creatures were connected אשה אל אחותה, "each one to its sister;" see also vis-à-vis cloths (Exod 26:3), buzzards (Isa 34:15), and sheep (Zech 11:9). It is the feminine-marked form of the term איש, "an individual, a member of a group," which may even include inanimate objects, like the stars in Isa 40:26.[7]

What sounds preferable in English? Since here marriage is assumed, "wife" is probably better, and the expression "to find a wife" is altogether better than "to find a woman." Interestingly, English "wife" originally meant "woman" without respect to marriage (alewife, fishwife) and secondarily "married woman." Given the context and English usage, I prefer "wife," even though she is not a wife before she has been found. The description that follows, however, portrays a married woman, a wife who tends to her husband and household. The elements in the description accord with the type of wife the poem's young man should have; her description is very specific to this context. The woman must manage a large household, a staff of servants, various types of domestic production, and business enterprises. She is wise (v. 26), suggesting that she may be educated.

Different attributes might be sought in, say, a queen, a shepherdess, a prophetess, or the wife of a poor man. This woman is not "everywoman," just as she is not "superwoman." One attribute that the Bible looks upon with favor in relation to women (also men) is beauty, yet in v. 30 it is minimized although not denigrated. (I agree with Fox on this point.) Other characteristics are more important, especially the fear of the Lord, a trope commonly associated with Wisdom thought. One should not be taken in by superficial appearance when choosing a wife any more than when choosing a king; in 1 Sam 16:7 God tells Samuel that one should not select a king based on his physical appearance. Beauty cannot make up for other deficits: "Like a gold ring in the snout of a pig, is a beautiful woman bereft of sense" (Prov 11:22). All this is good advice to the population at large, but it is especially relevant to a young man, who is more likely to be attracted by a woman's physical charms—"Do not lust for her beauty" (Prov 6:25). Another feminine quality that might be expected is fertility, although, of course, this cannot be ascertained before the marriage. It is hinted at indirectly in v. 28, where her children and her husband praise her. Having children in due time is assumed, for being a mother was important for all wives. It is not distinctive to the upper-class wife of this poem.

מי ימצא

The majority of translations render this phrase as a rhetorical question: *Who can find?* As such, it implies a negative response: no one can find such a woman. Some translations adjust the question, asking instead *how* to find such a wife (CEB, GNB). Yet that question is never answered; indeed, the point of the poem is what type of woman to seek, not how to find her. Only NJPS and CEV render the phrase as an exclamation rather than as a question. As Hurowitz explains, this is not actually a question—even a rhetorical one—but an exclamation; Bruce Waltke and M. O'Connor call it an exclamatory question.[8] Fair comparisons include both "O that I were appointed judge!" (מי ישמני שפט; 2 Sam 15:4) and "O that someone would give me water to drink!" (מי ישקני מים; 2 Sam 23:15); see also Exod 16:3; Num 11:29; 2 Sam 12:22. I would therefore translate מי ימצא, as "O to find!" or "O that he will find!"

ורחק מפנינים מכרה

Some translators render the conjunction *vav* by *for*, which makes it sound like the reason this wife cannot be found is that she is too expensive—that is, no one could afford her bride-price. However, that is not the sense of the verse. Others wisely leave the *vav* untranslated. The *vav* joins together the two parts of the verse but the nature of the relationship between the parts is left unspecified.

The precious stone has been rendered as *rubies, pearls, jewels* (*HALOT* says *corals* or *pearls of coral*). The stone has a reddish color (Lam 4:7), so *rubies* or *corals* work the best. The word means *pearls* in later Hebrew. Proverbs and other wisdom literature often use comparisons with precious metals and gems to illustrate the extreme value of priceless things like Wisdom (e.g., Prov 3:13–15; Job 28:15–19).[9] The point here is not, as NJPS suggests by the word *rare* (*What a rare find is a capable wife*), that it is so rare or unusual to find a suitable wife. According to v. 29, many exemplify חיל, so this woman is not unique. The point is that she is priceless; money cannot buy a woman like this. She is far beyond rubies. To be distant (רחק) from rubies implies not simply that she is worth more than rubies (presumably the most expensive gems), but, more aptly, that her value is not even in the same league with rubies. Job 28:15–19, in different words, makes the same point about Wisdom—it cannot be equated with precious stones and metals. The same goes for the wife, whose value cannot be estimated in financial terms, the way value is typically measured. This woman's value is immeasurable, incalculable—she is off the scale.[10] As Fox explains, the מכר is the bride-price, the price the groom pays to the bride's family; here it used figuratively.[11] No bride-price, however high, could approach this woman's worth.

To sum up: The opening verse of this poem counsels our young man to seek a suitable wife, one with the attributes that will complement his station in society. The benefit to him of such a wife is so immense that it is incalculable.

Comparing English translations is a simple exercise with two advantages. First, it reminds us that all translators, ancient and modern, have to juggle their understanding of the meaning of the Hebrew, often along with its traditionally accepted interpretation, with the needs and sensitivities of their readers. Not only do the readers speak a language different from biblical Hebrew, but they also live in a distinct cultural context, with nuances and frames of reference far removed from those of ancient Israel. Additionally, from a pedagogic point of view, comparing English translations opens students' eyes—even those who know no Hebrew—to the process of interpreting the Bible and to the fun of engaging in it.

Notes

[1] Michael V. Fox, *Proverbs 10–31: A New Translation with Introduction and Commentary*, A[Y]B 18B (New Haven: Yale University Press, 2009); Avigdor Hurowitz, *Proverbs: Introduction and Commentary; vol. 2: chs. 10–31*, Miqra leYisrael (Tel Aviv: Am Oved; Jerusalem: Magnes, 2012).

[2] Robert Alter, *The Wisdom Books: Job, Proverbs, and Ecclesiastes; A Translation with Commentary* (New York: Norton, 2010); Fox, *Proverbs 10–31*.

[3] Christine Roy Yoder, "The Woman of Substance (אשת חיל): A Socioeconomic Reading of Proverbs 31:10–31," *JBL* 122 (2003): 427–47; see also idem, *Wisdom as a Woman of Substance: A Socioeconomic Reading of Proverbs 1–9 and 31:10–31*, BZAW 304 (Berlin: de Gruyter, 2001).

[4] Fox, *Proverbs 10–31*, 904.

[5] See Hurowitz; see also Yair Zakovitch, "A Woman of Valor, *'eshet ḥayil* (Proverbs 31.10-31): A Conservative Response to the Song of Songs," in *A Critical Engagement: Essays on the Hebrew Bible in Honour of J. Cheryl Exum*, ed. David J. A. Clines and Ellen van Wolde (Sheffield: Sheffield Phoenix, 2011), 401–13.

[6] So too Samuel T. S. Goh, "Ruth as a Superior Woman of חיל? A Comparison between Ruth and the 'Capable' Woman in Proverbs 31.10–31," *JSOT* 38 (2014): 487–500.

[7] David E. S. Stein ("The Noun אִישׁ ['ÎŠ] in Biblical Hebrew: A Term of Affiliation," *JHebS* 8 [2008], article 1. Online: http://www.jhsonline.org/Articles/article_78.pdf.) points out that איש is not always an adult male but is a term of affiliation, an individual member of a group.

[8] Bruce K. Waltke and M. O'Connor, *Biblical Hebrew Syntax* (Winona Lake, IN: Eisenbrauns, 1990), 321.

[9] See Timothy J. Sandoval (*Discourse of Wealth and Poverty in the Book of Proverbs* [Leiden: Brill, 2006], 201–4) for the ways that terms of wealth are used to motivate the listener to gain wisdom.

[10] The CEV approaches this meaning: *most precious treasure a man can find*.

[11] Fox, *Proverbs 10–31*, 891–92.

9

Lost in Transmission, God: Shoah, Not Holocaust

Zev Garber
Los Angeles Valley College, Emeritus

The subject of the Holocaust/Shoah, the near total destruction of the Jews of Europe and others during World War II, is of great moral significance in the history of western civilization. Genocide, the obliteration of all members of a national group, is the most horrible of crimes and one of the most difficult to deal with in the field of social studies; it reveals the human race in its worst perspective. Researchers in the shadow of the Holocaust testify to the Shoah's persistence, "the past that weighs like a nightmare on the brain of the living," as Jean-Paul Sartre once described history.[1]

Advances in understanding the Shoah (causes, effects, and responses) have been dramatic in the second half of the twentieth century, and Holocaust studies have occurred in successive waves. The first recounted the horrors of the Nazi treatment of European Jews (1933–1945) in the historical context of deep-rooted religious anti-Judaism and secular anti-Semitism. Then came indictments against the German and Austrian nations, the Roman Catholic Church leadership, the French, English, and Soviet governments, and the free world for their failure to combat morally the threat of, and from, Nazism. Also in this second wave, questions of theology and theodicy arose—that is, issues regarding the interrelationship between human and divine responsibility after Auschwitz. In the last decades of the Century of Shoah and Genocide, a number of Jewish and Christian scholars exposed and debunked disingenuous Holocaust denial and revisionism. These scholars not only combated the denial of facts and the minimization of the event but also emphasized that moral bankruptcy in individuals, institutions, and governments who deny the historicity of the Shoah is an early warning sign of genocidal tendencies now and in the future. Finally, the rise of Jewish–Christian discussion groups, symposia, and conferences interfacing post-Holocaust morality and theology are notable in the last decades of the twentieth century and at the start of the twenty-first century.[2]

Holocaust Studies on American campuses stress history (cause and effect) and ideology, speak of victimization and witnessing, touch on religion and theology, and so forth. Of particular relevance, but less carefully studied, is language itself, including terminology selected advertently, inadvertently, or between. This essay is devoted to this topic. There are a number of questions that should be addressed. Why is there different terminology to describe, understand, and transmit knowledge from and about the European Judeocide? Arguably, Holocaust and *Shoah* have emerged as the terms of record. But how effective or ineffective are these titles in capturing the genocide of European Jewry? And how do survivors deal with shattered memories? Why do many in the Haredi ultra-Orthodox community (e.g., Satmar and Chabad) not feel the need to educate in this area? Does academic scholarship objectify their years of agony, pain, and torment? May this also explain decades of silence by a number of non-observant Jews whose experience has evolved a black hole around which their Jewish identity is spiraling? If cyanide has replaced Sinai and the State of Israel represents a hope risen from the ashes, then what should be said about the staying power (rituals and symbols) of the Jewish *religious* experience? What of Jewish theology after the Shoah and specifically the understanding and transmission of the Shoah passages in the Hebrew Bible?

Language Transmission: Holocaust

The sacred and the profane declare that humans constitute a unique species in the animal kingdom—s/he is a word producer. From the first embryonic word to the last word uttered by an expiring body, humans are the word-making animals. And in that rare species, those in education and religion are rarer still, for they know the awesome power of words and should be more careful regarding words and how to make use of them.

We must be more selective in our choice of words for criticism, praise, and sarcasm. We must avoid new words and overused words that mislead and confuse—words such as fundamentalism, ethnic cleansing, revisionism, "man's inhumanity to man." We must limit verbosity and repetitiveness for the overgrowth kills otherwise healthy words and ideas. We must discourage the cold, hot, lukewarm, and warmed-over war of words among scholars, which are not productive but destructive. We must practice more the basic words of humane vocabulary—words such as hello, sorry, you're OK–I'm OK, peace. In short, those who are practitioners of words and not merely believers in words are making one giant step forward to humanize mankind. So it is with language. Despite its omnipresence, many people usually do not think much about language as an instrument to do good or to enact evil, nor do they understand the working of its medium (words and syntax) in expressing how people think, feel, perceive, or desire.

Understanding the constraints of language on the (in)ability to ponder the imponderable became the focus of my initial study on the terminology of Judeocide. At the first international conference of Remembering for the Future (RFTF), Bruce Zuckerman and I called into question the validity of the label "Holocaust" to describe the extermination of European Jews during World War II.[3] We pointed to the shocking use of a specific religious term for the genocide, thereby making the Nazi murderers priestly officiants of divine propitiation. We challenged Elie Wiesel's attempt to make the (aborted) sacrifice of Isaac in Genesis the biblical analogy for the "Final Solution." Going far beyond questions of terminological propriety, we discerned basic psychological attitudes in the conventional Jewish view of the Shoah: that the Event is limited to Jewish victims of the Nazis and that it is a fulfillment of the Jews' traditional role as God's people, chosen to suffer for the redemption of mankind. We decried all this as theological gerrymandering, and instead we saw the Shoah as the tragedy of "Thou shall not murder," in which both murderers and victims are ordinary people in an extraordinary situation, a secular event without saints or demons.

Zuckerman and I fear that the attitudes behind the continual use of the term "The Holocaust" may lead to Jews being seen as Christ-like sacrificial "lambs of God" or extreme chauvinism. Still, on some profound level of meaningfulness, the Shoah (the biblical Hebrew term for "destruction, ruin," connoting no religious or sacrificial overtones) must be taken as emblematic. If it is to remain the paradigmatic genocide, then it must be a paradigm that shows true horror—what all people are capable of doing and what all people are capable of suffering; its message of survival must be shared with all who have suffered and will suffer.

At the second RFTF conference, Zuckerman and I probed the language of Shoah disputation, and we pointed out the many complications and difficulties that accompanied the Auschwitz Convent controversy.[4] More than a text of faith and "facts on the ground," the conflict is circumscribed by religious and cultural differences expressed in language predisposed by certain choices of interpretation. We are suggesting that people who speak different languages cannot share the same conceptual framework, and conversely different conceptual forms cannot be expressed in the same language.

For communication to occur, some prior agreement must exist between speaker/sender and hearer/receiver. But if the human need to communicate arises from social nature, then one's group identity determines a significant part of what one perceives to be moral goodness or blameworthiness, one's obligation to do right, be good, and damn evil. This may well explain why controversy and not communication prevailed at the Auschwitz Convent. The assumption is that the antagonists in the dispute must move beyond thought control and "herd mentality." We must rediscover—and in many cases, discover—the meaning of Auschwitz. Since meanings are not given independently of language, we must come up with a suitable hermeneutic that honors the dead and does not abuse the memory of the living. The cry of "Never Again" must never become the sub-text, "Never Again for Us." Loyalists of covenant or convent have created a virtual wall of words at Auschwitz, but it is better to believe that the wall is permeable. And by exploring the inside and outside of the language of bias, we can confront the cycle of contempt and move from strife to Shalom.[5]

Language Transmission: Shoah

To reiterate, Zuckerman and I contest the appropriateness of the word *Holocaust* to describe the genocidal tendency of German Nazi towards European Jewry. Lost in transmission are other victims of Nazi mass murder such as the Senti and Romi ("Gypsies"), the mentally and physically disabled, political opponents (e.g., Communists, Socialists, Unionists), religious dissidents (e.g., Jehovah Witnesses), Russian POWs, and civilians from Poland, the Soviet Union, and Yugoslavia. I would state emphatically that Nazi atrocities embraced the murder of non-Jews, including millions of Slavs and others. Perhaps this would mitigate the term *Holocaust* referencing *only* the mass murder of European Jews; see also the term *Shoah*. Semantically, *Holocaust* means the genocide of European Jews and others by the Nazis during World War II, and *Shoah* (Hebrew *sho'ah*) denotes only the murder of European Jews by the Nazis.[6] Gleanings from the appearance of the word Shoah in Hebrew Scriptures may suggest why this multi-faceted word is or is not appropriate to describe the Jewish calamity during WWII.

Biblical Passages[7]

Isaiah 6 recounts the prophetic call of Isaiah, son of Amoz (vv. 1–7), and his first mission (vv. 8–13); see Table 9.1. The first five chapters call on Judah and Jerusalem to repent, yet there is little positive response. Against the people's angst of possible political and social upheaval following the death of King Uzziah (780–741 BCE), Isaiah envisions God's enduring throne of glory to protect the people. But Isaiah's preaching leads not to return (*teshuva*), but to stubbornness. Alas, heavenly judgment against a sinful majority is requisite: Shoah and exile (vv. 11–12).

ויגע על-פי ויאמר הנה נגע זה על-שפתיך וסר עונך וחטאתך תכפר	(Isa 6:7) and he touched my mouth with it, and said: Lo, this hath touched thy lips; and thine iniquity is taken away, and thy sin expiated.
ואשמע את-קול אדני אמר את-מי אשלח ומי ילך-לנו ואמר הנני שלחני	(8) And I heard the voice of the LORD, saying: "Whom shall I send, and who will go for us?" Then I said: "Here am I; send me."

ויאמר לך ואמרת לעם הזה שמעו שמוע ואל-תבינו וראו ראו ואל-תדעו	(9) And He said: "Go, and tell this people: hear you indeed, but understand not; and see you indeed, but perceive not.
השמן לב-העם הזה ואזניו הכבד ועיניו השע פן-יראה בעיניו ובאזניו ישמע ולבבו יבין ושב ורפא לו	(10) Make the heart of this people fat, and make their ears heavy, and shut their eyes; lest they, seeing with their eyes, and hearing with their ears, and understanding with their heart, return, and be healed."
ואמר עד-מתי אדני ויאמר עד אשר אם-שאו ערים מאין יושב ובתים מאין אדם והאדמה תשאה שממה	(11) Then said I: "LORD, how long?" And He answered: "Until cities be *waste* without inhabitant, and houses without man, and the land become utterly *waste*,
ורחק יהוה את-האדם ורבה העזובה בקרב הארץ	(12) And the LORD have removed men far away, and the forsaken places be many in the midst of the land.
ועוד בה עשריה ושבה והיתה לבער כאלה וכאלון אשר בשלכת מצבת בם זרע קדש מצבתה	(13) And if there be yet a tenth in it, it shall again be eaten up; as a terebinth, and as an oak, whose stock remains, when they cast their leaves, so the holy seed shall be the stock thereof."

Table 9.1: Isa 6:7–13

Isaiah 10:1–4 is generally seen as the final section spelling indictment against the Northern Kingdom; see Table 9.2. This oracle castigates the rich and mighty who mistreat the poor and widows of the land. The theme resonates with the three strophes in the preceding chapter of Isaiah: the arrogance of Ephraim, particularly Samaria (9:7–11); Samaria's continual disobedience to the prophetic directive leads to calamity, for God removes mercy and protection (vv. 12–16); and the result is confusion, anarchy, and war (vv. 17–20). The people's disobedience leads to God's anger, displayed by the Assyrian conquest and destruction of the land: "For wickedness burns as the fire. . . and thickets of the forest roll upward in thick clouds of smoke. . . and the *sho'ah* will come from afar" (Isa 9:17; cf. 10:3). The onslaught by Assyria, "the rod of (God's) fury," is decreed until Zion's punishment is fulfilled. Yet the self-glorification of the Assyrian emperor Sennacherib—the "king of kings" who equates the God of Israel with useless heathen idols—will be short-lived: "And the light of Israel shall be for a fire, as the Holy One for a flame; and it shall burn and devour his thorns and his briers [i.e., the rank and file; see Isa 9:17] in one day" (Isa 10:17).

הוי החקקים חקקי-און ומכתבים עמל כתבו	(Isa 10:1) Woe unto them that decree unrighteous decrees, and to the writers that write iniquity;
להטות מדין דלים ולגזל משפט עניי עמי להיות אלמנות שללם ואת-יתומים יבזו	(2) To turn aside the needy from judgment, and to take away the right of the poor of My people, that widows may be their spoil, and that they may make the fatherless their prey!
ומה-תעשו ליום פקדה ולשואה ממרחק תבוא על-מי תנוסו לעזרה ואנה תעזבו כבודכם	(3) And what will you do in the day of visitation, and in the *ruin* which shall come from far? To whom will you flee for help? And where will you leave your glory?
בלתי כרע תחת אסיר ותחת הרוגים יפלו בכל-זאת לא-שב אפו ועוד ידו נטויה	(4) So as not to crouch under the captives, and fall under the slain. For all this His anger is not turned away, but His hand is stretched out still.

Table 9.2: Isa 10:1–4

Isaiah 47 is a taunting song against Babylon. The song mockingly portrays a mighty empire, hitherto unconquered but now sitting humiliated in the dust. The "virgin daughter sitting dethroned" (v. 1) signifies defeat, thereby setting the mood for a poignant poem depicting princess Chaldea stripped of royalty and riches (vv. 1–5). Babylonia's defeat of Judah was God's decision to punish a sinful people—not a natural extension of Babylonia's might. Her self-proclaimed haughtiness is the cause of her fall. Babylonia's fate is similar to Assyria's (Isa 10:5–15); see Table 9.3. Assyria's deportation of Israelites and Babylonia's deportation of Judahites (v. 10) are redeemed by divine judgment. By fire and smoke, an eternal *sho'ah*, "through justice, and through righteousness, the zeal of the LORD of hosts performs this forever" (Isa 9:6).

ועתה שמעי-זאת עדינה היושבת לבטח האמרה בלבבה אני ואפסי עוד לא אשב אלמנה ולא אדע שכול	(Isa 47:8) Now therefore hear this, you who are given to pleasures, that sit securely, who say in your heart: "I am, and there is none else beside me; I shall not sit as a widow, neither shall I know the loss of children";
ותבאנה לך שתי-אלה רגע ביום אחד שכול ואלמן כתמם באו עליך ברב כשפיך בעצמת חבריך מאד	(9) But these two things shall come to thee in a moment in one day, the loss of children, and widowhood; in their full measure shall they come upon you, for the multitude of your sorceries, and the great abundance of your enchantments.
ותבטחי ברעתך אמרת אין ראני חכמתך ודעתך היא שובבתך ותאמרי בלבך אני ואפסי עוד	(10) And you have been secure in your wickedness, you have t said: "No one can see me"; your wisdom and your knowledge, it has perverted thee; and you have said in thy heart. "I am, and there is no one else beside me."
ובא עליך רעה לא תדעי שחרה ותפל עליך הוה לא תוכלי כפרה ותבא עליך פתאם שואה לא תדעי	(11) Yet shall evil came upon you; you shall not know how to charm it away; and calamity shall fall upon you; you shalt not be able to put it away; and *ruin* shall come upon thee suddenly, before you know.

עמדי-נא בחבריך וברב כשפיך באשר יגעת מנעוריך אולי תוכלי הועיל אולי תערוצי	(12) Stand now with your enchantments, and with the multitude of your sorceries, wherein you have labored from your youth; if so you should be able to profit, if so you may prevail.
נלאית ברב עצתיך יעמדו-נא ויושיעך הברו שמים החזים בכוכבים מודיעם לחדשים מאשר יבאו עליך	(13) You are wearied in the multitude of your counsels; let now the astrologers, the stargazers, the monthly prognosticators, stand up, and save you from the things that shall come upon you.
הנה היו כקש אש שרפתם לא-יצילו את-נפשם מיד להבה אין-גחלת לחמם אור לשבת נגדו	(14) Behold, they shall be as stubble; the fire shall burn them; they shall not deliver themselves from the power of the flame; it shall not be a coal to warm at, nor a fire to sit before.
הנה היו כקש אש שרפתם לא-יצילו את-נפשם מיד להבה אין-גחלת לחמם אור לשבת נגדו	(15) Thus shall they be unto you with whom you have labored; they that have trafficked with you from thy youth shall wander everyone to his quarter; there shall be none to save you.

Table 9.3: Isa 47:8–15

The book of Ezekiel presents oracles of divine judgment against Gog—of the land of Magog—in chapters 38 and 39; see Table 9.4. The identity of Gog is unknown. Gomer, Magog, Meshech, Tubal, Togarmah are linked with Japhet, son of Noah, whose descendants are peoples of Asia Minor, Greece, and Europe (Gen 10:2–5). In traditional Jewish interpretation, Gog is transformed into a national symbol of evil against Israel and determined to wreak *sho'ah* over Israel's people and land. But on that (apocalyptic, eschatological, historical) day, the evil coalition's defeat will be imminent if the people of Israel honor the word of the Lord. Thus, in the intermediate Shabbat of the Feast of Tabernacles, Rabbinic tradition assigns Ezek 38:18–39:16 as the *Haftarah* to accompany Exod 33:12–34:26. Utter *sho'ah* (destruction) of hostile forces reflect Israel's acceptance of God's renewed covenant after the Golden Calf apostasy.

ויהי דבר-יהוה אלי לאמר	(Ezek 38:1) And the word of the LORD came unto me, saying:
בן-אדם שים פניך אל-גוג ארץ המגוג נשיא ראש משך ותבל והנבא עליו	(2) Son of man, set thy face toward Gog, of the land of Magog, the chief prince of Meshech and Tubal, and prophesy against him,
ואמרת כה אמר אדני יהוה הנני אליך גוג נשיא ראש משך ותבל	(3) and say: Thus saith the Lord God: Behold, I am against thee, O Gog, chief prince of Meshech and Tubal;
ושובבתיך ונתתי חחים בלחייך והוצאתי אותך ואת-כל-חילך סוסים ופרשים לבשי מכלול כלם קהל רב צנה ומגן תפשי חרבות כלם	(4) and I will turn you about, and put hooks into your jaws, and I will bring you forth, and all your army, horses and horsemen, all of them clothed most gorgeously, a great company with buckler and shield, all of them handling swords:
פרס כוש ופוט אתם כלם מגן וכובע	(5) Persia, Cush, and Put with them, all of them with shield and helmet;
גמר וכל-אגפיה בית תוגרמה ירכתי צפון ואת-כל-אגפיו עמים רבים אתך	(6) Gomer, and all his bands; the house of Togarmah in the uttermost parts of the north, and all his bands; even many peoples with you.
הכן והכן לך אתה וכל-קהלך הנקהלים עליך והיית להם למשמר	(7) Be you prepared, and prepare for yourself, you, and all your company that are assembled unto you, and be you guarded of them.
מימים רבים תפקד באחרית השנים תבוא אל-ארץ משובבת מחרב מקבצת מעמים רבים על הרי ישראל אשר-היו לחרבה תמיד והיא מעמים הוצאה וישבו לבטח כלם	(8) After many days you shall be mustered for service, in the latter years you shall come against the land that is brought back from the sword, that is gathered out of many peoples, against the mountains of Israel, which have been a continual waste; but it is brought forth out of the peoples, and they dwell safely all of them.
ועלית כשאה תבוא כענן לכסות הארץ תהיה אתה וכל-אגפיך ועמים רבים אותך	(9) And you shall ascend, you shall come like a *storm*, you shall be like a cloud to cover the land, you, and all your bands, and many peoples with you.

Table 9.4: Ezek 38:1–9

The book of Zephaniah proclaims judgment upon Judah and the inhabitants of Jerusalem. The superscription dates to the reign of King Josiah (639–608 BCE). The prophet addresses a despicable state of religious and social affairs, and chapter 2 divides into announcement (vv. 2–9) and enactment (vv. 10–18); see Table 9.5. The capital sin is idolatry coupled with religious pollution and assimilation. God's decisive judgment is extreme: darkness, clouds, and fire, as well as utter calamity and destruction (*sho'ah umesho'ah*). The alternative, however, is repentance and return (*teshuva;* see Zeph 2:1–4).

קרוב יום-יהוה הגדול קרוב ומהר מאד קול יום יהוה מר צרח שם גבור	(Zeph 1:14) The great day of the LORD is approaching, approaching most swiftly. Hark, the day of the LORD, wherein the mighty man cries bitterly.
יום עברה היום ההוא יום צרה ומצוקה יום שאה ומשואה יום חשך ואפלה יום ענן וערפל	(15) That day is a day of wrath, a day of trouble and distress, a day of *calamity and desolation*, a day of darkness and gloominess, a day of clouds and thick darkness,
יום שופר ותרועה על הערים הבצרות ועל הפנות הגבהות	(16) A day of the horn and alarm, against the fortified cities, and against the high towers.
והצרתי לאדם והלכו כעורים כי ליהוה חטאו ושפך דמם כעפר ולחמם כגללים	(17) And I will bring distress upon men, that they shall walk like the blind, because they have sinned against the LORD; and their blood shall be poured out as dust, and their flesh as dung.
גם-כספם גם-זהבם לא-יוכל להצילם ביום עברת יהוה ובאש קנאתו תאכל כל-הארץ כי-כלה אך-נבהלה יעשה את כל-ישבי הארץ	(18) Neither their silver nor their gold shall be able to deliver them in the day of the LORD'S wrath; but the whole earth shall be devoured by the fire of his jealousy; for he will make an end, yea, a terrible end, of all them that dwell in the earth.

Table 9.5: Zeph 1:14–18

In Psalm 35, the military leader or king cries for deliverance from persecution by military enemies (vv. 1–10) and by acquaintances and associates who bear false testimony (vv. 11–17). Divine intervention (God as warrior, or God's angelic forces) and invectives towards the enemy are invoked to mete out proper punishment. "Let *sho'ah* come upon (the enemy) unawares and let his net that he has hid catch himself; with *sho'ah* let him fall therein" (v. 8). A similar cry for justice comes against individuals who wrought enmity and false pretexts. Righteousness demands qualitative retribution, that is, rescue from God approved destructiveness/*sho'ah* (v. 17); see Table 9.6. The Psalm concludes with a plea to be judged in righteousness and to be remembered continuously by daily praising the Lord's righteousness (v. 19–28).

לדוד ריבה יהוה את-יריבי לחם את-לחמי	(Ps 35:1) A Psalm of David. Strive, O LORD, with them that strive with me; fight against them that fight against me.
יבשו ויכלמו מבקשי נפשי יסגו אחור ויחפרו חשבי רעתי	(4) Let them be ashamed and brought to confusion that seek after my soul; let them be turned back and be abashed that devise my hurt.
כי-חנם טמנו-לי שחת רשתם חנם חפרו לנפשי	(7) For without cause have they hid for me the pit, even their net, without cause have they dug for my soul.
תבואהו שואה לא-ידע ורשתו אשר-טמן תלכדו בשואה יפל-בה	(8) Let *destruction* come upon him unawares; and let his net that he has hid catch himself; with *destruction* let him fall therein.
ונפשי תגיל ביהוה תשיש בישועתו	(9) And my soul shall be joyful in the LORD; it shall rejoice in his salvation.
כל עצמותי תאמרנה יהוה מי כמוך מציל עני מחזק ממנו ועני ואביון מגזלו	(10) All my bones shall say: "LORD, who is like unto you, who delivers the poor from him that is too strong for him, yea, the poor and the needy from him that spoils him?"

אדני כמה תראה השיבה נפשי משאיהם מכפירים יחידתי	(17) LORD, how long will you look on? Rescue my soul from their *destructions*, mine only one from the lions.
אודך בקהל רב בעם עצום אהללך	(18) I will give you thanks in the great congregation; I will praise you among a numerous people.

Table 9.6: Ps 35:1, 4, 7–10, 17–18

In Psalm 63, the song leader reflects upon an anguished fleeing David in the wilderness of Judah and yearning to see the Jerusalem Temple and worship therein; see Table 9.7. Preceding Psalms express the same yearning; indeed Psalm 42 evinces identical language to Psalm 63. Psalm 63:9–11 depicts a plea for deliverance from lies and accusers. Their words inflict *sho'ah* on the innocent, but the accusers suffer *sho'ah* by the grace of God in the end.

דבקה נפשי אחריך בי תמכה ימינך	(Ps 63:9) My soul cleaves unto you; your right hand holds me fast.
והמה לשואה יבקשו נפשי יבאו בתחתיות הארץ	(10) But those that seek my soul, to *destroy* it, shall go into the nethermost parts of the earth.
יגירהו על-ידי-חרב מנת שעלים יהיו	(11) They shall be hurled to the power of the sword; they shall be a portion for foxes.
והמלך ישמח באלהים יתהלל כל-הנשבע בו כי יסכר פי דוברי-שקר	(12) But the king shall rejoice in God; every one that swear by him shall glory; for the mouth of them that speak lies shall be stopped.

Table 9.7: Ps 63:9–12

In the book of Proverbs, Wisdom (*khokhmah*, plural *khokhmot*) is personified as a woman who preaches the importance of learning and following the knowledge of the elders to avoid life's pitfalls and societal disaster (*sho'ah*, v. 27); see Table 9.8. Serious contrition does not suspend rightful punishment for wrongful acts. Punishment is rather a self-imposed reminder not to repeat wrongful deeds. The plural *khokhmot* underscores the intensity of this lesson.

תשובו לתוכחתי הנה אביעה לכם רוחי אודיעה דברי אתכם	(Prov 1:23) Turn you at my reproof; behold, I will pour out my spirit unto you, I will make known my words unto you.
יען קראתי ותמאנו נטיתי ידי ואין מקשיב	(24) Because I have called, and ye refused, I have stretched out my hand, and no man attended,
ותפרעו כל-עצתי ותוכחתי לא אביתם	(25) But ye have set at naught all my counsel, and would none of my reproof;
גם-אני באידכם אשחק אלעג בבא פחדכם	(26) I also, in your calamity, will laugh, I will mock when your dread cometh;
בבא כשאוה פחדכם ואידכם כסופה יאתה בבא עליכם צרה וצוקה	(27) When your dread cometh as a *storm*, and your calamity comes on as a whirlwind; when trouble and distress come upon you.
אז יקראנני ולא אענה ישחרנני ולא ימצאנני	(28) Then will they call me, but I will not answer, they will seek me earnestly, but they shall not find me.
תחת כי-שנאו דעת ויראת יהוה לא בחרו	(29) For that they hated knowledge, and did not choose the fear of the LORD;

Table 9.8: Prov 1:23–29

Proverbs 3 offers advice that wisdom and understanding vitalize the soul and preserve life. The proverb also admonishes the wicked who bring destruction (v. 25, *sho'ah*); see Table 9.9. The proverb provides guidelines for social interaction; for example, provide good for one who deserves it, do not inflict evil nor strive with one when uncalled for, and avoid the lawless and the devious, for they are an abomination before the Lord (vv. 27–32). The chapter concludes with a divine curse on the wicked and a contrasting blessing on the righteous (vv. 33–35).

בני אל-ילזו מעיניך נצר תשיה ומזמה	(Prov 3:21) My son, let not them depart from thine eyes; keep sound wisdom and discretion;
ויהיו חיים לנפשך וחן לגרגרתיך	(22) So will they be life unto thy soul, and grace to your neck.
אז תלך לבטח דרכך ורגלך לא תגוף	(23) Then you will walk in your way securely, and you will not dash your foot.
אם-תשכב לא-תפחד ושכבת וערבה שנתך	(24) When you lie down, you will not be afraid; yea, you will lie down, and your sleep will be sweet.
אל-תירא מפחד פתאם ומשאת רשעים כי תבא	(25) Be not afraid of sudden terror, neither of the *destruction* of the wicked, when it comes;
כי-יהוה יהיה בכסלך ושמר רגלך מלכד	(26) For the LORD will be your confidence, and will keep your foot from being caught.

Table 9.9: Prov 3:21–26

Job 38:1–42:6 dramatizes Job's cry of suffering, his direct encounter with God, and finally Job's vindication. God's voice out of the storm presents his infinite wisdom highlighted by his acts of creation and laws of nature. A paradoxical background is prevalent. Job 38:12–13 speak of wickedness and utter devastation (*sho'ah umesho'ah*) in the corners of the Earth before God's work commenced; see Table 9.10. The puzzled Job is asked if he could do any better in running the world more fairly. In sum, the discourse explains neither the suffering of the righteous Job nor the fullness of the wisdom of God.

הבאת אל-אצרות שלג ואצרות ברד תראה	(Job 38:22) Have you entered the treasuries of the snow, or have you seen the treasuries of the hail,
אשר-חשכתי לעת-צר ליום קרב ומלחמה	(23) Which I have reserved against the time of trouble, against the day of battle and war?

אי-זה הדרך יחלק אור יפץ קדים עלי-ארץ	(24) By what way is the light parted, or the east wind scattered upon the earth?
מי-פלג לשטף תעלה ודרך לחזיז קלות	(25) Who has cleft a channel for the torrents, or a way for the lightning of the thunder;
להמטיר על-ארץ לא-איש מדבר לא-אדם בו	(26) To cause it to rain on a land where no man is, on the wilderness, wherein there is no man;
להשביע שאה ומשאה ולהצמיח מצא דשא	(27) To satisfy the *desolate and waste* ground, and to cause the bud of the tender herb to spring forth?
היש-למטר אב או מי-הוליד אגלי-טל	(28) Has the rain a father? Or who has begotten the drops of dew?
מבטן מי יצא הקרח וכפר שמים מי ילדו	(29) Out of whose womb came the ice? And the hoar-frost of heaven, who has gendered it?
כאבן מים יתחבאו ופני תהום יתלכדו	(30) The waters are congealed like stone, and the face of the deep is frozen.

Table 9.10: Job 38:22–30

Conclusion

"Shoah" passages in the Hebrew Bible speak of catastrophic destruction, ruin, waste, and so forth. Collectively, they speak of judgment and judged, admonition and punishment, exile and return. God talk is passive, active, and rarely indifferent. Human actions are vulnerable and venerable. Saving a remnant is a response to Shoah. The use of *Holocaust* or *Shoah* to label the murder of European Jewry in WWII involves issues of motive and effect. *Holocaust* (Greek *holokaustos*) denotes a sacrificial offering that is totally consumed by fire. The root *`lh* occurs multiple times in the Tanakh, and the basic intent of *`olah* is a sacrificial offering to God. *Shoah* elicits similar catastrophic effect but *reconstructs* God's participatory role—that is, God creates, and humans redeem or prevent. In verses of *sho'ah* *umesho'ah*, for example, God brings forth tender vegetation out of preexistent *desolate and waste* (Job 38:27), and the wrathful day of the Lord is caused by humankind (Zeph 1:14–18).

In entering the abyss of evil, I choose the Hebrew term *Shoah*: it confronts the Nazi doer and sympathizer, questions the Gentile bystander, does not neutralize the Jewish victim, and—for the sake of God—keeps "Holocaust" in history. To repair the world (*tiqqun 'olam*) is the teaching lost in the whirlwind. "God: Shoah" is meant to convey that "never again" is "never to forget" that the voices from the ashes be heard in tribulation and awe: the living should do all in their power to ensure that the Event not become trivial and to ensure that the survival of the Jewish people (heritage, history, religion, and culture) is paramount.[8] And the Angels cry.

Notes

I am pleased to pay tribute to the academic work and achievement of Leonard Greenspoon. Master of translation and interpretation, who more than most, understands the importance of a biblical word (Greek and Hebrew) in transmission. A collegial friend who exemplifies the meaning of *menshlikeit* in friendship and scholarship. *Mit mazal und glick.*

[1]Thoughts expressed in this introductory paragraph are extracted from my article, "Holocaust," in *Encyclopedia of Religion in America*, ed. C. H. Lippy and P.W. Williams, 4 vols. (Washington, DC: CQ Press, 2010), 2:1027–32.

[2]One of the oldest annual Christian-Jewish discussion groups on faith responsibility related to the Shoah is the "Scholars Conference on the Holocaust and Churches" established by two American Protestant clergymen professors, Franklin H. Littell and Hubert G. Locke. The Scholars Conference convened in March of 1970 under the heading, "What can America Learn?" See Zev Garber, "A Citadel Fitly Constructed: Philo-Semitism and the Making of an American Holocaust Conference," in *The Impact of the Holocaust in America*, ed. Zev Garber, Casden Annual Review/The Jewish Role in American Life 6 (West Lafayette, IN: Purdue University Press, 2008), 191–217.

[3]For a discussion of the term "Holocaust" and the psychology behind its popular usage, see Zev Garber and Bruce Zuckerman, "Why Do We Call the Holocaust 'The Holocaust'? An Inquiry into the Psychology of Labels," *Modern Judaism* 9 (1989): 197–211; repr. in Zev Garber, *Shoah: The Paradigmatic Genocide; Essays in Exegesis and Eisegesis*, Studies in the Shoah 8 (Lanham, MD: University Press of America, 1994); a revised version of this article appears in Zev Garber and Bruce Zuckerman, *Double Takes: Thinking and Rethinking Issues of Modern Judaism in Ancient Contexts* (Lanham, MD: University Press of America, 2004).

[4]See Zev Garber and Bruce Zuckerman, "The Führer/Furor Over the Auschwitz Convent: The Inside and Outside of the Language of Bias," in *What Kind of God? Essays in Honor of Richard L. Rubenstein*, ed. Betty Rogers Rubenstein and Michael Berenbaum (Lanham, MD: University Press of America, 1995), 95–109; repr. in *From Prejudice to Destruction: Western Civilization in the Shadow of Auschwitz*, ed. G. Jan Colijn and Marcia Sachs Littell, (Münster: LIT, 1995), 167–79; a revised version of the article is found in Garber and Zuckerman, *Double Takes*, 57–78.

[5]Thoughts on RFTF I and II were presented at the Sixteenth Annual Symposium of the Klutznick Chair in Jewish Civilization held at Creighton University, September 14–15, 2003. See Zev Garber, "Language Violence: Auschwitz Convent Controversy," in *The Jews of Eastern Europe*, ed. Leonard J. Greenspoon, Ronald A. Simkins, and Brian Horowitz, Studies in Jewish Civilization 16 (Omaha: Creighton University Press, 2006), 329–38.

[6]Similar misuse of terminology is when anti-Semitism, exclusive hatred of Jews, embraces all Semitic peoples.

[7]In this section, the Hebrew and English biblical texts are from the 1917 JPS Tanakh.

[8]David Patterson ("Holocaust or Shoah: the Greek Category versus Jewish Thought," in *Maven in Blue Jeans: A Festschrift in Honor of Zev Garber*, ed. Stephen L. Jacobs, Shofar Supplements in Jewish Studies [West Lafayette, IN: Purdue University Press, 2009], 336–45, here 337) writes, "One scholar who resists the de-Judaization of the mass murder of the Jews is Zev Garber."

10

Translation versus Teaching: Competing Agendas in Samson Raphael Hirsch's Bible Project

Alan T. Levenson
University of Oklahoma

Does Rabbi Samson Raphael Hirsch (1808–1888) belong in a volume entitled *Found in Translation*? On a technical level, the case against Hirsch's methods of Bible translation—in his case, from Hebrew to German—are manifold. Hirsch consistently rendered hendiadys as offering two distinct teachings. He had no consistent method of treating the *vav*-consecutive.[1] He stuck more closely to the Hebrew word order (source language) than Moses Mendelssohn, who cared so much about elegant German (target language), but not as consistently as Buber–Rosenzweig.[2] The result is a German translation that can be called cumbersome (unlike Mendelssohn's) without being exciting (unlike the Buber–Rosenzweig rendering). Despite absolute fidelity to the Masoretic text versus any other possible version (e.g., the Septuagint, Syriac versions, the Samaritan Pentateuch),[3] Hirsch occasionally added clarifying words unsupported by the Masoretic text, thereby committing what Robert Alter has termed "the heresy of explanation" masquerading as translation.[4] Hirsch placed too much interpretive emphasis on vocalization and on cantillation marks which were added centuries after the biblical text achieved stabilization.[5] He did not adequately differentiate the two principal divine names used in the Torah, God (*Elohim*, rendered Gott) and Lord (*Yahweh*, also rendered Gott).[6] Above all, Hirsch used his theory of phonetic relationship (Lautverwandschaft) to derive all manner of teachings from three-letter Hebrew roots that often have little or nothing to do with each other.[7] Perhaps Hirsch's translation and commentary belong better in the category of "lost" than "found."

This litany of translational liberties appears ironic, given that Hirsch argued for over fifty years that the Bible must be understood on its own terms ("aus sich selbst verständet"). Hirsch's translation definitely has its flaws, and its sharpest critics question whether it even deserves attention in academic circles (see below). My goal is not to champion Hirsch, but rather to understand the role of his translation in the context of his Bible project overall. To state the obvious, Hirsch was well aware of the translations of Mendelssohn, Zunz, Philippson, and others, yet he decided to render his own, rather than using a preexisting translation, but supplying his own commentary, a road oft-taken. Hirsch clearly found his predecessors' efforts inadequate to his overarching goals, goals that seem worth articulating.

Hirsch's Premise: The Primacy of Oral Torah

As Jay Harris explains, Hirsch developed a novel view of the relationship between the Written and Oral Torahs.[8] Previous commentators regarded the Oral Torah as an explication of the Written Torah, thereby tacitly assigning pride of place to the latter. Hirsch reversed this relationship. For Hirsch, however, the Written Torah provided the "Cliffs Notes" to the Oral Torah, which God taught Moses directly at Mount Sinai and which Moses transmitted to the Sages. For forty years, Oral Torah existed as living Judaism without the Written Torah at all! Even after the Written Torah was given to Israel before Moses's death, it did not supplant the Oral Torah. In Hirsch's own words:

> The relationship between *torah sh'biktav* [Written Torah] and *torah sh'ba'al peh* [Oral Torah] is like that between brief notes taken on a scientific lecture, and the lecture itself. Students who attended the oral lecture require only their brief notes to recall at any time the entire lecture. They often find that a word, a question mark, an exclamation mark, a period, or the underscoring of a word, is sufficient to bring to mind a whole series of ideas, observations, qualifications and so forth. But for those who did not attend the instructor's lecture, these notes are not of much use.[9]

It is ironic and yet predictable that a self-conceived defender of tradition should introduce such a novelty. Despite Hirsch's self-consciously anti-historicist view of the Bible, he was very much a product of his age, and he did import some contemporary perspectives into his Bible project. Hirsch sought a timeless Torah that could be explained on its own terms, but such a quest is a chimera. Hirsch made rabbinic literature the *only* legitimate prism through which the Bible should be interpreted, and he implied that ancient Near Eastern analogues could never explain a biblical text.

Hirsch's position is frankly incompatible with two foundational premises of biblical scholarship, namely that scholarship can be an objective endeavor and that the biblical text can be analyzed as a humanly produced, historical document. When he discusses legal cases such as the acquisition of the Hebrew slave (Exodus 21), Hirsch claims that this text cannot represent the entire law of slavery. However, for Hirsch, the entirety of Ancient Israelite law on any and every point can be reconstructed by looking at the rabbinic literature! Scholars agree that the Hebrew Bible does not contain all the laws of ancient Israel; the Written Torah may even deal predominantly with exceptional cases or those cases requiring emphasis. Contemporary biblical scholars consider most laws customary, taken for granted, and therefore never recorded; the details have simply been lost in the sands of time. Such a degree of agnosticism, of course, would be unacceptable to Hirsch.

Hirsch's Books The Nineteen Letters *and* Horeb

Was Written Torah important to Hirsch? To follow Hirsch's metaphor to its logical end, if a student really knows the course material (the rabbinic tradition, in that case), does that student need the Cliffs Notes? Hirsch resoundingly answers affirmatively. Concerning haggadah, Written Torah is necessary for teaching;[10] regarding halachah, Written Torah is necessary for teaching the meaning of prescribed acts.[11] Hirsch believed the Bible required more attention than it had received in the immediate past, a viewpoint reflected in his critique on *pilpul*, a target of Mendelssohn and the entire Haskalah. Hirsch came from a household he described as "religiously enlightened," and like other Jewish Enlighteners, Hirsch wished to promote the centrality of the Hebrew Bible.[12]

The Nineteen Letters is best known for its German Romantic presentation of God, humanity, and the world (chs. 1–6) and for its embrace of Emancipation and modernity from a traditionalist perspective (chs. 16–19).[13] The heart of *The Nineteen Letters*, however (judging by its role as guide to the *Horeb*), was Hirsch's highly original classification of the commandments into six categories and their explication (chs. 7–15). Isidore Grunfeld wrote, "Hirsch seems to have been the first of our legal philosophers to try to classify the commandments of the Torah by exclusively using the terms used by the Torah (toroth, edoth, mishpatim, chukim, mitzvoth, avodah), and to interpret them in the manner set out at the beginning of this section."[14] Why did Hirsch try to do what earlier codifiers avoided? The answer seems to be that Torah's use of these terms is inconsistent, not distinguishing legal categories into which the commandments fall—even though Christian interpreters have long subdivided civil, ceremonial, and moral precepts.

As a law code, Hirsch's *Horeb* succeeded in making halachah familiar (by rendering it into German) and meaningful (by connecting it back to Scripture).[15] *Horeb* was intended as a modern, German-language law-code for Israel's "thinking young men and women," as the title page reads; expressly including female readership made Hirsch's work exceptional. Hirsch promised a companion work to *Horeb*, a biblically-based theology that would be entitled *Moriah*, but it never appeared; this has aroused considerable speculation.[16]

Horeb itself exemplifies Hirsch's bibliocentrism, though. Hirsch began every discussion with relevant biblical quotes, and he expounded their significance mainly through discussion of biblical passages. His procedure differed from earlier law codes, which focused more on rabbinic literature; no code that I know of assigned centrality to the Hebrew Bible in the way that Hirsch did. He famously noted how early in life his attitude toward scripture had coalesced:

> One word here concerning the proper method of Torah investigation [Thauroforschung]. Two revelations are open before

> us; that is, nature and the Torah. . . . In nature, all phenomena stand before us as indisputable facts, and we can endeavor a posteriori to ascertain the law of each, and the connection of all. . . . The same principles must be applied to the investigation of the Torah. In the Torah, as in nature, God is the ultimate cause. In the Torah, even as in nature, no fact may be denied, even though the reason and the connection may not be understood. . . . Its ordinances must be accepted in their entirety as undeniable phenomena, and must be studied in accordance with their connection with each other, and the subject to which they relate.[17]

When Hirsch likened "Torah" to "Nature," he meant the exact opposite of Spinoza's similar-sounding phrase in the *Theological-Political Treatise*, "The means of interpreting Scripture are not much different from those of interpreting nature." For Spinoza, interpreters engaged in a scientific dissection of the ancient text by assessing authorship, transmission, inclusion, and error. For Hirsch, the text simply cannot be questioned. For example, given three narratives regarding a Patriarch encountering a foreign ruler who would imperil the chastity of the Patriarch's wife—Abra(ha)m in Genesis 12 and 20 as well as Isaac in Genesis 26—the answer cannot be that ancient multiple sources are being preserved by a somewhat less ancient editor.[18] Similarly, if Deuteronomy gives new explanations of teachings in Genesis–Numbers, the reason cannot be that Deuteronomy comes from a seventh-century BCE milieu reflecting a more developed society. For Hirsch, the text we have is profoundly factual—*Torah* embodies God's Words just as the *world* embodies God's Creation.

Hirsch's Torah Commentary

Hirsch's *Der Pentateuch*, written in Frankfurt am Main from 1867–1878, was the product of decades of sermonizing and writing; his descendants claim that hardly an Orthodox home was found without it.[19] These years overlapped momentous events, such as the unification of Germany and the secession of Hirsch's Israelitische

Religionsgesellschaft (IRG) from the Jewish community. Hirsch's context clearly informed his interpretations. For example, in Exod 1:8, "a new Pharaoh arose who knew not Joseph," which prior commentators read as a native dynasty retaking control. Robert Liberles has shown that Hirsch saw the opposite: a foreign dynasty (analogous to Prussia) conquered and paid no heed to local history or custom, Joseph's service to the Egyptian nation.[20]

Hirsch applied his phonetic method (Lautverwandschaft),[21] and embraced the midrashic belief that Hebrew was humanity's original language.[22] He connected the second word of the Torah, *bara* ("create") with *barach, barah, perach, pereh* and *perah,* all of which, according to Hirsch, connote a striving to get out or to bring out. These relationships are dubious, but such word-play is replete in Hirsch's hand-written notebooks. I would argue that by stressing the Hebrew-ness of Hebrew Bible's language, Hirsch was in the mainstream of modern Jewish commentators.[23]

I would also describe Hirsch's commentary as Eurocentric, not as polemical.[24] Commenting upon Noah's three sons Shem, Ham and Japheth, Hirsch considers them eternal archetypes. Ham represents appetitive instincts; Japheth represents aesthetic beauty; and Shem shows that service to God is the highest calling. Genesis 9:27 is an admittedly problematic verse that has been used to support both slavery and racism. The text says that Japheth will live "in the tents of Shem" but that Canaan, the son of Ham, will be their servant/slave. Hirsch comments:

> When we look around in historical facts we can say: the stem of Japheth reached its fullest blossoming in the Greeks; that of Shem in the Hebrews, Israel who bore and bears the name of God through the world of nations. Right to the present-day it is only these two races, the descendants of Shem and Japheth, the Greeks and the Jews, who have become the real educators and teachers of humanity. . . . Japheth has ennobled the world aesthetically. Shem has enlightened it spiritually and morally. Hellenism and Judaism have become the great active forces in the educational work on mankind, and the rest of the world has been merely the passive material on which they worked.[25]

A final example of Hirsch's original mode of commentary comes from his discussion of "Hear O Israel!" known as the Shema (Deut 6:4), generally acknowledged as Judaism's central affirmation. The *dalet* at the end of the Shema (*Shema Yisrael, Adonai Eloheinu, Adonai ekhad*) is written larger. Hirsch explained that the *ekhad* is written with a large *dalet* on the Torah scroll to distinguish it from a *resh,* which would make the word *akher*, "another." This shows insight on Hirsch's part, for the *resh* in *akher* is likewise enlarged in Exod 34:14, which prohibits worship of "other" (*akher*) gods. Accordingly, Israel's God is not just "another" one of those foreign gods.

So far so good, but Hirsch then took these scribal niceties and inferred an entire kerygma: "The *resh* is the polytheistic thought and is accommodatingly round. The *dalet* of the Jewish truth is sharply angular. With the loss of this little sharpness, the *ehad* becomes *aher.*" Such an extreme position—that the actual shape and size of letters contain theological teachings—is also found in Jewish tradition, famously in Midrash Gen. Rab. 1:10 as to why God created the world with second letter [*bet*] rather than the first [*aleph*]. Still, it is a bit shocking to find this nineteenth-century commentator. I am reminded of Lenny Bruce's classic comic routine: "Jewish and Goyish." Is "resh" really a "goyish" letter and "dalet" a Jewish one?[26]

Assessing Hirsch as a Translator and Commentator

Hirsch has been grouped with Orthodox stalwarts such as Jacob Zvi Mecklenburg (1785–1865) and Meir Leibush Malbim (1809–1879), who not only rejected critical Bible scholarship but also unified written and oral Torah. But Hirsch has also been compared to Mendelssohn, who was both a translator and a commentator. Hirsch's translation differed greatly from Mendelssohn's. Mendelssohn freely rendered "units of meaning," whereas Hirsch's symbolic method demanded that he stay very close to each Hebrew word; his commentary was generated by listing similar verbal roots to the scriptural word and then deducing a theological teaching. Mendelssohn cared equally deeply about the translation and the commentary; for Hirsch, the translational choices mainly provided a platform for his theology.

Yet Hirsch's attitude toward Mendelssohn's achievement was not negative, but ambivalent. Like most German Jews, Hirsch venerated Mendelssohn as a model German Jew. Breuer tells us that Hirsch's admiration extended even to Mendelssohn's *Biur*, which had been condemned by Rabbi Raphael Kohen of Hamburg, the voice of tradition in Hirsch's hometown.[27] Indeed, it would have been very peculiar for any mid-nineteenth century German-Jewish thinker not to have been influenced by Mendelssohn's thought.[28]

Mendelssohn's influence is also evident in Hirsch's Bible Commentary as counter-example. In Gen 2:4, for instance, Hirsch savages Mendelssohn's rendering the Tetragrammaton as "Eternal." Hirsch writes:

> . . . a metaphysical transcendental conception which has scarcely any practical application to anything else certainly not to our own lives and existence. . . . The thought Eternal leaves our hearts cold, contains nothing for our lives and hence has no relationship whatsoever with *midat ha-rahamim* (the attribute of mercy).[29]

Mendelssohn's choice of Eternal was well known, and Hirsch's criticism has merit. Yet his own solution was problematic: Hirsch italicized God when it represented *Adonai*, did not italicize it when it represented *Elohim*, and left the double divine name unremarked except for two Hebrew letters. Unlike Mendelssohn, demonstrating the Scriptures' ability to speak in any language meant less to Hirsch than making sure readers step in as symbolic interpreters of the Hebrew word. Hirsch diverged from Mendelssohn in others ways, too. Translationally, Hirsch stuck closely to Hebrew word choice, verb stems (*binyanim*), and verb tense—at the expense of smooth reading. Just as there are minimalists and maximalists in the history of ancient Israel, Hirsch would be an exegetical maximalist, Mendelssohn a minimalist.

Hirsch nevertheless shared Mendelssohn's Orthodoxy vis-à-vis lower and higher criticism; his fundamental reliance on Jewish sources; his heteronymous view of the commandments; and his desire to sequester discussions of the Bible from a thoroughgoing historical-developmental model. The lengthy articles in *Jeschurun*,

"The Hypothesis of the Bible Critics and the Genesis Commentary of Rabbi S. R. Hirsch," exceeded Mendelssohn's already acerbic criticism of scholarly impiety. Hirsch's son-in-law, Joseph Gugenheimer, placed much of the blame for source criticism on Spinoza. Gugenheimer chided those who considered Moses more of a redactor than a vehicle for the divine; Gugenheimer was even more condemning of Jewish transgressors such as radical reformer David Einhorn. Unlike source critics' speculative procedure, Gugenheimer claimed that Hirsch's commentary was built "on the ground of a strictly rational scholarly exegesis."[30]

Hirsch cited Midrash Rabbah often in his *Pentateuch*; I believe Hirsch's debt to the early rabbinic masters has not been stressed sufficiently. While some have cast doubts on Hirsch's acumen as a Talmudist, he clearly had an eye for important rabbinic traditions. If he knew Tanach and rabbinic traditions less intimately than Eastern European contemporaries, that is hardly surprising, given that Hirsch was educated at public schools in Hamburg. He rarely stated his opposition to previous traditional commentators outright, although his dissent may be inferred, as in his comments to Genesis 1. Hirsch relied greatly on medieval figures such as Halevy and Nachmanides as well as modern figures such as Nieto, Mecklenburg, and Malbim. Hirsch's dependence on the early Sages is very great, and so is his debt to earlier German Jews. Most of all, Hirsch's originality as an exegete should not be minimized.

Hirsch's Pentateuch appears as the culmination of a lifetime of engagement with Torah. While he is rightly seen as going further than anyone in seeing the oral and written Torah as indivisible, Hirsch in no way disparaged studying the written Torah. In his early writings (*The Nineteen Letters* and *Horeb*) Hirsch promised a Jewish theology based on Tanach, insisted on the study of Tanach in Hebrew, and used terms in Torah to organize a legal classification of the commandments. Although some Ultra-Orthodox have tried to claim Hirsch as their own, a study of his Bible project reveals that Hirsch stands squarely in the German-Jewish tradition of elevating the Hebrew Bible and its religious teachings—his idiosyncrasies as a translator notwithstanding.

Conclusion

Hirsch's translation and commentary appear as the culmination of a lifetime's engagement in understanding the message of Torah. While Hirsch is rightly deemed to have gone further than anyone in seeing the Oral and Written Torah as indivisible, I have argued that this implies no disparagement of studying the Written Torah. In his early writings (*Nineteen Letters* and *Horeb*) Hirsch emphasized that Jewish theology could be based on the Bible, that Jewish law could be derived from biblical word-choice, and that the Torah's Hebrew-ness was indivisible from its nature.[31]

I am not sure if non-Jews read Hirsch, nor am I certain whether that criterion is most important for determining the significance of his work. I am sure, however, that Hirsch's *Pentateuch* (1867–1878) has had wide influence; it has appeared in several editions and has been translated into Hebrew, French, and twice into English. Hirsch appears in popular "Weekly Torah Portion" columns, including those of various Israeli newspapers, and he has been quoted by subsequent *Jewish* commentators. Without accepting Hirsch's translational procedures or agreeing with his theological assumptions, one can appreciate the psychological insights with which Hirsch illuminated biblical characters and scenes. His desire to validate every word of Torah engendered empathetic readings; although scholars may question whether these readings reflect authorial intent or Hirsch's eisegesis, lay readers probably do not care as much. And Jacob Rosenheim (1870–1965), an important leader of German Orthodoxy and a figure who bridged the gap between scholarly and devotional reading, has commented:

> I knew comprehensively, not from Talmud and not from Rashi's commentary, but rather from having studied Hirsch's *Commentary on the Torah*, the whole order of the offerings, the laws of *metzora* [skin disease] and ritual purity and the laws of custodians and damages, with all their manifold details, *more clearly and comprehensively than any yeshiva student.*[32]

In *The Making of the Modern Jewish Bible*, I claimed that Hirsch was even more important to the story of the modern Jewish Bible than was Abraham Geiger.[33] Professor Susannah Heschel, author of a seminal work on Geiger's role in nineteenth-century scholarship, objected to my characterization as follows:

> Hirsch wrote on a popular level and continues to be read in Orthodox circles; no one would be capable of reading Geiger's *Urschrift* other than highly-trained scholars. Theirs are two entirely different spheres of influence, and the impact of a work cannot be measured in terms of the numbers sold or read—*or we would conclude that* [Tim LaHaye and Jerry Jenkins's late-twentieth-century Christian dispensationalist] *Left Behind series is more influential than* [late-nineteenth-century biblical scholar Julius] *Wellhausen*. Never have I come across reference to Hirsch by any significant non-Jewish German Bible scholar, but Geiger's work was and is widely read, passionately debated, and ultimately has won some key debates.[34]

These are legitimate grounds for such criticism, and I certainly bow to Heschel's superior knowledge of the scholarly literature of this era. Nevertheless, I urge a more sympathetic assessment of what Hirsch accomplished.

Given Hirsch's learned style and diligent preparation, which are amply demonstrated in the numerous notebooks preserved in the Bar Ilan University Hirsch Chair archive, a closer analogy to the *Left Behind* series might be the early twentieth-century collection, *The Fundamentals*.[35] Either way, Heschel is arguing that Wellhausen's scholarship is more significant, if not more influential, than popular Protestant evangelical or fundamentalist writings. But I am not so sure. Without doubt, there is a huge gap between scholarly and devotional readings, between Bible scholarship and Bible study. This gap is a persistent feature of modern Bible reading, Jewish and Christian,[36] but I do *not* consider that gap to be absolute, or sufficiently addressed. Moreover, I think that academics ignore the needs, motives, and—dare I say—*hermeneutics* of the far larger number of devotional readers to the peril of the profession at large. To put it bluntly, the recent assault on the humanities in American life only deepens my concern, and if the general public is not confident that scholarly work matters, then scholars may not have successors.[37] We need much more investigation into the relationship between academic and devotional reading: this study of Hirsch's commentary serves only as a test-case. In conclusion, the significance of Hirsch's Bible teachings need not depend on the validity of his Bible translation.

Notes

Portions of this essay are adapted from Alan T. Levenson, *The Making of the Modern Jewish Bible: How Scholars in Germany, Israel, and America Transformed an Ancient Text* (Lanham, MD: Rowman & Littlefield, 2011), 50–62, in ch. 3: "Samson Raphael Hirsch: The Chimera of Self-Explanatory Scripture."

[1] Hirsch often used *da* (e.g. Gen 46:1), sometimes *und* (e.g. Gen 45:28), and sometimes neither.

[2] Everett Fox, *The Five Books Of Moses* (New York: Schocken, 1995), esp. ix–xxvi.

[3] Although traditional Jewish translators gave pride of place to the Masoretic text, Hirsch follows Nachmanides (Ramban) in refusing to elucidate Hebrew by cognate languages.

[4] Robert Alter, *The Five Books of Moses* (New York: Norton, 2004); Gen 37:14 offers an example of Hirsch's "addition":

לך-נא ראה את-שלום אחיך ואת-שלום הצאן והשבני דבר וישלחהו מעמק חברון ויבא שכמה ויאמר לו

Hirsch translates, "Gehe doch, sagte er ihm darauf, siehe nach dem Wohlbefinden deiner Brüder under den Wohlbefinden der Schaafe und bringe mir Antwort." Aside from the awkward rendering of Shalom as "Wohlbefinden," "*vayomer lo*" becomes "sagte er ihm darauf." Hirsch's understanding of Shechem typifies his apologetic approach. He makes Shechem the site of brotherhood and unity, basing this on the slaughter of Shechemites in Genesis 34, and the protests against royal power in 1 Kings 12. Surely, however, if one wishes to read Shechem symbolically, the text may represent violence as easily as brotherhood or unity. Another example of an explanatory addition comes in Gen 1:26, "Gott sprach: Wir wollen einen Adam (Stellvertreter) machen in einer unser würdigen Hülle. . . ." Hirsch's parenthetical (Stellvertreter) is explanation, not translation.

[5] Hirsch often adds exclamation and question marks where no obvious rabbinic support exists.

[6] At Gen 2:4 Hirsch renders the double divine name יהוה אלהים simply as Gott.

[7] Hirsch explicates Gen 40:5 *after* insisting on the seeming superfluity of all the words following ויחלמו חלום שניהם. Hirsch argues that the dreams of the cup-bearer and baker contain their own logic: God illumines his able, reasonable interpreter, "vernunftiger Mensch," as shown by the sound-alike of *piteron* (the root *pe, tav, resh*), which means "solution" with *peter* (the root *pe, tet, resh*) which means "opening." On Hirsch's derivation of this Lautverwandschaft method, see Michah Gottlieb, "Oral Letter and Written Trace: Samson Raphael Hirsch's Defense of the

Bible and Talmud," *JQR* 106 (2016): 316–51, here 334–35: "Dividing the Hebrew letters into the five categories of gutterals, palatals, dentals, labials, and sibilants, Hirsch claims that letters from the same category are cognates and so the meanings of words containing these cognates are related. While this approach has a basis in Rashi, Hirsch deploys it well beyond his predecessors."

[8]Jay Harris, *How Do We Know This? Midrash and the Fragmentation of Modern Judaism* (Albany: SUNY Albany Press, 1994). An example of interpreting Written Torah in light of Oral Torah may be seen in Gen 40:16, וירא שר-האפים כי טוב פתר, which Hirsch translates "dass er gut hatte gedeutet;" Hirsch insists that the verse can only mean "interpret correctly," not "interpret favorably," as argued in b. Ber. 55a–b; I believe the Bible intends to be ambiguous here.

[9]Hirsch, *Commentary to the Pentateuch*, Exodus 21:2. I have used the translation of Daniel Haberman, *The Hirsch Chumash* (Jerusalem-New York, 2000) for this quote, which more perfectly captures Hirsch's sense than the older Lewy rendering. On this passage, see Jay Harris, *How Do We Know This?* 223–28.

[10]Hirsch paid careful attention to word order and any variation from the usual biblical Hebrew order: verb, followed by the subject; even a seemingly trivial, unusual word order could yield an entire teaching for Hirsch. E.g., Hirsch translates Gen 41:33, ועתה ירא פרעה איש נבון וחכם וישיתהו על-ארץ מצרים, as "Un nun ersehe sich Pharao einen einsichtigen und weisen Mann und setzte ihn ueber das Land Mizraim." Does it really matter that נבון וחכם, einsichtigen und weisen, appear in this order? Hirsch thinks so.

[11]Hirsch wrote to his friend Z. H. May, "This book bearing the title *Horeb* represents an independent work; and only after the appearance of the book called *Moriah* will the *Horeb* form its second part. . . . The book *Moriah*, however, which will contain the fruit of my own study of Tanach, is intended to present a general conception of the essence of Jewish nationhood."

[12]Samson Raphael Hirsch, *Horeb: A Philosophy of Jewish Laws and Observances, vol. 1*, trans. Isidore Grunfeld (London: Soncino, 1962), cxli–cxlv.

[13]Samson Raphael Hirsch, *The Nineteen Letters of Ben Uziel: Being a Spiritual Presentation of the Principles of Judaism*, trans. Bernard Drachman (New York: Bloch, 1899).

[14]Hirsch, *Horeb*, lvi.

[15]Tellingly, the halachic work most similar to *Horeb*, is *Sefer ha-Chinuch*—not a law code at all, but a guide to the commandments and their biblical sources traditionally bestowed as a bar mitzvah present. Menahem Elon, "Codification of Law," *Encyclopedia Judaica* (5:628–56); idem, *Jewish Law* 3:1138–1452. I would like to thank my "Codes" teacher at the Academy for Jewish Religion, Rabbi Michael Pitkowsky, for bringing Elon's works to my attention.

[16]Scholars have speculated about *Moriah's* non-appearance. Grunfeld believed that the journal *Jeschurun* reflected Hirsch's views on the Bible. Rosenbloom believed that Hirsch backed away from an enormously difficult task. Shlomo Chertok, *Kankan Yashan Maleh Hadash* (Tel Aviv: Ha-kibbutz ha-meuchad, 2009) entertains the idea that Hirsch's *Chumash* is his *Moriah*, which I likewise think provides the best solution.

[17]Hirsch, *Neunzehn Briefe über Judentum* (Frankfurt: Kaufmann, 1901), footnote to Letter 18, 104–5. Available in English translation in Isidore Grunfeld's introduction to Hirsch, *Horeb*, lxx.

[18]E. A. Speiser, *Genesis*, AB 1 (Garden City, NY: Doubleday, 1964), xxxi–xxxiv, 150–52.

[19]This claim of the ubiquity of the Hirsch Pentateuch is given by Mordecai Breuer and others.

[20]Robert Liberles, *Religious Conflict in Social Context: The Resurgence of Orthodoxy on Frankfurt am Main, 1838–1877* (Westport, CT: Greenwood, 1985).

[21]Like Mendelssohn, Hirsch placed enormous importance on the Hebrew Bible as an oral/aural, sounded text. The Bible was meant to be in Hebrew and meant to be heard. For Buber-Rosenzweig, the repetition of theme-words (Leitwörter) provided a key to interpretation; for Mendelssohn, the fact that Moses heard everything on Sinai with full intonation and emphasis created a shield against misinterpretation. Hirsch incorporated Mendelssohn's view into his symbolic interpretation.

[22]Hirsch on Gen 11:7 led him to form a web of associations with any given biblical word.

[23]The Hebrew-ness of the Bible is something that has impressed Western diaspora Jews, who have generally remained committed to reading Torah in the original for liturgical purposes. In Israel, of course, this Hebrew is taken for granted, contemporary "Hebrew-lite" versions of the Bible such as *Tanach Ram* (Herziliya: Yediot Ahronot, 2010) notwithstanding. In Eastern Europe, commentators such as Malbim, Mecklenburg and Zvi Yehuda Berlin continued to write Torah commentaries in Hebrew. Hirsch insisted: "We must read the Torah in Hebrew—that is to say, in accordance with the spirit of that language. It describes but little, but through the rich significance of its verbal roots it paints in the word a picture of the thing. . . . It is as it were a semi-symbolic writing. With wakeful eye and ear, and with soul aroused to activity, we must read; nothing is told us of such superficial import that we need only, as it were, accept it with half roused dreaminess; we must strive ourselves to create again the speaker's thoughts to think them over or it will escape us." Letter two, in *The Nineteen Letters*. See Arnold Eisen, "Divine Legislation as Ceremonial Script," *AJS Review* 15 (1990): 239–67.

[24]*Pace* Tova Ganzel, "Explicit and Implicit Polemic in Rabbi Samson Raphael Hirsch's Bible Commentary" *HUCA* 81 (2010): 171–91.

[25]Hirsch on Gen 9:27.

[26]Regarding the teaching of Torah to one's children, in the first line of the "V'ahavta," the Israelite is enjoined to "teach them to one's children and talk about them." Once again, Hirsch takes a presumed hendiadys and breaks it down: "teach them/*shinantem*" = Written Torah, while "*dibarta bam*/talk about them" = Oral Torah. Hirsch goes even further with this verse by dividing students' historical-educational development into a three-fold injunction to study (1) Scripture, (2) Mishnah, and (3) Gemara. This three-fold division was occasioned only by the reluctant writing down of the Mishnah; originally, it was but two-fold: Written Torah and Oral Torah.

[27] Mordechai Breuer, *Modernity Within Tradition: The Social History of Orthodox Jewry in Imperial Germany*, trans. Elizabeth Petuchowski (New York: Columbia University Press, 1992), 80; Alexander Altmann, "Moses Mendelssohn As Archetypal German Jew," in *The Jewish Response to German Culture*, ed. Jehuda Reinharz and Walter Schatzberg (Hanover, NH: University Press of New England, 1985).

[28] "A comparison with Mendelssohn is very instructive here. Mendelssohn's Bible commentary had, throughout, a coolly rational and often apologetic tone, whereas Hirsch's Commentary on the Pentateuch expressed an aggressively affirmative joy and enthusiasm for tradition and duty" (Breuer, *Modernity Within Tradition*, 65).

[29] Hirsch on Gen 2:4.

[30] Joseph Gugenheimer, "Die Hypothesen der Bibelkritik" *Jeschurun* XIII (1867), XIV (1868), and XV (1886).

[31] See Hirsch on the "Forgotten Sheaf" in *Studies in Devarim (Deuteronomy)*, ed. Nehama Leibowitz; trans. Aryeh Newman (Jerusalem: World Zionist Organization, 1980), 246–47.

[32] Eliyahu Klugman, *Samson Raphael Hirsch* (Brooklyn: Mesorah Publications, 1996), 334, emphasis added.

[33] See now "Preface to the [2016] Paperback Edition," in Levenson, *Making of the Modern Jewish Bible*, xv–xxiii, here xix.

[34] Susannah Heschel, "Response to Alan Levenson," annual meeting of the Association for Jewish Studies, Chicago, IL, 17 December 2012, emphasis added.

[35] *The Fundamentals: A Testimony to the Truth*, 12 vols. (Chicago: Testimony Publishing Company, 1910–1915).

[36] Perhaps the gap between scholarly and devotional reading is less extreme within Jewish circles than within American Protestantism; knowing only one side of the equation, and that only partially, I am not in a position to judge, only speculate.

[37] Given recent trends in academia, scholars should definitely care about how many Assyriologists and Egyptologists will even be replaced upon their retirement. I am fairly sure that this Festschrift's honoree Leonard Greenspoon, having so successfully spoken to both scholarly and general audiences, cares about this issue.

11

Translating Poliscentrism: The Politics of Ethnicity and *Ethnos* related to Defining *Ioudaios*

Anthony Le Donne
United Theological Seminary

The translation of *Ioudaioi* in the Gospel of John remains an important debate in New Testament (NT) studies. There are two main options, both of which reveal underlying assumptions and engender negative consequences. On the one hand, the NT in general and the Fourth Gospel in particular have a catastrophic legacy—perhaps even an impetus—of anti-Jewish interpretation. Thus to enhance Jewish well-being and a better education for Christians, *hoi Ioudaioi* should not be translated as "the Jews" wherever this phrase connotes antagonism in the NT. On the other hand, if the broad term *hoi Ioudaioi* is rendered more narrowly "the Jewish leaders" or "the leaders" (for example, John 7 according to the CEV), translators may be sacrificing accuracy for sensitivity. Similarly, if the term *hoi Ioudaioi* is rendered geographically as "the Judeans" (for example, Steve Mason and Shaye Cohen),[1] translators risk erasing Jewish history and/or whitewashing Christian history.[2]

In his essay "Translating *Jesus* and *the Jews*,"[3] Leonard Greenspoon adds his inimitable voice to this important debate. His subtitle asks succinctly, "Can we eradicate the Anti-Semitism without also erasing the Semitism?" Greenspoon introduces the complexity of the problem and surveys several possible solutions. He commends efforts to create sensitivity in Christian readers, yet it is also worthwhile to emphasize Semitic names in the Gospels wherever they have been de-Judaized in translation. I agree wholeheartedly, and I would add that translators ought to convey the complexity of Jewish portraiture and Jewish culture in the NT. Having become required reading in my classrooms, Greenspoon's essay has two pedagogical effects. My Christian seminarians commonly express a "light-bulb moment" wherein they see the Gospels with new illumination. They also express a new appreciation for the importance of translation and the consequences of anti-Jewish bias. I cannot express enough gratitude to my friend and colleague for the positive impact he has had in my classrooms. What is remarkable about his essay is that it affects my students, not because it offers a concrete solution, but because it creates space for complexity.

In this chapter, I hope to continue in this spirit as I introduce another wrinkle to the complexity of translating *hoi Ioudaioi*. Reconsidering the problem of ethnic categories in the Second Temple period, I suggest that such categories were oriented by the cultural gravity of the *polis*. Accordingly, I suggest that *ethnos* is itself what I call a "poliscentric" category, and the same is especially true for *hoi Ioudaioi* vis-à-vis the Fourth Gospel.

Imagine No Religion

Over the last decade, a groundswell of dissatisfaction arose concerning the notion of "ancient religion." Many voices point out that there is no ancient word for "religion" as it is understood in the modern world. That is, the modern concept of religion coincides with the modern invention of the secular world. Only thereafter could religion signal a discrete area of human experience standing in contrast to other areas. To be "religious" now means choosing particular avenues within an otherwise secular landscape. Again, such a view is a modern invention; the landscape of the ancient world simply was not "secular" in any way that modern people could recognize.

Brent Nongbri's *Before Religion: A History of a Modern Concept* has forwarded this argument wonderfully.[4] Nongbri leans heavily on anthropologist Talal Asad, who writes:

> Religion has been part of the reconstruction of practical times and spaces, a restructuration of practical times and places, a rearticulation of knowledges and powers, of subjective behaviors, sensibilities, needs, and expectations in modernity. But that applies equally to secularism, whose function has been to try to guide that

> rearticulation and to define "religions" in the plural as a species of (non-rational) belief. . . . Secularist ideology, I would suggest, tries to fix permanently the social and political place of "religion."[5]

Asad writes in reply to the classic observation of Orientalist W. C. Smith: "I have not found [in eastern traditions] any formulation of a named religion earlier than the nineteenth century."[6] It is now common in the study of Buddhism, for example, to speak of Buddhist philosophy, with emphasis on the philosophical and not religious framework.

Steve Mason applies these insights to traditions associated with Christianity and Judaism. Religion, as a modern category, is "isolable from the rest of our lives: religious systems may be adopted or abandoned."[7] Such was not the case in antiquity, for "the category did not yet exist."[8] Mason explains, "I do not mean to say that our western forebears were not *religious*. Rather. . . the various elements that constitute our religion [were] inextricably bound up with other aspects of their lives."[9]

I can also point anecdotally to a similar notion in Christianity. In my youth I both heard and repeated this mantra: "Christianity is not a religion, but a relationship." A similar notion exists in the common refrain among my fellow Californians, "I'm not very religious, but I'm spiritual." I would imagine that this refrain exists elsewhere. One wonders if such statements serve to communicate "insider" sensibilities against the perceptions of outsiders. Consider this related statement—perhaps ahead of its time—by C. S. Lewis:

> The man I picture is a real Christian. But you would do him wrong by asking him to separate out, at such moments, some exclusively religious element in his mind from all the rest—from his hearty social pleasure in a corporate act, his enjoyment of the hymns (and the crowd), his memory of other such services since childhood, his well-earned anticipation of rest after harvest or Christmas dinner after church. They are all one in his mind. This would have been even truer of any ancient man, and especially of an ancient Jew. He was a peasant, very close to the soil. He had never heard of music, or festivity, or agriculture as things separate from religion, nor of religion as something separate from them. Life was one.[10]

Perhaps, then, "religion" is a concept imposed by outsiders onto the lives and thought-worlds of natives and native landscapes.

Daniel Boyarin and Tom Wright have suggested that something like religion begins to emerge alongside Christian doctrine. In their own ways, Boyarin and Wright have suggested that the emergence of Christianity *as an abstract system of beliefs* marks a sea change in sacred demarcation. Boyarin suggests that Judaism, as an abstract system of ideas, emerged in response to Christian anti-Judaism.[11] Tom Wright has recently called Paul the "first Christian theologian," since other Jewish thinkers did not utilize a constellation of abstract ideas in a way that became "load-bearing" for communal identity.[12] Each of these arguments has met controversy at varying levels of complexity. I will not attempt to detail their arguments or align myself with either of them. I will simply point out that representatives from varying ideological camps have converged on a similar hypothesis: Christianity represents a categorical shift toward religious abstraction in a world that did not conceive of religion as a discrete area of life.

Whether we point to the emergence of religion after the European Enlightenment or alongside Christian doctrine, speaking of "Second Temple Judaism" in terms of religion makes us vulnerable to category errors. More particularly, the application of the suffix "-ism" may be misleading from the start, for such an abstraction—given the paucity of the term *Ioudaismos*—is not well attested in the Second-Temple period.

From this perspective, the term *Ioudaios* is therefore not yet a religious category in the first century CE. Like many other designations for people groups, *Ioudaios* is a geographic and ethnic designation. Mason suggests that our modern concepts of "Jew" and "Judaism" might not capture the way that ancient minds would have perceived the people group in question. Rather, ancient writers thought in terms of place-bound identity that was determined by environmental factors and expressed in ethnic terms (Greek: *ethnos*). Just as the people of Athens were thought of as Athenians and just as Nabateans, Idumeans, and Samarians were named for their regional hubs, people associated with Judea were thought of in geographic and ethnic terms. Accordingly, *hoi Ioudaioi* ought to be translated as "the Judeans." In this way, the primary association is not religious, but regional. Mason sees his task as a philologist, separate from religious-liturgical concerns, and Mason intends his research for technicians; he does grant, though, that others who write for non-specialist audiences may have concerns beyond philology.[13] Region and ethnicity perhaps provide more stable and emic means of categorization.

At the same time, applying the categories of region and ethnicity to the Second-Temple period proves no less problematic than that of religion. Just as our concept of religious life is not theirs, our concept of ethnicity is not theirs either. In his seminal essay on the topic, Mason writes:

> In form, Ἰουδαῖος is cognate to Ἰουδαία and indicates a "person of Judaea": a Judaean. It bears precisely the same relationship to the name of the homeland that Ἄραψ, Βαβυλώνιος, Αἰγύπτιος, Σύρος, Παρθυαῖος, and Ἀθηναῖος have to the names of their respective homelands. If one asked where a Babylonian or Egyptian or Syrian or Parthian was from, in what laws and customs they had been educated, the answer was apparent in their ethnic label. That was also the case with Ἰουδαῖος (= of Ἰουδαία), which should therefore be translated "Judaean" by analogy. A hypothetically equivalent question today, "Where are Jews from?" would not admit of a straightforward answer. . . . Even in Israel many Jews consider themselves to be "from" Poland, Russia, Yemen, or Iraq, and some preserve Ashkenazi or Sephardi traditions in dress, diet, outlook, and speech. Since 1948 it has been possible for Jews also to be "from Israel," but the ethnicon that corresponds to this homeland is "Israeli," not "Jew." Since the modern English "Jew" does not mean "of Judaea" as Ioudaios did, the ancient term is more faithfully rendered "Judaean."[14]

Mason is close to the mark with his ambiguous genitive, "of Judaea." He is also quite close to the mark in emphasizing (as he does in several publications) that the νόμιμα (legal matters/precepts) and ἔθη (customs) of geography in question are crucial to determining *ethnos*. Yet it is clear in the quotation above that Mason really means "from Judaea." This is where I demur. The social construct of *ethnos* in the Second Temple period has much less to do with provenance—although this was one factor. Much more important in the construction of *ethnos* is the question of orientation: *to which* polis *are you and your people oriented?* In this way Mason's modern analogy of Israeli vs. Jew falls short.

Ethnicity and Race as Modern Constructs

The modern, western concept of ethnicity is socially constructed in relationship to the modern concept of race. The term "ethnicity" is only recently attested in English (1953) and was coined to reorient the study of race. Strategically, the term was etymologically linked to the Greek *ethnos*.[15] As such, this modern term coincides with a renaissance in social-scientific study, which rejects previously held notions of genetic determinism. The field of ethnic studies is in many ways a response to the pseudoscience of "racial theory" reified in Europe and North America from the eighteenth to twentieth centuries.

During the rise of racial science, many would-be scientists were preoccupied with phrenology, eugenics, and other theories that provided scientific fortification for racial stereotypes.[16] Such stereotypes doubtlessly existed long before the Enlightenment, but the pseudoscience of race gave them new momentum.[17] Many "scholars" were convinced that the study of skulls, brains, and other physical characteristics would serve to create a better society by locating the morally inferior races.[18] This work disastrously supported the notion of Aryan superiority and provided a platform for Joseph Arthur, Comte de Gobineau (1816–1882). Gobineau's "An Essay on the Inequality of the Human Races" showcased a "master race" ideology and undergirded the platforms of Nazism and various eugenic interests.[19]

The catastrophic violence of the Shoah/Holocaust had manifold consequences. Regarding racial theory, the impact was direct, and previous assumptions were ripe for reconsideration. The field of contemporary ethnic studies is thus a direct result of the failure of racial constructs in previous centuries. Within a few decades, ethnic studies became a dedicated field of study within universities. The felt need for new ways to think about race (cf. ethnicity) gained further momentum with the American Civil Rights Movement. The first to establish such a program was San Francisco State University:

> In 1968 and 1969 the Black Student Union, Third World Liberation Front, select staff and faculty, and members from the larger Bay Area community, organized and lead [sic] a series of actions against systematic discrimination. Protestors spoke out against lack of access, misrepresentation, and the overall neglect of indigenous peoples and people of color within the university's curriculum and programs. Their specific demands included the establishment of four departments: American Indian Studies, Asian American Studies, Black Studies, and La Raza Studies within a College of Ethnic Studies.[20]

Soon after, the University of California, Berkeley followed the same path. Berkeley's Ethnic Studies webpage explains its history similarly:

> The Department had its origins in the demands of students and others in the Third World Liberation Front on campus in 1969 for scholarly programs that would focus on the understudied histories and situations of African Americans, Asian Americans, Chicanos and Native Americans. In response to these demands—as well as to a resolution from the faculty Senate—four programs where established, with comparative Ethnic Studies added subsequently. The programs' intellectual rationale was grounded on the presumption that racially marginalized groups were not, and could not be, adequately represented or theorized in the existing disciplines (a rationale that remains very much at the heart of Ethnic Studies to this day). While student strikers initially proposed the creation of a Third World College, a number of factors have made that project impossible on campus to date. Of the different ethnic studies programs, African American Studies became a separate department in the College of Letters and Science in 1974. The Ethnic Studies Graduate Group was founded by faculty

> members of the Ethnic Studies and African American Studies departments in 1984.[21]

The two earliest established ethnic studies departments were thus created to answer systemic racism. These cases show clearly that the field of ethnic studies was conceptualized in counter-distinction to racial constructs. In short, the aim of the field has been to deconstruct the very concept of race and to introduce a better world of ideas.[22]

The primary object of contemporary ethnic studies is not race, but racism. Benjamin Isaac writes, "race does not exist, racism does," and "racism is never caused by the physical characteristics of the other."[23] Isaac does not represent every ethnologist in this statement, but such statements are commonplace in the field. He explains:

> Since the concept of race as such is merely theoretical, since it is a quasi-biological construct invented to establish a hierarchy of human groups and to delineate differences between them, and since it does not work in practice, attempts have been made from the beginning [of racial theory] to incorporate other features which are not physiological. The designation "race" in the sense of subspecies cannot be applied by definition to language groups (the Aryan race), national groups (the English race), religious groups (the Christian or Jewish race), groups with one or more physical features in common, such as skin color, or the entire species of humans (the human race): such usages are biologically and scientifically meaningless.[24]

Even if Isaac's view is extreme, he points to a common principle in ethnic studies: implicit in racial theory is the notion of superior and inferior races. Race is as much a matter of perception as it is anything else. At the same time, these perceptions have created realities in the modern world that cannot be ignored.[25] The racial categorization of society became the "commonsense" of the modern, western mind. A great many contemporary ethnologists are in the business of explaining how such real-world social constructs emerge.

When modern, western minds think of ethnicity, they either still think in racial categories betraying eighteenth- to twentieth-century pseudoscience, or they think through the category as a way to deconstruct such eighteenth- to twentieth-century pseudoscience; the former is perhaps more popular, and the latter is perhaps more academic. In either case, one's categories are derived from a social construct (racial science) that did not exist in the Second Temple period.

The Concept of Ethnos as a Hellenized Construct

Polis is a Greek word that is often rendered "city." Yet *polis* meant more in antiquity than is conveyed in the idea of an urban center. The concept of the *polis*—a carryover from the Greek city-state conceptual map—was a constellation of relationships between urban center, geography, law (or custom), worship, citizenship, wider community, governance, and (crucially) self-sufficiency. Those within the cultural orbit of a *polis* would be identified as in relationship to that *polis*. I emphasize that *cultural orbit* is a better way to think of this relationship than simple geographical association. This is what I mean by a "poliscentric" worldview.[26] My contention is that *ethnos* is a social construct that emerged from a poliscentric worldview.

To explain Poliscentrism, I begin with the more common reality of clan-centrism.[27] Clan-centric groups united (most often) around a father figure. Family honor and longevity of continuous progeny were key factors in determining what was good for the clan. As adapted by Greek and Roman cultures, the concept of *paterfamilias* (father of the family) betrays this foundational construct. The idealized father figure would control wealth, property, marriage, and most other major decisions.[28] Importantly, he would provide for those under his care and function as the public face of the wider clan. Aristotle summarizes: "The rule of a father over his children is royal, for he rules by virtue both of love and of the respect due to age, exercising a kind of royal power" (*Pol.* 1.12 1259b).[29]

Leading up to, and through, the Second Temple period, however, the *paterfamilias* was just one dynamic in play in a world of larger networks. Aristotle discusses this shift in terms of commerce:

> For the members of the family originally had all things in common; in a more divided state of society they still shared in many things, but they were different things which they had to give in exchange for what they wanted, a kind of barter which is still practiced among barbarous nations who exchange with one another the necessaries of life and nothing more; giving and receiving wine, for example, in exchange for coin, and the like. (*Pol.* 1.9 1257a)

For Aristotle, key factors that drive this move beyond clan-centrism (which he assumes are primitive) are the motives of necessity and self-sufficiency. Both are key themes throughout his *Politics*. As families grew and divided, more innovative ways to provide for them emerged, including exchange within and between clans. This development helps to explain the evolution from household to village. Aristotle considers this a necessary move toward a noble society, as he wants to define humans as political—or perhaps, poliscentric—animals.

Greek conceptual mapping involved processes of counter-distinction. That is, Greeks understood the world through binary sets. The default was not to study a phenomenon in isolation, but by contrast. Analytical reasoning sought antithetical relationships to construct mirrored, complementary opposites—hence the juxtapositions of household (*oikos* or *oikia*) and village (*kōmē*) and then village and *polis*.[30] In discussing the *polis*, I would suggest that a poliscentric worldview stands in contrast to earlier clan-centric views. It is important to point out, though, that the concept of *ethnos* does not stand in direct relationship to clan-centrism; instead, *ethnos* emerges as an extension of or in counter-distinction to the concept of the *polis*.

In Aristotle's ideal, size was an important point of distinction. As shown above, the size of the clan created the need for expansion and adaptation for new means of self-sufficiency. Size also was a key factor in defining the *polis*. The ideal *polis* must be larger than a village but small enough for all members of the community to know one another. Beyond this critical mass of intimacy, the participation of each individual in decision-making was nearly impossible (*Pol.* 7.4 1326b). The *polis* differed from the village because the *polis* was (relatively) self-governed and had an urban center. In this worldview, expansion and counter-distinction explain the evolution from household to village to *polis*.

These processes reveal the necessary link between *polis* and *ethnos*. In the antithetical world of the Greeks, *polis* and *ethnos* stood in a contrasting, but often necessary, relationship.[31] If a grouping of people became too large, it would cease to be a *polis*. Generally speaking, any large people group that could not be classified as a *polis* was called an *ethnos* (*Pol.* 7.4 1326b).[32] Edward Cohen points out that, in much of classical Greek literature, the term *ethnos* is often accompanied by its counterpart *polis*. If the writer wanted to speak of the entire population of the world, he would refer to "all cities (*poleis*) and nations (*ethnē*)." Cohen writes, "*polis* and *ethnos* together encompassed all units larger than a *kōmē*."[33] In *Politics*, Aristotle never uses the term *ethnos* without a mention of *polis*.

Ethnologists of Hellenistic thought often point to the contrasting relationship between *polis* and *ethnos* as a binary. Jean-Loup Amselle writes, "For the Greeks, the notion of *ethnos* was a political category. It constituted one pole in the hierarchization that evolved between the two principal forms of societies: *polis* and *ethnos*."[34] More recent studies demonstrate that the classical descriptions of Greek thought do not always represent the complexity of the relevant associations from which these categories derive. According to Kostas Vlassopoulos, "The *ethnos* is now envisaged not as an alternative to the *polis*, but as a complex organisational linking of political forms and communities both above and below the *polis*."[35] Whether a binary contrast or a more sophisticated network of relationships, the consensus is clear: in Hellenistic thought, the concept of *ethnos* was defined in relationship to *polis*. Where Amselle uses the qualifier "political" I would say "poliscentric;" *ethnos* was a poliscentric category.

According to C. P. Jones, Herodotus used both *genos* and *ethnos*, but not interchangeably. For Herodotus, *genos* refers to descent, whereas *ethnos* refers to a people unified as a geographical unit.[36] So, in simplest terms, ethnicity was related to geography. However, I have argued that "geography" is too imprecise.[37] The mapping of the Hellenistic world included gravitational centers of culture. Amselle helpfully explains that the *polis* "was a precisely defined and valorized category, one in which the Greeks found their plentitude of being." This is again what I would call poliscentrism.

Jones explains that *ethnos* is defined in counter-distinction: "the category of *ethnos*, in contrast [to *polis*], was vague and deprecatory."[38] One should nuance, though, that in some cases an *ethnē* orbited a *polis* center and was rendered distinct by this cultural force of gravity.[39] Athens, according to Cohen, is the quintessential example of such a relationship. In sum, while many *ethnē* were not oriented toward a *polis*, some very important *ethnē* were. Most importantly, the Greeks used the concept of *polis* to define the concept of *ethnos*.

It is safe to say that, in the Second-Temple period, Jerusalem was a *polis* with an orbiting *ethnos*. Delineating Jerusalem's variety of culture orbits, however, becomes quite complex. Diverse ideologies and power positions would have factored into varying expressions of investment in Jerusalem. *Ioudaioi* of Galilee, Idumea, among the Yahad, and in Diaspora *poleis* all over the Roman Empire had various ways of orienting themselves toward the *polis*. Indeed, the emerging consensus among ethnographic studies of the Second-Temple period is that *ethnos* was a flexible category that was conditioned by a variety of external factors.[40] It is worth noting that Aristotle criticizes Socrates for assuming too much homogeny in the ideal polis:

> For there is a point at which a (*polis*) may attain such a degree of unity as to be no longer a (*polis*), or [there is another point] at which, without actually ceasing to exist, it will become an inferior (*polis*), like harmony passing into unison, or rhythm which has been reduced to a single foot. The (*polis*). . . is a plurality, which should be united and made into a community by education. (*Pol.* 2.5 1263b)

Again, expansion and difference is at the forefront of Aristotle's thought, but here diversity is considered virtuous and is almost required for *polis* identity.

It makes sense, then, that *ethnos*—as a category more expansive than *polis* membership—would represent an even wider variety of diversity and require an even larger degree of flexibility. Such is the case with Diaspora communities of *Ioudaioi*. John Barclay explains that

> there were no 'typical' Diaspora conditions. Understanding the social milieu of Diaspora Jews requires attention to each individual site and period as well as the peculiar circumstances of Jewish individuals and communities in each environment. . . . 'Jewish identity' is, of course, a multi-faceted phenomenon. Jews had (and have) a triple identity: how they viewed themselves, how they were viewed by other Jews and how they were viewed by outsiders.[41]

The distinction between insiders' and outsiders' perspectives is crucial. In what follows, I offer one example of an insider perspective and one example of an outsider's perspective.[42]

From an insider's perspective, Philo's veneration of Jerusalem as the mother-*polis* of Diaspora *Ioudaioi* is important for my thesis in two ways: one is an echo of Aristotle's relation of *ethnos* to *polis*; the other is that *Ioudaioi* outside of Judea are defined as "Jews" by way of their orientation toward Jerusalem. Philo writes that

> no single country can contain the Jews because of their multitude, and for this reason they inhabit the most extensive and wealthiest districts in Europe and Asia both on islands and on mainlands, and while they regard the Holy City as their mother-city, in which is founded and consecrated the temple of the most high God, yet they severally hold that land as their fatherland which they have obtained by inheritance from fathers and grandfathers and great-grandfathers and still more remote ancestors for their portion to dwell in, in which they were born and reared.[43] (*Flacc.* 46)

Writing from Alexandria, Philo calls Jerusalem both holy city (*hieropolis*) and mother-city (*metropolis*). In keeping with Aristotle's definition of an *ethnos*, Philo emphasizes the large population of *Ioudaioi*. As shown above, the size of the population was an important factor in distinguishing a *polis* from an *ethnos*. Philo exemplifies an *ethnos* orbiting a *polis*, an orbit that extends to Alexandria. So the

Jewish *ethnos* is not contrasted with the *polis* in this case; rather the *ethnos* is defined in relation to Jerusalem positively. Since Jewish relationships with Jerusalem are primary, Philo viewed Diaspora *Ioudaioi* as a poliscentric people. A *Ioudaios* could easily have lived outside of Jerusalem his/her entire life and still have been oriented toward Jerusalem via custom, worship, ancestry, and common narrative.

From an outsider's perspective, Strabo provides a Greek perspective of Jewish political identity. He credits Moses for gathering and unifying *Ioudaioi* (themselves having an Egyptian heritage) and for leading them to Jerusalem. The fact that Moses guided them *to Jerusalem* was more determinative of their identity than the fact they came *from Egypt*. Strabo derides several customs, superstitions, and corruptions of the Jerusalem leadership but praises their relationship with the Acropolis (i.e., the temple mount):

> Respect, however, was paid to the Acropolis; it was not abhorred as the seat of tyranny, but honoured and venerated as a temple. This is according to nature, and common both to Greeks and barbarians. For, as members of a civil community, they live according to a common law; otherwise it would be impossible for the mass to execute any one thing in concert (in which consists a civil state), or to live in a social state at all.[44] (*Geogr.* 16.2.37–38)

Notice that Strabo assumes at least two of Aristotle's categories: one is the civil character of a poliscentric people; another is the question of size related to governance. For Strabo, the factors most important for explaining the identity of *Ioudaioi* relate to the story of Moses's leadership, the establishment and customs of Jerusalem, and Jerusalem's relationship with the Acropolis. I would render Strabo's comments about *Ioudaioi* as follows: "being *politikoi*, they live under a common constitutional order (*prostagma*); otherwise, it would be impossible for vast numbers to act together harmoniously with one another, which is just what it means to *politeuesthai*. . . ." These descriptions emphasize the poliscentrism of Jewish life.[45] Specialists of Second Temple literature might be inclined to retreat from categories like "religion" and "race" because they are anachronistic and too laden with modern conceptual baggage. However, retreating to the categories of ethnicity and *ethnos* proves equally problematic, for "ethnicity" is no less anachronistic and *ethnos* is no less complicated. Thus I conclude that rendering *Ioudaios* as "Judean" does not signal complexity well enough. Nevertheless, as Greenspoon commends, there is virtue in the attempt to translate in ways that engender sensitivity to the complexity of the ancient world and thus serve modern readers better. The remainder of this essay will explore the usefulness of poliscentrism as a category by using the Fourth Gospel as a window into the Second Temple period.

Is Jesus Jewish in the Fourth Gospel?

Jesus and *hoi Ioudaioi* are almost always set in opposition in the Fourth Gospel. Indeed, this adversarial relationship drives much of the plot. John 7:1 (NRSV) reads, "After this Jesus went about in Galilee. He did not wish to go about in Judea because the Jews were looking for an opportunity to kill him." Elsewhere Jesus says, "Even in your law it has been written that the testimony of two men is true" (8:17). The emphasis on "your law" gives the impression that it is the law of a perceived "other" and not the law of the speaker. The reader is given the impression that Jesus is opposed to *hoi Ioudaioi* in both geography and custom. Worse, *hoi Ioudaioi* are painted as monolithic "other" with murderous intentions. Regarding geography, the Fourth Gospel might convey that Jesus's status as a Galilean stands over and against his "Judean" counterparts—perhaps a Galilean vs. Judean rivalry. Mason's rendering of *Ioudaioi* as "Judeans" would thus be helpful. If so, John 7:1 could read, "After this Jesus went about in Galilee. He did not wish to go about in Judea because the *Judeans* were looking for an opportunity to kill him."

Yet this reading only works if Jesus's *ethnos* is determined by his provenance; he is not *from* Judea, so he is not a proper *Ioudaios*. However, I have argued that provenance is less important than orientation. Furthermore, this category error is exposed in Jesus's encounter with the Samaritan woman in John 4:7–42. This episode contains one of the few passages wherein Jesus is called a *Ioudaios* in the Fourth Gospel. This story begins by introducing a woman, identifying her by her *ethnos* and in counter-distinction to the *ethnos* of Jesus:

> A woman from Samaria came to draw water. Jesus said to her, "Give me a drink." (For his disciples had gone away into the city to buy food.) The Samaritan woman said to him, "How is it that you, a Jew [*Ioudaios*], ask for a drink from me, a woman of Samaria?" (For Jews [*Ioudaioi*] have no dealings with Samaritans.)

Remarkably, Jesus is categorized as *Ioudaios* in this passage by both the woman and the narrator. Jesus's candid statement that "salvation is from the *Ioudaioi*" (4:22) affirms the assumption. This is remarkable because the designation *Ioudaioi* is used in the Fourth Gospel almost exclusively as a designation for Jesus's enemies.

In John 4, not only is Jesus categorized as *Ioudaios*, he is aligned with those who believe that "Jerusalem is the place where people ought to worship" (4:20). The assumption here is that *Ioudaioi* are oriented toward the *polis* of Jerusalem, whereas Samaritans are not. We thus see here a poliscentric demarcation that divides these two peoples. Jesus claims, "You worship what you [Samaritans] do not know; we [Jews] worship what we know" (4:22). Notice the "you" (pl) and "we" in this statement. Notice also that Jesus implies that *Ioudaioi* are correctly oriented (they have a better knowledge) toward Jerusalem. So why is Jesus identified as *Ioudaios* when juxtaposed with a Samaritan but distanced from *Ioudaioi* elsewhere in the Fourth Gospel?

If indeed the designation *Ioudaios* is defined by one's *polis* orientation, perhaps John 4 represents a difference in orientation. Simply put, when juxtaposed against other *Ioudaioi*, Jesus stands in counter-distinction; when juxtaposed against a Samaritan, Jesus is more clearly seen as a properly poliscentric *Ioudaios*. Jesus is shown to be more closely aligned with Jerusalem-focused worship when the conversation partner represents a different *ethnos*.

If we adopt Mason's preference for "Judean," Jesus, the Samaritan woman, and the narrator misrepresent Jesus's regional ties in a way that conflicts with the rest of the narrative. While Jesus problematizes the virtue of any particular *polis* in this story,[46] he is clearly oriented toward Jerusalem in the Fourth Gospel. Even as a Galilean, Jesus travels often to Jerusalem for the festivals. In fact, given what I have argued about poliscentrism above, there is no clearer indication of Jesus' *ethnos* than statements like this: "The Passover of the Jews was near, and Jesus went up to Jerusalem" (2:13); "After this there was a feast of the Jews; and Jesus went up to Jerusalem" (5:1).[47]

Jesus's encounter with the Samaritan woman concludes by indicating that this was the custom of Galileans: "So when he came to Galilee, the Galileans welcomed him, having seen all that he had done in Jerusalem at the feast. For they too had gone to the feast" (4:45). While Jesus the Galilean is not *from* Judea and even farther geographically from Jerusalem than Samaria, he is more "Jewish/Judean" than the Samaritan woman because of his orientation towards the Jewish *polis*. In other words, Jerusalem was farther from Galilee but closer to the heart of Galileans when compared with Samaritans. At the same time, many Galileans continued to stand in hostile posture toward the urbanites of the South, as the rest of the Fourth Gospel showcases in devastating ways. In both cases, the perception of "otherness" is created from a poliscentric worldview.

Another example of this distance might be found in John 18 when Jesus is before Pilate. Pilate asks if Jesus is the "King of the *Ioudaioi*," to which Jesus responds by asking if Pilate has been prompted to ask this question (vv. 33–34). Pilate responds, "I am not a Jew [*Ioudaios*], am I? Your own nation [*ethnos*] and the chief priests have handed you over to me. . ." (v. 35). Here again, Jesus is only explicitly named as *Ioudaios* when he is in conversation with an outside *ethnos*—previously with a Samaritan and now with a Roman. Otherwise, Jesus's orientation to Jerusalem differs enough from his adversaries that he is disassociated from other *Ioudaioi*.

I suggest that poliscentrism, rather than geographical provenance, is the key to determining *ethnos* in this context. If so, the question is not *whether* Jesus is a proper *Ioudaios*, but *in what way* is Jesus a poliscentric *Ioudaios*.

Concluding Suggestions for Seminarians

As a Christian invested in Jewish well-being and Christian education, I am convinced that Christianity must become a philo-Jewish faith. Christianity's history of anti-Judaism (and its subsequent racial incarnation, anti-Semitism) has dehumanized both victims and perpetrators. Several passages from the NT—some discussed here—have perpetuated this dehumanization with catastrophic consequences. These passages will continue to do so without pedagogies designed to improve Jewish–Christian relations.

From one perspective, rendering *Ioudaios* in the NT as "Jew" has provided theological impetus for the oppression and murder of Jews. Too many Christians have associated Jesus's imagined adversaries with Jews of all times and all places. The designation "Judean" might serve to remind NT readers not only that Galileans and southern Judeans had a complicated relationship but also that NT controversies do not necessarily inform modern racial and religious realities. From this perspective, Steve Mason's preference for "Judean" might serve a contemporary liturgical-religious purpose even if this was not his motivation in translation.

Conversely, little is gained if Christians remain uneducated about the anti-Jewish and anti-Semitic legacies of NT-motivated applications. Ruth Sheridan writes, "We must not hide from the [Fourth] Gospel's tragic reception history as it affected actual Jews."[48] In affirmation of her statement, translating NT occurrences of *Ioudaios* as "Jew" prompts an opportunity for students of the NT to reflect on this legacy. There is a possibility that translating *Ioudaios* as "Judean" perpetuates Christian amnesia of this legacy. Analogous here is the designation "Pharisees" which is almost entirely pejorative in Christian memory. It remains so because most Christians are unaware that many modern Jews trace their heritage to the historical Pharisees. Thus most Christians do not realize that denigrating the Pharisees of the NT is offensive to many modern Jews. Rendering *Ioudaios* as "Judean" might have a similar impact of obscuring the connection between modern Jews and their ancient forebears. Furthermore, Adele Reinhartz writes:

> I am all for historical precision and sharply attuned to potential anti-Semitism. Yet as a scholar and a Jew, I am alarmed by the growing invisibility of Jews and Judaism in English translations of ancient texts and scholarship about them. The use of "Judeans" to translate all occurrences of *ioudaioi* achieves neither the scholarly precision nor the ethical high ground that scholars claim. On the contrary, the proliferation of Judeans inadvertently creates confusion and misunderstanding and merely sidesteps the issue without addressing the anti-Jewish or even anti-Semitic potential of texts such as the Gospel of John.[49]

Reinhartz's alarm at the inadequacies of Christian memory is not unwarranted. I will take her concern a step further by asking, *Can Christians be trusted with their own sacred texts?* History suggests otherwise. For this reason, translating *Ioudaios* in a text like the Fourth Gospel is best done in inter-religious dialogue.

Here we are confronted with an almost insoluble problem. Recent incarnations of Jewish–Christian dialogue have valued an appreciation of differences and an allowance for complexity as we perceive the other. If these values guide us, the Fourth Gospel's use of *Ioudaios* is just a doorway into a larger, ongoing, and more complex conversation. But, by contrast, the role of the translator is often to decide, to be definitive. After all, translators must choose one word or phrase in translation over/against others.

I will conclude with two suggestions for seminarians and educators of seminarians. First, we ought to continue translating *Ioudaios* as "Jew" in the NT and remind students that the category emerged from complexity and has evolved alongside a host of new complexities in the modern world ("Jew/Judean" may be a way to emphasize the complexity). Thus the ancient written text should be informed by contemporary oral teaching. Second, our teaching should include a robust discussion of the violent legacies associated with miscategorizing and therefore misunderstanding first-century Jews. Christian seminarians in particular should be sensitized to the role the NT has played in this history.

Notes

[1]Steve Mason, "Jews, Judaeans, Judaizing, Judaism: Problems of Categorization in Ancient History," *JSJ* 38 (2007): 457–512; Shaye J. D. Cohen, *The Beginnings of Jewishness: Boundaries, Varieties, Uncertainties* (Berkeley: University of California Press, 1999). Mason and Cohen are representative of a much wider conversation and have themselves published more widely on this topic.

[2]On the erasure of Jewish history, see Ruth Sheridan, "Hiding from the Fourth Gospel's Tragic Reception History," in *Jew and Judean: A Forum on Politics and Historiography in the Translation of Ancient Texts, Marginalia | Los Angeles Review of Books*, 26 August 2015. Online: http://marginalia.lareviewofbooks.org/hiding-fourth-gospels-tragic-reception-history/. On the whitewashing of Christian history, see Adele Reinhartz, "The Vanishing Jews of Antiquity," in *Jew and Judean*, 24 June 2014. Online: marginalia.lareviewofbooks.org/vanishing-jews-antiquity-adele-reinhartz/.

[3]Leonard Greenspoon, "Translating *Jesus* and *the Jews*: Can We Eradicate the Anti-Semitism without Also Erasing the Semitism?" in *Soundings in the Religion of Jesus*, ed. Bruce Chilton, Anthony Le Donne, and Jacob Neusner (Minneapolis: Fortress, 2012), 11–27.

[4]Brent Nongbri, *Before Religion: A History of a Modern Concept* (New Haven: Yale University Press, 2013).

[5]Talal Asad, "Reading a Modern Classic: W. C. Smith's *The Meaning and End of Religion*," *HR* 40 (2001): 205–22.

[6]W. C. Smith, *The Meaning and End of Religion: A New Approach to the Religious Traditions of Mankind* (New York: Macmillan, 1963), 61.

[7]Mason, "Jews, Judaeans, Judaizing, Judaism," 482.

[8]Mason, "Jews, Judaeans, Judaizing, Judaism," 480.

[9]Mason, "Jews, Judaeans, Judaizing, Judaism," 481.

[10]C. S. Lewis, "Reflections on the Psalms" in *C. S. Lewis: Selected Books* (New York: Harper Collins), 334. Lewis neglects to recognize the diversity of Jewish life in the ancient world, but his point stands nonetheless.

[11]Daniel Boyarin, *Border Lines: The Partition of Judaeo-Christianity*, Divinations: Rereading Late Ancient Religion (Philadelphia: University of Pennsylvania Press, 2006).

[12]N. T. Wright, "Why and How Paul Invented 'Christian Theology,'" lecture presented at Duke Divinity School, 11 November 2014. Online: https://www.youtube.com/watch?v=Y4CY73psVFQ.

[13]Steve Mason, *Josephus, Judea, and Christian Origins: Methods and Categories* (Peabody, MA: Hendrickson, 2009), ch. 5. See also his reflections and stated motives in idem, "Ancient Jews or Judeans? Different Questions, Different Answers," in *Jew and Judean*, 26 August 2014. Online: http://marginalia.lareviewofbooks.org/ancient-jews-judeans-different-questions-different-answers-steve-mason/.

[14]Mason, "Jews, Judaeans, Judaizing, Judaism," 489.

[15]Nathan Glazer and Daniel Patrick Moynihan, *Ethnicity: Theory and Experience* (Cambridge: Harvard University Press, 1975), 1.

[16]See John Greene, "Biology and Social Theory in the Nineteenth Century: Auguste Comte and Hebert Spencer," in *Critical Problems in the History of Science*, ed. Marshall Clagett (Madison: University of Wisconsin Press, 1959), 419–46.

[17]Benjamin H. Isaac, *The Invention of Racism in Classical Antiquity* (Princeton: Princeton University Press, 2004), 55–79.

[18]According to Martin N. Marger (*Race and Ethnic Relations: American and Global Perspectives* [Belmont, CA: Wadsworth, 2012], 408), the "popularly used physical features to define races" tend to be the most easily recognizable features like "skin pigmentation, hair type, lip size," etc.

[19]It is noteworthy that Jesus "historian" Ernst Renan was also deeply invested in racial theories. So close was his research to Gobineau's that he accused Renan of plagiarism. It is therefore not inconsequential that Renan's Jesus became Aryan in race and the "destroyer of Judaism"; see Susannah Heschel, *The Aryan Jesus: Christian Theologians and the Bible in Nazi Germany* (Princeton: Princeton University Press, 2010), 37.

[20]Online: http://ethnicstudies.sfsu.edu/home2.

[21]Online: http://ethnicstudies.berkeley.edu/history.php.

[22]According to John Hutchinson and Anthony D. Smith ("Introduction," in *Ethnicity*, ed. John Hutchinson and Anthony D. Smith [Oxford: Oxford University Press, 1996], 3–16, here 6–7), an ethnicity is now defined by one introduction as a people with varying combinations of (1) a common proper name; (2) a myth of common ancestry; (3) shared commemoration; (4) one or more elements of common culture, e.g. religion, customs, language; (5) a link with a (physical or symbolic) homeland; (6) "a sense of solidarity on the part of at least some sections of the *ethnie*'s population."

[23]Isaac, *Invention of Racism*, 33.

[24]Isaac, *Invention of Racism*, 33.

[25]Along these lines, it is important to note the instrumental functions of ethnicity toward political and economic ends; see Jonathan Hall, *Ethnic Identity in Greek Antiquity* (New York: University of Cambridge Press, 1997).

[26]Previous generations emphasized the distinction between *atsu* (life nearer to the urban center) and *chora* (life in the countryside), yet recent scholarship has blurred this distinction; see, e.g., Neville Morley, "Cities in Context: Urban Systems in Roman Italy," in *Roman Urbanism: Beyond the Consumer City*, ed. Helen M. Parkins (London: Routledge, 1997), 44–45.

[27]One might think of this as "tribalism," but the negative associations with that category remain problematic.

[28]I discuss this more fully in my *The Wife of Jesus: Ancient Texts and Modern Scandals* (London: Oneworld, 2014).

[29]All quotations of *Politics* are from Benjamin Jowett, trans., *The Politics of Aristotle* (Oxford: Clarendon, 1885); online: http://classics.mit.edu/Aristotle/politics.html. The most up-to-date treatments of ethnographic study in Hellenism treat Aristotle's *Politics* as primary and central to the discussion; see, e.g., Kostas Vlassopoulos, *Unthinking the Greek Polis: Ancient Greek History beyond Eurocentrism* (Cambridge: Cambridge University Press, 2007).

[30]Edward Cohen, *The Athenian Nation* (Princeton: Princeton University Press, 2000), 23: "In the fourth century [BCE], numerous nouns were available to denote a farrago of differentiable sites smaller than a *polis*—*kōmion, khōrian, topos, epineion, amphodon, limēn, hieron, tonos, manteion, polikhnē*, and many others—but all were encompassed within the general term 'village,' itself a contrast to 'household' (*oikos* or *oikia*)."

[31]It was possible for an *ethnos* to become self-sufficient through several collaborating villages, which would have no urban center. Yet such a network of villages was not a *polis* according to Aristotelian standards.

[32]Cohen (*Athenian Nation*, 28) argues that urban groupings like Athens and Babylon would have been too large to be considered *poleis*. Indeed, some urban groupings would have been larger than many nations and would have therefore been *ethnē*. Cohen concedes, however, that Herodotus calls Babylon a *polis* in *Histories* 1.90–91.

[33]Cohen, *Athenian Nation*, 24.

[34]Jean-Loup Amselle, *Mestizo Logics: Anthropology of Identity in Africa and Elsewhere*, trans. Claudia Royal (Stanford: Stanford University Press, 1998), 6.

[35]Vlassopoulos, *Unthinking the Greek Polis*, 194

[36]C. P. Jones, "Ethnos and Genos in Herodotus," *ClQ* 46 (1996): 315–20, here 316: "Herodotus uses *ethnos* in a very restricted way, and practically every case can be translated 'people' or 'nation.'" See also Vlassopoulos's nuances that "the supposed tribal affinities of the *ethnos* are fictive; the Greeks of the *ethnē* were capable of inventing and forging ties of political, social and religious kinship, as the Greeks of *poleis* were" (*Unthinking the Greek Polis*, 194). If Vlassopoulos is correct, then a more sustainable emic definition of *ethnos* rests on the myth of a shared tribe rather than any genotypical connection to the past.

[37]See Catherine Morgan, "Ethnic Expression on the Early Iron Age and Early Archaic Greek Mainland: Where Should we be Looking?" in *Ethnic Constructs in Antiquity: The Role of Power and Tradition*, ed. T. Derks and N. Roymans (Amsterdam: Amsterdam University Press, 2009), 11–36; this essay serves as an excellent starting point for assessing the relationship(s) between *ethnos* and *polis*.

[38]Amselle, *Mestizo Logics*, 6.

[39]Thucydides (*Hist.* 2.9.4) describes Khios and Lesbos as *ethnē* encompassing *poleis*.

[40]See survey and bibliography in Eric Barreto, *Ethnic Negotiations: The Function of Race and Ethnicity in Acts 16*, WUNT 2/294 (Tübingen: Mohr Siebeck, 2010), esp. chs. 1 and 2. Barreto suggests that in the Acts of the Apostles, "Like ethnicities, ethnic terminologies are flexible and subject to change in different narrative contexts" (p. 24).

[41]John M. G. Barclay, *Jews in the Mediterranean Diaspora: From Alexander to Trajan (323 BCE–117 CE)* (Berkeley: University of California Press, 1996), 399, 400.

[42]I deal with this more fully in my "Complicating the Category of *Ethnos* toward Poliscentrism: A Possible Way Forward within Second Temple Ethnography" in

Cities of God? Early Christian Engagement with the Ancient Urban Environment, ed. David Gill, Paul Treblico, and Steve Walton (Grand Rapids: Eerdmans, 2017).

[43]Translated by H. Box, *Philonis Alexandrini In Flaccum* (London: Oxford University Press, 1939); quoted in Sarah Pearce, "Jerusalem as 'Mother-City' in the Writings of Philo of Alexandria," in *Negotiating Diaspora: Jewish Strategies in the Roman Empire*, ed. John M. G. Barclay, LSTS 45 (London: T&T Clark, 2004), 19–36, here 19.

[44]Translated by W. Falconer, *The Geography of Strabo*, 3 vols. (London: George Bell & Sons, 1903), 3:179.

[45]A fuller study might compare and contrast this relationship with the arrangement of Idumeans and Jerusalem. Idumea seems to become poliscentric by way of reorientation to Jerusalem thus becoming *Ioudaioi* in the eyes of many.

[46]In John 2:19–22, the narrator associates Jesus's own body with the Jerusalem Temple. Perhaps one consequence of shifting the poliscentrism to Jesus is the possibility of a new *ethnos*.

[47]An exception is John 6, where Jesus presumably does not travel to Jerusalem for the second of three Passovers in the Gospel.

[48]Sheridan, "Hiding from the Fourth Gospel's Tragic Reception History."

[49]Reinhartz, "The Vanishing Jews of Antiquity."

12

Proclamation, Translation, Implication: Addressing the Vilification of "the Jews"

Amy-Jill Levine
Vanderbilt University

Leonard Greenspoon, Philip M. and Ethel Klutznick Chair in Jewish Civilization at Creighton University, is a Jew who teaches in a Department of Theology at Creighton University, a Catholic school. Imagine that—a Jew teaching a predominantly Christian student body about Jewish texts and Christian origins. Prof. Greenspoon has built a distinguished career around the subject of translating: from Hebrew to Greek (with a focus on the Septuagint), from Jewish to Christian (with a concern to explain Jewish concepts and practices to non-Jews), and from ancient text to popular culture (with attention to the Bible in the news).

Translations matter, and translation matters: how a text is read can impact not only the individual reader but social conscience and political practice. The following essay, in Prof. Greenspoon's honor, attends to matters of translation, as well as to Jewish-Christian relations and popular culture, in its focus on how Christian homileticians speak about "the Jews."

Jesus of Nazareth, charged with sedition as "King of the Jews," dies on a Roman cross. But Jews—the collective, the people, all Jews in all times—become known as "Christ-killers."[1] As Cynthia Baker summarizes, "For the writer of the Gospel of John, as for later theologians like Augustine and Martin Luther, *the Jews*, definite plural, names a problem and an evil seldom condensed or essentialized into the singular."[2]

In the wake of the Shoah and, two decades later, of *Nostra Aetate* (1965), homileticians have struggled with proclaiming the texts that led to this charge. The approaches, designed to deny what the texts (apparently) say, are both creative and, ultimately, neither convincing nor even helpful.

The Texts

In 1 Thessalonians, likely the earliest document in the New Testament, Paul writes, "For you, brothers [and sisters], became imitators of the churches of God in Christ Jesus that are in Judea (*Ioudaia*), for you suffered the same things from your own compatriots as they did by the Jews (*Ioudaioi*), who killed both the Lord Jesus and the prophets, and drove us out; they displease God and oppose everyone. . . " (2:14–15). One could limit these *Ioudaioi* to the inhabitants of Judea, and thus insist that the "Judeans" killed Jesus. Yet Paul nowhere else delimits the term to the Judean population: he self-identifies as a *Ioudaios* (Gal 2:15), although he is from Tarsus, and his opposition of "Jews and Greeks" (Rom 1:16; 2:9, 10; 3:9; 10:12; 1 Cor 1:22, 24; 10:32; 12:13; Gal 3:28) is not restricted to the inhabitants of Jerusalem and Athens.

In Matthew, "all the people" (*pas ho laos*) call for Jesus's death with the narratively stunning but historically improbable line, "His blood be on us and on our children." "All the people" could be the Jews in Judea, or in Jerusalem that day, although this approach undermines Matthew's earlier claim that Jesus had come to save "his people" (*laos*) from their sins. Such delimitation also undermines the ending of the Gospel, where *laos*, a technical term for Matthew,[3] makes its final appearance. According to the Evangelist, the chief priests and the Pharisees (27:62) are concerned that the disciples might tell "the people" (*laos*) that Jesus has been raised (27:64). Jesus had restricted the disciples mission to the Jewish people, the "lost sheep of the house of Israel" (10:5b–6 cf. 15:24), and the gentile mission will not begin until 28:19, so "the people" have to be "the Jews."

The chief priests together with the elders then develop an alternate explanation for the empty tomb: "to give a large sum of money to the soldiers, telling them, 'You must say, 'His disciples came by night and stole him away while we were asleep.' If this comes to the governor's ears, we will satisfy him and keep you out of trouble.' So they took the money and did as they were directed. And this story is still told among the *Ioudaioi* to this day" (28:11b–15). The story is as improbable as the blood cry:

no Roman soldiers would admit to falling asleep, and had they fallen asleep, they could have not seen the disciples steal the body. The narrative, no matter how improbable, does make one entirely probable connection: "All the people" who hear the controlled story become *Ioudaioi*, Jews.

John's Gospel solidifies this communal guilt.[4] Following several earlier altercations between "the Jews" (*Ioudaioi*) and Jesus, John writes, "the Jews were seeking all the more to kill him, because he was not only breaking the Sabbath, but was also calling God his own Father, thereby making himself equal to God" (5:18). The term *Ioudaioi*, used seventy-one times in the Gospel, can at times be delimited to the residents of Judea (as in 7:1, "Jesus went about in Galilee. He did not wish to go about in Judea because the *Ioudaoi* [here "Judeans" is a viable translation] were looking for an opportunity to kill him"); however, the cumulative effect of John's uses suggests "all Jews." By the Passion Narrative, the chief priests and the "Jews" are assimilated into one, toxic group. "(Pilate) said to the Jews, 'Here is your King!' They cried out, 'Away with him! Away with him! Crucify him!' Pilate asked them, 'Shall I crucify your King?' The chief priests answered, 'We have no king but the emperor'" (19:14–15). Finally, the Gospel implies, several times, that Jesus and his followers are distinct from the "Jews." Jews themselves, Joseph of Arimathea and the disciples act "for fear of the Jews" (19:38; 20:19; cf. 7:13).

In Acts 2:22–23, Peter addresses "Parthians, Medes, Elamites, and residents of Mesopotamia, Judea and Cappadocia, Pontus and Asia, Phrygia and Pamphylia, Egypt and the parts of Libya belonging to Cyrene, and visitors from Rome, both Jews (*Ioudaioi*) and proselytes, Cretans and Arabs" (Acts 2:9–11) with the collective: "You that are Israelites" and then charges this group with having handed Jesus over to be "crucified and killed by the hands of those outside the law" (Acts 2:22–23). Who crucified Jesus? The Jews, from Judea and the Diaspora; those born into Jewish families and those who became proselytes. Place of birth and native language are irrelevant in the charge; membership in the Jewish people is what matters.

Peter repeats the point in the next chapter: "Men, Israelites. . . Jesus, whom you handed over and rejected in the presence of Pilate, though he had decided to release him. But you rejected the Holy and Righteous One and asked to have a murderer given to you, and you killed the Author of life. . . " (Acts 3:12–15). Rome is exculpated and Israel, the Jews, is guilty of Jesus's death.

Despite these verses and others, numerous people choose to read John in a way that does not vilify Jews. They are guided by more than linguistics; they are also guided by morality. *Nostra Aetate*, the Vatican II document that denies the claim of deicide, reads:

> True, the Jewish authorities and those who followed their lead pressed for the death of Christ; still, what happened in His passion cannot be charged against all the Jews, without distinction, then alive, nor against the Jews of today. Although the Church is the new people of God, the Jews should not be presented as rejected or accursed by God, as if this followed from the Holy Scriptures. . . . Furthermore, in her rejection of every persecution against any man, the Church, mindful of the patrimony she shares with the Jews and moved not by political reasons but by the Gospel's spiritual love, decries hatred, persecutions, displays of anti-Semitism, directed against Jews at any time and by anyone.

Given that the Nazi atrocities were within the memory of every participant at Vatican II, recognition of Jews as a people and not just Judaism as a religion, was a necessary move.

Fifty years after *Nostra Aetate*, the need to repeat such concerns continues. It is needed for people whose memories do not include the Shoah, whose education overlooked it, and especially for those persuaded that it never happened. With the uptick in anti-Jewish and antisemitic statements and events throughout the globe in 2016–2017, the need for sensitive preaching about "the Jews" in Churches—Protestant, Catholic, Orthodox—is especially acute. An unthinking comment voiced from the pulpit on a Sunday morning, or from the cozy chair at the Wednesday evening Bible study, can reinforce or inculcate prejudice. Therefore, clergy and religious educators have to determine how to proclaim the Gospel without vilifying the Jews.[5]

Addressing the Texts

There are six approaches by which the problematic material has been addressed. None is ideal, and there is no quick fix, no catch-all approach for avoiding the problem. Further, what works in one congregation may not work in another. The six options are:

1. Excision (or, if you prefer, exorcism): cast it out, either literally with a scissors or academically with an argument about authorship.
2. Appropriate: re-enact the events and participate in them.
3. Christologize: turn Jesus's opponents into crypto-Christians.
4. Historicize: explain the text within its own cultural context.
5. Substitute terminology: re-label the target of the invective.
6. Acknowledge the problem, and address it.

Excision

The first option is excision: take a scissors to the offending passages, or, for the modern iteration, hit the delete key for verses we don't like. This approach has good American precedent. Thomas Jefferson, unable to accept the historicity of the New Testament's supernatural elements, including Christological claims, made those elements disappear in his 1803 Bible, and then in its 1819 revision.[6] No angelic annunciation, no virginal conception, no cleansing those suffering from leprosy, no walking on water or rising from the dead: Jefferson's Bible is one that any humanist would appreciate. Jefferson also eliminated Matt 27:24–25, Pilate's handwashing and the "blood cry," and most of John's references to "the Jews."

Two centuries later, Dr. Howard Thurman spoke of excision for reasons of justice rather than rationality. Thurman recounted what his grandmother, a former slave, told him:

> Sometimes the plantation owner's minister would be permitted to hold a religious service for the slaves, and he always preached from the same text: 'Slaves, be obedient to your masters, for this is right in the Lord.' My grandmother said that she made up her mind then and there that if she ever learned to read or if freedom ever came she would never read that part of the

> Bible. So all the years that I was growing and had the job of reading to her every day, I could never read any of the Pauline letters, except now and then the 13th chapter of I Corinthians.[7]

The story has morphed into the common sermon illustration that Thurman's grandmother, once she learned to read herself, took a scissors to the text and excised Paul's writings from the New Testament.

In different ways, a form of excision is how both Judaism and Christianity liturgically deal with problematic texts. Given that the biblical canons, whether Christian (with various books) or Jewish, are too long for a complete annual proclamation, authorities determined what passages would be read on days the congregation met. These determinations became for Jews the *Parashat Hashavua* and for some Christian congregations, the lectionaries of various communions, Catholic, Orthodox, and Protestant. Thus, there are at least two canons for every church and synagogue: what is written, and what is proclaimed.

In the synagogue, the Torah is read, aloud, in Hebrew, whether on an annual or a triennial cycle. Some congregations proclaim the full *parashah*; some read selections, but something from Torah is read. However, only select Prophetic passages appear in the *Haftarah* readings. Of import for Jewish–Christian dialogue, the passages from Isaiah 61 in Jesus's famous "synagogue sermon" (Luke 4:17–19, paraphrasing Isa 61:1–2) are not proclaimed in the synagogues today. For another example, in some (more liberal) Jewish congregations, the last two chapters of the book of Esther, which describe the massacre of the Persians, are read, at Purim, in an undertone, with an introductory warning, followed by sober discussion, or not read at all.[8]

In some churches, biblical readings are determined by lectionaries. Matthew 27:25, the "blood cry," is part of the Revised Common Lectionary (RCL) Year A: Lent, Liturgy of the Passion (the full reading is Matt 27:11–54). In the Roman Catholic Church, the verse is part of the Palm Sunday reading (either Matt 26:14–27:66 or the shorter 27:11–54).[9] John 20, where the disciples hide behind locked doors "for fear of the Jews," appears in all three annual readings for the Second Sunday of Easter. For Roman Catholics, John 20:1–9 is read on Easter Sunday. Acts 2:22–23, wherein Peter accuses Israel of killing the Christ, surfaces in Year A, the Second Sunday of Easter, in the context of Acts 2:14a, 22–32. In the Roman Catholic Church, these verses are proclaimed on Monday within the Octave Easter. If the faithful miss services that year, they will hear the charge repeated: Acts 3:12–19, the second charge against the Jews, is read in Year B, the Third Sunday of Easter (or, for Roman Catholics, a Thursday within the Octave of Easter). John 8:44, wherein Jesus accuses the Jews of being "Children of the Devil," did not make the RCL or Roman Catholic cut; neither does 1 Thess 2:14–16. The good news is that these difficult verses will not be proclaimed in the churches on Sunday morning. Yet the presence of these verses in the canon remains, and the lack of liturgical focus removes the possibility of the homiletician's confronting them. The expression "damned if you do/damned if you don't" comes to mind.[10]

Precedent for not proclaiming texts, for skipping verses, thus exists in synagogues, churches, and even in U.S. history. There is both good news and bad news with this approach in regard to the New Testament's less-than-positive comments about Jews. The good news is that there will be fewer prompts for inculcating or reinforcing anti-Jewish views. The bad news is that the homiletician will be less likely to address the verses, and so too the problems they can create. If we excise problematic verses from the liturgy, we also excise the history of how those texts were understood, and the memory of those who were harmed because of how those texts were proclaimed. Christians who read the Bible outside of liturgical context will have less guidance on how to interpret the difficult verses.

For Evangelical Churches, a sermon series might spend several weeks on one book. Pastors may choose to skip verses, but few do, for to skip verses would be to disrespect the words of the text. For such settings, excision may not be an option.

Excision also faces an epistemological problem. All readers determine what texts best speak to their needs and what texts to ignore. But what concerned Jefferson was not what concerned Thurman's grandmother. Designer canons eliminate ecclesial community even as they threaten to eliminate history.

A variant on the excision move is to claim that because the texts are not historically accurate, they have lesser import or can even be ignored. For example, the view that Paul did not write

1 Thess 2:14b–16 has gained increasing traction over the past several decades,[11] as has the correlate view that Paul did not write 1 Cor 14:33b–36, which attempts to silence women (or at least wives) in churches. Claims that 1 Thess 2:14b–16 is an interpolation follow from three arguments, all three ultimately apologetic and none of them conclusive.

First, the passage can be seen as inconsistent with later passages, such as Rom 9:4–5; 11:28b–29, "They are Israelites, and to them belong the adoption, the glory, the covenants, the giving of the law, the worship, and the promises; to them belong the patriarchs, and from them, according to the flesh, comes the messiah. . . as regards election they are beloved, for the sake of their ancestors; for the gifts and the calling of God are irrevocable." Ralph Waldo Emerson wrote, "A foolish consistency is the hobgoblin of little minds, adored by little statesmen and philosophers and divines."[12] Emerson also named several thinkers who, because of this apparent lack of consistency, would be misunderstood: Pythagoras, Socrates, Jesus, Luther, Copernicus, Galileo, and Newton. He could have included Paul. That Paul may have changed his mind is possible; that he adapted his message to the needs of his assemblies, such that to the gentiles in Thessalonica an anti-Jewish screed was pastorally helpful, but to the gentiles in Rome, where relations with the local Jewish community were of concern, such polemic would be inappropriate.

A second argument for removing the verses is that they can be removed without harming the rhetorical flow. The argument is not cogent, for there is no smooth transition from 1 Thess 2:14a to 2:17. Even were we to begin the excision with 2:14a, v. 17 remains the beginning of a new thought.

The third argument is that the comment, "God's wrath has overtaken them at last" (1 Thess 2:16) refers to the destruction of Jerusalem, an event that occurred after Paul died. 1 Thessalonians may well date ca. 41,[13] but even in this short period of time between Jesus's death and Paul's writing, bad things happened in Judea.[14] Alternatively, Paul may be speaking eschatologically: the disaster is the failure of Israel to recognize the role of the Christ in salvation history. For Paul, the Jews, in general, are damned.

The greatest problem with the excision move is demonstrated by the correlate attempts to remove 1 Cor 14:33b–36. That is, the text remains in all printed versions of the Bible. Were well-meaning homilists to omit these verses "because Paul did not write them," then conservative readers, unimpressed with text-critical claims, would be left with no resource to address the problem.

Upshot: the excision model—whether by scissors or by academic argument—is not going to resolve the problems, and it is surely not going to resolve the problems in the Evangelical congregations that regard the entire Bible as sacred scripture. The Christian witness, and the Christian Gospel, is not based on some anterior scholarly construct of what happened; it is based in the words of the Bible as interpreted by the faithful community, and so one must deal with those words.

Appropriate

The appropriating or participatory model places the congregation in the role of "the Jews." When congregants liturgically recite "His blood be on our heads and on our children," they recognize that they are the sinners for whom Jesus died. This is the model connected with Christmas pageants and Passion Plays, performances of Bach's passion, and even "The Passion of the Christ," which depicts Mel Gibson's own hand driving the first nail into Jesus/Jim Caviezel. It is modeled in a famous seventeenth-century hymn by Johann Heermann, "Ah Holy Jesus," with its line, "Who was the guilty? Who brought this upon thee? Alas, my treason, Jesus, hath undone thee! 'Twas I, Lord Jesus, I it was denied thee; I crucified thee." The approach creates a theology that attributes the cross primarily to human sin rather than to Jewish evil.

The problems with appropriating the role of the Jews are two-fold. First, those in the Church who appropriate responsibility for Jesus's crucifixion are the same people who claim the baptism of forgiveness. They never forget their insider position, so that their claiming the guilt is at best temporary (i.e., for as long as the lectionary reading or the hymn or even Good Friday lasts). Coupled with the potential feelings of guilt or shame are the actual feelings of salvation. Second, many Christians are well aware that the Jewish people as a whole do not move from guilty opponents to redeemed confessors. Indeed, by appropriating the guilt and then being exculpated by belief, the Christian risks reinforcing the damnation of the Jews. I am not suggesting that all people who call themselves "Christians" believe that people outside their communion are all damned; there are numerous views of soteriology expressed in the pulpit and in the pew. I am rather noting the potential difficulty of appropriating the role of "guilty Jew."

Another appropriation by which "the Jews" become the Christian sinners occurs in some readings of Matthew 23, Jesus's excoriation of the scribes and Pharisees. Jesus's rhetoric is severe: "Woe to you, scribes and Pharisees, hypocrites! For you are like whitewashed tombs, which on the outside look beautiful, but inside they are full of the bones of the dead and of all kinds of filth. . . inside you are full of hypocrisy and lawlessness. . . . You snakes, you brood of vipers! How can you escape being sentenced to hell?" (Matt 23:27–33). This is not the sort of language typically classified as civil discourse today, no matter how normative it was in antiquity.

Reading ancient Pharisees as stand-ins for present day Christians has a pastoral pay-off. Nevertheless, the "scribes and Pharisees," or the Jews in John's Gospel remain the negative exemplars. Substituting "woe to you, Mexicans" or "African-Americans, hypocrites" should demonstrate the problem. U.S. readers of a certain age might recall adults telling our rambunctious younger selves, "Stop acting like wild Indians." Whoever the "Indians" were, I knew that whatever they were doing, it wasn't good. Today, we recognize this as bigoted language. Reading Matthew 23 has the same impact.

As long as the words "scribes and Pharisees" are in the text, we will have a problem, for the scribes and Pharisees come to represent how not to behave. Further, not all congregants hear the allegory; they hear the text as confessing the sins of the Jews, not of themselves.

Christologize

Along with appropriating Matt 27:25, congregations can also read the verse not primarily as a death wish for Jesus but as an ironic plea for redemption: "his blood be on our heads" becomes the Jewish people's way of asking for Jesus's blood to redeem them from sin. This reading appears, *inter alia*, in the second of Pope Benedict XVI's "Jesus" books: The blood of Jesus "is not poured out against anyone; it is poured out for many, for all. . . . these words are not a curse, but rather redemption, salvation."[15] Anders Runesson suggests something similar: "Unlike the Pharisees, the people of Jerusalem are also, unknowingly, instrumental in providing for the sacrificial replacement that will save the people once the temple is destroyed."[16] And Boris Repschinski asserts:

> the prediction of [Matthew] 1:21 ['he will save his people (λαός) from their sins'] finally gains fulfillment as the readers realize that the events before Pilate's court bring about the prediction at Jesus' Last Supper that his blood would be given for the forgiveness of sins. Again, Matthew plays with different meanings on different levels: just as λαός signifies the crowd before Pilate on the level of the plot and the people of Israel on the level of guiding the reader, so αἷμα ἐφ'ἡμάς καὶ ἐπὶ τὰ τέκνα ἡμῶν signals the crowd's guilt before Pilate on the level of the plot, while it affirms the salvation of Israel on the level of the story.[17]

This approach redeems the verse theologically—the text becomes not a perpetual curse but a perpetual blessing. It may also be true to the evangelist's intent. Matthew may be reflecting on the destruction of the Temple in 70 and regarding Jesus as replacing the soteriological import of the sacrificial system.

And yet. . . this theological reading does not obviate the difficulties with the approach. The presentation of the people's accepting Jesus's sacrifice suggests that the Jewish crowd desired to be redeemed by Jesus's blood; it infers that Judaism apart from the Christian message is ineffective; it turns the Jewish crowd into crypto-Christians.

Historicize

The fourth approach, historical contextualization, is the darling of the academy. It is used to explain the circumstances that gave rise to the text as we have it, and it extends that explanation to defuse some of the negative rhetoric's power. It can also suggest that some narratives lack historical credibility. In each case, however, the historical argument remains at best a hypothesis; in some cases, it rests on apologetic views; in some others, it backfires by reinstating a negative view of Jews and/or Judaism.

One popular historical approach, found in traditional Christian teaching as well in academic biblical studies, is the claim that both the First and the Fourth Gospels—Matthew and John—were written by Jews, and that both were written for predominantly Jewish communities. Therefore, so the historicizing argument goes, these Gospels cannot be anti-Jewish. They represent, rather, internal Jewish disagreements. Negative language would be expected in response to being exiled from synagogues (so John 9, 12, 16) or persecuted therein (Matt 23:34; Luke 21:12). While internal community difficulty is historically plausible—Paul does describe synagogue discipline (2 Cor 11:24)—the result of this claim does not much help the homilist. If the rhetoric is inner-Jewish polemic, then the cause is "Jewish" behavior.

The dirty little secret of New Testament studies is the circular argument by which readers achieve such interpretations: read the text and determine, on the basis of its contents, both author and audience; then interpret the text on the basis of the reconstruction. We know neither who wrote the Gospels nor the community to which they were addressed, if indeed they were addressed to a specific group. Claims of a target audience (e.g., Mathew as written for a Jewish or partly Jewish congregation; John addresses a group recently expelled from the synagogue because of the *birkhat ha-minim*, the "benediction against heretics") are suspect. Matthew's Gospel may well have been addressed to all followers of Jesus rather than to a Jewish conventicle.[18] The First Gospel is the most quoted and, as far as we can tell, most copied of any of the Gospel material in the first few centuries. There is no historical proof for Christ-confessors being expelled from synagogues in the first two centuries; to the contrary, Paul speaks of internal discipline. Even the famous two-level reading of John's Gospel—the story of the Johannine community mapped onto the story of Jesus—popularized by J. Louis Martyn in the late 1970s,[19] has faced its own expulsion from much of Johannine studies.

The argument of an inner-Jewish polemic also fails to resolve the problem, in that (a) it puts the onus for the harsh rhetoric on the Jews; (b) it presumes that Jews cannot engage in anti-Jewish discourse; (c) it can serve to excuse the polemic by rendering it understandable; and (d) it goes against the narratives of both Matthew and John, who locate the "Jews" (*Ioudaioi*) as at best those who deny the resurrection (Matt 28:15) or worse, who are "children of the devil" (John 8:44).[20]

The historicizing explanations, already hypothetical given that they are based on disputed reconstructions of the Gospels' authors and target audiences, wind up blaming the victim: harsh rhetoric is explained (or explained away) as a reaction to the "persecution" of Jesus's followers even as the synagogue is condemned for maintaining its own practices or attempting to preserve its safety in the Diaspora. For a final problem: historical-critical analysis tends not to work well from the pulpit.

Language substitution

The most popular move may be retranslation, or language substitution. This approach begins by acknowledging that the biblical text, as traditionally read, can create prejudice. In his editing of the Bauer-Arndt-Gingrich *Greek-English Lexicon of the New Testament and Other Early Christian Literature*, Frederick Danker writes, "Incalculable harm has been caused by simply glossing *Ioudaios* with 'Jew,' for many readers or auditors of Bible translations do not practice the historical judgment necessary to distinguish between circumstances and events of an ancient time and contemporary ethnic-religious-social realities, with the result that anti-Judaism in the modern sense of the term is needlessly fostered through biblical texts."[21] Anticipating Danker, already in 1976 Malcolm Lowe labeled the translation "Jew" as a "philological error" as well as the source of "a constant excuse for anti-Semitism."[22]

There are several options for replacing "the Jews." None is ideal. One is to translate according to context. Attempting to narrow the focus of villainy, and often with good support from the pericope in question, some homilists adapt their translations based on narrative context. This is a fine translation technique (words always change meaning depending on context). For example, while, positively speaking, "salvation is from the Jews (*Ioudaioi*)" in John 4:22 (what this verse says about *Samaritan* worship is a related issue), the

Ioudaoi who say to Jesus, "Now we know that you have a demon" (John 8:52) might be the "Jewish leaders," "religious leaders," or "Judeans." People hearing the text read in Greek would not hear such shifts, and given John's literary artistry, probably should not.[23] There are other reasons to question these alternatives.

Another option is to translate *Ioudaioi* as "Jewish leaders," which sometimes fits the narrative context. John 19:6–7 provides a test case. The first verse states, "When the chief priests and the police saw him, they shouted, 'Crucify him! Crucify him!' Pilate said to them, 'Take him yourselves and crucify him; I find no case against him.'" Then, in v. 7, the *Ioudaioi* answer, "'We have a law, and according to that law he ought to die because he has claimed to be the Son of God.'" Translating these *Ioudaioi* as "Jewish leaders" makes sense, given that "the chief priests and the police" are among the Jewish leaders. The NLT takes this approach; it reads, for John 19:7, "The Jewish leaders replied. . . ." Similarly, it is not "the Jews" (John 19:14) who call out "Away with him! Away with him! Crucify him!" (John 19:15a), but the "Jewish leaders."

Aside from erasing John's own rhetorical use of *Ioudaioi*, the move does not exculpate "Jews" in general; the people are responsible for their leaders, whether by commission (election, popular acclaim) or omission (failure to rebel). Further, as long as the term "Jewish" remains, so does the problem.

A variant on "Jewish leaders" is "religious leaders,"[24] and there is textual warrant here as well. After depicting "the Jews" as advocating for Jesus's death, John writes, "Pilate asked them, 'Shall I crucify your king?' The chief priests answered, 'We have no king but Caesar'" (John 19:15b). Thus, it is the priests, "religious leaders" who promoted Jesus's death.

This option may be worse, as it reduces the conflict to a matter of "religion" and thus sets up for the church congregation a "Judaism vs. Christianity" scenario. It also reinforces the relationship between the people and their "leaders": one cannot always choose one's "political leaders," but one can choose religious leaders. Josephus suggests that the Jewish population followed the teachings of the Pharisees, not that of the priests (as a priest himself, Josephus is a tad miffed at what he regards as disloyalty to the priests, the supposedly authorized teachers). Finally, as long as the term

"Jewish" or even "religious" becomes attached to these "leaders," the problem of blaming the Jews is not resolved. If the congregation begins with the perspective of Jews as legalistic, the negative impression is increased.

The CEB from the American Bible Society opts simply for "leaders."[25] The problem here is that the reader does not know the answer to the question, "Leaders of whom?"

"Judean" is a legitimate translation of the Greek; it indicates the connection between the Judean people and the land of Judea, and it locates the *Ioudaioi* among the other nations of the world. "Judean," which derives from the land of "Judea," indicates the ethnic component of the Jewish people; an ethnic group has a homeland, and Judea is the homeland of the Judeans.[26] Unlike the term "Jew," which lacks the "d" (the German *Jude* does resolve the Jew/Judean problem, but putting a German term into an English liturgy comes with its own difficulties) and therefore the stronger connection to "Judea," "Judean" anchors the people to the land. Therefore, keeping the focus on the ethnically charged "Judean" rather than "Jew," which has as religious component, is historically correct.

Whether it is the best translation to use, particularly in a liturgical context, is another question. For some scholars, the translation "Judean" *appropriately* severs any connection between Jews today and those Judeans in antiquity. Adele Reinhartz cites Philip Esler's 2007 claim that the translation of "Jew," especially for the Gospel of John, mistakenly creates "a persistence of identity between the *Ioudaioi* of John's time and the Jews of ours."[27] However, there *is* a persistence of identity. This is precisely the critique Joshua Garroway names in his article on *Ioudaios* in the *Jewish Annotated New Testament*: "The removal of 'Jews' from ancient texts also undermines the Jews' own sense of continuity."[28] Twenty-first century Jews still hold a connection to those first-century ancestors, just as twenty-first century Greeks claim a connection to Plato and Aristotle, or some Palestinian Christians regard themselves as the descendants of those who participated at Pentecost.[29]

To translate the term "Judean" is to follow, intentionally or not, the view that until the Mishnah or even the Talmud, there were no "Jews" per se, but only "Judeans." As Reinhartz trenchantly puts it, "At stake for these scholars is not so much the question of 'who is a Jew'—a preoccupation of many Jewish communal organizations—but whether there were any Jews at all, anywhere, prior to the third or fourth centuries CE."[30] In my own study of the use of "Judean" in popular culture (I plugged "Jew," "Judean," and "Jesus" into a Google search), I found KKK and neo-Nazi websites. This was to be expected: if there are no Jews in the New Testament, and Jesus is a "Galilean" rather than a Judean, then clearly Jesus cannot be a Jew. And if there are no Jews in the first century in the territory of the current nation-state of Israel, then Jews today can have no claim to the land. The replacement of "Judean" for "Jew" may be based on benevolent premises, as they are, for example, for Danker and Lowe. The replacements may also be based on the attempt to be historically accurate, as they are for Mason. Regardless of the basis, however, Jonathan Klawans makes clear the result: "let's face it," he writes, "there are two ideologies that are well-served by disconnecting contemporary 'Jews' from 'Judeans.' The first ideology is anti-Zionism and the second is anti-Semitism."[31]

The major source, particularly for the liberal Christian pastor today in the U.S., for the replacement of "Jew" by "Judean," is the writing of Creighton University Professor Bruce Malina (1933-1917). For Malina, one cannot talk about "Jews" prior to the codification of the Talmud; therefore, "Judean" is the only appropriate translation of *Ioudaios*. Malina further claims, "the fact is that most of those Central European Jews and hence most U.S. Jews from Central Europe are descended from Khazars, a people who accepted the Jewish religion in the 8th century A.D."[32] His major point then is both to sever connections between Jews (however defined) and Jesus and then to sever the connection of Jews, at any time or place, to the land of Israel.

The translation "Judean" does not resolve the problem of negative proclamation. Regardless of all the arguments regarding emic and etic approaches, historical implications, authorial intent, literary-critical sensitivity, and even the compassionate view that "Judeans" sounds "less anti-Jewish," "Judean" still sounds like "Jew"—enough so that only the densest in the congregation will not make the connection. Worse, reading "Hiding behind locked doors for fear of the Judeans" will sound, to the skeptical congregant, like a "politically correct" (with all the negative connotations that term can have) reading. No one is fooled. And were that dense congregant to ask, "Who are the Judeans," the answer will have to be, "the Jews." And should the congregant look at the pew Bible—from the NRSV (liberal Protestant) to the NIV (Evangelical) to the NABR (Roman Catholic), the text will say "Jews," so "Judean" creates a disconnect. The translation "Judean" might also cause worry, among the conservatives in the Church, that the homilist is playing with more than just one text and is therefore potentially heretical.

In speaking of the "Hebrew" Bible, Leonard Greenspoon wisely notes, "In my carefree youth, I blithely conceived of a perfect sort of translation that would fulfill all needs for all people. I have learned, and been chastened to learn, that it just ain't so."[33] Amen to that.

Admit the problem

We come finally to our sixth option: admit to the problem that certain verses in the New Testament can lead to anti-Jewish views, and deal with it. Once we admit the problem, using allegory, or relativizing, or retranslating, or any of the other options, is at least honest. In his 1970 Fordham University Dissertation, L. Augustine Grady documented "The History of the Exegesis of Matthew 27.25: A Study of Early Medieval Commentaries (650–1000) on Matthew's Gospel."[34] Grady begins the dissertation by quoting *Nostra Aetate* and then observing, "the council clearly repudiates any interpretation of Scripture that depicts all Jews as objects of the divine displeasure. It does not, however, affirm that such an interpretation has never been made; rather, it says that this interpretation does not represent the true tradition of the Church."[35]

Grady's point is apt: for an anti-Jewish reading to be removed from the pulpit, the groundwork also will have to be done by theologians and ethicists, and the implementation remains the task of the preachers and the teachers; historians, no matter what we conclude, do not have the information or the authority on our own to change the sermons and Bible studies.[36] As Grady shows, not all theologians of the early Church promulgated the idea of a perpetual blood guilt, which means that an anti-Jewish reading (however defined) is not a necessary one.

Acknowledging the problem has both historical and theological warrant. If we erase the difficult verses, we threaten to erase or obscure part of the reason why Jews have been persecuted over the past 2,000 years,[37] and we lose an opportunity to educate the next generation.

Christians should no more be expected to develop an anti-Jewish attitude upon reading the Bible than Jews should become anti-Egyptian given centuries of slavery followed by an attempted genocide. We choose how to read, and those choices require guidance from childhood education on.

There are no quick fixes, and what works in one church might not work in another. Some homileticians may choose to read difficult passages in an undertone, or with body movement and placement to indicate the harm some interpretations have caused; some may choose to put a note in the order of worship; some might opt for a gloss on the reading itself; some may base their sermon on the difficult parts of the text.

Afterword

One cannot enter the same river twice, and the saying holds for texts as well. Texts speak different messages depending upon with whom, when, how, where, and why the reading occurs. This polyvocality may be particularly true of the Bible, which speaks in its own historical context, through the centuries, and to those who hold the text sacred as well as to the academic (sometimes the categories overlap) today. Leonard Greenspoon has provided instruction on what biblical texts meant, how their meaning changed over time and over language, and how they are appropriated today, religiously and popularly (sometimes these categories, too, overlap).

He provides one more gift to readers, and one that is particularly of value when addressing difficult topics such as potentially harmful texts. Professor Greenspoon's writings and his conferences convey a sense of playfulness and joy. These traits keep creativity alive, and—when it comes to difficult texts—they prevent despair.

Notes

An earlier version of part of this essay appeared in "Holy Week and the Hatred of the Jews," *ABC [Australian Broadcasting Commission] Religion and Ethics*, 4 April 2012: http://www.abc.net.au/religion/articles/2012/04/04/3470618.htm.

[1]See Jeremy Cohen, *Christ Killers: The Jews and the Passion from the Bible to the Big Screen* (New York: Oxford University Press, 2007).

[2]Cynthia M. Baker, *Jew*, Key Words in Jewish Studies (New Brunswick: Rutgers University Press, 2016), 11.

[3]Other Matthean uses are 2:4 ("chief priests and scribes of the people"); 2:6 ("my people Israel"); 4:16 ("people who sat in darkness," cf. Isa 42:7); 4:23 ([Jewish] people in Galilee); 13:15 ("people's heart has grown dull," cf. Isa 6:20); 15:8 ("This people honors me with their lips," cf. Isa 29:13); 21.23; 26:3; 26:47; 27:1 ("chief priests and elders of the people"); and 26:5 (concern that "there may be a riot among the [Jewish] people [in Jerusalem]).

[4]For the argument that John had familiarity with Matthew's Gospel, see James W. Barker, *John's Use of Matthew*, Emerging Scholars (Minneapolis: Fortress, 2015).

[5]See Marilyn J. Salmon, *Preaching Without Contempt: Overcoming Unintended Anti-Judaism*, Fortress Resources for Preaching (Minneapolis, Augsburg Fortress, 2006); Ron Allen, *Interpreting Difficult Texts: Anti-Judaism and Christian Preaching* (Harrisburg: Trinity Press International, 1989). See also the blog, "Faith not Fault: Affirming Christianity without Faulting Judaism"; https://faithnotfault.wordpress.com. The Standing Commission on Liturgy and Music of the Episcopal Church began an "Addressing Christian Anti-Judaism Project" in 2006, and the committee addressed the question in 2012–2015. The website indicates, as part of a report to the 78th general convention [2015], a resolution: "A062: Address Christian Anti-Judaism in Liturgical Texts: *Resolved*, the House of (Deputies) concurring, That the 78th General Convention direct the Standing Commission on Liturgy and Music to continue to collect, review, and disseminate materials to address Christian anti-Judaism expressed in and stirred by portions of Christian scriptures and liturgical texts. Explanation: This resolution asks the Standing Commission on Liturgy to continue work first directed in Resolution 2006-C001, calling for 'materials to assist members of the Church to address anti-Jewish prejudice expressed in and stirred by portions of Christian scriptures and liturgical texts'" (https://extranet.generalconvention.org/staff/files/download/12780.pdf). The Vatican Commission for Religious Relations with the Jews published in 1985 "Notes on the correct way to present the Jews and Judaism in preaching and catechesis in the Roman Catholic Church" (http://www.vatican.va/roman_curia/pontifical_councils/chrstuni/relations-jews-docs/rc_pc_chrstuni_doc_19820306_jews-judaism_en.html); the problem with this fine and well-intended text is that it gives few examples on the *how* of homiletics. Today there are few homiletic guides on *how* to preach "without contempt" for Judaism, and the subject is often unaddressed or quickly passed over in homiletics courses.

[6]Thomas Jefferson, *The Jefferson Bible: The Life and Morals of Jesus of Nazareth* (reprint of *The Philosophy of Jesus of Nazareth, extracted from the account of his life and doctrines, as given by Matthew, Mark, Luke, and John; being an abridgement of the New Testament for the use of the Indians, unembarrassed with the matters of fact or faith beyond the level of their comprehension*; Radford, VA: A&D Publishing, 2007).

[7]Mary E. Goodwin, "Racial Roots and Religion: An Interview with Howard Thurman" (http://genius.com/Mary-e-goodwin-racial-roots-and-religion-an-interview-with-howard-thurman-annotated), cf. Howard Thurman, *Jesus and the Disinherited* (Nashville: Abingdon, 1949), 30–31, where a variant of the story appears: "During the days of slavery," she said, "the master's minister would occasionally hold services for the slaves. Also, the white minister used as his text something from Paul. 'Slaves be obedient to them that are your masters. . . as unto Christ.' Then he would go on to show how, if we were good and happy slaves, Christ would bless us. I promised my Maker that if I ever learned to read, and if freedom ever came, I would not read that part of the Bible."

[8]See, inter alia, the *Tikkun Magazine* essays at http://www.tikkun.org/nextgen/rabbi-dev-noilly-and-others-on-the-book-of-esther.

[9]From the USCCB website: http://www.usccb.org/about/divine-worship/liturgical-calendar/upload/2017cal.pdf.

[10]Addressing the RCL directly is the helpful volume by Ronald James Allen and Clark M. Williamson, *Preaching the Gospels Without Blaming the Jews: A Lectionary Commentary* (Louisville: Westminster John Knox, 2004).

[11]The seminal study is by Birger A. Pearson, "1 Thessalonians 2:13–16: A Deutero-Pauline Interpretation," *HTR* 64 (1971): 79–94.

[12]Ralph Waldo Emerson, *Essays: First Series/Self-Reliance* (1847).

[13]See Gerd Lüdemann, *The Earliest Christian Text: 1 Thessalonians* (Salem, OR: Polebridge, 2013).

[14]Markus Bockmuehl, "1 Thessalonians 2:14–16 and the Church in Jerusalem," *TynBul* 52 (2001): 1–31.

[15]Pope Benedict XIV (Joseph Ratzinger), *Jesus of Nazareth, Part Two. Holy Week: From the Entrance into Jerusalem to the Resurrection*, trans. Vatican Secretariat of State (San Francisco: Ignatius Press, 2011), 187. The same idea appeared earlier in Timothy Cargal, "'His Blood Be upon Us and upon Our Children': A Matthean Double Entendre?" *NTS* 37 (1991): 101–12 and Desmond Sullivan, "New Insights into Matthew 27.24-5," *NBf* 73 (1992): 453–57. See Catherine Hamilton, "'His Blood Be upon Us': Innocent Blood and the Death of Jesus in Matthew," *CBQ* 70 (2008): 82–100.

[16]Anders Runesson, *Divine Wrath and Salvation in Matthew: The Narrative World of the First Gospel* (Minneapolis: Fortress, 2016), 306 (cf. n. 234).

[17]Boris Repschinski, "For He Will Save His People from Their Sins" (Matthew 1:21): A Christology for Christian Jews," *CBQ* 68 (2007): 248–67, here 263.

[18]E.g., Richard Bauckham, ed., *The Gospel for All Christians: Rethinking the Gospel Audiences* (Grand Rapids: Eerdmans, 1998).

[19]J. Louis Martyn, *History and Tradition in the Fourth Gospel*, 3rd ed. (Louisville: Westminster John Knox 2003). For a positive recent study of the thesis which argues that the expulsion passages are historical but date ca. 30, to the time of Jesus himself, see Jonathan Bernier, *Aposynagōgos and the Historical Jesus in John: Rethinking the Historicity of the Johannine Expulsion Passages*, BibInt 122 (Leiden: Brill, 2013). Bernier's volume has an up-to-2013-date for bibliography on the expulsion passages.

[20]See Amy-Jill Levine, "Anti-Judaism and the Gospel of Matthew," in *Anti-Judaism and the Gospels*, ed. William R. Farmer (Valley Forge: Trinity Press International, 1999), 9–36, esp. 16 on the question of popular rhetoric.

[21]Cited in Amy-Jill Levine, *The Misunderstood Jew: The Church and the Scandal of the Jewish Jesus* (New York: HarperOne, 2007), 159–60 as well as by Adele Reinhartz, "The Vanishing Jews of Antiquity," in *Jew and Judean: A Marginalia Forum on Politics and Historiography in the Translation of Ancient Texts*, ed. Timothy Michael Law and Charles Halton, *Marginalia | Los Angeles Review of Books*, 24 June 2014, 10–23, here 19. This edited collection offers several essays on the problem of the translation. See also now the helpful summary of Johannine Jew/Judean discussion in Wendy E. S. North, *A Journey Round John: Tradition, Interpretation and Context in the Fourth Gospel*, LNTS 534 (London: Bloomsbury T&T Clark, 2015), 6–8. For additional discussion of Danker's lexical views, see Baker, *Jew*, 22–25.

[22]Malcolm Lowe, "Who Were the IOUDAIOI," *NovT* 18 (1976): 101–30; see also his "Ioudaioi of the Apocrypha: A Fresh Approach to the Gospels of James, Pseudo-Thomas, Peter and Nicodemus," *NovT* 23 (1981): 56–90, cited inter alia, in Reinhartz, "Vanishing Jews," 20. Lowe develops his arguments in "Concepts and Words," in *Jew and Judean Forum*, 77–87. See also David M. Miller, "Ethnicity Comes of Age: An Overview of Twentieth-Century Terms for Ioudaios," *CBR* 10 (2012): 293–311.

[23]Arguments for distinct translation of *Ioudaios* based on context are most thoroughly discussed by Daniel Schwartz, *Judeans and Jews: Four Faces of Dichotomy in Ancient Jewish History* (Toronto: University of Toronto Press, 2016); see also idem, "The Different Tasks of Translators and Historians," in *Jew and Judean*, 42–47.

[24]See, e.g., the recommended "service for Tenebrae" by James H. Charlesworth, published by the United Methodist Church; online: https://www.umcdiscipleship.org/resources/a-service-of-tenebrae. The site explicitly notes that Charlesworth "accurately translates John 18:1 –19:42, with special sensitivity to Jews, Judaism, Jesus's Jewishness, and the Jewish origins of Christianity."

[25]"Uncompromising simplicity marked the American Bible Society's (ABS) translation of the Contemporary English Version (CEV) that was first published in 1995. The text is easily read by grade schoolers, second language readers, and those who prefer the more contemporized form. The CEV is not a paraphrase. It is an accurate and faithful translation of the original manuscripts" (https://www.biblegateway.com/versions/Contemporary-English-Version-CEV-Bible/). Greenspoon notes regarding the CEV, "Its text of the New Testament has been singled out for its efforts to

eradicate any possible anti-Jewish sentiments." Leonard J. Greenspoon and Harvey Minkoff, *The Holy Bible: A Buyer's Guide* (Washington, DC: Biblical Archaeology Society, 2013 [updated], 30.

[26] For an example of such ethnic interpretations of *Ioudaioi*, see the essay by Anthony Le Donne in this volume.

[27] Philip Esler, "From Ioudaioi to Children of God: The Development of a Non-Ethnic Group Identity in the Gospel of John," in *In Other Words: Essay on Social-Science Methods and the New Testament in Honor of Jerome H. Neyrey*, ed. Anselm C. Hagedorn, Zeba A. Crook, and Eric Stewart, SWBA 2 (Sheffield: Sheffield Phoenix, 2007), 106–37, cited in Reinhartz, "Vanishing Jews," 20.

[28] Joshua Garroway, "Ioudaios," in *The Jewish Annotated New Testament*, 2d rev. edition, ed. Amy-Jill Levine and Marc Z. Brettler (New York: Oxford University Press, 2017), 596-99.

[29] Naim Ateek's "Pentecost and the Intifada" (in *Reading from this Place, vol. 2: Social Location and Biblical Interpretation in Global Perspective,* ed. Fernando F. Segovia and Mary Ann Tolbert [Minneapolis: Fortress, 1995], 69–81, here 69) begins, "Palestinian Christians trace their Christian faith to apostolic times." Mitri Raheb (*I am a Palestinian Christian*, trans. Ruth C. L. Gritsch [Minneapolis: Fortress, 1995], 8) writes, "The Evangelist Luke reports in Acts 2:11 that Arabs were present at the first feast of Pentecost. Thus, Arab Christians were among the very first Christians."

[30] Reinhartz, "Vanishing Jews," 12.

[31] Jonathan Klawans, "An Invented Revolution," in *Jew and Judean*, 88–95, here 90.

[32] Malina, "Was Jesus a Jew? Was Aristotle a Greek-American? Translating 'Ioudaios,'" online: http://assemblyoftrueisrael.com/Documents/Yahshuawasnojew[1].htm. Malina repeats this material in his (and Richard Rohrbaugh's) *Social Science Commentary on the Gospel of John* (Minneapolis: Fortress, 1998), which is quoted by James Crossley, "What a Difference a Translation Makes! An Ideological Analysis of the Ioudaios Debate," in *Jew and Judean*, 107–20, here 108–9. The quotation ends, "in all of the sixty-nine other instances in John where the term *Judeans* (Greek *Ioudaioi*) appears, there is nothing of the modern connotations of 'Jew' or 'Jewishness.'" See also Joan Taylor, "'Judean' and 'Jew', Jesus and Paul," in *Jew and Judean*, 27–32.

[33] Leonard Greenspoon, "Another Perspective—Jewish Translations of the Bible," *SBL Forum*, August 2005; online: https://www.sbl-site.org/publications/article.aspx?ArticleId=96

[34] *ETD Collection for Fordham University*. Paper AAI7108717. Grady mentions, among others, Haymo of Auxerre (ca. 850) who "spoke with favor of the Jewish sins which enriched the world by bringing about the crucifixion of Christ" (p. 12); such friends we do not need. Nor does Bede's conviction that the destruction of the Temple in 70 indicate "it is a religion that God's anger has turned against, not a people on whom he has taken vengeance" (p. 118) help much.

[35] Grady, "History of the Exegesis of Matthew 27.2," 1–2.

[36]See Amy-Jill Levine, "Matthew, Mark, and Luke: Good News or Bad?" in *Jesus, Judaism, and Christian Anti-Judaism: Reading the New Testament after the Holocaust,* ed. Paula Fredriksen and Adele Reinhartz (Louisville: Westminster John Knox, 2002), 77–98, esp. 77–78.

[37]See especially Ruth Sheridan, "Hiding from the Fourth Gospel's Tragic History," in *Jew and Judean*, 96–106.

Index